TAKE BACK
THE NIGHT

Women on Pornography

TAKE BACK THE NIGHT

Women on Pornography

Edited by Laura Lederer

WILLIAM MORROW AND COMPANY, INC.
New York   1980

Library of Congress Cataloging in Publication Data

Main entry under title:

Take back the night.

"Morrow quill paperbacks."

Bibliography: p.
Includes index.
1. Pornography—Addresses, essays, lectures.
2. Pornography—Social aspects—United States.
3. Pornography—Moral and religious aspects.
4. Pornography—Psychological aspects. 5. Sex
crimes—United States. 6. Feminism—United States.
I. Lederer, Laura.
[HQ471.T27 1980]   363.4′7   80-23701
ISBN 0-688-03728-3
ISBN 0-688-08728-0 (pbk.)

Printed in the United States of America

5   6   7   8   9   10

BOOK DESIGN BY MICHAEL MAUCERI

To the thousands of women in this country and abroad who recognize the hatefulness and harmfulness of pornography, and who are organizing to stop it now.

An Open Letter

We live in cities like the tame pheasants who are hand-raised and then turned loose for hunters to shoot, an activity called sport. The hunting, maiming, the mutilation and murder of ourselves, our mothers, our grandmothers, our daughters, our granddaughters is the stuff of a vast industry. Just as the National Rifle Association spends millions whenever restriction of hunting is considered in an area like the one I live in, where more dogs are shot every year than deer, so the corporate woman-desecrators hire the best legal talent to keep their violence against women on the streets, in the theaters, in the combat zones of every city. They use all the arsenal of weapons available to those with money and position: they use economic pressure against newsstand vendors: if you don't take these flesh magazines, you can't have the others you need. They use muscle. They use threats and injunctions and sympathetic or bought judges. They use male intellectuals who consider arousal sacred, no matter whether it is caused by a caress or the sight of a disemboweling. The link between sex and violence must be broken in our generation and broken for good if we are to survive into a future fit for our children to inhabit.

—Marge Piercy

In Gratitude:

To my parents, Creighton and Natalie Lederer, without whose sustained support the book would never have seen the light of day. Also to my sister, Carrie Lederer, whose faith and love and encouragement were ever present though she was 3,000 miles away.

To Kathleen Barry, a friend, a mentor, an energizer. Our long, animated conversations moved me constantly toward completion of the book.

To those who listened: Susan Lurie, Shawn Bronzli, Weji Louise, Dr. Robert Burnstein, and Ruth van Leeuwen. Among these names special mention needs to be made of feminist therapist Pat Hoornstra of Cleveland, Ohio.

To those who wrote: Andrea Dworkin, Marty Lee, and Dr. David Noel Freedman. Their letters buoyed me up when the book work was weighing me down.

Throughout the gathering of material, the editing, the drafts and redrafts, Mitchell Botney was there. A special thanks to him for lending a hand where he could, listening far beyond the call of duty, encouraging when encouragement was needed.

There are many women who helped me with parts of the book. Important contributions were made by Ann Jones, Adrienne Rich, Andrea Dworkin, and Beth Goldberg. Lynn Campbell deserves a special thanks for her hand in the early development of this project.

The first grant that funded the *Women Against Violence in Pornography and Media Newspage,* which I edited, was given by The L. J. and Mary C. Skaggs Foundation. A special thanks to Philip M. Jelley and Jillian Steiner for their understanding and encouragement at a time when no one else dared. Other donations which funded the Feminist Perspectives on Pornography conference (out of which this book grew) were given by The Ms. Foundation and The Eastman Foundation.

To the women who typed the manuscript goes a huge thank-you: Susan Shaw, Kathleen MacRae, Carolyn Borchardt; and to Jody Grasgreen for her fast, efficient work on the bibliography.

Finally, I owe a large debt to my editors, Julie Weiner and Toni Burbank, and to my agent, Frances Goldin, who have worked hard alongside me. The quality of the book is much improved for their help.

9

Contents

11

Introduction

—Los Angeles, 1976: Outraged by a billboard of a woman in chains with bruises on her legs and face, and a caption reading "I'm black and blue from the Rolling Stones and I love it," feminists from Southern California stage a demonstration and a national press conference, and force Warner Brothers to remove the advertisement.

—Rochester, N.Y. 1977: *Snuff*, a movie billed as a pornographic thriller in which a woman is supposed to have actually been tortured, mutilated, and murdered for sexual stimulation, appears at a local theater. A demonstration is called, a window in the theater is broken, and four women are arrested for malicious destruction. Stating that "It is illegal to destroy an ad for a film in which women are savagely dismembered and killed for sexual entertainment, but it is not illegal to show such films," the women stand trial.

—San Francisco, 1978: Women Against Violence in Pornography and Media, a membership organization of 1,000 women, organizes a national conference entitled "Feminist Perspectives on Pornography" (November 17–19, 1978). For the first time in history, women from across the country gather to discuss the destructive consequences of pornography, to exchange information and analysis, and to plan strategies for eliminating pornography. In conjunction with the conference, a Take Back the Night March is staged through San Francisco's pornography district. Over 5,000 women from thirty states participate and return to their own communities to continue the work.

—New York, N.Y., 1979: Biweekly tours of Forty-second Street are being offered by a new organization called Women Against Pornography. The tours take groups of twenty women around Times Square to expose them to the thriving pornography industry. Tour leaders believe that once women see for themselves the brutality of the industry they will be better equipped to fight it. In one year over two thousand women toured New York City's pornography strip. Many later participated in a large March on Times Square.

These events and others across the country are a sign that women

15

are claiming pornography as a feminist issue. In the last few decades women have been bombarded with ever-increasing numbers of pornographic images in liquor stores, bookstores, and drugstores; in supermarkets; in the hands of fathers, uncles, brothers, sons, husbands, lovers, and boyfriends; in movies, in films, and on street-corner newsstands; on the covers of record albums, on the walls of poster stores, and in shop windows. The media have subjected women to dramatized rapings, stabbings, burnings, beatings, gaggings, bindings, tortures, dismemberments, mutilations, and deaths in the name of male sexual pleasure or sheer entertainment.

In the meantime, women have been increasingly and ever-more-gruesomely raped and brutalized on the streets and in homes. In its annual publication, *Crime in the United States*, the FBI states that a woman is raped every eight minutes. Lieutenant John Jordan of the San Francisco Police Department says that the Sex Crimes Division sees fewer "clean" rapes and more rapes in which women are brutalized, blatantly humiliated, and tortured as well as sexually assaulted. Jordan referred to cases in which women reported their faces were rubbed in the dirt, cigarettes were stubbed out on their bodies, or degrading words were spoken to them during the assault. In reaction, whistles, dog repellents, Mace, tear gas canisters, sirens, extra keys, dead-bolt locks, security buildings, and peepholes have become the norm in our society, as Kate Roberts pointed out in her introduction to the Conference on Feminist Perspectives on Pornography.

At first, women viewed each violent crime as a separate but crucial problem. Rape-crisis centers were set up, and after that, battered-wives shelters, and following that, child-abuse councils. But slowly we came to see that these crisis-care organizations were not enough. A comparison can be made with health care in America. Until recently doctors limited their attention to the treatment of acute medical problems. Within the last decade, the concept of "preventive medicine" has emerged. Feminists too began to realize that although we must deal directly with acute care problems like rape and wife-beating, we must also remove the images which promote a climate in which these crimes are possible. We noted the inconsistency in allowing (and even encouraging) women and young girls to be set up as sexual objects and willing victims in all forms of mass media, while at the same time protesting the victimization of females in real life. We began to make the connections between media violence to women and real-life violence to them, to recognize the threat which pornography poses to our lives and livelihood, and to speak out against it. As sociologist Diana E. H. Russell points out in an article entitled "Pornography, A Feminist Perspective":

> There are no piecemeal solutions to rape, woman-battering, the murder of women by men, or the molestation of young girls by their fathers. All of these crimes against women are linked. They all involve the acting out of male power over, and often hatred toward, women.

In recent years the debasement of women in pornographic magazines and films has increased steadily. The California Department of Justice estimated several years ago that pornography was a $4-billion-a-year industry in the United States alone. Large cities across the country have experienced the proliferation of "porn strips"— blocks of storefront shops which display pornographic magazines, movies, peep shows, and live sex shows. Paralleling this growth, there has been a change in the kind of material available. Professor John H. Court of Flinders University in South Australia has studied current trends in pornography and sex crimes around the world. In "Pornography and Sex Crimes: A Re-evaluation in Light of Recent Trends Around the World," an article published in the *International Journal of Criminology and Penology*, Dr. Court refers to "a chain reaction with people constantly seeking stronger stuff," and an "increased availability of material dealing with sadomasochism, bondage, abuse of young children . . . exploitation of racial prejudice . . . and ritual torture and murder for sexual pleasure."

In one three-month period, a group of researchers from Women Against Violence in Pornography and Media viewed twenty-six pornographic films in San Francisco. Twenty-one had rape scenes, sixteen had bondage and torture scenes, two were films of child molestation, and two featured the killing of women for sexual stimulation. Feminist researchers also monitored pornographic magazines. We divided these into two categories: blatantly violent magazines, usually found only in pornography shops and costing anywhere from five dollars to fifteen dollars, and the more familiar "tabletop pornography" magazines. Here are some examples of the images and themes we found:

- A *Penthouse* magazine spread entitled "The Joy of Pain," illustrated with a large needle piercing a woman's painted fingernail and finger.

- An article in *Oui* magazine (published by *Playboy*) entitled "Jane Birkin in Bondage," in which Jane "explains the solution to all disciplinary problems." It is illustrated with several color photos of Jane Birkin handcuffed, gagged, whipped, and beaten.

• *Hustler* magazine's "Chester the Molester." Until 1978 Chester was a regular feature of *Hustler*. Each month he molested a different young girl, using techniques like lying, kidnapping, and assault.

• A magazine called *Bondage*, in which women are tied up and scissors, hot irons, torches, and knives are held to their breasts and vaginas.

• A magazine entitled *Brutal Trio*, in which three men successively kidnap a woman, a twelve-year-old girl, and a grandmother, and beat them senseless, kicking them in the face, head, and body. After they have passed out, they are raped and beaten again.

• A *Hustler* magazine item called "About Face," in which a man sticks a gun into a woman's mouth and forces her to suck it. A variation of this theme is seen in a magazine called *Dynamite*, available for fifty cents. One month this magazine featured a cover story called "Women Under the Gun," in which a gun is shown pointed at a woman's head on the cover of the magazine, and at her breasts, vagina, and buttocks in three separate pictures in the centerfold.

These are just a few examples of the violence to and degradation of women which have become a staple of pornographic magazines and movies. Some of these magazines have become household commodities in the last decade. Others, like *Dynamite*, are available to adults and minors alike from street-corner boxes in large cities across the country.

Recently we noticed a "ripple effect": Violent pornography has moved from special hard-core magazines and shops to the larger mass media. Along the way it may be airbrushed and spruced up, but although the form changes, the content remains the same. Thus, in the last decade, consumers, fashion-minded women, and musically inclined youngsters all have been subjected to this new form of media:

• A *Vogue* magazine fashion spread which features a couple modeling jumpsuits. The photos, taken by Richard Avedon, portray a young man viciously slapping his companion. She is reeling in pain as she cries out. We asked Mr. Avedon for permission to reprint this picture in our book. He refused. (*Vogue* magazine, December 1975, p. 149.)

• A record album called *Wild Angel* by Nelson Slater, produced by RCA Records. The cover shows a smooth and plastic-looking woman with her head pulled back and her throat exposed by a chain resembling a horse's bit which is run through her mouth.

• Advertisements in major daily newspapers for pornographic movies with illustrations featuring scantily clad women in handcuffs and chains.

The implications of current trends in pornography are overwhelming. While it may be argued that reading magazines like *Playboy*, *Penthouse, Oui,* and *Hustler,* and viewing pictures such as those described are entertaining, it is also clear that these media forms contribute to a culture in which real violence against women is not only perpetrated but accepted as normal.

The title of this book, *Take Back the Night*, reflects this growing realization of the links among crimes against women. The pollution of our media with sexist articles, programming, and advertisements, and the increasing amounts of pornography readily available, are hardly questioned. Rapes, muggings, and sexual harassment of women at all times, but especially at night, are the norm. That we have been unable to walk the streets after dark without a male to protect us from all the rest of the men has been assumed in this society for so long that people can hardly imagine a culture in which this would not be the case. The slogan Take Back the Night was first used in the United States as a theme for a national protest march down San Francisco's pornography strip. The march took place at night and was in the spirit of many similar events taking place all over the world. Take Back the Night was a profound symbolic statement of our commitment to stopping the tide of violence against women in all arenas, and our demand that the perpetrators of such violence—from rapists to batterers to pornographers—be held responsible for their actions and made to change.

Until recently there have been only two sides to the pornography issue: the conservative approach, which argues that pornography is immoral because it exposes the human body; and the liberal approach, which presents pornography as just one more aspect of our ever-expanding human sexuality. This book presents a third and feminist perspective: That pornography is the ideology of a culture which promotes and condones rape, woman-battering, and other crimes of violence against women. It is a concrete tribute to what we have done and where we intend to go. We pass on this body of knowledge, ideas, and expertise in the hope that it will be helpful in the fight against pornography and other violent crimes against women.

—LAURA LEDERER

SECTION I.

What Is Pornography?

Man in his lust has regulated long enough this
whole question of sexual intercourse. Now let
the mother of mankind, whose prerogative it is
to set bounds to his indulgence, rouse up and
give this whole matter a thorough, fearless examination.

—ELIZABETH CADY STANTON
Letter to Susan B. Anthony,
1853

Questions We Get Asked Most Often

Diana E. H. Russell with Laura Lederer

In 1976 a group called Women Against Violence in Pornography and Media was formed out of a growing recognition of the need for feminists to act in some organized fashion to fight pornography. Its first action was a 600-woman march down Broadway, the biggest pornography strip in San Francisco, to protest pornography as "anti-woman propaganda." Six months later, WAVPM published the first issue of its newsletter. At the same time, the group began a series of speaking engagements at libraries, town houses, colleges, and women's apartments, using a pornography display and a slide show to demonstrate visually some of the kinds of images women were fighting. During these first months of organizing in the Bay Area, people repeatedly asked the same questions about pornography. The public was confused on the issue, WAVPM discovered, but a few well-formed answers made it possible for many to see why women were upset about pornography. The November 1977 issue of the WAVPM newsletter tackled some of those basic questions and gave short, concrete answers. This issue of the newsletter became a basic educative tool and a short introduction to the complexities of the pornography problem.

Since that time, over 5,000 copies of the article have been distributed across the country. Requests for the newsletter came from as far as Puerto Rico, Germany, and Australia and from as close to home as the housewife around the corner. Since the article raises, in short form, many of the questions that the rest of this book deals with at length, we have used it as an introduction to this section.

Q: *What is Women Against Violence in Pornography and Media (WAVPM), and how did you come into existence?*

A: We are a group of Bay Area (California) feminists who have been meeting because we share a common concern about the prevalence of violence against women. Our primary focus is on the relationship between such violence and the image of women in the media, particularly in pornography. The group evolved out of a Conference

23

on Violence Against Women which was sponsored by San Francisco
Women's Centers and San Francisco State University in December
1976. The workshops on pornography and media merged on the last
day of the conference, and we have been meeting ever since.

Q: *What are your goals?*

A: Our goals are:

—To educate women and men about the woman-hatred expressed
in pornography and other media violence to women, and to increase
understanding of the destructive consequences of these images;

—To confront those responsible—for example, the owners of pornographic stores and theaters, those who devise violent images on
record covers, newspapers that give a lot of space to advertising pornographic movies, politicians who give out permits for "live shows,"
pornographic bookstores, etc.;

—To put an end to all portrayals of women being bound, raped,
tortured, killed, or degraded for sexual stimulation or pleasure. We
believe that the constant linking of sexuality and violence is dangerous.

Q: *What kinds of images are you talking about when you say you
are opposed to "violence in pornography and media"?*

A: We are talking about films like the ones shown in the Kearny
Cinema in San Francisco. The titles are self-explanatory. *Expectant
Pain, Cry Rape, Black and Chained, Love Gestapo Style, Slave Girl,
Angels in Pain, Corporal Punishment, Club Brute Force.* We are talking about books and magazines that depict women being bound,
beaten, and abused. We are protesting the message of these images—
that beating and raping women, urinating and defecating on women,
is erotic and pleasurable for men, and that women desire this kind of
treatment, or at least expect it.

We are talking about record album photos, fashion and men's-
magazine layouts, department-store window displays and billboards,
in which women are shown bound, gagged, beaten, whipped, and
chained.

Q: *But not all pornography is violent. Do you object to pornography in which there is no violence?*

A: Yes. Not all pornography is violent, but even the most banal
pornography objectifies women's bodies. An essential ingredient of
much rape and other forms of violence to women is the "objectification" of the woman. This is not just rhetoric. It means that women
are not seen as human beings but as things. Men are reared to view
females in this way, pornography thrives off this and feeds it, and
rape is one of the consequences.

Q: *Is there any proof that these kinds of images really affect us? How can you be sure that it bothers people?*

A: If it doesn't bother people to see women being raped or beaten or killed for sexual stimulation, then something is wrong. This is exactly our point—if we see enough victimization of women, then we are going to become desensitized to it. Natalie Shainess, a psychoanalyst in New York, points out that as rape becomes more common in the media, rapists stop seeing themselves as abnormal. Imagine the public outcry that would occur if there were special movie houses in every city across the country where viewers could see whites beating up Blacks, or Christians beating up Jews. But if it's called pornography and women are the victims, then you are seen as a prude to object.

Q: *But still, you haven't told me what* proof *is available.*

A: Many people do not realize that there is now a substantial body of research which proves that adults and children behave more violently after viewing movies in which violence occurs.[1] In a standard experiment, for example, people who have just witnessed a violent episode in a movie give greater levels of shock to other people than those who have witnessed a nonviolent movie.* Yet pornographic movies and live shows are getting increasingly violent, and the media continue to promote violence in the name of entertainment.

Q: *Do you know of any specific cases outside of experimental situations in which watching a violent movie has led to violent acts?*

A: There have been several articles in the news recently about the effect of TV violence. Men who have seen "Dirty Harry," "Helter Skelter," and "Kojak" have subsequently committed crimes. Currently there is a case in the California courts which concerns a nine-year-old girl who was raped with a beer bottle by three schoolgirls four days after they saw a movie on TV called "Born Innocent." † The movie

---

* Ed. Note. For a full explanation of this experiment, see Section IV, Research on the Effects of Pornography, page 198.

† Ed. Note: The case is *Niemi* v. *NBC*. At this writing, all final briefs are in, and both sides are getting ready to argue their cases. The case, which was thrown out of court three times in judgments without trials, is now in the appellate court. Attorney Marvin Lewis says that he is sure that whoever loses will appeal to the California Supreme Court, and that the case will go from there to the United States Supreme Court. He feels confident that the United States Supreme Court will take the case this time, not only because of the important issue involved—namely, should the First Amendment deny damages to a person wrongfully injured by one who had a legal duty not to do so?—but also because the Court denied previously a writ on the merits of the case applied for by NBC to stay the trial.

has a scene in which several girls use a "plumber's helper" to rape a girl.

In a study in which prison inmates were asked whether or not their criminal activities had ever been influenced by what they saw on TV, three out of the fifty-nine rapists (5 percent) said that they had felt inspired or motivated to commit rape as a result of something they had seen on TV; of the thirty-one men serving life sentences for murder, two (6 percent) said their crimes had been television-influenced; and "of the 148 men who admitted to committing assault, about one out of six (17 percent) indicated that his crime had been inspired or motivated by something he saw on TV." *

Q: *But that's violence. Are there any studies which prove that pornography is harmful?*

A: First, it is important to know that pornography usually combines some sort of violence with sex. WAVPM has monitored dozens of pornographic movies in the past year. In addition, we have researched the current trends in pornographic books and magazines. Some of the pornography we have seen was nothing *but* violence. In one movie a doctor takes a nurse by surprise, binds her into a wheelchair, and gets off by gassing her to death. In others, women are kidnapped, tied up, beaten, tortured, and hung upside down like pieces of meat. And that's the end of the movie. Domination and torture is what it's about.

Research to date on the effect of pornography is sketchy and inadequate. There is very little data on the long-term effects of pornography, and particularly on the development of negative, distorted, and dangerous views of women.

Q: *What do you mean by "long-term effects"?*

A: Most studies on pornography suffer seriously from male biases —especially from an insensitivity to the problem of sexism. Research is conspicuously meager on whether pornography reinforces and increases contempt and hatred of women; whether it glorifies, trivializes, or demeans the suffering of raped and battered women; whether it makes it more difficult for men and women to relate to one another as human beings.

Another thing to remember is that past research was done before

---

* *TV Guide*, January 29, 1977. In addition, nine out of the ten men interviewed in this prison survey said that they learned "new tricks" by watching TV crime programs. Another survey of prisoners by Gladys Denny Shultz reports that of a group of seventy sex offenders, half (50 percent) indicated pornography as an influence toward crime. ("What Sex Offenders Say About Pornography," *Reader's Digest*, July, 1971)

the proliferation of the pornographic magazines of the 1970's. Younger children are viewing pornography daily on display racks in drugstores, and we have no idea what effect this is having. In addition, very little is known about the effect of pornography on women.

Q: *Has any research been done on the effect of pornography on women?*

A: Very little. But the results from a recent questionnaire-study by Judith Bat-Ada of Case Western Reserve University do show that women are adversely affected by pornography. Bat-Ada concluded that women are beginning to view themselves in a negative manner after comparing themselves with pictures in pornographic magazines. Almost exclusively, the consumers of pornography are men. Most women don't even realize what it is that men are buying. Women have turned a blind eye to this aspect of male culture. Hence, it has been an issue long neglected by the Women's Movement. And those outside the movement who have acted against pornography have usually ignored the misogyny (woman hatred) expressed in it.

Q: *What about films which have sexual scenes in them—are you saying that ALL films and pictures showing explicit sex have a destructive effect?*

A: Not at all. WAVPM has no objection to explicit sex, nor do we object to depictions of nudity per se. Movies put out by the National Sex Forum, for example, use explicit sex, but they are designed to educate. Pornography is not made to educate but to sell, and, for the most part, what sells in a sexist society is a bunch of lies about women and sex. Women are portrayed as enjoying being raped, spanked, or beaten; tied up, mutilated, or enslaved; or they accept it as their lot as women to be victims of such experiences. In the less sadistic films, women are portrayed as turned on and sexually satisfied by doing anything and everything that men order them to do, and what this involves is for the most part totally contrary to what we know about female sexuality; that is, it is almost totally penis-oriented, often devoid of "foreplay," tenderness, or caring, to say nothing of love and romance. In short, pornographic movies, pictures, and stories are a celebration of male power over women and the sexist wish that women's sexuality and values be totally subservient to men's.

Q: *Why has the amount of pornography available increased so much over the past few years?*

A: We see this proliferation of pornography, particularly violent pornography and child pornography, as part of the male backlash to the Women's Liberation Movement. Enough women have been rejecting the traditional role of subordination to men to cause a crisis in the collective male ego. Pornography is a male fantasy-solution that inspires nonfantasy acts of punishment for uppity females. As Gloria Steinem points out (*Ms.*, August 1977), "It is one logical, inevitable result of raising boys to believe they must control or conquer others as a measure of manhood, and producing men who may continue to believe that success or even functioning—in sex as in other areas of life—depends on subservience, surrender, or some clear tribute to their superiority." As women have become stronger and more assertive, some men find it easier to feel powerful with young girls, including children. Hence the enormous increase in child pornography in recent years.

Q: *I had heard that watching pornography and other violent movies had a cathartic effect. That is, that they actually help get rid of the viewers' sexual and violent urges in a safe way. What do you think of this argument?*

A: We have already mentioned research and cases that disprove such a contention. But, in addition, we want to ask you what you would think of a suggestion that parents who feel an urge to beat their children should have available to them movie houses in every town, showing parents battering and torturing their children and some of the children enjoying the experience. Do you honestly believe that such movies would prevent rather than promote child abuse? If not, then let's be consistent and recognize that pornography is no safety valve but encourages the acting out of violent urges toward women.

Q: *But after all, women choose to act in these movies, or to model for pornographic photographs. How then can you say they're being abused and exploited?*

A: First of all, we must consider the impact of pornography on all women, not just the models. Second, it is incorrect that all models choose to be such. We are not simply arguing that all models have no other survival choice, though this may be the case in many instances. We are referring to the fact that some pornography models are coerced. For example, some models are actually sold by their parents. Sometimes their parents are the moviemakers. And some young women are kidnapped; others, broken down by the use of violence and/or drugs, become "willing" models.

Whatever the route to becoming a pornography model, the women's vulnerability to physical abuse on the job is also great. In one movie we saw, boiling candle wax was dripped onto a bound woman's breasts. Had she consented beforehand? Even if she had, this is clearly a violent act—one which was followed by her acting the willing and adoring lover of her torturer. Even where models have consented to participate, they don't necessarily know what they're in for, and often they are in no position to maintain control.

Q: *So what can be done to prevent such abuse of pornography models?*

A: Because pornography is detrimental to all women, not just the models, we think that the solution to the abuse suffered by these models is *not* merely to try to improve their conditions of work. We want to see banned all pornography which portrays rape, torture, murder, and bondage for erotic stimulation and pleasure.

Q: *But wouldn't banning pornography jeopardize some people's freedom of speech?*

A: We think not. WAVPM stands firm in our dedication to freedom of speech. Pornography is an *abuse* of the right to freedom of speech, and the First Amendment was never intended to protect material that condones and promotes violent crimes against any group—be it women, children, Third World people, Jews, old people, etc. The fact that the issue of "censorship" is raised so readily when women are the victims, in contrast with other groups, suggests that a political ploy is being used to confuse and intimidate us.

Q: *But wouldn't banning pornography just create a black market for this material?*

A: Probably. But we will never be rid of pornography totally until we are rid of the sexist society in which we live. It is better to have it underground than to see it flourish as an accepted part of our culture. Feminists must demand that society find the abuse of women both immoral *and* illegal.

Excerpt on Pornography from *Against Our Will: Men, Women and Rape*

Susan Brownmiller

The following is an excerpt from Susan Brownmiller's book, *Against Our Will: Men, Women and Rape*, published in 1975 by Simon & Schuster. It is famous now because it opened the debate between feminists and liberals on what should be done about pornography.

Pornography has been so thickly glossed over with the patina of chic these days in the name of verbal freedom and sophistication that important distinctions between freedom of political expression (a democratic necessity), honest sex education for children (a societal good) and ugly smut (the deliberate devaluation of the role of women through obscene, distorted depictions) have been hopelessly confused. Part of the problem is that those who traditionally have been the most vigorous opponents of porn are often those same people who shudder at the explicit mention of any sexual subject. Under their watchful, vigilante eyes, frank and free dissemination of educational materials relating to abortion, contraception, the act of birth and female biology in general is also dangerous, subversive and dirty. (I am not unmindful that a frank and free discussion of rape, "the unspeakable crime," might well give these righteous vigilantes further cause to shudder.) Because the battle lines were falsely drawn a long time ago, before there was a vocal women's movement, the anti-pornography forces appear to be, for the most part, religious, Southern, conservative and right-wing, while the pro-porn forces are identified as Eastern, atheistic and liberal.

But a woman's perspective demands a totally new alignment, or at least a fresh appraisal. The majority report of the Commission on

Obscenity and Pornography (1970), a report that argued strongly for the removal of all legal restrictions on pornography, soft and hard, made plain that 90 percent of all pornographic material is geared to the male heterosexual market (the other 10 percent is geared to the male homosexual taste), that buyers of porn are "predominantly white, middle-class, middle-aged married males" and that the graphic depictions, the meat and potatoes of porn, are of the naked female body and of the multiplicity of acts done to that body.

Discussing the content of stag films, "a familiar and firmly established part of the American scene," the commission report dutifully, if foggily, explained, "Because pornography historically has been thought to be primarily a masculine interest, the emphasis in stag films seems to represent the preferences of the middle-class American male. Thus male homosexuality and bestiality are relatively rare, while lesbianism is rather common."

The commissioners in this instance had merely verified what purveyors of porn have always known: hard-core pornography is not a celebration of sexual freedom; it is a cynical exploitation of female sexual activity through the device of making all such activity, and consequently all females, "dirty." Heterosexual male consumers of pornography are frankly turned on by watching lesbians in action (although never in the final scenes, but always as a curtain raiser); they are turned off with the sudden swiftness of a water faucet by watching naked men act upon each other. One study quoted in the commission report came to the unastounding conclusion that "seeing a stag film in the presence of male peers bolsters masculine esteem." Indeed. The men in groups who watch the films, it is important to note, are not naked.

When male response to pornography is compared with female response, a pronounced difference in attitude emerges. According to the commission, "Males report being more highly aroused by depictions of nude females, and show more interest in depictions of nude females than (do) females." Quoting the figures of Alfred Kinsey, the commission noted that a majority of males (77 percent) were "aroused" by visual depictions of explicit sex while a majority of females (68 percent) were not aroused. Further, "females more often than males reported 'disgust' and 'offense.'"

From whence comes this female disgust and offense? Are females sexually backward or more conservative by nature? The gut distaste that a majority of women feel when we look at pornography, a distaste that, incredibly, it is no longer fashionable to admit, comes, I think, from the gut knowledge that we and our bodies are being stripped, exposed and contorted for the purpose of ridicule to bolster that "masculine esteem" which gets its kick and sense of power from viewing females as anonymous, panting playthings, adult toys, dehumanized objects to be used, abused, broken and discarded.

This, of course, is also the philosophy of rape. It is no accident (for what else could be its purpose?) that females in the pornographic genre are depicted in two cleanly delineated roles: as virgins who are caught and "banged" or as nymphomaniacs who are never sated. The most popular and prevalent pornographic fantasy combines the two: an innocent, untutored female is raped and "subjected to unnatural practices" that turn her into a raving, slobbering nymphomaniac, a dependent sexual slave who can never get enough of the big, male cock.

There can be no "equality" in porn, no female equivalent, no turning of the tables in the name of bawdy fun. Pornography, like rape, is a male invention, designed to dehumanize women, to reduce the female to an object of sexual access, not to free sensuality from moralistic or parental inhibition. The staple of porn will always be the naked female body, breasts and genitals exposed, because as man devised it, her naked body is the female's "shame," her private parts the private property of man, while his are the ancient, holy, universal, patriarchal instrument of his power, his rule by force over her.

Pornography is the undiluted essence of anti-female propaganda. Yet the very same liberals who were so quick to understand the method and purpose behind the mighty propaganda machine of Hitler's Third Reich, the consciously spewed-out anti-Semitic caricatures and obscenities that gave an ideological base to the Holocaust and the Final Solution, the very same liberals who, enlightened by Blacks, searched their own conscience and came to understand that their tolerance of "nigger" jokes and portrayals of shuffling, rolling-eyed servants in movies perpetuated the degrading myths of Black inferiority and gave an ideological base to the continuation of Black oppression—these very same liberals now fervidly maintain that the hatred and contempt for women that find expression in four-letter words used as expletives and in what are quaintly called "adult" or "erotic" books and movies are a valid extension of freedom of speech that must be preserved as a Constitutional right.

To defend the right of a lone, crazed American Nazi to grind out propaganda calling for the extermination of all Jews, as the ACLU has done in the name of free speech, is, after all, a self-righteous and not particularly courageous stand, for American Jewry is not currently threatened by storm troopers, concentration camps and imminent extermination, but I wonder if the ACLU's position might change if, come tomorrow morning, the bookstores and movie theaters lining Forty-second Street in New York City were devoted not to the humiliation of women by rape and torture, as they currently are, but to a systematized, commercially successful propaganda machine depicting the sadistic pleasures of gassing Jews or lynching Blacks?

Is this analogy extreme? Not if you are a woman who is conscious of the ever-present threat of rape and the proliferation of a cultural ideology that makes it sound like "liberated" fun. The majority report of the Commission on Obscenity and Pornography tried to pooh-pooh the opinion of law enforcement agencies around the country that claimed their own concrete experience with offenders who were caught with the stuff led them to conclude that pornographic material is a causative factor in crimes of sexual violence. The commission maintained that it was not possible at this time to scientifically prove or disprove such a connection.

But does one need scientific methodology in order to conclude that the anti-female propaganda that permeates our nation's cultural output promotes a climate in which acts of sexual hostility directed against women are not only tolerated but ideologically encouraged? A similar debate has raged for many years over whether or not the extensive glorification of violence (the gangster as hero; the loving treatment accorded bloody shoot-'em-ups in movies, books and on TV) has a causal effect, a direct relationship to the rising rate of crime, particularly among youth. Interestingly enough, in this area—nonsexual and not specifically related to abuses against women—public opinion seems to be swinging to the position that explicit violence in the entertainment media does have a deleterious effect; it makes violence commonplace, numbingly routine and no longer morally shocking.

More to the point, those who call for a curtailment of scenes of violence in movies and on television in the name of sensitivity, good taste and what's best for our children are not accused of being pro-censorship or against freedom of speech. Similarly, minority group organizations—Black, Hispanic, Japanese, Italian, Jewish, or American Indian—that campaign against ethnic slurs and demeaning portrayals in movies, on television shows and in commercials are perceived as waging a just political fight, for if a minority group claims to be offended by a specific portrayal, be it Little Black Sambo or the Frito Bandido, and relates it to a history of ridicule and oppression, few liberals would dare to trot out a Constitutional argument in theoretical opposition, not if they wish to maintain their liberal credentials. Yet when it comes to the treatment of women, the liberal consciousness remains fiercely obdurate, refusing to be budged, for the sin of appearing square or prissy in the age of the so-called sexual revolution has become the worst offense of all.

Erotica and Pornography: A Clear and Present Difference

Gloria Steinem

Perhaps one of the greatest debates about pornography is the question of how to distinguish pornography from erotica. Here, in an article first printed in *Ms.* magazine, Gloria Steinem provides a practical test for making a distinction between the two.

Human beings are the only animals that experience the same sex drive at times when we can and cannot conceive.

Just as we developed uniquely human capacities for language, planning, memory, and invention along our evolutionary path, we also developed sexuality as a form of expression; a way of communicating that is separable from our need for sex as a way of perpetuating ourselves. For humans alone, sexuality can be and often is primarily a way of bonding, of giving and receiving pleasure, bridging differentness, discovering sameness, and communicating emotion.

We developed this and other human gifts through our ability to change our environment, adapt physically, and, in the long run, affect our own evolution. But as an emotional result of this spiraling path away from other animals, we seem to alternate between periods of exploring our unique abilities to forge new boundaries, and feelings of loneliness in the unknown that we ourselves have created; a fear that sometimes sends us back to the comfort of the animal world by encouraging us to exaggerate our sameness with it.

The separation of "play" from "work," for instance, is a problem only in the human world. So is the difference between art and nature, or an intellectual accomplishment and a physical one. As a result, we celebrate play, art, and invention as leaps into the unknown; but any imbalance can send us back to nostalgia for our primate past and the conviction that the basics of work, nature, and physical labor are somehow more worthwhile or even more moral.

In the same way, we have explored our sexuality as separable from conception: a pleasurable, empathetic bridge to strangers of the same species. We have even invented contraception—a skill that has probably existed in some form since our ancestors figured out the process of birth—in order to extend this uniquely human difference. Yet we also have times of atavistic suspicion that sex is not complete—or even legal or intended-by-god—if it cannot end in conception.

No wonder the concepts of "erotica" and "pornography" can be so crucially different, and yet so confused. Both assume that sexuality can be separated from conception, and therefore can be used to carry a personal message. That's a major reason why, even in our current culture, both may be called equally "shocking" or legally "obscene," a word whose Latin derivative means "dirty, containing filth." This gross condemnation of all sexuality that isn't harnessed to childbirth and marriage has been increased by the current backlash against women's progress. Out of fear that the whole patriarchal structure might be upset if women really had the autonomous power to decide our reproductive futures (that is, if we controlled the most basic means of production—the production of human beings), right-wing groups are not only denouncing pro-choice abortion literature as "pornographic," but are trying to stop the sending of all contraceptive information through the mails by invoking obscenity laws. In fact, Phyllis Schlafly recently denounced the entire Women's Movement as "obscene."

Not surprisingly, this religious, visceral backlash has a secular, intellectual counterpart that relies heavily on applying the "natural" behavior of the animal world to humans. That application is questionable in itself, but these Lionel Tiger-ish studies make their political purpose even more clear in the particular animals they select and the habits they choose to emphasize. For example, some male primates (marmosets, titi monkeys, night monkeys) carry and/or generally "mother" their infants. Tiger types prefer to discuss chimps and baboons, whose behavior is very "male chauvinist." The message is that females should accept their "destiny" of being sexually dependent and devote themselves to bearing and rearing their young.

Defending against such reaction in turn leads to another temptation: merely to reverse the terms, and declare that all nonprocreative sex is good. In fact, however, this human activity can be as constructive or destructive, moral or immoral, as any other. Sex as communication can send messages as different as life and death; even the origins of "erotica" and "pornography" reflect that fact. After all, "erotica" is rooted in "eros" or passionate love, and thus in the idea of positive choice, free will, the yearning for a particular person. (Interestingly, the definition of erotica leaves open the question of gender.) "Pornography" begins with a root "porno," meaning "prostitution" or "female captives," thus letting us know that the subject is not mutual love, or love at all, but domination and violence against women. (Though, of course, homosexual pornography may imitate this violence by putting a man in the "feminine" role of victim.) It ends with a root "graphos," meaning "writing about" or "description of," which puts still more distance between subject and object, and replaces a spontaneous yearning for closeness with objectification and voyeurism. The difference is clear in the words. It becomes even more so by example.

Look at any photo or film of people making love; really making love. The images may be diverse, but there is usually a sensuality and touch and warmth, an acceptance of bodies and nerve endings. There is always a spontaneous sense of people who are there because they want to be, out of shared pleasure.

Now look at any depiction of sex in which there is clear force, or an unequal power that spells coercion. It may be very blatant, with weapons of torture or bondage, wounds and bruises, some clear humiliation, or an adult's sexual power being used over a child. It may be much more subtle: a physical attitude of conqueror and victim, the use of race or class difference to imply the same thing, perhaps a very unequal nudity, with one person exposed and vulnerable while the other is clothed. In either case, there is no sense of equal choice or equal power.

The first is erotic: a mutually pleasurable, sexual expression between people who have enough power to be there by positive choice. It may or may not strike a sense-memory in the viewer, or be creative enough to make the unknown seem real; but it doesn't require us to identify with a conqueror or a victim. It is truly sensuous, and may give us a contagion of pleasure.

The second is pornographic: its message is violence, dominance, and conquest. It is sex being used to reinforce some inequality, or to create one, or to tell us that pain and humiliation (ours or someone else's) are really the same as pleasure. If we are to feel anything, we must identify with conqueror or victim. That means we can only experience pleasure through the adoption of some degree of sadism or masochism. It also means that we may feel diminished by the role of conqueror, or enraged, humiliated, and vengeful by sharing identity with the victim.

Perhaps one could simply say that erotica is about sexuality, but pornography is about power and sex-as-weapon—in the same way we have come to understand that rape is about violence, and not really about sexuality at all.

Yes, it's true that there are women who have been forced by violent families and dominating men to confuse love with pain; so much so that they have become masochists. (A fact that in no way excuses those who administer such pain.) But the truth is that, for most women—and for men with enough humanity to imagine themselves in the predicament of women—pornography could serve as aversion-conditioning toward sex.

Of course, there will always be personal differences about what is and is not erotic, and there may be cultural differences for a long time to come. Many women feel that sex makes them vulnerable and therefore may continue to need more sense of personal connection and safety than men do before allowing any erotic feelings. Men, on the other hand, may continue to feel less vulnerable, and therefore more open to such potential danger as sex with strangers. Women now frequently find competence and expertise erotic in men, but that may pass as we develop those qualities in ourselves. As some men replace the need for submission from childlike women with the pleasure of cooperation from equals, they may find a partner's competence to be erotic, too.

Such group changes plus individual differences will continue to be reflected in sexual love between people of the same gender, as well as between women and men. The point is not to dictate sameness, but to discover ourselves and each other through a sexuality that is an exploring, pleasurable, empathetic part of our lives; a human sexuality that is unchained both from unwanted pregnancies and from violence.

But that is a hope, not a reality. At the moment, fear of change is increasing both the indiscriminate repression of all nonprocreative sex in the religious and "conservative" male-dominated world, and the pornographic vengeance against women's sexuality in the secular world of "liberal" or "radical" men. It's almost futuristic to debate what is and is not truly erotic, when many women are again being forced into compulsory motherhood, and the number of pornographic murders, tortures, and women-hating images are on the increase in both popular culture and real life.

Together, both of the above forms of repression perpetuate that familiar division: wife or whore; "good" woman who is constantly vulnerable to pregnancy or "bad" woman who is unprotected from violence. Both roles would be upset if we were to control our own sexuality. And that's exactly what we must do.

In spite of all our atavistic suspicions and training for the "natural" role of motherhood, we took up the complicated battle for reproductive freedom. Our bodies had borne the health burden of endless births and poor abortions, and we had a greater motive than men for separating sexuality and conception.

Now we have to take up the equally complex burden of explaining that all nonprocreative sex is not alike. We have a motive: our right to a uniquely human sexuality, and sometimes even to survival. As it is, our bodies have too rarely been enough our own to develop erotica in our own lives, much less in art and literature. And our bodies have too often been the objects of pornography and the woman-hating, violent practice that it preaches. Consider also our spirits that break a little each time we see ourselves in chains or full labial display for the conquering male viewer, bruised or on our knees, screaming a real or pretended pain to delight the sadist, pretending to enjoy what we don't enjoy, to be blind to the images of our sisters that really haunt us—humiliated often enough ourselves by the truly obscene idea that sex and the domination of women must be combined.

Sexuality is human, free, separate—and so are we.

But until we untangle the lethal confusion of sex with violence, there will be more pornography and less erotica. There will be little murders in our beds—and very little love.

Pornography, Oppression, and Freedom: A Closer Look

Helen E. Longino

A question which is often asked at the beginning of any discussion on pornography is "How do you define it?" The answer is difficult. A good clear definition of pornography has eluded everyone. Twenty years ago, the United States Supreme Court was defining pornography as material which "taken as a whole appeals to prurient interest." Ten years later, Justice Potter Stewart said, "I can't define it, but I know it when I see it." Today federal law states that the definition of pornography is to be left up to the individual communities to decide. This, of course, has totally confused the country. What seems to be acceptable in San Francisco may be appalling in a small town, and communities themselves are having trouble deciding what they think is "patently offensive" and without "serious literary, artistic, political or scientific value." Feminists have a further objection to this definition: If pornography does not offend local community standards, we say, then something is wrong because it should!

In this paper, published here for the first time, feminist philosopher Helen Longino puts forth a serious definition of pornography which we believe withstands a rigorous and critical examination and which may prove helpful to teachers, doctors, laypeople, and jurists—anyone, in fact, who is interested in a good working definition of the term. She goes on to apply this definition to the question of pornography and the First Amendment.

I. Introduction

The much-touted sexual revolution of the 1960's and 1970's not only freed various modes of sexual behavior from the constraints of social disapproval, but also made possible a flood of pornographic material. According to figures provided by WAVPM (Women Against Violence in Pornography and Media), the number of pornographic magazines available at newsstands has grown from zero in

1953 to forty in 1977, while sales of pornographic films in Los Angeles alone have grown from $15 million in 1969 to $85 million in 1976.[1]

Traditionally, pornography was condemned as immoral because it presented sexually explicit material in a manner designed to appeal to "prurient interests" or a "morbid" interest in nudity and sexuality, material which furthermore lacked any redeeming social value and which exceeded "customary limits of candor." While these phrases, taken from a definition of "obscenity" proposed in the 1954 American Law Institute's *Model Penal Code*,[2] require some criteria of application to eliminate vagueness, it seems that what is objectionable is the explicit description or representation of bodily parts or sexual behavior for the purpose of inducing sexual stimulation or pleasure on the part of the reader or viewer. This kind of objection is part of a sexual ethic that subordinates sex to procreation and condemns all sexual interactions outside of legitimated marriage. It is this code which was the primary target of the sexual revolutionaries in the 1960's, and which has given way in many areas to more open standards of sexual behavior.

One of the beneficial results of the sexual revolution has been a growing acceptance of the distinction between questions of sexual mores and questions of morality. This distinction underlies the old slogan, "Make love, not war," and takes harm to others as the defining characteristic of immorality. What is immoral is behavior which causes injury to or violation of another person or people. Such injury may be physical or it may be psychological. To cause pain to another, to lie to another, to hinder another in the exercise of her or his rights, to exploit another, to degrade another, to misrepresent and slander another are instances of immoral behavior. Masturbation or engaging voluntarily in sexual intercourse with another consenting adult of the same or the other sex, as long as neither injury nor violation of either individual or another is involved, are not immoral. Some sexual behavior is morally objectionable, but not because of its sexual character. Thus, adultery is immoral not because it involves sexual intercourse with someone to whom one is not legally married, but because it involves breaking a promise (of sexual and emotional fidelity to one's spouse). Sadistic, abusive, or forced sex is immoral because it injures and violates another.

The detachment of sexual chastity from moral virtue implies that we cannot condemn forms of sexual behavior merely because they strike us as distasteful or subversive of the Protestant work ethic, or because they depart from standards of behavior we have individually adopted. It has thus seemed to imply that no matter how offensive we might find pornography, we must tolerate it in the name of freedom from illegitimate repression. I wish to argue that this is not so, that pornography is immoral because it is harmful to people.

II. What Is Pornography?

I define pornography as *verbal or pictorial explicit representations of sexual behavior that,* in the words of the Commission on Obscenity and Pornography, *have as a distinguishing characteristic "the degrading and demeaning portrayal of the role and status of the human female . . . as a mere sexual object to be exploited and manipulated sexually."* [3] In pornographic books, magazines, and films, women are represented as passive and as slavishly dependent upon men. The role of female characters is limited to the provision of sexual services to men. To the extent that women's sexual pleasure is represented at all, it is subordinated to that of men and is never an end in itself as is the sexual pleasure of men. What pleases women is the use of their bodies to satisfy male desires. While the sexual objectification of women is common to all pornography, women are the recipients of even worse treatment in violent pornography, in which women characters are killed, tortured, gang-raped, mutilated, bound, and otherwise abused, as a means of providing sexual stimulation or pleasure to the male characters. It is this development which has attracted the attention of feminists and been the stimulus to an analysis of pornography in general.[4]

Not all sexually explicit material is pornography, nor is all material which contains representations of sexual abuse and degradation pornography.

A representation of a sexual encounter between adult persons which is characterized by mutual respect is, once we have disentangled sexuality and morality, not morally objectionable. Such a representation would be one in which the desires and experiences of each participant were regarded by the other participants as having a validity and a subjective importance equal to those of the individual's own desire and experiences. In such an encounter, each participant acknowledges the other participant's basic human dignity and personhood. Similarly, a representation of a nude human body (in whole or in part) in such a manner that the person shown maintains self-respect—e.g., is not portrayed in a degrading position—would not be morally objectionable. The educational films of the National Sex Forum, as well as a certain amount of erotic literature and art, fall into this category.

While some erotic materials are beyond the standards of modesty held by some individuals, they are not for this reason immoral.

A representation of a sexual encounter which is not characterized by mutual respect, in which at least one of the parties is treated in a manner beneath her or his dignity as a human being, is no longer simple erotica. That a representation is of degrading behavior does not in itself, however, make it pornographic. Whether or not it is pornographic is a function of contextual features. Books and films may contain descriptions or representations of a rape in order to explore the consequences of such an assault upon its victim. What is being shown is abusive or degrading behavior which attempts to deny the humanity and dignity of the person assaulted, yet the context surrounding the representation, through its exploration of the consequences of the act, acknowledges and reaffirms her dignity. Such books and films, far from being pornographic, are (or can be) highly moral, and fall into the category of moral realism.

What makes a work a work of pornography, then, is not simply its representation of degrading and abusive sexual encounters, but its implicit, if not explicit, approval and recommendation of sexual behavior that is immoral, i.e., that physically or psychologically violates the personhood of one of the participants. Pornography, then, is verbal or pictorial material which represents or describes sexual behavior that is degrading or abusive to one or more of the participants *in such a way as to endorse the degradation*. The participants so treated in virtually all heterosexual pornography are women or children, so heterosexual pornography is, as a matter of fact, material which endorses sexual behavior that is degrading and/or abusive to women and children. As I use the term "sexual behavior," this includes sexual encounters between persons, behavior which produces sexual stimulation or pleasure for one of the participants, and behavior which is preparatory to or invites sexual activity. Behavior that is degrading or abusive includes physical harm or abuse, and physical or psychological coercion. In addition, behavior which ignores or devalues the real interests, desires, and experiences of one or more participants in any way is degrading. Finally, that a person has chosen or consented to be harmed, abused, or subjected to coercion does not alter the degrading character of such behavior.

Pornography communicates its endorsement of the behavior it represents by various features of the pornographic context: the degradation of the female characters is represented as providing pleasure to the participant males and, even worse, to the participant females, and there is no suggestion that this sort of treatment of others is inappropriate to their status as human beings. These two features are together sufficient to constitute endorsement of the represented behavior. The contextual features which make material pornographic are intrinsic to the material. In addition to these, extrinsic features, such as the purpose for which the material is presented—i.e., the sexual arousal/ pleasure/satisfaction of its (mostly) male consumers—or an accompanying text, may reinforce or make explicit the endorsement. Representations which in and of themselves do not show or endorse degrading behavior may be put into a pornographic context by juxtaposition with others that are degrading, or by a text which invites or recommends degrading behavior toward the subject represented. In such a case the whole complex—the series of representations or representations with text—is pornographic.

The distinction I have sketched is one that applies most clearly to sequential material—a verbal or pictorial (filmed) story—which represents an action and provides a temporal context for it. In showing the before and after, a narrator or film-maker has plenty of opportunity to acknowledge the dignity of the person violated or clearly to refuse to do so. It is somewhat more difficult to apply the distinction to single still representations. The contextual features cited above, however, are clearly present in still photographs or pictures that glamorize degradation and sexual violence. Phonograph album covers and advertisements offer some prime examples of such glamorization. Their representations of women in chains (the Ohio Players), or bound by ropes and black and blue (the Rolling Stones) are considered high-quality commercial "art" and glossily prettify the violence they represent. Since the standard function of prettification and glamorization is the communication of desirability, these albums and ads are communicating the desirability of violence against women. Representations of women bound or chained, particularly those of women bound in such a way as to make their breasts, or genital or anal areas vulnerable to any passerby, endorse the scene they represent by the absence of any indication that this treatment of women is in any way inappropriate.

To summarize: Pornography is not just the explicit representation or description of sexual behavior, nor even the explicit representation or description of sexual behavior which is degrading and/or abusive to women. Rather, it is material that explicitly represents or describes degrading and abusive sexual behavior so as to endorse and/or recommend the behavior as described. The contextual features, moreover, which communicate such endorsement are intrinsic to the material; that is, they are features whose removal or alteration would change the representation or description.

This account of pornography is underlined by the etymology and original meaning of the word "pornography." *The Oxford English Dictionary* defines pornography as "Description of the life, manners, etc. of prostitutes and their patrons [from πόρνη (porne) meaning "harlot" and γράφειν (graphein) meaning "to write"]; hence the expression or suggestion of obscene or unchaste subjects in literature or art." [5]

Let us consider the first part of the definition for a moment. In the transactions between prostitutes and their clients, prostitutes are paid, directly or indirectly, for the use of their bodies by the client for sexual pleasure.* Traditionally males have obtained from female prostitutes what they could not or did not wish to get from their wives or women friends, who, because of the character of their relation to the male, must be accorded some measure of human respect. While there are limits to what treatment is seen as appropriate toward women as wives or women friends, the prostitute as prostitute exists to provide sexual pleasure to males. The female characters of contemporary pornography also exist to provide pleasure to males, but in the pornographic context no pretense is made to regard them as parties to a contractual arrangement. Rather, the anonymity of these characters makes each one Everywoman, thus suggesting not only that all women are appropriate subjects for the enactment of the most bizarre and demeaning male sexual fantasies, but also that this is their primary purpose. The recent escalation of violence in pornography—the presentation of scenes of bondage, rape, and torture of women for the sexual stimulation of the male characters or male viewers—while shocking in itself, is from this point of view merely a more vicious extension of a genre whose success depends on treating women in a manner beneath their dignity as human beings.

III. Pornography: Lies and Violence Against Women

What is wrong with pornography, then, is its degrading and dehumanizing portrayal of women (and *not* its sexual content). Pornography, by its very nature, requires that women be subordinate to men and mere instruments for the fulfillment of male fantasies. To

---

* In talking of prostitution here, I refer to the concept of, rather than the reality of, prostitution. The same is true of my remarks about relationships between women and their husbands or men friends.

accomplish this, pornography must lie. Pornography lies when it says that our sexual life is or ought to be subordinate to the service of men, that our pleasure consists in pleasing men and not ourselves, that we are depraved, that we are fit subjects for rape, bondage, torture, and murder. Pornography lies explicitly about women's sexuality, and through such lies fosters more lies about our humanity, our dignity, and our personhood.

Moreover, since nothing is alleged to justify the treatment of the female characters of pornography save their womanhood, pornography depicts all women as fit objects of violence by virtue of their sex alone. Because it is simply being female that, in the pornographic vision, justifies being violated, the lies of pornography are lies about all women. Each work of pornography is on its own libelous and defamatory, yet gains power through being reinforced by every other pornographic work. The sheer number of pornographic productions expands the moral issue to include not only assessing the morality or immorality of individual works, but also the meaning and force of the mass production of pornography.

The pornographic view of women is thoroughly entrenched in a booming portion of the publishing, film, and recording industries, reaching and affecting not only all who look to such sources for sexual stimulation, but also those of us who are forced into an awareness of it as we peruse magazines at newsstands and record albums in record stores, as we check the entertainment sections of city newspapers, or even as we approach a counter to pay for groceries. It is not necessary to spend a great deal of time reading or viewing pornographic material to absorb its male-centered definition of women. No longer confined within plain brown wrappers, it jumps out from billboards that proclaim "Live X-rated Girls!" or "Angels in Pain" or "Hot and Wild," and from magazine covers displaying a woman's genital area being spread open to the viewer by her own fingers.* Thus, even men who do not frequent pornographic shops and movie houses are supported in the sexist objectification of women by their environment. Women, too, are crippled by internalizing as self-images those that are presented to us by pornographers. Isolated from one another and with no source of support for an alternative view of female sexuality, we may not always find the strength to resist a message that dominates the common cultural media.

The entrenchment of pornography in our culture also gives it a significance quite beyond its explicit sexual messages. To suggest, as

* This was a full-color magazine cover seen in a rack at the check-out counter of a corner delicatessen.

pornography does, that the primary purpose of women is to provide sexual pleasure to men is to deny that women are independently human or have a status equal to that of men. It is, moreover, to deny our equality at one of the most intimate levels of human experience. This denial is especially powerful in a hierarchical, class society such as ours, in which individuals feel good about themselves by feeling superior to others. Men in our society have a vested interest in maintaining their belief in the inferiority of the female sex, so that no matter how oppressed and exploited by the society in which they live and work, they can feel that they are at least superior to someone or some category of individuals—a woman or women. Pornography, by presenting women as wanton, depraved, and made for the sexual use of men, caters directly to that interest.* The very intimate nature of sexuality which makes pornography so corrosive also protects it from explicit public discussion. The consequent lack of any explicit social disavowal of the pornographic image of women enables this image to continue fostering sexist attitudes even as the society publicly proclaims its (as yet timid) commitment to sexual equality.

In addition to finding a connection between the pornographic view of women and the denial to us of our full human rights, women are beginning to connect the consumption of pornography with commiting rape and other acts of sexual violence against women. Contrary to the findings of the Commission on Obscenity and Pornography a growing body of research is documenting (1) a correlation between exposure to representations of violence and the committing of violent acts generally, and (2) a correlation between exposure to pornographic materials and the committing of sexually abusive or violent acts against women.[6] While more study is needed to establish precisely what the causal relations are, clearly so-called hard-core pornography is not innocent.

From "snuff" films and miserable magazines in pornographic stores to *Hustler*, to phonograph album covers and advertisements, to *Vogue*, pornography has come to occupy its own niche in the communications and entertainment media and to acquire a quasi-institutional character (signaled by the use of diminutives such as

* Pornography thus becomes another tool of capitalism. One feature of some contemporary pornography—the use of Black and Asian women in both still photographs and films—exploits the racism as well as the sexism of its white consumers. For a discussion of the interplay between racism and sexism under capitalism as it relates to violent crimes against women, see Angela Y. Davis, "Rape, Racism, and the Capitalist Setting," *The Black Scholar*, Vol. 9, No. 7, April 1978.

"porn" or "porno" to refer to pornographic material, as though such familiar naming could take the hurt out). Its acceptance by the mass media, whatever the motivation, means a cultural endorsement of its message. As much as the materials themselves, the social tolerance of these degrading and distorted images of women in such quantities is harmful to us, since it indicates a general willingness to see women in ways incompatible with our fundamental human dignity and thus to justify treating us in those ways.* The tolerance of pornographic representations of the rape, bondage, and torture of women helps to create and maintain a climate more tolerant of the actual physical abuse of women.† The tendency on the part of the legal system to view the victim of a rape as responsible for the crime against her is but one manifestation of this.

In sum, pornography is injurious to women in at least three distinct ways:

1. Pornography, especially violent pornography, is implicated in the committing of crimes of violence against women.

2. Pornography is the vehicle for the dissemination of a deep and vicious lie about women. It is defamatory and libelous.

3. The diffusion of such a distorted view of women's nature in our society as it exists today supports sexist (i.e., male-centered) attitudes, and thus reinforces the oppression and exploitation of women.

Society's tolerance of pornography, especially pornography on the contemporary massive scale, reinforces each of these modes of injury: By not disavowing the lie, it supports the male-centered myth that women are inferior and subordinate creatures. Thus, it contributes to the maintenance of a climate tolerant of both psychological and physical violence against women.

---

* This tolerance has a linguistic parallel in the growing acceptance and use of nonhuman nouns such as "chick," "bird," "filly," "fox," "doll," "babe," "skirt," etc., to refer to women, and of verbs of harm such as "fuck," "screw," "bang" to refer to sexual intercourse. See Robert Baker and Frederick Elliston, " 'Pricks' and 'Chicks': A Plea for Persons." *Philosophy and Sex* (Buffalo, N.Y.: Prometheus Books, 1975).

† This is supported by the fact that in Denmark the number of rapes committed has increased while the number of rapes reported to the authorities has decreased over the past twelve years. See *WAVPM Newspage,* Vol. II, No. 5, June, 1978, quoting M. Harry, "Denmark Today—The Causes and Effects of Sexual Liberty" (paper presented to The Responsible Society, London, England, 1976). See also Eysenck and Nias, *Sex, Violence and the Media* (New York: St. Martin's Press, 1978), pp. 120–124.

IV. Pornography and the Law

Congress shall make no law respecting the establishment of religion, or prohibiting the free exercise thereof; or abridging the freedom of speech, or of the press; or the right of the people peaceably to assemble, and to petition the Government for a redress of grievances.

—FIRST AMENDMENT, BILL OF RIGHTS
OF THE UNITED STATES CONSTITUTION

Pornography is clearly a threat to women. Each of the modes of injury cited above offers sufficient reason at least to consider proposals for the social and legal control of pornography. The almost universal response from progressives to such proposals is that constitutional guarantees of freedom of speech and privacy preclude recourse to law.[7] While I am concerned about the erosion of constitutional rights and also think for many reasons that great caution must be exercised before undertaking a legal campaign against pornography, I find objections to such a campaign that are based on appeals to the First Amendment or to a right to privacy ultimately unconvincing.

Much of the defense of the pornographer's right to publish seems to assume that, while pornography may be tasteless and vulgar, it is basically an entertainment that harms no one but its consumers, who may at worst suffer from the debasement of their taste; and that therefore those who argue for its control are demanding an unjustifiable abridgment of the rights to freedom of speech of those who make and distribute pornographic materials and of the rights to privacy of their customers. The account of pornography given above shows that the assumptions of this position are false. Nevertheless, even some who acknowledge its harmful character feel that it is granted immunity from social control by the First Amendment, or that the harm that would ensue from its control outweighs the harm prevented by its control.

There are three ways of arguing that control of pornography is incompatible with adherence to constitutional rights. The first argument claims that regulating pornography involves an unjustifiable interference in the private lives of individuals. The second argument takes the First Amendment as a basic principle constitutive of our form of government, and claims that the production and distribution of pornographic material, as a form of speech, is an activity protected by that amendment. The third argument claims not that the pornographer's rights are violated, but that others' rights will be if controls against pornography are instituted.

The privacy argument is the easiest to dispose of. Since the open commerce in pornographic materials is an activity carried out in the public sphere, the publication and distribution of such materials, unlike their use by individuals, is not protected by rights to privacy. The distinction between the private consumption of pornographic material and the production and distribution of, or open commerce in, it is sometimes blurred by defenders of pornography. But I may entertain, in the privacy of my mind, defamatory opinions about another person, even though I may not broadcast them. So one might create without restraint—as long as no one were harmed in the course of preparing them—pornographic materials for one's personal use, but be restrained from reproducing and distributing them. In both cases what one is doing—in the privacy of one's mind or basement—may indeed be deplorable, but immune from legal proscription. Once the activity becomes public, however—i.e., once it involves others—it is no longer protected by the same rights that protect activities in the private sphere.*

In considering the second argument (that control of pornography, private or public, is wrong in principle), it seems important to determine whether we consider the right to freedom of speech to be absolute and unqualified. If it is, then obviously all speech, including pornography, is entitled to protection. But the right is, in the first place, not an unqualified right: There are several kinds of speech not protected by the First Amendment, including the incitement to violence in volatile circumstances, the solicitation of crimes, perjury and misrepresentation, slander, libel, and false advertising.† That there are forms of proscribed speech shows that we accept limitations on the right to freedom of speech if such speech, as do the forms listed, impinges on other rights. The manufacture and distribution of material which defames and threatens all members of a class by its recommendation of abusive and degrading behavior toward some members of that class simply in virtue of their membership in it seems

---

* Thus, the right to use such materials in the privacy of one's home, which has been upheld by the United States Supreme Court (*Stanley* v. *Georgia*, 394 U.S. 557), does not include the right to purchase them or to have them available in the commercial market. See also *Paris Adult Theater I* v. *Slaton*, 431 U.S. 49.
† The Supreme Court has also traditionally included obscenity in this category. As not everyone agrees it should be included, since as defined by statutes, it is a highly vague concept, and since the grounds accepted by the Court for including it miss the point, I prefer to omit it from this list.

a clear candidate for inclusion on the list. The right is therefore not an unqualified one.

Nor is it an absolute or fundamental right, underived from any other right: If it were there would not be exceptions or limitations. The first ten amendments were added to the Constitution as a way of guaranteeing the "blessings of liberty" mentioned in its preamble, to protect citizens against the unreasonable usurpation of power by the state. The specific rights mentioned in the First Amendment—those of religion, speech, assembly, press, petition—reflect the recent experiences of the makers of the Constitution under colonial government as well as a sense of what was and is required generally to secure liberty.

It may be objected that the right to freedom of speech is fundamental in that it is part of what we mean by liberty and not a right that is derivative from a right to liberty. In order to meet this objection, it is useful to consider a distinction explained by Ronald Dworkin in his book *Taking Rights Seriously*.[8] As Dworkin points out, the word "liberty" is used in two distinct, if related, senses: as "license," i.e., the freedom from legal constraints to do as one pleases, in some contexts; and as "independence," i.e., "the status of a person as independent and equal rather than subservient," in others. Failure to distinguish between these senses in discussions of rights and freedoms is fatal to clarity and understanding.

If the right to free speech is understood as a partial explanation of what is meant by liberty, then liberty is perceived as license: The right to do as one pleases includes a right to speak as one pleases. But license is surely not a condition the First Amendment is designed to protect. We not only tolerate but require legal constraints on liberty as license when we enact laws against rape, murder, assault, theft, etc. If everyone did exactly as she or he pleased at any given time, we would have chaos if not lives, as Hobbes put it, that are "nasty, brutish, and short." We accept government to escape, not to protect, this condition.

If, on the other hand, by liberty is meant independence, then freedom of speech is not necessarily a part of liberty; rather, it is a means to it. The right to freedom of speech is not a fundamental, absolute right, but one derivative from, possessed in virtue of, the more basic right to independence. Taking this view of liberty requires providing arguments showing that the more specific rights we claim are necessary to guarantee our status as persons "independent and equal rather than subservient." In the context of government, we understand independence to be the freedom of each individual to participate as an equal among equals in the determination of how she or he is to be governed. Freedom of speech in this context means that an individual may not only entertain beliefs concerning government privately, but may express them publicly. We express our opinions about taxes, disarmament, wars, social-welfare programs, the function of the police, civil rights, and so on. Our right to freedom of speech includes the right to criticize the government and to protest against various forms of injustice and the abuse of power. What we wish to protect is the free expression of ideas even when they are unpopular. What we do not always remember is that speech has functions other than the expression of ideas.

Regarding the relationship between a right to freedom of speech and the publication and distribution of pornographic materials, there are two points to be made. In the first place, the latter activity is hardly an exercise of the right to the free expression of ideas as understood above. In the second place, to the degree that the tolerance of material degrading to women supports and reinforces the attitude that women are not fit to participate as equals among equals in the political life of their communities, and that the prevalence of such an attitude effectively prevents women from so participating, the absolute and fundamental right of women to liberty (political independence) is violated.

This second argument against the suppression of pornographic material, then, rests on a premise that must be rejected, namely, that the right to freedom of speech is a right to utter anything one wants. It thus fails to show that the production and distribution of such material is an activity protected by the First Amendment. Furthermore, an examination of the issues involved leads to the conclusion that tolerance of this activity violates the rights of women to political independence.

The third argument (which expresses concern that curbs on pornography are the first step toward political censorship) runs into the same ambiguity that besets the arguments based on principle. These arguments generally have as an underlying assumption that the maximization of freedom is a worthy social goal. Control of pornography diminishes freedom—directly the freedom of pornographers, indirectly that of all of us. But again, what is meant by "freedom"? It cannot be that what is to be maximized is license—as the goal of a social group whose members probably have at least some incompatible interests, such a goal would be internally inconsistent. If, on the other hand, the maximization of political independence is the goal, then that is in no way enhanced by, and may be endangered by, the tolerance of pornography. To argue that the control of pornography would create a precedent for suppressing political speech is thus to confuse license with political independence. In addition, it ignores a crucial basis for the control of pornography, i.e., its character as libelous speech. The prohibition of such speech is justified by the need for protection from the injury (psychological as well as physical or economic) that results from libel. A very different kind of argument would be required to justify curtailing the right to speak our minds about the institutions which govern us. As long as such distinctions are insisted upon, there is little danger of the government's using the control of pornography as precedent for curtailing political speech.

In summary, neither as a matter of principle nor in the interests of maximizing liberty can it be supposed that there is an intrinsic right to manufacture and distribute pornographic material.

The only other conceivable source of protection for pornography would be a general right to do what we please as long as the rights of others are respected. Since the production and distribution of pornography violates the rights of women—to respect and to freedom from defamation, among others—this protection is not available.

V. Conclusion

I have defined pornography in such a way as to distinguish it from erotica and from moral realism, and have argued that it is defamatory and libelous toward women, that it condones crimes against women, and that it invites tolerance of the social, economic, and cultural oppression of women. The production and distribution of pornographic material is thus a social and moral wrong. Contrasting both the current volume of pornographic production and its growing infiltration of the communications media with the status of women in this culture makes clear the necessity for its control. Since the goal of controlling pornography does not conflict with constitutional rights, a common obstacle to action is removed.

Appeals for action against pornography are sometimes brushed aside with the claim that such action is a diversion from the primary task of feminists—the elimination of sexism and of sexual inequality. This approach focuses on the enjoyment rather than the manufacture of pornography, and sees it as merely a product of sexism which will disappear when the latter has been overcome and the sexes are socially and economically equal. Pornography cannot be separated from sexism in this way: Sexism is not just a set of attitudes regarding the inferiority of women but the behaviors and social and economic rules that manifest such attitudes. Both the manufacture and distribution of pornography and the enjoyment of it are instances of sexist behavior. The enjoyment of pornography on the part of individuals will presumably decline as such individuals begin to accord women their status as fully human. A cultural climate which tolerates the degrading representation of women is not a climate which facilitates the development of respect for women. Furthermore, the demand for pornography is stimulated not just by the sexism of individuals but by the pornography industry itself. Thus, both as a social phenomenon and in its effect on individuals, pornography, far from being a mere product, nourishes sexism. The campaign against it is an essential component of women's struggle for legal, economic, and social equality, one which requires the support of all feminists.*

* Many women helped me to develop and crystallize the ideas presented in this paper. I would especially like to thank Michele Farrell, Laura Lederer, Pamela Miller, and Dianne Romain for their comments in conversation and on the first written draft. Portions of this material were presented orally to members of the Society for Women in Philosophy and to participants in the workshops on "What Is Pornography?" at the Conference on Feminist Perspectives on Pornography, San Francisco, November 17, 18, and 19, 1978. Their discussion was invaluable in helping me to see problems and to clarify the ideas presented here.

SECTION II.

Pornography: Who Is Hurt

In education, in marriage, in religion, in everything, disappointment is the lot of women. It shall be the business of my life to deepen this disappointment in every woman's heart until she bows down to it no longer.
   —LUCY STONE
      "Disappointment Is the Lot of Women" speech, October 17–18, 1855

Then and Now:
An Interview with a Former
Pornography Model

Laura Lederer

The question often arises, "Why do women star in pornographic films and model for pornographic magazines?" Many people suggest that feminists are aimed in the wrong direction: We should, they say, attack the women who pose for and act in such degrading films and photographs.

Presumably our society is set up so that women have a free choice as to what we want to do. If women can be convinced to stop modeling for pornographic magazines and films, goes the argument, then the industry will shut down. But the truth is, as long as we have a patriarchal culture which encourages women to use their bodies to get male approval and which rewards young girls for being sexy objects, we can expect to see many females turn to pornography, prostitution, and other forms of sex-ploitation to stay alive or even to earn prestige and social acceptance.

The following interview with Jane Jones (for purposes of anonymity her name has been changed) is one woman's story of how she got involved in the pornography industry and what it was like to be a pornography model. New first-person accounts, like Linda Lovelace's *Ordeal*, and new evidence and research by women like Kathleen Barry (*Female Sexual Slavery*) and Diana E. H. Russell (*International Tribunal on Crimes Against Women*) suggest that her story is not atypical.

Jane Jones (JJ): My family life wasn't the greatest. I was the only female child. Both my parents were alcoholics and both were child abusers; though neither one admitted they were themselves, they used to accuse one another of mistreating us kids.

There were a lot of sexual imbalances in my family. For instance, I had my own room because I was the only girl, but I wasn't allowed to lock it, also because I was a girl. If I tried to lock it, my father or older brothers would use that as an excuse to burst in on me. One time I didn't have anything on and grabbed a sweater to cover myself. My brother ripped it off me. He had to pay for a new sweater, but no one said anything about how it was ripped off or why.

If I was in the shower, my father would come in and turn off the hot water or throw ice cubes into the shower. Just a joke, of course, but I would have to jump out or yell. My father was sexually provocative. He was always touching me. My mother encouraged it in a strange way by not validating my experience when I would object. If my father fondled my butt and I protested to her, she would say, "But he's your father!" No one ever believed my problems. My father was my grandmother's only and precious son. There was a sense in my family that if I didn't put up with these jokes or antics, I was being paranoid, or a bad sport, or I had a dirty mind. It was always in *my* imagination.

My first experience with the camera was for high school graduation. My mother fixed me up to wear a low-cut black blouse which was deliberately suggestive. This was in the decade when females wore Peter Pan blouses and circle pins. I remember I felt extremely sexy. I had never liked my body, mostly because of the suggestive innuendos of my father as I developed. I always thought I was plain-looking. But I photographed differently than I looked, and I found that out very quickly. I found out that I had a marketable commodity.

Laura Lederer (LL):   *How did you get started in the nude modeling business?*

JJ: It was in 1967. I was just out of high school. I had run away from home. I was rebellious—"living in sin" with my boyfriend. We had a two-bedroom house, actually a little shack in the inner city, complete with rats and cockroaches, which we shared with a seven-and-a-half-month pregnant woman. I wasn't able to keep the jobs I had tried to get. I was fired from one job because of ill health. I remember feeling trapped. I had no real skills I could market in order to stay alive. That particular month was a hard one, and we ended up not having enough money to pay the rent. We needed a fairly large amount of money quickly. I looked in the want ads in the *L.A. Free Press*. There was an ad which read: "Models, $50.00/day, 18 and over." I called, and they asked me my height and weight and hired me that first day.

LL: *Why do most women model for these agencies? Why do women come in the door in the first place?*

JJ: A lot of women are hurt or crazy—women under stress. Yes, most women come in under a lot of stress. They're usually desperate when they first come in—maybe they need money for some emergency, like I did, or they've gone as long as they can doing odds and ends or working at shit jobs, and they finally just have to pay their bills. I met a woman whose kid was in the hospital, and I met lots of women who were financially strapped. There were also many illegal aliens there who couldn't work regular jobs even if they had the skills because they didn't have their green cards.

LL: *Does the agency exploit this need?*

JJ: I don't know. Well, they certainly know how to get you to do what they want. Some women are so bad off that they just go immediately into hard-core films.

Take the average woman who graduates from high school. Vast numbers of us are not skilled at anything but marketing our bodies, usually to get husbands, but sometimes to get money or fame. We spend all our time and money making ourselves pretty, being well made up. What I'm trying to say is that I don't see what is so unusual about a woman going to a modeling agency. It's just the logical extension of everything that is taught us at home and in school. The only difference is in the degree. Most of the women who came to the agency were poor, or in extreme times of crisis, or both. They were women from all walks of life. Runaways are a very big part of the business. This fed right into the 1960's hippie movement. I remember feeling nudity was okay and natural, so photos of it must be okay too —except that it didn't feel good.

LL: *How did your agency work?*

JJ: First, they took nude pictures of you. They had this huge book of photos of women. Most of the women were posed in high heels with no clothes on. There are a variety of poses—standing, sitting, back, front, side, and sometimes a closeup of the face. They had two books—one was of white women, one was of Black women and other women of color. Then they had a third portfolio, which was commonly known as the "Freaks" book—women who (in their eyes) were grotesquely overweight, or had some deformity or something abnormal like a tattoo. I remember feeling badly for them, not because they were overweight, but because they were treated much worse than the other women. It was almost as if they weren't human.

LL: *Why did they have one book for white women and another one for women of color?*

JJ: I suppose because there are bigots in this business too—it's no different than the rest of society.

LL: *Could you talk more about the agency procedure?*

JJ: There was a legal-size sheet of paper. It's actually your contract (at least it was in my agency). On the sheet there was a check-list of what types of modeling were available. There were boxes which you could check off—"hard core," "soft core," "pretty girl." "Pretty girl" was like the pin-up bathing suits, negligees, and "tasteful" nudity, always posed so the crotch was hidden. There were also boxes labeled "nude modeling" and "movies" and "hostessing." In another space on the contract, the agency checked off what age you could look. I could look as young as eleven, which was a benefit, since "young girls" were in big demand.

There was a place on the sheet to check off whether you were on the pill. The agency encouraged women to go on the pill because it made your breasts bigger. There was a large market for women with big breasts. They had a whole portfolio of these women which they called "Tit Rags" or "Mammary Reviews." If you got the job, pho-tographers frequently asked you when your period was due and scheduled the photography session just before so your breasts were at their biggest. Photographers would come in and look at pictures in the portfolio and write down your code number and name. The agency had code numbers supposedly for your own protection, but also for their protection—so that the women wouldn't get jobs with-out giving the agency their cut. After the photographer had chosen a model, the agency would call you and you would appear for an audition. The audition usually consisted of you stripping and walking around the room. A lot of times you had to wear stockings, garters, and high heels without any underwear. I hated that part—it really made me feel creepy. Occasionally the photographer would take test shots before you were hired.

There was a lot of competitiveness between women at the agency. Most women were out to get the job, and women would cut one another down before the auditions. Almost every model was con-nected to a man. Contrary to popular belief that there are a lot of les-bians in the business, almost every woman I met there was hetero, as far as I knew.

It was a lonely sort of business in that you rarely worked with one another, but always in competition. Once in a while the agency would send two women on a job together, but that was the excep-tion rather than the rule, and even then there was a competitive atmosphere. Sometimes they would have what's called a "cattle call," and all the women would line up. Cattle calls were very demeaning.

The photographers ranged from nice to real pricks. Some were old, grandfatherly types. Others were freelancers with no idea where they would sell their photographs. Some worked for specific magazines. Some men treated you okay, but most acted like you weren't even human and didn't give you lunch breaks or anything. There were some lecherous types who figured that once they had "paid" for you, you owed them more than just photographs.

LL: What were some of your first jobs?

JJ: On my first job there was a woman who had just had a baby two days prior to the assignment. She was bleeding. She was doing the movie to try to get the kid out of the hospital. She had this tampon—or two of them—in her to try to stop the bleeding, even though she wasn't supposed to use tampons right after birth. Our job was to simulate lesbian love. That was the first and last time I did that. I really disliked the woman-on-woman stuff. Most women asked for lesbian scenes. In fact, several women told me that I was crazy not to work with women because then I wouldn't get the clap. But I was very male-identified at that time and extremely homophobic, so I requested hetero scenes. In retrospect, it is easy for me to see that I was fighting my own sexuality.

The male image of lesbian love seems to dictate that it be violent and/or include a male voyeur. There is a very big demand for this sort of lesbian love scene in pornography.

It seems to me that it is important for male photographers to portray lesbian love in as repugnant a way as possible. They have very bizarre notions of women's sexuality. None of the gentle loving comes through. Male portrayal of lesbian sex is a real PR job for heterosexual sex.

I also had to do a simulated lesbian sadomasochism job. (At that time I was not a lesbian.) I was terrified. The woman who was playing the "S" was really into it (she wasn't a lesbian either), and that came out in the film. The photographer thought it was just great.

Another movie I did was called *Five the Hard Way*. The plot revolved around this guy who was supposedly incredibly endowed. Women pursued him everywhere until he was exhausted from having to deal with them. In desperation he staged his own funeral. The last scene is at the grave. All the women who "love" him weep and take off their clothes. As they do, the dead man gets this monumental erection (which they manufactured with a Phillips screwdriver).

LL: What other assignments did you have?

JJ: I did an album cover for an English group that was released here. Their music was terrible. I know the cover was what sold the album because of reviews I've read. It didn't sell well in the first issue, but they reissued it with the new cover and the album sold 50,000 copies in one day. It was written up in *Rolling Stone*—people were buying the album, tossing the record out, and taking the cover home to display. The picture on the cover was a crotch shot of me leaping high in the air to simulate flying. I had to go through hell to get that photo.

LL: What do you mean?

JJ: For the cover shot I jumped eighty-seven times off a coffee table onto a hard mat. I counted because it was such a nightmare. I had to resist my natural impulse to break my fall until the last possible moment. The photographer was underneath, taking pictures, straight up. Then he drove me out to the desert for the shot for the inside cover. I went alone with him.

LL: Wasn't that dangerous?

JJ: Yes—incredibly dangerous. But things like that happened all the time, and I never thought twice about them in those days. It was ridiculous. I put myself into all sorts of dangerous situations.

I rationalized it because I had been referred to the job by a photographer I knew, and because I was really impressed with the credentials of the guy taking the pictures—he had done several other album covers. Anyway, he said he wanted a photograph with no telephone poles on the horizon, but that also meant I was away from anyone else with a man in the desert, and I was nude. There was one point when I was very scared. He propositioned me, and I refused. I remember thinking, "I could easily get raped out here." After that I started leaving the license number of the photographer with my boyfriend so that if anything happened to me he could track me down.

LL: Why did you put up with situations like that?

JJ: At that time, it was just part of the job for me. Women are socialized to put up with a lot—to passively accept tremendous amounts of pain, indignity, and humiliation. They used to do the most ridiculous things to you—like paint your whole body or put glitter all over you.

LL: They still do. The cover of the Ohio Players album is called Honey, *and in the picture they have poured honey all over a woman —as if she were a thing to be consumed.*

JJ: That's it exactly. Women are portrayed, seen, and treated as "little treats." There aren't many other images to choose from when you're growing up. I was taught that I was a "sweet thing," and when I grew up, I found that I was a marketable commodity—which is exactly what a woman is in our society in one form or another. One of the porn series I was in used food names for the women, like Taffy, Candy, Cookie.

LL: What jobs did you like and dislike?

JJ: The jobs that were okay were the ones in which I could just sit there and get photographed. That allowed me to stay detached. As much as possible I tried to keep detached from the pictures, from how they were being taken, and where they would be going. I never thought about that. I never thought about the conditions under which I worked. I would try to think about what was going to happen later —what I would do when I got home or on the weekend, and how I would spend the money I had made.

The jobs I hated most were the ones where you had to "emote." Emote means the guy would say something like "Pretend you're really getting it," or "Make love to the camera."

LL: *What was the pay like?*

JJ: The average pay was very good. For one job I got $150 for twenty-five pictures. It took a half hour to take them. You could make forty-five dollars for a half hour of filming for a peep show. In those days (1968) that was quite a bit of money; but you couldn't count on regular work—it was very sporadic, and the agency took between 25 and 30 percent of everything I took in.

LL: *And the photos were published here?*

JJ: A lot of the photos were used in a magazine called *Jaybird*, which was supposed to be a magazine of nudists in nudist camps, but was really just a cover for legitimizing the pornography business. Their attitude was "the secret camera"—spying on the nudists. *Jaybird* photographed nudes swimming in a pool or hanging out in the sun. The interesting thing was that they were always pictures of naked *females.*

LL: *What about your boyfriend? Did he approve?*

JJ: He thought it was great. He was really turned on by the whole idea and came to watch me several times. He encouraged it a lot. He felt proud because my job was a sign that I was a "sexy chick," and that was a big reflection on him. I was "his." When his friends found out, they made weird sexual allusions and propositioned me. Once they knew I was doing the modeling, they thought I was free for the taking. There was this immediate assumption by men that I was turning tricks on the side. Men would ask me, "Did you get off on it?" or "Would you do it for your friends?" If a woman showed disapproval of what I was doing, my boyfriend would say, "She's just jealous that she can't do it."

The relationship between a man who is lovers with a woman who does nude modeling is just like the relationship of a pimp to a prostitute. In my household I bought the goodies and made the food and paid the rent. My boyfriend lived off me. It's ironic—when I look back now, I realize that I could have done much better without him and his drug habits. I could have supported myself, but back then I didn't believe I could do it alone.

LL: What would you say are the similarities and differences between the prostitute and the pornography model?

JJ: A prostitute is just being more honest about what she's doing. A pornography model can fool herself, and we did. We called what we were doing "modeling" or "acting." Pornography models have the illusion that they're not hooking. It's called acting instead of sex. Or it is labeled "simulated sex"—even sometimes when it's not simulated, it's called simulated. But it's all a form of rape because women who are involved in it don't know how to get out.

LL: When did the big money, the glamour, and the fun start to fade?

JJ: Fairly soon after I started modeling, the agency started to pressure me to do hard-core films. I would come in for a job, and they would say, "There's nothing available in the area you want, but I've got this other job—you really should think about it."

You would be furious and frustrated, but they would break you down little by little. You get more and more pressed to take what is available. And what is available becomes less and less attractive the longer you stay in the business.

I was always trying to get "softer" jobs and not stoop to doing films that were hard core. These standards might seem funny to people outside the modeling business, but it is a way for the model to maintain self-respect and some control over what is happening.

There is a real demand for women who haven't been photographed before. If you're a new person, everyone wants you because you're new. "Fresh meat" they call it. You think it is going to continue like that forever. When I first started modeling, I was offered several jobs every day, and I had my choice of anything I wanted to do. After I'd been around, they started to offer me less jobs, and things became tighter and tighter. The agency was always calling me and saying, "What about *this* job? It's really something you should take. And he doesn't even mind that you're not twenty-one." That was another thing: Many photographers didn't want you unless you were a legal adult, so that was one more thing the agency held over your head if you were younger.

LL: Why do women resist the pressure to do hard-core films?

JJ: Once you do hard core, you can't ever go back to the more "legitimate" modeling. There is this illusion of virginity lost when you do a hard-core pornography movie or magazine. Supposedly you are more "hard bitten." You have gone lower than the acceptable low. *Playboy* initiated that whole attitude back in the fifties. They were very picky about what flesh they exposed. They would never take any woman who had already been in a porn movie—especially a hard-core porn movie. When I was told that *Playboy* wouldn't take you if you'd ever had nude pictures published before, I was very angry because that meant I'd blown my chance! My great ambition in those days was to be a *Playboy* bunny—that was the direction I was headed in.*

LL: Why do women do hard-core movies then?

JJ: A good analogy is to think of the pollution standard in Los Angeles. The air is dirty; the EPA measurement says it's beyond the acceptable level. But instead of cleaning up the air, pressure is just put on the EPA to lower its standards. That way Los Angeles air still falls within the acceptable category, and people go on living and thinking they have clean air when they really don't. The same thing happens in modeling. Your standards go down—they're forced down by circumstances. You become fearful that you'll never be able to work at anything else. You hook into the money, but that doesn't continue unless you'll do more and more things you don't want to do.

LL: Did you ever think about getting older—about what would happen then?

JJ: Yes. I was always aware of my body as a commodity. I couldn't have tan marks, so I never went out into the sun unless I could be nude. I worried about scars; I fussed over wrinkles. There was a woman at the front desk who was older. She was the wife of the man who owned the agency. She was also an ex-model. She had gargantuan silicone breasts. One of the first things I noticed when I came to the agency was a huge photo—a crotch shot of this woman when she was younger. Now she was sitting behind the desk encouraging other young women to go the same route.

There is no provision for aging in this business. She's lucky she's got the job behind the desk.

* Ed. Note: This sort of prejudice against pornography models is common knowledge among fledgling actresses and models. Cecil Smith, of the *Los Angeles Times* ("Katie, Inside the World of a Centerfold." *Los Angeles Times,* Pt. IV, October 23, 1978, p. 18) recently asked a young model turned actress if she ever posed in the nude. When she answered no, he asked why: "Well, it's a kind of social thing," she said. "If you do centerfold, you're, well, in a different class. I don't like that word 'class,' but it's a different social order." She was discussing the thesis that models who pose in the nude for pornographic magazines are destined after that to work "in the kind of semiporno back street of modeling."

LL: Was there physical violence on your job?

JJ: There is a great deal of physical abuse on the job that is taken for granted. Most of these operations were low-budget cram-course films, and the men would work you to death. At the end of the day, I was often exhausted and sometimes in tears.

Sometimes I would show up on location and have to leave. I lost two jobs because I refused to wear the costumes. They were crusty with vaginal secretions and sperm. Women who work in the pornography business always have vaginal trichomoniasis or some infection from the working conditions, which run from bad to simply intolerable. At one point there was an epidemic of hepatitis and mononucleosis. The communicable diseases spread quickly.*

Oftentimes women were put in physically dangerous positions. I knew a model who broke her leg trying to pose in a movie of a nude circus act. She fell off a trapeze because she just wasn't trained to do that sort of thing. Another example of this was a woman who received bad rope burns from a pose which required her to slide up and down a rope. There was also a woman who had an allergic reaction to paint. They sprayed her with paint (that was in the late sixties when psychedelic body painting was in). Her skin reacted, and the whole top layer peeled off. They weren't able to photograph her, so she never got paid for her trouble.

The most common kind of abuse was emotional abuse. There were suggestive sexual comments. You were treated like a piece of meat. Sexism is a given in that business. In those days I didn't understand the meaning of the word sexism and all its political ramifications, but I sure knew how the crap came down on a day-to-day basis. Many times there were hard sexual overtures at the end of a working day.

Another thing about pornographic films is that the men always referred to you in the third person. You would be standing right there, and they would talk about you or about your body. It was very degrading and humiliating.

In the casting and scripting of the films, women are not given real names. For instance, while the hero of the film may be called something like "Robert Swashbuckler," all the females are called by "types" such as "Goldilocks" or "Negress" or "Cleopatra" or "Miss

---

* Ed. Note: Another pornography model I interviewed told me she had a herpes infection that hung on for years. When I expressed dismay, she said she was lucky: Another friend in the business had dozens of the open sores on her vagina. The model called it an "occupational hazard" of the business. For a full list of occupational hazards of pornography modeling, read Linda Lovelace, *Ordeal* (Secaucus, N.J.: Citadel Press, 1980).

Muffet." Sometimes the character types are taken from fairy-tale images. Others were named "Heaven" and "Sin."

LL: Did you personally ever experience violence on the job?

JJ: Yes. One day I went on a modeling assignment with a photographer. We went on location to a very fancy Los Angeles home. It was an assignment for a typical fake, nudist magazine. He brought his assistant (a woman), his eight-year-old daughter, and another female model. All four of us got into the swimming pool and swam nude while he took pictures. The setting was gorgeous, and I remember thinking that every assignment should be so good.

After the photographing he brought out this enormous strawberry pie and a glass of milk for each of us. I went in to make a phone call, and he followed me. A few seconds later my legs buckled out from under me, and I felt dizzy and out of control. I know now that he drugged me, but at the time I didn't understand what was happening. He carried me to a large bed and raped me. I was conscious but groggy and unable to move a muscle. After it was over he went to a picture on the wall and lifted it. Underneath it were markings, like this: 𝍢𝍩 | . He added another one and put the picture back down. Afterward he drove me home. Later when I reported it to my agency, they brushed it off saying that they couldn't believe that I didn't know about his reputation as a "ladies' man." They also told me that he was a big client, and they weren't going to harass him over such a "little thing." That "Oh, it's nothing" attitude was pervasive—later I saw the same photographer at a nude-modeling contest. He couldn't understand why I became hysterical when he walked over to say hello.

LL: When did you stop modeling?

JJ: Around 1970 I was exhausted. I wasn't sleeping at night. I was having nightmares and throwing up. I was physically sick from the long hours of work, and I was getting bladder infections from the work conditions and the general uncleanliness. The last straw was when the agency tried to coerce me into signing a contract for a terrible hard-core pornography film without letting me see the script. In a rage I asked them for my contract, and when they gave it to me, I ripped it into shreds and walked out. I remember I felt absolutely exhilarated—I was free—but also absolutely terrified. I was asking myself, "How am I going to make a living?"

LL: And now?

JJ: Things won't ever be the same for me. My sex life has never been normal. I can't equate sex with affection. I have these images that never stop running in my head. They're fantasies of women as passive victims. All the scenes disgust me, but I can't stop them. I want to be able to be in a loving situation without having these scenarios going through my head. I hate myself if I have the fantasies, and if I don't have them I don't get off sexually. It seems to me that having masochistic fantasies is indicative of how I view myself as a woman. Even though I was socialized into it by a traumatic background, I can't forgive the part of me that is sexual in that way.

I've been in years of therapy. Some therapists say you can change; some say you just have to accept your fantasies. But I just feel damaged. I relate sexually to women now, and I feel that is a more loving and natural way for me. But the psychic damage has never really healed. Eventually I hope it will.

LL: How do you feel now about having been in the pornography business?

JJ: I have a very deep fear that my picture will show up somewhere, somehow, in the future. I was naïve. I used my real name. Most women change their names or use false names, but at that time I had no conception of a future that might be different for me.

Even when photographers give back the negatives, you can never be sure. They might have kept one or made new negatives or something. I am positive that my past is going to come back to me. It already has a couple of times. Once a man I knew (but not well) went into a camera store and saw a shot of me. He mentioned it to me the next time he saw me, and I felt raped—I really did. Suddenly he seemed to have this power over me. Another time a male friend in the army saw a picture of me pinned to some man's locker. I was obsessed to know what the picture looked like—not out of vanity but out of fear. Now that I am a feminist and active politically, there is all the more reason to be fearful. Photos like that can really be used.

LL: That actually happened to a leading feminist—did you know that? She did some nude modeling a long time ago, and when her book was published, Hustler *magazine got hold of the nude photos of her and published them in their magazine as a political slap in the face.*

JJ: Yes, because as soon as you've signed a model's release form, you've signed away those pictures for life. It doesn't hit you at the time how long a period that can be, or how differently a photo can appear from what you think is being taken. The thing is, with enough stress or enough need, any woman will do things she never thought she would do before. And if a woman is disenfranchised, poverty-stricken, or an illegal alien, she really doesn't have much choice—she makes her money any way she can. Woman are not on the controlling end of the pornography business, just as they are not on the controlling end in the rest of our society.

LL: So women should concentrate on pressuring those who are on the controlling end rather than on the pornography models who are themselves the victims of pornography?

JJ: Yes. It isn't just the "Ms. Enameled Floors" in the suburbs who put me down. It's also feminists that are supposed to be my sisters. It's politically incorrect to talk about it. The taboos keep us apart.

I've never had anybody from a poor or working-class background give me the "How could you have done anything like that?" question, but middle-class feminists have no consciousness about what it is like out there. You have to remember who's the real enemy—who has the power—who you're selling it to, who you're looking up at and trying to please. It's not other women.

LL: Were there "snuff" films then?

JJ: I heard about "snuff" films right after I stopped modeling. Stories came down the grapevine. One agency in Los Angeles sent a woman out on an assignment with a man who killed her and took pictures of how he tortured her. The business just froze. Models went to work with their boyfriends, and some stopped coming in altogether. Everyone was terrified. That didn't last long though. People need money in order to live. My agency told me that that man had come to them, and that they had checked out his credentials and found that they were false. Obviously the murdered woman's agency didn't check. We valued ourselves so little.

LL: Have there been changes in the pornography industry since you modeled?

JJ: Yes, there's been a big change in pornography. The hating way in which women are portrayed has escalated so fast. They used to be afraid to portray it all, but now you see everything—women being skewered, women being killed. When I was modeling, I never saw any of what is now called hard core. It may have been around somewhere, but it was definitely underground.

There may have been allusions to struggle or antagonism between the sexes in the script, but there was never the out-and-out hatred that is seen in pornography today. Back then it was very "clean-cut" nudist, All-American, with photos of white underwear and tennis shoes. The sexuality was barely suggested. Back then hard core meant simply out-front sex. Now it means violence, brutality, sadomasochism. The people have harder-looking, subhuman faces.

LL: What do you think women can do to make the world a safer place for ourselves?

JJ: To tell you the truth, I'm not very optimistic. I've seen the worst of it. In order to change the industry, society and its view of women both have to change fundamentally. You can make an impact on some areas, but others are a lost cause. Damage is being done daily to young kids because at that age they are just forming an image of themselves, even though they don't know it. The media is marketing younger and younger girls.

I have a feeling of powerlessness. Women must get together and realize that it's not the women being photographed but the images they are forced to portray by the men in control that we must confront. The misogyny I see today is so blatant and so accepted as a matter of fact that when we challenge it, we're seen as irrational or bad sports, or lacking a sense of humor, much like my father viewed me when I objected to his incestuous advances. When you're not being oppressed by it, it seems harmless to you. I'm convinced we're training little girls and boys to view sadomasochistic behavior as normal by allowing pornography to proliferate so openly. Women are inevitably the victims in this scenario, since it's done for the benefit of the men who buy it. We must organize boycotts against the people who profit from it. They won't listen to our feelings, but they'll listen to our money. If we don't organize, all women will suffer. To me the acceptability of pornography is the clearest statement about the acceptability of women-hating and of women's real status in society.

Child Pornography

Florence Rush

"I do not think it is an accident that the ideal of femininity is fast becoming the infantilized woman," says Florence Rush, former social worker and author of a book on child sexual abuse. "Men are attracted to a woman who has the helplessness of a child. They prefer children, whether they are large size or little size. Today our society either makes the child look like a woman or the woman look like a child."

Child pornography is very big business. According to researchers and reporters, child models are not difficult to recruit: Many magazine publishers and film producers use their own children; others advertise to parents. A recent advertisement in Al Goldstein's magazine *Screw* offered $200 for young girl-child models. It brought dozens of responses from parents with female children. A writer who followed up the ad reports:

> Some parents appeared in the movie with their children; others merely allowed their children to have sex. One little girl, age 11, who ran crying from the bedroom after being told to have sex with a man of 40 protested, "Mommy, I can't do it." "You have to do it," her mother answered. "We need the money." And of course the little girl did.[1]

The last two years have brought much attention to the growing problem of child pornography, and fairly quick action has been taken by legislatures in our country. But while protecting our children is an important part of the feminist battle against pornography, educational and legal activity should not stop there. It is easier for us to become outraged by what is happening to young children than by what happens to grown women. We forget that young girls grow up to be women. About the time they reach the age of consent, what protection there is stops and the legalized exploitation starts again.

We do not have a history of taboos against the sexual use of children. Until recently, children were a paternal property and could be legitimately exploited, sold, or even killed by their masters.[2] And since minors were also a sexual property, sex between male adults and children has been sanctioned, or at the very least tolerated, in

71

our institutions of marriage, concubinage, slavery, prostitution, and pornography.

Today we expect the adult world to protect the young from sexual exploitation, but because we have neglected simultaneously to deprive men of their sexual privileges, our prohibitions represent the same confusion as do all laws and attitudes which arise from a double standard. Recently I heard a woman protest the marriage between a man of twenty and a woman of thirty. The bride was a "cradle snatcher," she said. When the protester was reminded of a male friend of seventy who was living with a woman of thirty, she spontaneously approved with "Good for John. I'm glad the old boy still has it in him." This common approbation of sex between young females and older males is also reflected in the law. In 1962 the American Law Institute recommended that the legal age of consent to sex* (now between sixteen and eighteen, depending upon the state) be uniformly dropped to age ten.[3] And until recently, the legal age of consent in the state of Delaware was seven; if a man of forty had sex with a child of seven or over, he did so legally.[4]

There is little doubt that men are sexually attracted to children, and entrepreneurs and advertisers attempt to capture this market. A good huckster will associate his product with a longed-for desire. Image-makers assure a man that if he uses the right shaving cream, a sexy woman will appear and obligingly demand that he "take it all off." And for those attracted to females of smaller dimensions, our media transform the most nonsexual items into an erotic garden of childish delights. Bell Telephone at one time circulated a picture of a twelve-year-old girl standing on a phone book reaching for something unseen. The caption read, "Are you using your phone book properly?" The message ostensibly instructed that the phone book is for finding numbers rather than adding height, but by posing the little girl with provocatively exposed buttocks, the picture made a direct appeal to male sexual interest in little girls. The message was so obvious that a group of women lawyers finally had the picture removed.[5] Today underwear companies have tots and teens modeling "demure briefs" and "sensuous thongs." Caress soap pushes its product with a T-shirt on which the word "Caress" invitingly covers a preteen bosom. In popular periodicals one can find a full-page photograph of a child about eight made up to look like Marilyn Monroe, holding a Teddy Bear, with the captioned promise that Baby Soft Cosmetics will give you that "clean irresistible baby smell grown up enough to be sexy." [6] In the sixties Romania Power

* Ed. Note: In other words, the age below which sex is termed statutory rape.

(Tyrone's daughter), age fourteen, became the model of high fashion, and Twiggy, the British model, age seventeen, stood five feet six inches, but weighed no more than ninety pounds; small, infantile, and childish was beautiful. Women who shopped at Bloomingdale's and Lord & Taylor could not find clothes long enough to cover their private parts. In the seventies *Harper's Bazaar* stated: "Just look at the movies. The kids are taking over Hollywood . . . Tatum O'Neal and Jodie Foster are already femme fatales and Chastity Bono is sure to be the tiny terrific of TV land." [7]

But if the little girl is to be a sexual commodity, the rift between common decency on the one hand and male desire and the profit motive on the other must somehow be reconciled. Many devices are used to mitigate this rift. One is the naughty but sophisticated dirty joke. William Burroughs in his book *Naked Lunch* had one child molester say to another, "May all your troubles be little ones." [8] Weather forecaster Tex Antoine, after hearing a report of the rape of an eight-year-old, quipped: "Confucius say if rape is inevitable, relax and enjoy it." [9] The coast-to-coast show, Mary Hartman, Mary Hartman, made an exhibitionistic flasher grandfather (flashers usually expose themselves to children) both funny and lovable. Another strategy employed to make the sexual use of children more palatable is art—preferably rebellious art. In the late nineteenth and early twentieth centuries, western society was obsessed with the image of the pure, innocent, sexless little girl. Several men of letters and art, who had never before made a political statement, suddenly found a cause. In opposition to her idealistic representation, they portrayed the female child as carnal. Cinderella kept a clean house and Alice in Wonderland had excellent manners, but Lolita was preferred. The prominent photographer O. G. Rejlander, the painters Jules Pascin and Balthus, and the currently popular photographer David Hamilton have portrayed the female child as either sexually aggressive, wantonly exuding sex, or depraved and harlot-like.

In Dostoyevsky's *The Possessed*, the downtrodden twelve-year-old Matroysha, first frightened when seduced by Stavrogin, soon becomes an unpleasant aggressor:

> Finally, such a strange thing happened suddenly which I will never forget and which astonished me: the little girl grabbed me around my neck with her arms and suddenly began really kissing me herself. Her face expressed complete delight. I got up almost in indignation—this was all so unpleasant for me, in such a little creature.[10]

And in *Crime and Punishment*, the fifty-year-old pedophile, Svidri-gailov, dreamed of a lustful five-year-old:

> There was something shameless and provocative in the quiet childlike face; it was depravity, it was the face of a harlot . . . now both eyes opened wide . . . they laughed . . . there was something infinitely hideous and shocking in that laugh, in those eyes. . . . "What, at five years old," muttered Svidrigailov in genuine horror. "What does it mean?" And now she turned to him her little face aglow, holding out her arms.[11]

While Dostoyevsky may have been using the seduction and corruption of children as a symbol of absolute moral degeneracy, nonetheless the frequent use of child sexuality by nineteenth-century authors contributed to the real use, abuse, and sexual manipulations of children.

O. G. Rejlander posed his eleven-year-old model, Charlotte Baker, in the nude and seminude so that her immature body communicated incongruous adult sexuality. Pascin painted his female children as seductive, cheap, and available. Later Balthus exhibited the immature female body to sharpen erotic reaction,[12] and today the popular photographer David Hamilton has his pubescent and prepubescent models pose vacant-faced and trance-like as they are sexually involved with themselves or each other. The novelist Alain Robbe-Grillet, in admiration of Hamilton's work, describes one Hamilton girl (addressing another) as follows:

> "She is an idiot. She understands nothing. She sleeps like an overripe fruit." Then come back toward the bed and whisper lowly into her ear, saying clearly: "You are nothing but a little whore, a slut, a damp meadow, a half-open shell." [13]

In this last decade we've had films like *Taxi Driver*, in which a twelve-year-old prostitute happily gratifies any male whim in order to please her loathsome pimp. Jodie Foster, who played the adolescent prostitute, was so well received in the role that she soon starred in *The Little Girl Who Lives Down the Lane*, in which she performed as a thirteen-year-old bundle of budding sexuality.

And then, of course, there is *Pretty Baby*. *Pretty Baby* is an invention of the French film director Louis Malle. It tells the story of a twelve-year-old prostitute, Violette, who was born and raised in a New Orleans brothel in the early twentieth century. On her twelfth birthday, the child's virginity is auctioned off to the highest bidder. Unaware of another existence, Violette takes her initiation into "the life" with pride and equanimity. When the brothel is closed by irate citizens, she moves in with the bearded photographer Bellocq, whom she seduces. Critic Vincent Canby saw the film as a "parable about life and art," but despite his enthusiasm for "art," he did not seem to care about the skill of Brooke Shields, the twelve-year-old actress who played the leading role. "I have no idea whether Brooke Shields can act in any real sense," he wrote. But to Canby, as well as to Malle, her skill (or lack of it) was irrelevant. Shields was a sex object and nothing more. "She has a face that transcends the need to act," said Canby.[14] Judith Crist, on the other hand, found *Pretty Baby* to be visually beautiful but "pointless"—especially the gratuitous flashing of "the heroine's prepubescent nudity." [15] For all its artistic trappings, I found the film no more than a pandering to pedophilic interests.

Pretty Baby was patterned after an actual child prostitute who lived in an actual brothel. But in the face of hard evidence that of the prostitutes who worked in the brothel, no less than one out of twelve suffered the ravages of venereal disease, drugs, and bodily abuse, Malle preferred fantasy to reality and insisted that in this brothel world there was neither a victim nor a violator.[16] And if a depiction of a child prostitute can be accomplished without showing a victim or a violator, then the statement, however artistic, can be no more than a legitimization of a man's right to purchase a child for sexual use. The poet Christina Rossetti said of the artist that he paints the female "not as she is but as she fills his dream." [17] And if the artistic creator of the female child refuses to acknowledge the power of one sex over the other and of the mature over the immature, then whether the little girl is fashioned as an *objet d'art* or a slut, by an artist or a hack pornographer, her representation can be nothing more than an insulting reflection of her creator's mind's eye.

And when in the name of humor, art, or the rebellious spirit, sex remains a metaphor for contempt and hostility, the step from humor, art, or the rebellious spirit to pornography is a short, easy one. The illustrator Aubrey Beardsley, Felix Salten, author of *Bambi*, and Guy de Maupassant all contributed to child pornography.

Aubrey Beardsley in *Under the Hill* described an orgy in which children pleasured carefree guests.[18] *The Memoirs of Josephine Mutzenbacher* is attributed to Felix Salten. Josephine, a prepubescent prostitute, shares the details of her profession with her readers:

> I was so worked up by this time that I went off as soon as I felt the head of it entering my vagina. His face was still sober, but he must have gone also as I felt my pussy getting all wet. He remained quiet, always with that grave look. Putting his hands

under my ass and pressing me tight to him, with one more shove
. . . I felt his whole cock entering me. It was a short thick one
but . . . it was all inside me.[19]

Guy de Maupassant in *The Colonel's Nieces* has a father assist his
his son in raping a child. " 'Give it to her,' muttered the father, who
was feeling the lad's balls, . . . 'Ain't she a beauty, boy? What a
tight little cunt she's got . . .' " [20]

And if the progression from the erotization of children in art and
humor to pornography is short, the step from pornographic fantasy
to acting out the fantasy as a real-life experience is negligible. Sex
biographers such as Casanova, Frank Harris, and the anonymous
author of *My Secret Life* all boasted of seducing children. Casanova
suggested that a child could be more easily seduced in the presence
of someone she trusted—an older sister perhaps.[21] Harris recommended India "as the happy hunting ground for little girls," [22] and
Walter (the main character in *My Secret Life*) found a plentiful sup-
ply of "young quims" [23] among the hungry children who wandered
the London slums.

The Marquis de Sade, currently resurrected as a philosopher and
revolutionary, even in fantasy never inflicted his atrocities upon
equals; he reserved his sexual torture for women, children, and members of the lower classes. But if de Sade's life did not match his imagination, it was not for lack of effort. He was finally arrested for
sticking young girls with knives, feeding them aphrodisiacs, whipping
them, and other such delights.[24]

As our threshold for shock diminishes and we become more and
more immune to the dangers of pornography, we conjure up all sorts
of rationales to perpetuate this voracious industry. In England in
1966, Pamela Hansford Johnson, who covered the trials of the sex
mutilator and murderer of children Ian Brady and his assistant Esther
Hindly, was impressed by the fact that over fifty volumes of sadomasochistic material was found in Brady's room with the Marquis de Sade
as his major hero. In Johnson's opinion, in mine, and in that of many
others, the violence found in pornography is "suggested to us, even
urged upon us." [25] George Steiner commented:

> There may be deeper affinities than we as yet understand be-
> tween the "total freedom" of the uncensored erotic imagination
> and the total freedom of the sadist. That these two freedoms have
> emerged in close historical proximity may not be coincidence." [26]

Actual living examples of a connection between criminal sexual assaults against children and pornography are too frequent to ignore. Police records throughout the country carry accounts of adult men and of juvenile offenders who have been found with pornographic material either on their persons, in their cars, or in their rooms. Social workers, district attorneys, and police officers are consistently making connections between sexual assaults against children and pornography. Here is a typical example from the San Antonio, Texas, police force:

> A 15 year old boy grabbed a 9 year old girl, dragged her into the brush and was ripping off her clothes. The girl screamed and the youth fled. The next day he was picked up by the police. He admitted that he had done the same thing in Houston, Galveston and now in San Antonio. He said his father kept pornographic pictures in his top dresser drawer and that each time he pored over them the urge would come over him.[27]

And this from Jacksonville, Florida:

> We have four felony charges pending in our criminal courts . . . wherein adults are charged with various sexual offenses involving minor children. In each of these four cases . . . obscene literature and other pornographic materials were used to entice minor children . . .[28]

Statistics *

The kiddy-porn industry is extremely clandestine. Most statistics therefore are a loose approximation. In my opinion the numbers offered here represent only the tip of the iceberg.

- Of the $2.5 billion porn industry, about $1 billion is from kiddy porn.

- In 1975 Houston police uncovered a warehouse filled with child pornography, and among the collection were 15,000 color slides of children, 1,000 magazines, and thousands of reels of film.

- At Crossroads Store in New York City, a group of investigators found, among the usual displays of *Lollitots, Moppets,* and other kiddy-porn magazines, nineteen films on kiddy porn, and an additional sixteen on incest alone.

* From "Children—A Big Profit Item for the Smut Producers," John Hurst, *Los Angeles Times,* May 26, 1977.

- One and a half million children under sixteen are used annually in commercial sex (prostitution or pornography).

- Most runaways can survive only as prostitutes or by posing for pornography. Each year there are one million runaway children whose ages range from eight through eighteen.

- Covenant House in New York City shelters 5,000 runaways each year. Over 2,000 are involved in pornography and prostitution, and of this number, 1,000 are under twelve.

- Los Angeles police have estimated that 30,000 children are sexually exploited in Los Angeles alone every year.

Child pornography is a thriving business. The money is good, easy. As in any other profitable business, pumping out kiddy porn has become routine. Ron Sproat, a writer, who worked in a "porno factory" (until he quit), described the formula he was instructed to use for kiddy porn:

> I was given a guideline. It said: "Emphasis on the innocence of children and the lechery of adults. Boys from six to thirteen and girls from six to fifteen. Emphasize hairlessness—tiny privates, lack of tits.[29]

Until recently, much child porn sold in America was smuggled from abroad, but now most of it originates here. Robin Lloyd, reporter and author of *For Money or Love*, a book on boy prostitution, collected 264 different child-porn magazines, each costing an average of seven dollars. *Where the Young Ones Are*, a sex guide for pedophiliacs, contains a listing of 378 places in fifty-nine cities where the young can be found, and has sold over 70,000 copies.[30]

There are over one million runaways each year, and more often than not they survive by prostitution and posing for the pornography trade. Father Ritter, director of Covenant House, a shelter for runaways in New York City, said, "These children cannot go home, cannot find jobs nor take care of themselves. First they are approached to pose in the nude, and it is a quick progression to engage in sexual acts for movies or in strip joints along Eighth Avenue for $100 for four performances."[31]

What about our anti-obscenity and anti-pornography laws, one might ask? The fact is that anti-obscenity and anti-pornography rulings have existed since the eighteenth century, but have rarely been enforced, and if enforced at all, it was usually for political rather than moral reasons. Actually it was not until the early twentieth century, when women began agitating for sexual equality and the right to control their own bodies and reproductive functions, that obscenity laws were seriously executed. Margaret Sanger and Annie Besant were imprisoned for writing and distributing "obscene" literature on birth control. But while women and some men were persecuted for advocating sexual equality, no one prevented the American and European markets from being flooded with hard-core pornography.[32] Actually men like Henry Miller, Frank Harris, and D. H. Lawrence were innocent victims of censorship. They never favored female emancipation, and when it became clear that both creative writers and hack pornographers never intended the "sexy" female to be a sexual equal, censorship relaxed.

By the mid-1950's, a series of Supreme Court decisions resulted in progressively lenient attitudes toward sexually explicit material, and in 1970 the Commission on Obscenity and Pornography published a report which concluded that pornography is not harmful, it is even educational, encourages frank discussions between parents and children, releases inhibitions, is not a factor in the causation of crime, and is therefore not a matter of public concern.[33]

But nothing could better illustrate the commission's lack of moral interest than its refusal to deal with the exploitation and victimization of vulnerable children in pornography. The commission reported such gross inaccuracies as "Pedophilia is outside the interests of pornography," or, in referring to stag films, "the taboo against pedophilia remains inviolate," and "the use of prepubescent children is almost nonexistent." [34] It really takes very little research to discover that as soon as the camera was invented, dirty postcards of breastless, hairless children and of pregnant, naked child prostitutes appeared. And from the liberated sixties until today, "avant-garde" publications advertise films entitled *Infant Love, Children and Sex, Little Girls*, etc., in which one can see spread shots of children from six to thirteen as they perform oral sex. I never even found it necessary to browse in Forty-second Street sex shops for my research. From San Francisco to New York, in every airport, train, and bus station, the most respectable bookstores and newsstands carry such titles as *Uncle Jake and Little Paula, The Child Psychiatrist, Lust for Little Girls, Adults Balling Children*, ad nauseam. With little difficulty one can easily obtain *Lollitots*, which introduces Patti, "the most exotic ten-year-old you'll ever meet," or *Little Girls*, which offers pictures of ten- and twelve-year-olds in intercourse with adult males. For forty-five dollars one can purchase a film in living color and see a nine-year-old getting fucked by two Arab boys, then by an adult.

The commission's ability to ignore child pornography could only stem from a conscious or unconscious determination to tolerate male sexual interest in children and not to interfere in the lucrative child pornography industry. The commission managed to rationalize this determination by assuming that legal restraints on pornography could be justified only by proving bad effects upon the consumers. Admittedly pornography does not harm its all-male consumer population. It harms the items consumed. Unlike hair dyes and cigarettes, the items consumed in pornography are not inanimate objects but live women and children who are degraded and abused in the process. By adopting a "consumer-beware" attitude, however, the commission satisfied itself with the fact that juveniles rarely purchase explicit materials. Therefore, once such materials are labeled "For Adults Only" or "Parental Guidance Recommended," the commission felt its obligation to the young was fulfilled.[35]

Some members of the commission produced studies, testimony, and authoritative evidence which proved that pornography was physically dangerous to the young, that it encouraged child molestation and rape, and that it destroyed both the public image and the self-image of children. The commission, however, paid little heed to these protests from a minority of its members, and recommended the repeal of laws restricting the sale of pornography.

By 1973 the Supreme Court abandoned a national standard definition of obscenity, and allowed individual states to establish their own guidelines.[36]

In the name of freedom many jumped on this strange bandwagon, and currently our most progressive and radical elements prefer to defend pornographers rather than to organize against them. Others have argued that if "forbidden fruit" is available, prurient material would soon become boring and interest would wane. Nothing could disprove this more than our current avalanche of child pornography. In 1977 Dr. Judith Densen-Gerber unleashed a crusade against this overwhelming onslaught, and quickly discovered that putting this industry out of business was not easy. The Supreme Court ruling which permits communities to determine what is obscene allows individual judges to translate the sexual use of children into a "liberating and educational" experience.[37] The child-pornography industry is today in excellent health.

It is estimated that 1.2 million children under sixteen are involved yearly in commercial sex—either prostitution, pornography, or both.[38] Those who have been a part of the struggle for a woman's right to a legal abortion have said that if men could become pregnant abortion would be a sacrament. And if women and children were the prime consumers of pornography and men the objects to be degraded and endangered, would the Commission on Obscenity and Pornography not then have declared pornography to be a crime? I think it would have!

Testimony Against Pornography: Witness from Denmark

edited by Diana E. H. Russell

Since Denmark lifted its censorship laws on pornography a decade ago, it has been referred to repeatedly as proof that sexual offenses decrease when pornography is allowed to flourish. In 1970, for example, the Commission on Obscenity and Pornography cited two Danish studies which claimed that sex crimes were down in Denmark as a result of liberalized pornography laws. The commission used those statistics to bolster its own finding—that pornography was "harmless." But recent research shows these studies were incomplete, inadequate, and biased on several counts. Section IV of this book discusses these shortcomings at length.

It is also important to note, as Jean-Claude Lauret points out, that pro-pornography arguments from Denmark are suspect: Pornography is the third largest industry (after agriculture and furniture-making) in Denmark, bringing in $60 million per year.[1] This is a strong incentive to the government to keep stories and statistics of rape and violence under cover. In his paper, "Danish 'Permissiveness' Revisited," Belgian professor of communications, Victor Bachy, notes that since the legalization of pornography in Denmark, tremendous changes have taken place in the landscape of Danish cities:

> Southwest of the Copenhagen Central Railroad Station lies the old neighborhood of Vesterbro . . . The people who used to live there were of small means, working men and craftsmen whose heartiness, spirit of mutual aid and sense of community compensated for their misery. The neighborhood had acquired a reputation throughout Denmark for its spirit. . . . The liberation of pornography has transformed the center of the neighborhood. Sex shops and porno shops, projection theatres, massage parlours and shops of sexy underwear invaded all streets.[2]

Most of these shops, says Bachy, now recruit their personnel from among the socially handicapped of this area. He claims that drugs are rampant, and that the businesses are "kept under strict control" by high-class criminals and international gangsters. "Methods of recruiting female personnel resemble those of international procurers"—what feminists call female sexual slavery. Knowledge of this expropriation and deterioration of a poor neighborhood, and the outright exploitation of young, poor females is just as important as statistics gathered on the increase of violent sexual crimes in Denmark.*

- In 1930 a law removed adultery, homosexuality, and zoophilia from the Penal Code [of Denmark], but retained the provisions relating to written and other representations of obscenity.
- In 1954 a law abolished prior censorship for theatrical productions.
- In 1964 the lawsuit against the editors of the translation of *Fanny Hill, Memoirs of a Woman of Pleasure* by John Cleland failed. The Minister of Justice assigned the problem of obscenity to the care of the Permanent Commission of penal law (created in 1960).
- In June 1966, the report of the Permanent Commission was made. It concluded that it was improbable that the influence of pornographic literature was harmful.
- On June 4, 1969 the Penal Code of Denmark was changed to read: "Any person who sells obscene pictures or objects to a person less than sixteen years of age incurs a fine." This liberated pornography in the form of texts, pictures, and objects for those aged sixteen and over.

The following testimony is from *The International Tribunal of Crimes Against Women*, edited by Diana E. H. Russell, in which a young Danish female testified against pornography in her country.

———

On July 1, 1969 pictorial pornography was legalized in Denmark. Prior to this there was a big debate about whether or not to legalize it. One of the strongest arguments for changing the law was that women would not be raped as much as they had been before. So we should be happy, because men who would like to rape us will go out and buy a pornography magazine instead. But it is a big fat lie. With the legalizing of pornography it is also legal to regard women as sex objects, to rape and accost according to need, because pornography ideologically establishes that a woman's innermost wish is to subject herself to men.

It is a crime against women that some make a profit out of such an ideology. It is violence against women to be exhibited as sex objects and nothing else. So why did our government agree to legalize pornography? Who does it serve other than capitalists? Even before the change in the law they made money by sending magazines and films abroad. Uncensored pornography means even more profit.

Who are the women who agree to be photographed for pornography? They are housewives, young women who can't earn enough

* Ed. Note: Bachy also noted a few important dates which I have summarized here:

money, women students who haven't enough understanding of what it is to be a real woman, women who do not have the possibility of becoming economically independent of men. Should we blame these women who have been told their whole lives that they are sex objects, and that this is their most important role in life?

This society is organized according to the needs of capitalism and men, and it is a threat to capitalism and male structures if women start to believe in themselves, because then they will start to struggle against every form of economic and ideological oppression. It is quite clear that it is in society's interest to legalize pornography, because pornography helps to deepen woman's alienation from herself. It alienates her from her own body and her own sexuality. It is a way to strengthen and justify the male ethic that men can direct their potency and aggression towards women, and that women shall passively submit to them. But here in Denmark we are so sexually liberated, or so it is said, that it is considered to be in women's interests that everything is allowed, pornography too.

Let us go back to those who let themselves be photographed. Yes, I am one of them. I believed that I was so liberated that nothing could touch me. Nobody could exploit me. Why did I do it? I had to get a lot of money fast and that was the easiest way. It paid well. But how I felt doing it was something else! I felt it as a violence against my body to be exhibited like a piece of meat, and as a violence against all women. All women suffered because I supported the pornography industry.

The many women I talked to during my three months as a pornography model often hated themselves. But it was very often of bitter necessity that they did it. They had to. Their husbands drank, or they were single mothers. Others felt they had to compete by wearing smarter clothes. For some it was just to be the one time, because they wanted to buy this or that. But for me it was many times. For me too it was almost impossible to get out again. The money is good and for many women it is easy to get into drinking during the photography sessions. Why do the models often hate themselves? Most of the male models think it is ok. But it's the women who have a prick in their mouths, who have to be tied up, who have to do everything so that a man can get his orgasm, who are exhibited as wet cunts and nothing else. I learned quickly to hate my body and myself for supporting capitalists and their easy money, and for supporting this society's decay. And I learned too that it is men who have the upper hand in this situation.

Who should I accuse because I was a pornography model? Yes, I did it of my own free will, and the other women I talked to did too. Nevertheless, I accuse the government for making a law that supports a capitalistic, patriarchal society with its ideology of women as sexual objects and nothing else; that gives life to men's sexual fantasies; that reduces women to passive objects to be abused, degraded, and used. I say that this is violence against women, because now every woman is for sale to the lowest bidder, and to all men. I accuse the government for supporting the pornography industry and for continuing to exploit women economically so that women still have very limited possibilities to control their own lives.

I believe that only by overthrowing this society will the violence against women cease. And I am prepared to use violence against an ideology that says that women are inferior to men. And I am prepared to fight against a government and the capitalist economic system which strengthens such an ideology.*

* Ed. Note: It is interesting to note that in several countries where capitalism has been overthrown by workers' socialist revolutions, organized crime was driven out and pornography and the exploitation of women as prostitutes virtually eliminated. Most striking are the examples of China and Cuba. Before the revolutions in those countries, Shanghai and Havana were the "sin capitals" of their respective hemispheres; poor peasant women and children from all over the countries were forced by excruciating poverty and unemployment into prostitution—often by their own families. Since the revolutions, government policy in both countries has discouraged pornography and prostitution. In recent years, they have begun to return, at least underground.—L.L.

Pornography in Sweden:
A Feminist's Perspective

An Interview with Britta Stövling

In Sweden detailed facts on rape, pornography, and sexual offenses are difficult to obtain. Pornography has been circulating freely since 1960 when the Swedish government lightened the penalty on this material, but researchers complain of a dearth of information from that country. Many of the studies conducted in Denmark have not even been attempted in Sweden. Official information is guarded; the Swedish people themselves seem unsure of their definitions of what constitutes a sexual offense against a woman. *The Spectator*, an English magazine, reports that Sweden suffers "a continuing increase of rape, of crimes of violence . . . a burgeoning of pornographic magazines and a trebling of their circulation in the past decade." [1]

The following is an interview with Britta Stövling, a Swedish feminist writer. She is the author of a book on the feminist movement in the United States, and is currently finishing research on feminists in North and South America. Because so many people refer to Sweden and Denmark as countries where liberalized laws have solved the pornography problem, we asked Britta to give us a feminist perspective of the situation in her country. She stressed that the Swedish feminist movement does not get major media coverage in her country because its position is contrary to the formal government position and the current social trends. One of our responsibilities as feminists is to help such voices to be heard.

Laura Lederer (L): *Can you speak about the pornography situation in Sweden?*

Britta Stövling (B): Well, believe it or not, it is a relief to be here in the United States, where one is not constantly confronted with pornographic pictures. In Sweden when you go to the drugstore, or even to the local co-op (which is a people's co-op—run by the people and for the people—a part of the "people's movement"), you see pornographic magazines everywhere. There are two in my local

86

co-op with women lying spread-eagled and bare-breasted on the front covers. Almost all our stores have it—drugstores, grocery stores, kiosks. It is concentrated in the urban areas. The only place there isn't much pornography is in the rural areas, where there is a ban on it because of the pressure of women who are customers of the local shops. But where I live, in Stockholm, women and children see it all the time. Schoolboys can get hold of the magazines because there is no law against buying the materials no matter how young you are.

In Sweden thirty million copies of pornographic magazines are sold annually. There are only four million men (we have eight million people), so you get an idea of the kind of problem we have.

L: What kind of pornography are you talking about?

B: There is hard-core and soft-core pornography, both aimed at men. Not only do they use young, beautiful women, as you have in the United States, but also what are considered fat, old, ugly women who have leering expressions on their faces. There are two magazines which are especially popular. They feature articles on social affairs, men's sports (like hunting), and women's pictures in the centerfold. Many pornographic magazines use children, and some specialize in Third World children. You can find this child pornography in the most elegant and chic parts of Stockholm, as well as in the poorer sections of town. There are pictures of small Black children with gigantic penises in their mouths.

L: Why do you think there is this "specialization" in Third World children?

B: Well, first, it is easier to exploit or abuse Asian children. There is a regular, respectable governmental business which deals in "adoption" of Third World children (mainly from Ceylon, Vietnam, and India). This legitimate agency has in some ways opened the door for underground trafficking in children for money-making purposes. These children are sold for pornographic purposes because it is considered more exotic for white men to have sex with children who are not white. The final reason for this specialization is, of course, so that one does not identify that girl in the picture with one's own daughter.

L: Does Sweden have any laws which apply to pornography?

B: We have what is called an "indecency law," which states that you cannot earn money from other people's bodies. This means that prostitution is legal, but it is against the law to be a pimp. We have tried to get the police to use the indecency laws to prohibit pornography on the grounds that pornographers are pimps (i.e., they make money off women's bodies through newspapers and magazines), but this attempt has been unsuccessful to date.

L: What are the rape statistics like in Sweden? Has any research been done comparing rape and pornography figures?

B: In Sweden everything is researched except rape, wife-battering, prostitution, and pornography. This is due partly to our social climate. For instance, you might not allow yourself to feel raped in Sweden because it is a very liberal country. So far, the Swedish women's movement does not have a clear-cut definition of what it is to be raped like you do in the United States. Therefore, it is difficult to gather accurate figures.

On the other hand, there are some good things about my country. A woman can get an abortion very quickly there, with no waiting or humiliation or monetary troubles. Also, there is no such thing as illegitimacy. There is little societal pressure to marry, and more and more women are not bothering to be wives. They are just having their children.

But many people still promote pornography as healthy. The truth is that it is extremely bad for children and adults. Young boys are insecure, uptight, and tense. They call young girls "cunt" even in kindergarten. Violent sex and pornography are things they learn about very early. We still have a male identification of what sex is. Perhaps an older woman can say, "No, it is on my terms or not at all," but young females get kicked around and beaten up, and they suffer. Pornography helps entrench these male attitudes. We just heard about *Playgirl* magazine, and we thought, "Well, maybe that trunaround will be good for a while, just to show people how degraded women are." But actually *Playgirl* does nothing to lift women out of their degradation, so it does not really help.

L: Is there other media-abuse of women?

B: Fragmentation of women is also very common in Sweden. Female lips or buttocks or breasts are blown up larger than life and plastered on ads or billboards. There are also ads which use nude women's bodies. One suntan ad shows a photo of a deeply tanned nude woman lying on a beach. Women got up on the billboard and painted the ♀ symbol with the slogan "Get up, woman!" on it.

L: That is a good example of an action women have taken. Have feminists done anything else?

B: Yes. Women have attacked pornography. We have picketed stores, and we have painted the woman symbol on pornography shops. We have made reports to the police and written many articles.

Some women jammed the coin boxes which carry pornographic magazines. In Swedish the word "purse" refers to money, but it also means "testicles or balls." So if you stop the purse, the source of the money . . .

We also went to our co-op to demand that they remove the pornographic magazines. They said they wanted to keep them because of freedom of the press. We retorted that there is no freedom of the press for women—our magazines, our articles, our statements, and our feelings are censored every day. When we said that, they replied that they are only interested in selling what people (meaning men) want to buy.

L: Can you talk in more detail about one specific action which feminists in Sweden have taken against pornography?

B: Several years ago, women attacked *Dagens Nyheter,* the largest daily newspaper in Stockholm, because they were running ads for pornographic theaters and shops. The women's movement used the indecency laws to point out that the paper was a pimp—it was making money off women's bodies through its ads. Women organized and put pressure on the paper from the outside, and women journalists on the paper also organized and put pressure on it from within, saying that they wanted a voice in the kinds of articles and ads which were placed in the paper. Under pressure from these groups, the paper cut down its ads. They adopted a policy in which there are no pictures, only words (and no "blatant" words), in ads for pornography shops.

L: Here in America we have what we call "organized crime" which runs most of the pornography industry (or at least so it is rumored—it is difficult to obtain any information, facts, or figures on this hypothesis). Do you have a similar problem in Sweden?

B: Yes. That is a good question. We have International Organized Crime, and that is one of the reasons why there is so little known about the subjects I mentioned before—rape, prostitution, pornography. There was a group of feminists who were doing their master's theses on prostitution. They were going out and interviewing prostitutes, and researching the subject from a feminist perspective. When they were finished with the first part of their research, they stopped. They said they did not dare to continue because they did not want to end up as a parcel in one of the canals. They had been threatened. The whole pornography industry is connected with drugs and crime. Every so often there is a story in the newspaper about a prostitute who is found dead in her apartment. When the police go to examine her possessions, they find phone books and numbers of really big names—very powerful men in business and government. But they never seem to catch these men. Only the small sharks are arrested and sent to jail.

L: What can women do? What is your advice as to how we should be approaching the pornography problem?

B: First of all, I do not want to make light of what my sisters and I have been doing to fight pornography. I think all our small actions and confrontations help enormously. But I think women must realize that we are facing an overwhelming problem. It is like a quagmire—it sucks you under unless you are prepared. We should continue to confront pornographers and the pornography industry, but we should use tactics, psychological strengtheners. I think we should attack in waves—one wave after another—advance and retreat. We can go out into the world to fight, but then we should withdraw and recover our energies for the next battle. Then we can go out again. If we have a long-term plan, and if we realize that it is going to take a lot of energy over a long period of time, then we will surely win!

Lesbianism and Erotica in Pornographic America

Charlotte Bunch

───

A key issue among women working against pornography has been the exploitation of lesbians in pornography, and the suppression of true lesbian art, erotica, and culture in our society. Charlotte Bunch addressed these issues in a speech she gave at the March on Times Square in November 1979, organized by Women Against Pornography. This is a reprint of that speech.

───

We are here today to demand and to organize an end to violence against women in pornography. But we are also here to ask some questions of America: What kind of society is it that calls love and affection between two women perverse, while male brutality to women is not only considered not perverse but made profitable? What kind of society is it that takes a child away unwillingly from a loving mother simply because she is a lesbian, while another child can be used by her parents to produce child pornography? What kind of society is it where the lifelong partnership of two women has no standing in court, while a husband can batter and rape his wife under protection of the law? You can add to the list—it is endless.

It is a pornographic society; America is a pornographic patriarchy. We are here to say it is not the kind of society that we want. We are here to say that it is going to change; we are demanding better of America. Last week at the National Gay Rights Rally in Washington, over 100,000 people marched to demand better of our society. We demanded the right to control our bodies, including our sexuality, and we demanded an end to social degradation and violence against lesbians and gay men. Today, many lesbians are here marching again to demand that same right as women—to control our bodies and to protect all women from the violence of pornography. The demands of these two rallies are two sides of the same coin. Both are about the absolute right of all people: to the dignity of our sexuality, to the control of our own bodies, and to an end to all forms of violence and degradation against us.

I was once asked to speak on the topic "Why Lesbianism Is Natural, Healthy, and Good." Yes, that was the title they gave me. I realized that there was only one way to answer: To ask instead, "What kind of society makes such a topic possible?" And the answer was the same as the answer I speak about today: patriarchy. The issue is how patriarchy is unnatural, unhealthy, and bad for women, for children, and even for men. And nothing highlights that issue more clearly than the violence against women that masquerades as sexuality in pornography.

Lesbians are tired of having our love labeled "pornographic," while the real pornographers go free and make money off all women's bodies and oppression. Lesbians know what love, sex, and eroticism of the female body is: We know it and we love it. And we know that it has nothing to do with pornography, which is based on woman-hatred, not woman-love. Indeed, it is only in woman-hating pornography in which men exploit lesbianism for their own ends, that the portrayal of lesbianism becomes okay to patriarchy. Lesbian love is for ourselves, for women. It is abused precisely because it is outside of male control; the label "pornographic" is used against lesbianism just as the term "dyke" was used against feminism—to frighten women and to give men greater control over their lives. All women, lesbian and heterosexual, must reject the association of lesbianism with pornography.

Lesbians are tired of having our love, our culture, and our publications threatened by these labels of "perversion," and we will continue fighting for our right to proclaim and portray our love and our sexuality openly. But we will not be intimidated into silence about the real perversions of pornography—the perpetrators of violence and hatred against women—by the fear that we will be called "pornographic" if we oppose them. We will not be pushed into a closet of blindness toward pornography and the culture it thrives on. Lesbian oppression is a part of that same pornographic culture, and bringing lesbianism out of the closet is not contrary to, but goes hand in hand with, exposing the woman-hating basis of most pornography.

We have seen the exploitation of lesbian love in pornography. We can tell how phony are the lesbian scenes in which our reality is distorted to fit male fantasies and to contribute to the male consumption of female sexuality. As lovers of our sex and our sexuality, if we had even one quarter of the money that goes into pornography, we could produce some genuine erotica about lesbian love, portraying the real beauty of women and of women loving women for ourselves, not for men. And I promise you—there would be a difference. Our productions would have nothing in common with woman-hating pornography.

Some people ask: Where do you draw the line? But every woman that I know, lesbian and heterosexual, can draw the line. We can tell the difference between eroticism and anti-female pornography. We don't all like or respond to the same things sexually, but we do all know the distinction between eroticism, which celebrates our sexuality, and pornography, which degrades us.

In seeking to change society's view of women and of the role of pornography in our oppression, feminists can and must begin to draw some lines. If a Ku Klux Klansman says that he gets off at the sight of a lynching or a burning cross (and, given the links between sex, racism, and power in our society, some probably do), do we therefore label his reaction as sexual rather than violent and racist? Do we "tolerate" it simply as "freedom of sexual expression"? I hope not. Yet that is precisely what *Snuff* and thousands of other forms of pornography do regularly to women.

Male control depends on the appropriation of all sexuality, and this, in a woman-hating society, means men retain the right to degrade and do violence to women. Yes, women can draw lines between eroticism and degradation, and it is time that we did so publicly.

Finally, pornography is not just symbolic violence against women. It is part of an international slave traffic in women that operates as a multinational corporation, where our bodies are the product, often procured unwillingly and always abused. Our fight against the violence in pornography in its widest implications is therefore a global fight. It extends from local street actions to the United Nations, where reports on the slave trade in women have been covered up for decades. In fact, that cover-up makes Watergate look like peanuts.

As in all international struggles, we begin in our own streets, and nowhere is that more appropriate than here on Forty-second Street— Times Square—the pornography capital of America. We begin by reclaiming our bodies and our sexuality for ourselves. We begin by demanding that a society which punishes us for loving ourselves and each other, and then demeans our bodies for the profit of men, must change. We begin by no longer tolerating a pornographic and hetero-sexist patriarchy in any of its aspects. We begin by drawing lines and fighting back and organizing. We begin by calling on America to do better—to take violence and degradation out of so-called sexuality in order to discover fully and celebrate the joy and eroticism of female sexuality.

Coming Apart

Alice Walker

These three paragraphs by Alice Walker tell why she wrote *Coming Apart*. "Many Black men see pornography as progressive because the white woman, formerly taboo, is, via pornography, made available to them. Not simply available, but in a position of vulnerability to all men. This availability and vulnerability diminishes the importance and *power* of color among men and permits a bonding with white men *as men*, which Black men, striving to be equal, not content with being different, apparently desire.

"Many Black women also consider pornography progressive and are simply interested in equal time. But in a racist society, where Black women are on the bottom, there is no such thing as equal time or equal quality of exposure. It is not unheard of to encounter 'erotica' or pornography in which a Black woman and a white woman are both working in 'a house of ill-repute,' but the Black woman also doubles as the white woman's maid.* The Black man who finds himself 'enjoying' pornography of this sort faces a split in himself that allows a solidarity of gender but promotes a rejection of race. 'Beulah, peel me a grape' has done untold harm to us all.

"I have, as we all have, shared a part of my life—since the day I was born—with men whose concept of woman is a degraded one. I have also experienced, like the woman in this piece, Forty-second Street; I felt demeaned by the selling of bodies, threatened by the violence, and furious that my daughter must grow up in a society in which the debasement of women is actually *enjoyed*."

A middle-aged husband comes home after a long day at the office. His wife greets him at the door with the news that dinner is ready. He is grateful. First, however, he must use the bathroom. In the bathroom, sitting on the commode, he opens up the *Jiveboy* magazine he has brought home in his briefcase. There are a couple of Jivemate poses that particularly arouse him. He studies the young women—blonde, perhaps (the national craze), with elastic waists and inviting eyes—and strokes his penis. At the same time, his bowels stir

* Ed. Note: This is the situation in the movie version of *The Story of O*.

with the desire to defecate. He is in the bathroom a luxurious ten minutes. He emerges spent, relaxed—hungry for dinner.

His wife, using the bathroom later, comes upon the slightly damp magazine. She picks it up with mixed emotions. She is a brownskin woman with black hair and eyes. She looks at the white blondes and brunettes. Will he be thinking of them, she wonders, when he is making love to me?

"Why do you need these?" she asks.

"They mean nothing," he says.

"But they hurt me somehow," she says.

"You are being a) silly, b) a prude, and c) ridiculous," he says. "You know I love you."

She cannot say to him: But they are not me, those women. She cannot say she is jealous of pictures on a page. That she feels invisible. Rejected. Overlooked. She says instead, to herself: He is right. I will grow up. Adjust. Swim with the tide.

He thinks he understands her, what she has been trying to say. It is *Jiveboy*, he thinks, the white women.

Next day he brings home *Jivers*, a Black magazine, filled with bronze and honey-colored women. He is in the bathroom another luxurious ten minutes.

She stands, holding the magazine: on the cover are the legs and shoes of a well-dressed Black man, carrying a briefcase and a rolled *Wall Street Journal* in one hand. At his feet—she turns the magazine cover around and around to figure out how exactly the pose is accomplished—there is a woman, a brownskin woman like herself, twisted and contorted in such a way that her head is not even visible. Only her glistening body—her back and derriere—so that she looks like a human turd at the man's feet.

He is on a business trip to New York. He has brought his wife along. He is eagerly sharing Forty-second Street with her. "Look!" he says, "how *free* everything is! A far cry from Bolton!" (The small town they are from.) He is elated to see the blonde, spaced-out hookers, with their Black pimps, trooping down the street. Elated at the shortness of the Black hookers' dresses, their long hair, inevitably false and blonde. She walks somehow behind him, so that he will encounter these wonders first. He does not notice until he turns a corner that she has stopped in front of a window that has caught her eye. While she is standing alone, looking, two separate pimps ask her what stable she is in or if in fact she is in one. Or simply "You workin'?"

He struts back and takes her elbow. Looks hard for the compliment implied in these questions, then shares it with his wife: "*You know you're foxy?*"

She is immovable. Her face suffering and wondering. "But look," she says, pointing. Four large plastic dolls—one a skinny Farrah Fawcett (or so the doll looks to her) posed for anal inspection; one, an oriental, with her eyes, strangely, closed, but her mouth, a pouting red suction cup, open; an enormous eskimo woman—with fur around her neck and ankles, and vagina; and a Black woman dressed entirely in a leopard skin, complete with tail. The dolls are all life-size, and the efficiency of their rubber genitals is explained in detail on a card visible through the plate glass.

For her this is the stuff of nightmares because all the dolls are smiling. She will see them for the rest of her life. For him the sight is also shocking, but arouses a prurient curiosity. He will return, another time, alone. Meanwhile, he must prevent her from seeing such things, he resolves, whisking her briskly off the street.

Later, in their hotel room, she watches TV as two Black women sing their latest hits: the first woman, dressed in a gold dress (because her song is now "solid gold!"), is nonetheless wearing a chain around her ankle—the wife imagines she sees a chain—because the woman is singing: "Free me from my freedom, chain me to a tree!"

"What do you think of that?" she asks her husband.

"She's a fool," says he.

But when the second woman sings: "Ready, aim, fire, my name is desire," with guns and rockets going off all around her, he thinks the line "Shoot me with your love!" explains everything.

She is despondent.

She looks in a mirror at her plump brown and blackskin body, crinkly hair and black eyes and decides, foolishly, that she is not beautiful. And that she is not hip, either. Among her other problems is the fact that she does not like the word "nigger" used by anyone at all, and is afraid of marijuana. These restraints, she feels, make her old, too much like her own mother, who loves sex (she has lately learned) but is highly religious and, for example, thinks cardplaying wicked and alcohol deadly. Her husband would not consider her mother sexy, she thinks. Since she herself is aging, this thought frightens her. But, surprisingly, while watching herself become her mother in the mirror, she discovers that *she* considers her mother— who carefully braids her average length, average grade, graying hair every night before going to bed; the braids her father still manages to fray during the night—*very* sexy.

At once she feels restored.

Resolves to fight.

"You're the only Black woman in the world that worries about any of this stuff," he tells her, unaware of her resolve, and moody at her months of silent studiousness.

She says, "Here, Colored Person, read this essay by Audre Lorde."

He hedges. She insists.

He comes to a line about Lorde "moving into sunlight against the body of a woman I love," and bridles. "Wait a minute," he says. "What kind of a name is 'Audre' for a man? They must have meant 'An*dré*.' "

"It *is* the name of a woman," she says. "Read the rest of that page."

"No dyke can tell me anything," he says, flinging down the pages.

She has been calmly waiting for this. She brings in *Jiveboy* and *Jivers*. In both, there are women eating women they don't even know. She takes up the essay and reads:

> This brings me to the last consideration of the erotic. To share the power of each other's feelings is different from using another's feelings as we would use a Kleenex. And when we look the other way from our experience, erotic or otherwise, we use rather than share the feelings of those others who participate in the experience with us. And use without consent of the used is abuse.

He looks at her with resentment, because she is reading this passage over again, silently, absorbedly, to herself, holding the pictures of the phony lesbians (a favorite, though unexamined, turn-on) absentmindedly on her lap. He realizes he can never have her again sexually, the way he has had her since their second year of marriage, as though her body belonged to someone else. He sees, down the road, the dissolution of the marriage, a constant search for more perfect bodies, or dumber wives. He feels oppressed by her incipient struggle, and feels somehow as if her struggle to change the pleasure he has enjoyed is a violation of his rights.

Now she is busy pasting Audre Lorde's words on the cabinet over the kitchen sink.

When they make love she tries to look him in the eye, but he refuses to return her gaze.

For the first time he acknowledges the awareness that the pleasure of coming without her is bitter and lonely. He thinks of eating stolen candy alone, behind the barn. And yet, he thinks greedily, it is better than nothing, which he considers her struggle's benefit to him.

The next day she is reading another essay when he comes home from work. It is called "A Quiet Subversion," and is by Luisah Teish. "Another dyke?" he asks.

"Another one of your sisters," she replies, and begins to read aloud, even before he's had dinner:

> During the Black Power Movement, much cultural education was focused on the Black physique. One of the accomplishments of that period was the popularization of African hairstyles and the Natural. Along with (the Natural) came a new self-image and way of relating. It suggested that Black people should relate to each other in respectful and supportive ways. Then the movie industry put out *Superfly,* and the Lord Jesus Look and the Konked head, and an accompanying attitude ran rampant in the Black community. . . . Films like *Shaft* and *Lady Sings the Blues* portray Black "heroes" as cocaine-snorting, fast-life fools. In these movies a Black woman is always caught in a web of violence. . . .
>
> A popular Berkeley, California, theater featured a porno-graphic movie entitled *Slaves of Love.* Its advertisement por-trayed two Black women, naked, in chains, and a white man standing over them with a whip! How such *racist* pornographic material escapes the eye of Black activists presents a problem. . . .

Typically, he doesn't even hear the statement about the women. "What does the bitch know about the Black Power Movement?" he fumes. He is angry at his wife for knowing him so long and so well. She knows, for instance, that because of the Black Power Movement (and really because of the Civil Rights Movement before it) and not because he was at all active in it—he holds the bourgeois job he has. She remembers when his own hair was afro-ed. Now it is loosely curled. It occurs to him that, because she knows him as he was, he cannot make love to her as she is. Cannot, in fact, *love* her as she is. There is a way in which, in some firmly repressed corner of his mind, he considers his wife to be *still* Black, whereas he feels himself to have moved to some other plane.

(This insight, a glimmer of which occurs to him, frightens him so much that he will resist it for several years. Should he accept it at once, however unsettling, it would help him understand the illogic of his acceptance of pornography used against Black women: that he has detached himself from his own blackness in attempting to identify Black women only by their sex.)

The wife has never considered herself a feminist—though she is, of course, a "womanist." A "womanist" is a feminist, only more common.* So she is surprised when her husband attacks her as a "women's liber," a "white women's lackey," a "pawn" in the hands of Gloria Steinem, an incipient bra-burner! What possible connection could there be, he wants to know, between her and white women—those overprivileged hags, now (he's recently read in *Newsweek*) marching and preaching their puritanical horseshit up and down Times Square!

(He remembers only the freedom he felt there, not her long pause before the window of the plastic doll shop.) And if she is going to make a lot of new connections with dykes and whites, where will that leave him, the Black man, the most brutalized and oppressed human being on the face of the earth? (*Is it because he can now ogle white women in freedom and she has no similar outlet of expression that he thinks of her as still Black and himself as something else?* This thought underlines what he is actually saying, and his wife is unaware of it.) Didn't she know it is over these very same white bodies he has been lynched in the past, and is lynched still, by the police and the U. S. prison system, dozens of times a year *even now!*?

The wife has cunningly saved Tracey A. Gardner's essay for just this moment. Because Tracey A. Gardner has thought about it *all*, not just presently, but historically, and she is clear about all the abuse being done to herself as a Black person and as a woman, and she is bold and she is cold—she is furious. The wife, given more to depression and self-abnegation than to fury, basks in the fire of Gardner's high-spirited anger.

She begins to read: †

---

* "Womanist" encompasses "feminist" as it is defined in Webster's, but also means *instinctively* pro-woman. It is not in the dictionary at all. Nonetheless, it has a strong root in Black women's culture. It comes (to me) from the word "womanish," a word our mothers used to describe, and attempt to inhibit, strong, outrageous or outspoken behavior when we were children: "You're acting *womanish*!" A labeling that failed, for the most part, to keep us from acting "womanish" whenever we could, that is to say, like our mothers themselves, and like other women we admired.

An advantage of using "womanist" is that, because it is from my own culture, I needn't preface it with the word "Black" (an awkward necessity and a problem I have with the word "feminist"), since Blackness is implicit in the term; just as for white women there is apparently no felt need to preface "feminist" with the word "white," since the word "feminist" is accepted as coming out of white women's culture.

† The excerpts that follow are taken from an earlier, longer version of Tracey A. Gardner's essay, "Racism in Pornography and the Women's Movement."

Because from my point of view, racism is everywhere, including the Women's Movement, and the only time I really need to say something special about it is when I *don't* see it—and the first time that happens, I'll tell you about it.

The husband, surprised, thinks this very funny, not to say pertinent. He slaps his knee and sits up. He is dying to make some sort of positive dyke comment, but nothing comes to mind.

American slavery relied on the denial of the humanity of Black folks, on the undermining of our sense of nationhood and family, on the stripping away of the Black man's role as protector and provider, and on the structuring of Black men and women into the American system of *white* male domination.

"In other words," she says, "white men think they have to be on top. Other men have been known to savor life from other positions."

The end of the Civil War brought the end of a certain "form" of slavery for Black folks. It also brought the end of any "job security" and the loss of the protection of their white enslaver. Blacks were now free game, and the terrorization and humiliation of Black people, especially Black men, began. Now the Black man could have his family and prove his worth, but he had no way to support or protect them, or himself.

As she reads, he feels ashamed and senses his wife's wounded embarrassment, for him and for herself. For their history together. But doggedly, she continues to read:

After the Civil War, "popular justice" (which meant there usually was no trial and no proof needed) began its reign in the form of the castration, burning at the stake, beheading, and lynching of Black men. As many as 5,000 white people turned out to witness these events, as though going to a celebration. (*She pauses, sighs: beheading?*) Over 2,000 Black men were lynched in the ten-year period from 1889–1899. There were also a number of Black women who were lynched. (*She reads this sentence quickly and forgets it.*) Over 50 percent of the lynched Black males were charged with rape or attempted rape.

He cannot imagine a woman being lynched. He has never even considered the possibility. Perhaps this is why the image of a Black woman chained and bruised excites rather than horrifies him? It is the fact that the lynching of her body has never stopped that forces the wife, for the time being, to blot out the historical record. She is not prepared to connect her own husband with the continuation of that past.

She reads:

> If a Black man had sex with a consenting white woman, it was rape. (*Why am I always reading about, thinking about, worrying about, my man having sex with white women? she thinks, despairingly, underneath the reading.*) If he insulted a white woman by looking at her, it was attempted rape.

"Yes," he says softly, as if in support of her dogged reading, "I've read Ida B.—what's her last name?" *

> "By their lynching, the white man was showing that he hated the Black man carnally, biologically; he hated his color, his features, his genitals. Thus he attacked the Black man's body, and like a lover gone mad, maimed his flesh, violated him in the most intimate, pornographic fashion. . . ."
>
> I believe that this obscene, inhuman treatment of Black men by white men . . . has a direct correlation to white men's increasingly obscene and inhuman treatment of women, particularly white women, in pornography and real life. White women, working toward their own strength and identity, their own sexuality and independence, have in a sense become "uppity niggers." As the Black man threatens the white man's masculinity and power, so now do women.

"That girl's onto something," says the husband, but thinks, for the first time in his life, that when he is not thinking of fucking white women—fantasizing over *Jiveboy* or clucking at them on the street— he is very often thinking of ways to degrade them. Then he thinks that, given his history as a Black man in America, it is not surprising that he has himself confused fucking them *with* degrading them. But what does that say about how he sees himself? This thought smothers his inward applause for Gardner, and instead he casts a bewildered, disconcerted look at his wife. He knows that to make love to his wife as she really is, as who she really is—indeed, to make love to any other human being as they really are—will require a soul-rending look into himself, and the thought of this virtually straightens his hair.

* Ida B. Wells, also known as Ida Wells Barnett, Black radical investigative reporter and publisher of the Memphis-based *Free Speech*. She wrote *On Lynchings: A Red Record, Mob Rule in New Orleans: Southern Horrors* (New York: Arno Press, 1969; first published 1892), a brilliant analysis of lynching in America. Wells led the anti-lynching movement in this country.

His wife continues:

> Some Black men, full of the white man's perspective and values, see the white woman or Blond Goddess as part of the American winning image. Sometimes when he is with the Black woman, he is ashamed of how she has been treated, and how he has been powerless, and that they have always had to work together and protect each other. (*Yes, she thinks, we were always all we had, until now.*)

> (*He thinks: We are all we have still, only now we can live without permitting ourselves to know this.*)

> Frantz Fanon said about white women, "By loving me she proves that I am worthy of white love. I am loved like a white man. I am a white man. I marry the culture, white beauty, white whiteness. When my restless hands caress those white breasts, they grasp white civilization and dignity and make them mine." (*She cannot believe he meant to write "white dignity."*)

She pauses, looks at her husband: " 'So how does a Black woman feel when her Black man leaves *Playboy* on the coffee table?' "

For the first time he understands fully a line his wife read the day before: "The pornography industry's exploitation of the Black woman's body is *qualitatively* different from that of the white woman," because she is holding the cover of *Jivers* out to him and asking: "What does this woman look like?"

What he has refused to see—because to see it would reveal yet another area in which he is unable to protect or defend Black women—is that where white women are depicted in pornography as "objects," Black women are depicted as animals. Where white women are at least depicted as human bodies if not beings, Black women are depicted as shit.

He begins to feel sick. For he realizes that he has bought some if not all of the advertisements about women, Black and white. And further, inevitably, he has bought the advertisements about himself. In pornography the Black man is portrayed as being capable of fucking anything . . . even a piece of shit. He is defined solely by the size, readiness and unselectivity of his cock.

Still, he does not know how to make love without the fantasies fed to him by movies and magazines. Those movies and magazines (whose characters' pursuits are irrelevant or antithetical to his concerns) that have insinuated themselves between him and his wife, so that the totality of her body, her entire corporeal reality is alien to him. Even to clutch her in lust is to automatically shut his eyes. Shut his eyes, and . . . he chuckles bitterly . . . dream of England. For years he has been fucking himself.

At first, reading Lorde together, they reject celibacy. Then they discover they need time apart to clear their heads. To search out damage. To heal. In any case, she is unable to fake response—he is unwilling for her to do so. She goes away for a while. Left alone, he soon falls hungrily on the magazines he had thrown out. Strokes himself raw over the beautiful women, spread like so much melon (he begins to see how stereotypes transmute) before him. But he cannot refuse what he knows—or what he knows his wife knows, walking along a beach in some Black country where all the women are bleached and straightened and the men never look at themselves; and are ugly, in any case, in their imitation of white men.

Long before she returns he is reading her books and thinking of her—and of her struggles alone and his fear of sharing them—and when she returns, it is 60% *her* body that he moves against in the sun, her own Black skin affirmed in the brightness of his eyes.

Racism in Pornography and the Women's Movement

Tracey A. Gardner

Third World women find themselves in a doubly oppressed position in today's society. They are subject to the racist prejudices of a predominantly white society in power and, in addition, they are oppressed as women.

In this paper, first presented at the Feminist Perspectives on Pornography conference in 1978, Tracey A. Gardner traces the historical and intertwining development of sexism and racism for the Black woman in America, providing a backdrop for understanding the unique way Black and other Third World women are exploited in pornography.

There is a group of women, all-white, marching outside a pornography shop, passing out leaflets, and talking about how men are exploiting and abusing women.

A Black woman, holding a little Black boy by the hand, averts her eyes, embarrassed and angry, when a white demonstrator tries to give her a leaflet and a speech.

The white woman turns back to her group and mumbles, "But doesn't she realize how we're being hurt? If she'd only look at what they're doing to Black women too."

When I began writing this lecture, I said to myself, racism in pornography? So what? Because from my point of view, racism is everywhere, including the Women's Movement, and the only time I really need to say something special about it is when I *don't* see it —and the first time that happens, I'll tell you about it.

When I talk about pornography and racism, I want you to understand who I am, my feelings and experiences, and what it means for me to be talking to you. I want you to understand that when a person of color is used in pornography, it's not the physical appearance of that person which makes it racist. Rather, it's how pornography capitalizes on the underlying history and myths surrounding and oppressing people of color in this country which makes it racist.

The real meaning and dimensions of the crime done people of color in pornography, in sexual assault, in just living in this country will remain inaccessible to white people if you continue to be ignorant or unconcerned about our history.

What I'm going to tell you is not the "Truth," but rather a starting point from which we can begin discussing the issue. It must be understood that I am *a Black* woman. I cannot represent Hispanic, Asian, or Native American women. I cannot even represent Black women. I am only one Black woman, and you should be listening just as hard to what any other woman of color has to say.

I know that I hold some of the stereotypes that white people have created about other races of color. I'm not going to attempt to make any cross-cultural analysis between different groups of color. No one at this time could do so, with all that still remains buried of our herstories and what we actually feel and experience today.

What I'm going to do is talk about what I have direct experience of—being Black. I hope by opening up my history and feelings and showing their neglected complexity, you will realize how little you know about other races. It is this ignorance which prevents the unification of all women in the struggle to expose and end violence against women.

* * * * *

What was in the minds of the white European invaders when they dragged Black men, women, and children in chains from their homeland and way of life? Even before the Europeans had "discovered" Africans, their religions had made a clear distinction between black and white. White was purity and morality; black was carnality, Satanic, diabolical. This symbolic use of black was extended to language: blackmail, black market, blacklist, black sheep, and so on.

When white Europeans first came upon Africa, they were amazed by two things: the dark skin of the people and the ape population. They confused the two and wrote about how the apes were like men, and how the African males were beastlike, being half-man and half-ape, with human faces, long tails, and huge genitals. It was even imagined that Africans had sex with apes.

To the Europeans, although Africans bore a physical resemblance to human beings, their living habits appeared to be those of animals. Africans had no recognizable culture, so the white men rationalized that they were doing Africans a great service by introducing them to real civilization. The white male Europeans enslaved the African people.

Who were these kidnapped Black people? They came primarily from West Africa, a region where tribes and societies were fairly unified, having similar language structures and cultures. West African civilization had well-organized, complex economic and political systems; intricate religions; numerous structures which served various societal needs (such as police and insurance); and highly developed arts.

In some societies in West Africa, the mother and the grandmother were the heads of the family. The father had an essential place, and did much of the providing. Often it was all men who sat on the councils, and the man received his soul from his father. But it was his maternal line that determined his place in society. If parents separated, children went with the mother, not because they were her burden but because their primary affinity was with the mother; it was she who begat them.

To marry, all that was required was the approval of both families. There was no need for the consent of the whole tribe or society, the state as we know it, or any religious body. The African family unit was a large extended family. It was not unusual for children to live with relatives outside the immediate family, especially if those relatives had resources or skills to offer.

Women traditionally managed much of the family's resources and often were traders in the open market. This earned them their economic independence. If a woman was dissatisfied with her husband, she was able to take her children and leave him. Later if she found another man she liked, she would enter into a new marriage.

I have not been able to find any indication that pornography existed in African society. This could be because there has not been enough investigation into African sexual practices. Or it could be because Africa was not technologically developed enough to produce pornography. (For pornography to become a common feature of a society, a technology is needed that can reproduce images and the written word on a mass scale.) Or it could be that because of the sex-role types particular to West African culture and how the African woman was valued (which is not to say that there were not always ways in which she was oppressed), pornography could not be a natural outgrowth of that culture.

When African people arrived in the New World, they were confronted by a drastic cultural shock. Their families were broken up, their native tongues outlawed, their customs and arts forbidden. Africans have the distinction of being the only race brought to this land of the free against their will.

The tremendous coping ability Africans showed in surviving slavery was later used by white men in the 1960's as justification for further injustices. Unsettled by the sixties riots, white men tried to explain away the current unrest among Blacks by claiming that the price Blacks had paid for surviving the "unfortunate" institution of slavery was that they had become an immoral and culturally deprived people.

Black folks are not deprived, we are denied. Our culture was not destroyed by slavery, it just went underground, and it is what we stand on. We have been forced to take on white cultural forms in order to survive, but the meaning we give to things is still our own.

Stereotypes are, in part, based on the realities of how people have had to adapt themselves in order to deal with oppression. Take the stereotypes of Black people and sex. There is definitely some reality to it. Black people *are* really sexy. But you have to put it in the context of our very rich and earthy heritage and our relationship to our land, which was quite different from puritanical Europe.

Writer James Weldon Johnson said,

> In the core of the heart of the American race problem the sex factor is rooted, rooted so deeply that it is not always recognized when it shows at the surface. Other factors are obvious and are the ones we dare to deal with; but regardless of how we deal with these, the race situation will continue to be acute as long as the sex factor persists.

American slavery relied on the denial of the humanity of Black folks, on the undermining of our sense of nationhood and family, and on the structuring of Black men and women into the American system of *white* male domination.

Much of this was achieved through the sexual exploitation, brutalization, and degradation of the enslaved people. Sexual and racial oppression in America are inseparable for both Black women and men. The raping of enslaved women and the castration of enslaved males were common practices.

White men, in their treatment of Black males, were motivated by two other myths of their own invention: (1) Black men are phallic symbols. Just the sight of an African's dark skin told you he had a monster penis. (2) Bigness connoted power, and the measure of masculinity was a man's power over other men and over women. The size of a penis was a significant factor in determining the latter. White men feared Black men as sexual rivals.

White people, men and women, came out of the puritanical European tradition, which alienated them from their bodies. They were simultaneously threatened and drawn to what they believed to be the uninhibited, guilt-free sexuality of Blacks. The unmentionable sexual feelings as well as the unacceptable acts of aggression of the white people were easily projected onto the enslaved Africans. Thus, many white men who feared that Black men would rape white women were daily raping Black women.

It was said that Black folks could not know love, only lust, whereas white people did not lust, they loved and protected. It was also said, and by many of the same people, "You are not a man until you sleep with a nigger."

In the eighteenth and nineteenth centuries in the United States, it was common for white men to have two families, one white and one Black. If anything was regarded as wrong about having that second, not so hidden family, it was not that the white man economically and physically forced the Black woman's sexual services. No, what was wrong was that the offspring made for the pollution of white blood. The crime was to acknowledge that a white man could be in a "relationship" with a Black woman.

What were the societal positions available to Black women? To be the sexual object of the white enslaver was perhaps the best, most protected and rewarding position because the Black woman was then subjected to the abuse of only one man. Then there was being a house servant and mammy, taking care of the white woman's home and children, while she had no place she could call her own and her children had to look after themselves. She might be a breeder woman who had children every nine months, most of whom she'd never get to know. Finally, there was the position of field mule. If a field mule got pregnant, she was treated special—two weeks before she was due, there was no punishment if she did not finish her work. A Black woman could serve in all these positions in her lifetime.

What were white women doing? Some tried to intercede on behalf of the enslaved people. Most did not. They were oppressed by their own position as mute ornaments in society.

Sometimes white women would confuse who their real oppressors were, and they would be active accomplices in the victimization of the enslaved. Often white women would blame Black women for "tempting" their husbands. There are accounts of white women's vindictiveness and cruelty toward Black women. They would pull out their teeth; have them stripped, chained, and flogged until bleeding; drop hot sealing wax on their breasts; damage their sexual organs by various means.

At the same time the white man was exploiting the Black woman, he was obsessive about protecting the white woman from the Black man. White women were told that the Black man was unnatural and dangerous, having an ape's penis, which, if it were to penetrate her, would split her vagina and cause permanent damage. The Black man was held up as one more reason why the white woman needed the protection of the white man.

The white man projected his own savagery upon the Black man, and one myth he employed to this end was that of the Pathological Black Rapist of white women.

This is not to say that Black men did not rape white women. They were fed fantasies about white women, that they were a delicacy to be protected, while Black women were trash, thrown out too many times.

But most of the interracial rapes in this country were committed by white men. White men have always had the power: social, economic, political, military, and psychological. Black men had to be more realistic about living out their fantasies. They got killed for just looking. Social writers of that time affirmed the myth that rape was a crime committed exclusively by Black men, and they explained the "rampant raping" by Black men as being the result of the "talk of social equality," which just excited the "ignorant nigger" and made him uppity. And as late as 1944 a study of white people's opinions about Blacks showed that they thought that Black people desired— over and above political, economic, and social justice—sex with white people.

After the Civil War, "popular justice" (which meant there usually was no trial and no proof needed) began its reign in the form of the castration, burning at the stake, beheading, and lynching of Black men. As many as 5,000 white people turned out to witness these events, as though going to a celebration. Over 2,000 Black men were lynched in the ten-year period from 1889–1899. There were also a number of Black women who were lynched. Over 50 percent of the lynched Black males were charged with rape or attempted rape.

Actor James Earl Jones said about lynching:

> By their lynching, the white man was showing that he hated the
> Black man carnally, biologically; he hated his color, his features,

his genitals. Thus he attacked the Black man's body, and like a lover gone mad, maimed his flesh, violated him in the most intimate, pornographic fashion. When a white man makes such a personal involvement and takes the time to strip off or cut off penises and torture, beat and lynch a Black man it has got to be sexual, it's the result of repressed sex. It's finding a way out.

I believe that this inhuman treatment of Black men by white men, in reality based to some extent upon the economic threat free Black men posed,* has a direct correlation to white men's increasingly obscene and inhuman treatment of women, particularly white women, in pornography and real life. White women, working toward their own strength and identity, their own sexuality and economic independence, have in a sense become "uppity niggers." As the Black man (and Black woman) threatens the white man's masculinity and power, so now does the white woman.

Eventually lynchings were replaced by police bullets and state executions. In Louisiana from 1900 to 1950, forty Black men were legally hanged or electrocuted for the rape of women, white women. During that time, only two white men were put to death for that crime. Both were immigrants, and their deaths happened before 1907.

Many Black women tried to protect their menfolk from this terrorization, either physically or by trying to expose the lies and savagery of white people. But they had to try to protect themselves as well, for the counterpart to the myth of the Black Man as Rapist was the myth of the Bad Black Woman.

White men still needed slave women on whom to force their "manhood." As Lorraine Hansberry said, a white man assumes that "if you're Black you must be selling." It was thought that a Black man having a relationship with a white woman degraded the white woman. There were laws in almost every state against interracial sex and marriage, which were usually enforced only when the man in the relationship was of color, and it was not until 1967 that the Supreme Court declared these laws unconstitutional. Sixteen states still had these laws on the books at that time. Yet, when a white man had a relationship with a Black woman or took sexual services from her, she was elevated in the world. By the 1950's the image of the Black woman was still that of a slut who could take anything sexually.

* Ed. Note: For more information on the economic factors involved in lynching, see Ida B. Wells, *On Lynchings: A Red Record, Mob Rule in New Orleans: Southern Horrors,* and Margaret Truman's *Women of Courage* (New York: William Morrow & Co., Inc., 1976).

The Black Liberation Movement is restoring the history and dignity of our people. But often it has remained trapped within the mores and attitudes of our white European male oppressors. Its efforts go toward proving that Black folks are *just as good* as whites, rather than showing that we are *different* and that it is not just slavery which affected the sex roles and relationships of Black men and women, but also who we were before slavery. Because of this misleading emphasis, the dominant motif of the Black Movement has been Black masculinity.

Black women are sometimes the target of the Black man's efforts to restore his sense of power, rather than the white man who has been the one out to destroy it. Sometimes when the Black man is with the Black woman, he is ashamed of how she has been treated, and how he has been powerless, and that they have always had to work together and protect each other. Some Black men, full of the white man's perspective and values, see the white woman or Blond Goddess as part of the American winning image.

Frantz Fanon said about white women,

> By loving me she proves that I am worthy of white love. I am loved like a white man. I am a white man. I marry the culture, white beauty, white whiteness. When my restless hands caress those white breasts, they grasp white civilization and dignity and make them mine.

So how does a Black woman feel when her Black man leaves *Playboy* on the coffee table?

"It's a white folks' thing, and it's corrupting our men."

That is what several Black women I have talked to think. Pornography speaks to the relationship *white* men and women have always had with each other. Because they have been forced to live under the values of white people, the identity of Afro-Americans has been distorted and belittled to the point where pornography also speaks in part to our relationships.

The pornography I am reacting to is *soft-core* pornography, which objectifies but at least retains the woman's body in one piece. Most women in this country, white and Third World, are unaware of the nature of hard-core pornography and how widespread it is. I know that if any woman of color were to see some of the brutal and deadly hard-core pornography around, she would be outraged by it no matter what the color of the woman being exploited was.

But when you talk about soft-core pornography, it's difficult for a Black woman to identify totally with what white women feel about it.

Soft-core pornography is an extension of mass advertising and the beauty market; it is the Beauty Queen revealed. Until recently the Beauty Queen was by definition white: fair complexion, straight hair, keen features, and round eyes. Soft-core pornography was the objectification of white purity, white beauty, and white innocence.

To little Black, Asian, or Hispanic girls, growing up with dark skin, kinky hair, African, Asian, or Latin features, everything around them —in storybooks and the media, in dolls in stores—announced that something was wrong with them. They could be whores but not beauty queens. There used to be a lot of Black women who used bleaching creams and stayed out of the sun, and there are still many who straighten their hair because they feel they have to, not because they want to. There also have been Asian women who have had eye- lid operations. It is not so much that women of color are trying consciously to become white as that they are trying to look beautiful in a white-dominated society.

This has been changing somewhat. What is beautiful now also includes that which is unusual or exotic, such as women of color. We have started appearing in *Vogue* and in *Playboy*.

Black women were allowed in *Playboy* in the last ten years as a result of the sixties riots, which also won a few Black men the right to wear business suits and carry briefcases and have wives who stayed at home. So, Black women have been elevated from the status of whore to "Playmate." Now white boys can put them in *Playboy* without damaging the magazine's respectability too much (though after the first appearance of Black women in *Playboy*, there were some angry letters to the editor saying "get them niggers out").

Black men are exploited in pornography too. In 1978 *Hustler* magazine ran a full-page cartoon of a white man sitting on a raised chair and a Black shoeshine boy at his feet who is looking surprised as he is polishing the white man's gigantic penis.

I have noticed that while white men like Black women "looking baaad" in leather with whips, Black men like Black women in bondage, helpless and submissive. Check out the album covers of groups like the Ohio Players and New York City.

The Black man, like the white man, is buying pornography. He is beating, raping, and murdering all kinds of women. Black women are going to have to deal with him on this. But when we do, we must deal with the Black man as a Black man, not as a white man. In this country it is the *white* man who is producing pornography, and it is the *white* man who is profiting from it.

We need to hear from other races in this country, especially those, such as the Japanese, who have had their own highly developed tradition of violent pornography. We need to know how *all* women of *all* cultures are affected by violence within their communities and in the larger, white, male-dominated society.

Unification of all women in the struggle to end violence against women can happen only if women of color share their experiences, hurts, and confusions with white women. Before this can happen though, white women must understand that while sexism might be the ultimate oppression for many of them, it is only *one* of the ways in which women of color are oppressed. White women must recognize the ways in which they have bought into the oppression and stereotyping of communities of color.

As a Black woman, I find myself in limbo. My experiences and concerns don't quite fit—not in the Black Liberation Movement, nor in the Women's Movement. Because my Black brother and I speak the same language and go back a ways, he usually can hear me, but either he doesn't want to answer me or he can't, so he gets ashamed of himself and pissed off at me.

I believe white women have the resources to answer me and, for the most part, would like to, but you don't hear me because you never take the time to listen; so often you are afraid of me.

But if you're going to call the white man to task for his racism, it's your obligation to know who people of color are, and what women of color think of you, the images and concerns we have about white women. Too often what has been between us has not been a relationship but usage. The only times you remember women of color are on the occasions when it would be an embarrassment to be without us. And as women of color, when we're in need we don't call on you, because half the time you are part of our trouble, and our association with you makes it more difficult to bring the issue of our rights to our communities of color.

It cannot continue this way. No one wants it to. We must find ways to share and merge our experiences. We must create a movement that really moves for all oppressed people.

A Quiet Subversion

Luisah Teish

In the last decade new pornographic magazines have appeared on the market that are aimed specifically at Third World men (*Swank* and *Players* are the best known). Many Black authors, recording artists, and sports figures are as notorious as white men for their sexist attitudes. What is to be done? Here for the first time, a Black woman directly addresses the issue of the harm pornography does to Black women and appeals to the Black community for action.

In comparison with pressing issues such as South African liberation, infant mortality, and the slow death of affirmative action, pornography may seem a "low man" on the totem pole of Black feminists' priorities. But just as right-wing moves like the Bakke decision and anti-abortion laws serve to reverse the gains of the civil rights struggle, the media are quietly pressing forth dangerous images of Black women, a reverse of our *cultural* development and self-image.

Hints of Aunt Jemima, Bubbling Brown Sugar, and the "Tragic Mulatto" stereotypes can be seen on billboards, TV, and magazine covers. But today's versions of those stereotypes have gained the dubious addition of black leather and a space in the pornography market. It is important that the images of women born out of the Black Women's Liberation Movement be realistic images. Pornography serves to distort our image.

The history of America is largely one of systematic physical and symbolic exploitation of the Black woman's body. On the slave ships and plantations, she served as an easy target for the slave owners' carnal pleasures. At any time and without provocation, the Black woman could be raped and beaten, without defense. In addition to being the white man's concubine, she was also mated to the "Black buck" in order to produce the best "stock" for next year's slave sale. Again she had no choice in the matter.

Through historical stereotyping, a myth has developed that the

Black concubine was a privileged "house nigger" who wielded power in the "big house" while others worked in the field. More often than not the woman worked in the field like the other slaves, was raped at an early age, and bore children to the white man, without compensation. Although a few Black women earned their freedom or that of their children, the inheritances left them were not enough to give any significant number of Black people anything even slightly resembling advantage in this country.

What it may have left us with is an inherited sense of abandonment and powerlessness. With Black men unable to defend Black women under penalty of death, it soon became a part of the slave culture for them to stand by with only a prayer.

Today we see vestiges of that inheritance in the exploitation of women's bodies through prostitution and pornography and denial of reproductive rights.

The stereotype of the big Black mammy, who wants nothing more from her life than a job in the big house and a shack full of pickaninnies, has helped to make Black women victims of birth-control experimentation and sterilization abuse. Decisions are being made for them by doctors who sterilize them without their consent. Approximately 30 percent of America's *married* Black women have been sterilized. Far too many television comedy shows portray Black families without fathers, and the mothers on these shows are Aunt-Jemima-looking women with a shack full of pickaninnies. Our children watch these shows and absorb the projected values.

Prostitution has been called a victimless crime. But the fact that the number of Black "working girls" on Prostitution Row is disproportionate to our number in the society bespeaks an economic and cultural crime. Facing the greatest degree of discrimination in education, jobs, and federal aid, some poor Black women have been forced to the streets. Here they sell interracial fantasies to suburban businessmen: Friday Night in the Ghetto. And here they are exploited by the Pimp, the Peddler, and the Police.

Media images have significant bearings on the life choices of many young Black Americans. Young Black girls, through the media and environmental reinforcement, can be led to believe that their only choices are Aunt Jemima or Bubbling Brown Sugar.

During the Black Power Movement, much cultural education was focused on the Black physique. One of the accomplishments of that period was the popularization of African hairstyles and the Natural. Along with the Natural came a new self-image and way of relating. It suggested that Black people should relate to each other in respectful and supportive ways. Then the movie industry put out *Superfly* and the Lord Jesus Look and the Konked head, and an accompanying attitude ran rampant in the Black community. These films preceded a rise in black-on-black crime and undermined activism in the Black community. Films like *Shaft* and *Lady Sings the Blues* portray Black "heroes" as cocaine-snorting, fast-life fools. In these movies a Black woman is always caught in a web of violence. In these movies the "Black Lady of the Night" is glorified.

These movies warranted reactions from responsible Black citizens. "Blaxploitation" was exposed in *Ebony* magazine, and Black actors rose to the challenge of protecting the Black image.*

A popular Berkeley, California, theater recently featured a pornographic movie entitled *Slaves of Love*. Its advertisement portrayed two Black women, naked, in chains, and a white man standing over them with a whip! How such *racist* pornographic material escapes the eye of Black activists presents a problem. Pornography is a branch of the media that Black-activist feminists have considered a "white market." It is clearly an ignored area that deserves further investigation. The pornography industry's exploitation of the Black woman's body is qualitatively different from that of the white woman. While white women are pictured as pillow-soft pussy willows, the stereotype of the Black "dominatrix" portrays the Black woman as ugly, sadistic, and animalistic, undeserving of human affection.

Black women like Ruby Dee, Maya Angelou, and Cicely Tyson have fought courageously for more realistic images of Black women on stage and screen. While occasionally the entertainment industry concedes to "historical specials" like *Roots* and *Harriet Tubman*, usually they romanticize the image of the battered Black woman. The music industry, for example, offers us an album entitled *The Best Of New York*, recorded by a group called New York City, with a cartoonish cover depicting a Black woman running for her life, being chased by four Black men. And the Ohio Players' album, *Pleasure*, shows a Black woman in bondage!

Some will argue that this is just the white man's device to sell *his* product, but—Black people buy that product. And what is the Black artist's position? Is he standing by with only a prayer? What is being

---

* Ed. Note: "Blaxploitation" is the particular name given to films projecting negative, violent images of Black people. Critics said that they were void of historical/social accuracy, and were made primarily to perpetuate white stereotypes of Black people and to exploit Black people's hunger to see themselves on screen. This term is very well known in the movie industry and the Black artistic community.

peddled in the white man's market—Black music or the Black woman's body?

The cover of the New York City album should be a picture of Harlem. Must we wait until the problem is epidemic before we take action? It is the responsibility of Black feminists and Black artists to demand that this be stopped.

SECTION III.

―――――――――――――――――――――――――――――――――――――

Pornography:
Who Benefits

―――――――――――――――――――――――――――――――――――――

Hitherto, instead of being a help meet to man, in the highest, noblest sense of the term, as a companion, a co-worker, an equal; she has been a mere appendage of his being, an instrument of his convenience and pleasure, the pretty toy with which he whiled away his leisure moments, or the pet animal whom he humored into playfulness and submission.
—ANGELINA GRIMKE
  Letters to Catherine Beecher, Number 11, 1836

"Playboy *Isn't Playing,*" An Interview with Judith Bat-Ada

Laura Lederer

Judith Bat-Ada has earned a doctorate in Mass Media and Speech Communications at Case Western Reserve University. She has conducted research on the influence of sexual media, such as *Playboy* and *Penthouse* magazines, on female identity. Her work revolves around trends in pornography, changes in the portrayal of females and female sexuality in the industry, and the effect of those changes on women and men. She has focused on big pornography producers like Hugh Hefner, Bob Guccione, and Larry Flynt, examining their use of advertising techniques, slick tricks, and cartoons to break down sexual taboos and to further exploit and objectify women.

Laura Lederer (LL): Judy, what kind of work are you doing?
Judith Bat-Ada (JB): We have placed what we call the *Playboy* genre in a systems-analysis perspective, viewing it not as a collection of disjointed "girlie magazines," but rather as an integrated whole. We have been examining the evolution of the so-called soft-core pornography, whose images pervade the media—from the 1950's "38D" fantasy to the present trend toward pedophilia (the view and use of children as sexual objects). Our analysis has revealed a "hidden agenda" which is different from the overtly expressed aims and goals of the particular pornographic magazines. *Playboy*'s successive manipulations and distortions of the image of women typifies the pornography-conditioning process. As the most influential and pioneering magazine of its kind, it laid the groundwork for the whole media sexploitation movement which we are in the midst of right now.

LL: Can you talk more about the trends you mention? What do you see happening and why is it happening?
JB: In sheer numbers, newstand pornographic publications have increased from zero in 1953 to well over forty in the last five years.

121

Historically, male culture has devised techniques to keep women powerless and to shut us out of mainstream society. It is not a casual coincidence that *Playboy* began eight years after the end of World War II, when women were getting restless; *Penthouse* and the rest of the pornography industry merely followed the path *Playboy* had blazed. They picked up steam in 1965, right after the publication of Betty Friedan's *The Feminine Mystique*. These magazines began by peddling the female as "other." They are now unabashedly peddling the dehumanization of women, and, as a result of cultural conditioning and pressures, young girls and women are buying the images.

LL: What does this mean for women?

JB: A decade ago Gloria Steinem said, "A woman who has Playboy in the house is like a Jew who has *Mein Kampf* on the table." The *Playboy* genre is programming a female identity which features female masochism during our youth and early twenties, and female obsolescence when we have barely achieved womanhood. This programming is based upon the dehumanization of women, and the "object" erotization of homo sapiens. In other words, as the commercial establishment inundates us with images of women as "objects," the rewards for women who grow and become strong decrease, while the rewards for women who present themselves as sexual objects increase. There is a strong female tendency to "be" whatever the male society demands at the time: Victorian in one period, and explicit and erotic objects in another. The process of identity is a learned one, and millions of women are accepting the culturally preferred, dehumanized sex-object symbols of themselves.

LL: Do you think this is really happening?

JB: There is ample evidence for this transformation in the past few years. One of the more telling instances is the *Hustler* magazine competition, which offers prize money (or just instant fame) for the "best" or most pornographic photo of a wife, sister, or girl friend. Some daughter photos have been submitted as well.

LL: You talked about a trend from "38D" to "pedophilia." Can you explain that?

JB: Saturation with straightforward female sexual stimulus leads slowly but inevitably to the need for, and the acceptance of, such things as child molestation, incest, and sexual violence. Hard-core pornography is like any other marketed product—it needs to be revamped periodically to stimulate flagging sales. We have made women easy and accessible targets for sexual violence, so there are very few final taboos left to break—children and incest are the last.

The American media have moved into an acceptance of pedophilia, and are progressing very rapidly toward the endorsement of incest. I believe the final taboo now being breached is child sadism. For example, a recent edition of *Forum* magazine, published by Bob Guccione of *Penthouse,* carried no less than twenty accounts of adult-child sex (the children being from eight to twelve years of age) in the first quarter of its pages. The issue then moved on to incest, which it has cozily familiarized under the title "Home and Family Sex." *Forum* claims it is simply reflecting readership views, but I think the selling of incest is part of a process whereby a particular kind of pornographic imagery percolates through all the media until it has saturated them, and then a new level of degradation begins to become acceptable.

The May/June 1977 issue of *UCLA Monthly* magazine ran an article entitled "Help for the Child Abuser." One paragraph in particular caught my eye: "Adolescents have been the primary targets of sexual abuse, but there is a *recent sharp increase* in oral venereal disease among children under five years of age, who have been infected by their fathers, older brothers, or boyfriends of the mother." This "sharp increase" is a national phenomenon and can reasonably be related to the breaking of taboos against incest. The *Playboy* genre has been the original educator in this breakdown from a broad social perspective.

LL: How does this breakdown of the taboos work?

JB: Taboos are broken by the use of advertising techniques and slick tricks, which *Playboy, Penthouse,* and *Hustler* have learned from the major marketing industries of this country. Patterns are visible when these magazines are studied over a period of years. We first began to realize this when we noticed a spate of what I used to call "incest" cartoons and features. I now call this trend "malecest," since it is almost always males who commit incest. *Playboy* began its malecest push with joking little features. One I remember distinctly pictured a girl sleeping on Mickey Mouse sheets holding a Raggedy Ann doll. The caption underneath read: *"Baby Doll.* It's easy to feel paternalistic to the cuddly type above. Naturally she digs forceful father figures, so come on strong, Big Daddy." That was in November 1971. Since then there have been hundreds of short pieces, letters, and cartoons which poke fun at the taboos against father-daughter sex, and rhapsodize about adult male-little girl sexual relationships.

According to sociologist Donald Johanson, human beings have a biological need to care. The roots of pornography are in hostility and violence. It must attack and negate the caring sentiments of its consumers in order to maintain its readership and attract potential customers.

The language used in *Playboy*-genre magazines is emphatically negative toward the loving aspects of human beings. In cartoons, photographs, drawings, and text, there is a clear isolation of the male from the traditional view of male-female, father-child relationships, which, although patriarchal, at least involved some norm of responsibility and concern. *Playboy* readers are conditioned by text and images to disavow their sentiments of caring, and to abdicate their social responsibility for respect in female-male relationships and for nurturance in adult-child relationships. The *Playboy* way of life portrays men as play-boys—boys forever playing. A boy plays, and women are his toys. Woman cannot be mate, companion, lover —she must be his thing, his pet, his chick, his "bunny," as *Playboy* puts it. Boys cannot produce children because children mean responsibility—they make a boy into a man. That is why the realities of everyday life are hidden in *Playboy*. You rarely see a father and children, you rarely see a man and his wife or woman friend having a good nonsexual conversation. You rarely see mothers, daughters, mothers-in-law, or sisters engaged in nonsexual family relationships. You rarely see a recognition of women menstruating, you never see people growing old together. All this MUST be invisible in the *Playboy* way of life because it threatens the isolated, mechanistic, aggressive male life-style the magazine is promoting.

The idealized *Playboy* man, the "winner" male, is depicted as reasonably, pleasantly sexually exploitive. This stance requires the dehumanization of woman and the ridicule of family members, relatives, and children. Thus, a staple joke image of the *Playboy* genre is the devalued wife. In thousands of repetitions over and over again, females are depicted as nonhuman, as whores, as animals— thereby removing any obligation on the part of the male to treat them as equal beings.

By socializing the view of women as unreal sex objects, *Playboy* and the magazines that have followed its lead have contributed to the increasing antagonism and subsequent violence between males and females, methodically helping break down the ability and need to care which, if Johanson is correct, human beings are born with and which, as social animals, we need in order to survive.

This breakdown in social relations between women and men is directly attributable to the current pressures being exerted by men against the incest taboo. Up until now this taboo has offered some protection to children in our country against sexual exploitation by adults. The acceptance of pedophilia requires the blurring of age distinctions between mature women, teens, adolescents, and children. Thus, if *Playboy* conditions men to consider females as sex objects, then children as sex objects, eventually and naturally female children in our own homes become sex objects as well. This completes the *Playboy* family: a sexually exploitive father; a dehumanized, ridiculed mother; and a sexually precocious and eroticized child. This "family scene" has become the repeated vocabulary within the *Playboy* game plan.

LL: How do magazines like Playboy *and* Penthouse *get men to accept this view of females and female children?*

JB: Getting readers used to the forbidden requires subtle but clever devices. *Playboy* uses what I call "groundbreakers" for the construction of new attitudes. These groundbreakers include cartoons, skillfully contrived photographs, and an extensive use of symbols which are aimed at invading both the conscious and unconscious mind. A few examples will help the reader understand how it is done:

One favorite technique is to publish photographs of women simulating children, or imitating children and their behavior. For example, the April 1976 cover of *Playboy* magazine featured a very young-looking female seated on a stool surrounded by Teddy Bears, Raggedy Ann dolls, and wearing patent-leather Sunday-School shoes and a "virgin-white" petticoat, while the word "virginity" appeared to the right of the picture in another context. Pictures of women in these childhood trappings combined with glaring erotic exposure pave the way for real sexual abuse of children.

Another favorite technique is the use of fairy tales in cartoons. I believe this technique is carefully planned. Fairy tales take us back to our childhood, and unconscious childhood memories short-circuit our conscious, rational thinking processes. Thus, cartoons about fairy tales can be used to disarm the reader. Common themes in *Playboy*-genre fairy tales are the wolf molesting Little Red Riding Hood, the Seven Dwarfs raping Snow White, Goldilocks sleeping with Baby Bear, etc. Fairy tales are exploited by pornographers in order to block out objections to rape, molestation, and violence by defining the imagery as "fantasy." Many men, if confronted directly with a violent sexual image would reject it—and the magazine! The idea is to put these vicious crimes into a context which infers that it is "just a joke" or "all in good fun." After all, who can object to that —except a woman without a sense of humor?

LL: Why would pornographers want to do this?

JB: A chief concern of pornographers is the social availability-acceptance factor. Men are using mass media to break apart old values and create new cultural patterns. In addition, our legal system is put under pressure and is changing, as are this generation's lawyers and judges, nursed at the *Playboy* nipple.

Men want women to be available to them sexually, and in order to make younger and younger women available, it is necessary to change the existing laws. In Sweden, where there are liberal laws concerning pornography, the age of consent has recently been lowered to fifteen years of age, and now a bill is being considered which would eliminate it altogether! This would make small girls legal adults, and it would also leave them open to sexual exploitation without any legal reprisals. Such legal change can hardly be brought about by the power lobby of little girls.

LL: Do you think this violent pornography reflects a trend toward sadomasochism in our society?

JB: When the media talk, they always label grossly sadistic pornography "S and M" (sadomasochism). But it is not S and M, it's just sadism—no cutesy letters or hyphens and no "masochism" either because it is being foisted on us. By labeling violent and degrading depictions of women "sadomasochism," the media-makers cleverly take the onus off themselves and make it sound as though we participate by mutual agreement. But we have no say in the matter. In fact, healthy, self-respecting females do not want to see *Playboy, Penthouse,* or any other pornographic magazines in drugstores, grocery stores, and markets. The pornographers know this and have devised insidious methods to accomplish their ends. For example, there is something called the "high-percentage" rule in distribution and display terminology. This refers to an agreement between the store owner/manager and the distributor in which extra money is paid to the storeowner to display pornographic magazines. In other words, storeowners are given an extra percentage to put pornographic magazines in the front racks instead of behind the counter. Moreover, in some cases storeowners get a 100 percent return rate on pornographic magazines. They buy them for a dollar and sell them for two dollars. Lately we have seen a large increase in front-rack displays of *Playboy* and *Penthouse.**

* Ed. Note: A small-bookstore owner in San Francisco told us that he is forced to carry *Playboy* and *Penthouse* if he wants to get any magazines at all. His distributor will not deliver other publications unless he includes pornographic magazines as a "package deal."

LL: Many people claim that "soft-core" pornography is passé. I have read that Playboy *is having trouble with its circulation, and that* Hustler *has more readers now than either* Playboy *or* Penthouse. *What do you think of this?*

JB: I don't believe it for a second. I have read all those figures too, but this is not an accurate interpretation of them. Generally, men are not abandoning one pornographic magazine for another. They are now reading two or three instead of just one. You get different types of violence to women in each of the leading magazines. I consider *Playboy* the most dangerous because it is the leader and the "philosopher," precisely as Hugh Hefner likes to claim. The hatred of women in *Playboy* is much more insidious and evil than in the other pornographic magazines. *Hustler* is simply the gross exaggeration of *Playboy* and *Penthouse*. It is filled with hate, but at least it is hate you can see. *Playboy* has made its fortune on creating a soft focus for the hate.

LL: You have referred to the Playboy *philosophy as "sexual fascism." Can you explain that term?*

JB: Well, let us begin with the term fascism. The psychology of fascism is a view of people as "others"—as less than you. It is a belief that you can take control—to secure whatever power you want without regard for how that may affect other human beings. It is a belief in one's own superiority, and that feeling of superiority allows you to hurt and sometimes destroy another person without feeling, empathy, or human compassion. It is a total divorcing of oneself from other human beings, and a glorification of power, violence, and aggression.

Sexual fascism is the fascist mentality applied to our sexuality. *Playboy* (and the *Playboy* philosophy) makes woman the "other" just as the nazis made the Jews the "other," and just as the white man made Black People and American Indians and migrant workers the "others." For women, sexual fascism means that men, and in particular a few powerful men, control our behavior, attitudes, fantasies, concepts of love and caring, integrity, that in which we believe and hope, as well as the ways in which we love and to whom and how we make our genitalia available. In this society we have no choice but to follow these dictates. In the case of sexual fascism there is a triumvirate—Hugh Hefner, Bob Guccione, and Larry Flynt—who are every bit as dangerous as Hitler, Mussolini, and Hirohito, the political fascist triumvirate of World War II.

These men can be held clearly responsible for a great deal of the current desperate, sick, and cruel trends in sexuality and human behavior. Just as the nazis built prisons around the Jews, and the white man put chains on the Black women and men, so pornographers have put women into equally constricting "genital service" structures. The only trouble is that the contemporary fascist form is more insidious because we cannot see the bars or the chains. When we insist we are chained and barred, we are told—no, it is only our imaginations, our "repressions" at work. Nonsense! We are longing for the freedom to be human. But we have no freedom, no language, no behavior to call our own. All the special glitter that this male society produces for women—the makeup, the high-heeled shoes, the tight little dresses—single us out as women as effectively as did the yellow stars on the coats of the Jews in nazi Germany. Only today it is all done in the name of "fashion." It is interesting that one high-fashion trend is getting more and more constricting and more and more violent-looking—blood-red nails, spike heels, black leather jackets and suits, actually aping the nazi costume as "style." What's more, by adopting such a costume as "style" one intrinsically adopts its ideology as value.

The *Playboy* genre is given enormous assistance by television, magazine, and film magnates of a similar fascistic bent, of course, but I think it is important to name Hefner, Guccione, and Flynt for what they are: the philosophical leaders of this view of woman as "other." Recall Hitler, Mussolini, and Hirohito—one need not have the best interests of the human race at heart to be "der leader"— they were simply sufficiently psychotic to inspire fear and a following of frustrated men. It is vital to recognize the inherent danger of accepting the idea that women are alien just because we are women. We must realize that we are being groomed by a male power elite for "object" or "other" status on this earth. This male power elite is currently assisted by an unconscionable, female, elite, professional force, which acts as lackeys for the established "instant gratification for men" power structure.

LL: What do you think about the idea that today's woman has reaped benefits from the sexual revolution (of which pornography is a part), so she can now be "freer sexually"—less hung up, etc.?

JB: I think we are being sold a lie. As women get societal rewards for offering themselves up as sexual objects, we communicate and receive the message that a "real woman" is one who will take off her clothes at the drop of a hat, who will perform sexually, who is "ready anytime," who will sell (or rather rent) herself. We can be said to be breeding a nation of whores. If we accept the fact that the media directly affects behavior in today's world and we note that they are selling women the concept of the glamorous woman as whore, then the whole idea of pornographic modeling or prostitution as a "choice" women can make becomes a lie, because for a young girl to function, to be liked, it is important to be an accepted part of our culture. And if the culture encourages her to be a sexual object, that is what she will be.

In its November 1979 issue, *Playboy* published an interview with Masters and Johnson. In it Masters and Johnson (funded to the tune of $300,250 *Playboy* dollars, incidentally) talk about sexual trends, and mention that some heterosexuals as well as homosexuals perform anal intercourse. They add that although there is "discomfort" upon "initial penetration" and "thrusting," women can enjoy anal intercourse. But this article neglects to mention the homosexual men who are in hospitals receiving treatment for acute or chronic problems related to anal intercourse. That such intercourse is generally uncomfortable at best and dangerous at worst is obfuscated by their carefully worded "scientific proclamations."

Later in the interview, Masters and Johnson are asked about the size of the male penis, and they decline to comment. When pressed as to why they refuse to specify penis size, Masters and Johnson replied that such a statement would have a direct impact on male readers! They felt that "everybody would have been using a measuring stick," resulting in complexes and even impotence!

But though they observed only seven heterosexual couples engaging in anal intercourse, they refer to it as a "dimension of erotic stimulation" and encourage such "variance" in sex. This in a pornographic magazine dedicated to measuring and cataloging of the female in minute detail. Masters and Johnson know very well that their statements have a direct impact on women who read the magazine, and on men who read it and then try to push their wives and lovers into having anal sex with them. None of the pornographic magazines help to "free women sexually." They only make heavier the burden of male-oriented and male-identified sex which we already carry around inside us.

LL: Does this sort of sexual propaganda force women to pretend to themselves and the world that they are something they are not?

JB: It does more than that. Women hate themselves for not being like the magazine models they see men panting after. We don't measure up to the measurements touted by the magazines, and we know it. We despair (as Masters and Johnson worried that men might about penis size), but because there is nowhere to go with that despair it turns inward and becomes self-hatred.

I have been conducting a field study now for six months. I carry a measuring tape around with me, and I measure the bust, waist, and hips of every woman who will cooperate. My findings are very interesting: *Not once* have I encountered a female who measures the 38–22–34-inch size that *Playboy* used to claim its centerfold was. I have not come across one female with a natural 22-inch waist! For example, you are almost as thin as my thirteen-year-old cousin. Let me measure you—but, first, what size do you think your waist is?

LL: Probably 24 inches, but I don't know—I haven't measured it lately.

JB: Here. See—your waist is 25 inches, and that's with your stomach sucked in. Everywhere I have found the same sort of statistics: The average slender young female aged sixteen to twenty-six has a waist of 26 to 27 inches. Many are significantly larger than that. *And these are not fat women!* A two-month-old baby already has a waist of 16 or 17 inches! Yet *Playboy* would like us to believe that the perfect woman's waist is 21 or 22 inches. I suggest that *Playboy* has a tendency to lie about its models' measurements.

My field study is composed of two parts. After asking a woman what her measurements are and recording her answer, I ask her to take the tape measure and measure herself. Every woman who did this gained an inch or two in the waist and hips and lost an inch or two in the bust (from what she had originally stated her measurements were). Every woman expressed embarrassment at this, and many apologized to me saying things like, "Oh, I didn't realize how fat I was," or "Gee, I must have gained weight since the last time I measured myself." Next I say, "Here let ME measure you now, and don't suck in your waist or push out your chest." I hold the tape measure loosely around all three areas—not loose around the bust and tight around the waist and hips like most women do when they measure themselves. When I measure them naturally, I get gains of up to 4 inches in the waist and 1 to 2 inches in the hips, and losses of 1 to 3 inches in the bust from the original figures these women quoted to me. This field study, in conjunction with three years of survey data covering over 700 women, has established that we do a great deal of wishing we were something we are not—a lot of covering up of the facts of how we look and who we really are, and a lot of lying to try to measure up. In other words, a lot of self-hatred. This "perfect female body" concept also stimulates male hatred of women—their wives and lovers especially. Readers feel short-changed when a woman does not look and act the part of the *Playboy* model. It is an insult to their masculine capacity to get what they want because in this society the female is, after all, a reflection of how much he can get. He cannot seem to attract the good-looking model in *Playboy*; instead he is stuck with a woman who has borne three children, gained weight, grown older with time. It makes him hate her. And it makes him turn to the younger female daughters in the family, which is why *Playboy* is cleverly exploiting that lust now.

LL: You spoke earlier of a "hidden agenda" in Playboy *magazine. Do you believe this agenda is conscious?*

JB: Yes. Absolutely. *Playboy* is an outstanding success in the sale of products. One of the magazine's biggest claims is that readers heed the advertisements more than other magazine ads and purchase products they see in the magazine. *Playboy* knows that the exploitation of women's bodies is what keeps men buying the magazine. Billions of dollars are involved in this industry. People say *Playboy* is "just an entertainment magazine for men," but much, much more than that is at stake. *Playboy* is selling a way of life, and its way of life is not love and respect of human beings, but love of commodities —and women and children are regarded as commodities.

Nothing *Playboy* does is accidental. The publication of a successful magazine is big business, and you must plan ahead if you are in a big business or you go under. You plan not just for a year or two but for five years, for decades. Hefner knows marketing techniques inside out. He is advised by some of the sharpest people in the country: for example, Philip Kotler of Northwestern University, a major marketing figure in the United States. In addition, *Playboy* paid Yankelovich, Skelly, and White, Inc., in New York City, one of the biggest and most famous marketing research companies in the world to do a wide range of psychological services, surveys, and tests.

Playboy is moving into film, video, and TV. It has its finger in every liberal political pie in the nation. It has even been funding many women's organizations and women's issues in order, ultimately, to gain control of our issues and our political organizations, three of the most important of which are NOW, ERA, and abortion! The Hefner empire is not interested in publishing "girlie" magazines. It is interested in becoming more and more powerful, and the more dependent people become on the *Playboy* way of life, the more powerful *Playboy* is. That is why I like to say that *Playboy* isn't playing.

LL: What should women do?

JB: There are many things I feel women must do.

First: We must recognize our leadership role and our own personal expertise in the matter of what is offensive and pornographic. The research conducted until now overwhelmingly confirms women's rejection of commercial pornographic materials, despite the pressures to conform by their loved ones and by society. Even research which finds sexual arousal in females toward pornographic material also finds rejection of the same material by the women responding. Interestingly, most researchers have tended to explain this contradiction in typically sexist language, e.g., *women* are out of step due to "cultural conditioning." This is hardly the case. I contend this rejection is simply a still-functioning survival instinct—the instinctive recognition of the danger, hate, and unbridled violence inherent in pornographic ideas and images, however well they are designed and sugar-coated. Anger toward this female hate propaganda is a healthy sign for women in contemporary society. Women must understand that and sense it, feel it, believe it before we will feel comfortable challenging (often) husbands, friends, colleagues, and other women. We must understand that it is not we who are out of step. Indeed, it is the male-dominated world which is out of step, as it has been before so regularly.

Second: It becomes vitally important to speak out clearly regarding the rejection of pornography in your private spheres, with those close to you at home, at work, and in organizations. We should practice in these areas as it were, to get our voices, our courage.

Third: Although single voices do carry weight, group action is the best, the speediest way to be effective. NOW has established a boycott of national significance to help win us Equal Rights Amendment. This kind of action must be imposed on all pornographic images. Pornography is a hate campaign; make no "liberally sophisticated" mistake about that. It is a campaign to humiliate and brutalize all females, women, and children. If it continues to succeed, we will be back at the bottom of the barrel—all of us—and for generations to come.

Fourth: A coalition of all women needs to be established, regardless of race, color, creed, religion, or political persuasion. No discriminatory "radicals-only" concept will do. The idea of divide and conquer is still effective. Women have been divided; we must reunite throughout the nation on this one basic issue. A coalition is central to our survival . . . all women who refuse to accept the contemporary sexualized definition of women must agree to work together on this issue. Disagreements on other issues can be dealt with when fewer of us are being murdered, beaten, tortured, and raped. There will be that many more votes to count.

Fifth: Pressure must be put on NOW and *Ms.* magazine, and on other women's organizations and magazines, to advertise a national boycott of any media materials and supporting products which we believe in any way, shape, or form demean women. I find it disturbing that literally nothing has come out of any liberated women's magazines which squarely treats the *Playboy* ethic for what it is—a threat to our very lives as human and humane beings, ERA notwithstanding. The opportunities for communication and education on this issue are enormous due to the number of women's periodicals and their outreach. With this in mind, all women's magazines should be encouraged to sanction and publicize as one unified body, such national boycott action or risk the loss of female readership.

Sixth: Legal action must be taken wherever possible on a national organizational scale. So much needs to be done on the legal front. There must be protection for women and children from pornographic hate propaganda.

Seventh: Now we get to a rather touchy and controversial point: Our problem is not just *men* in power. All oppressors worth their salt have employed members of the exploited class to do their dirtiest work. This is just as much a reality for women today. The 1976 April cover of *Playboy*, which featured the clearest emphasis on malecest and pedophilia, was photographed by a woman. The publisher of *High Society* magazine is a woman. Women are being offered excellent opportunities throughout the mass media to serve as collaborators, producing vile sexist propaganda. This is to be expected. As the tempo of exploitation is increased, more confederates are hired to create the soft patina of credibility.

There are always those who need to dehumanize others and who will exploit the weakest group at hand. Since contemporary culture prohibits exploitation and denigration on the basis of race, creed, color, or religion, it would appear that the only "group" now legally at hand is sexual—the female sex specifically. We have to take very seriously the treatment we and our children are receiving in the mass media. I believe current media trends are destroying female sexuality and the male-female relationship. It is time that we stop serving the worst of the male culture, and make our own definitions of what being a woman and being female means to us. This is not a pretty time. If my assessment is correct, it is a time of war. We are dealing with a fragile hold upon humaneness. Let us also remember that we are up against a powerful media industry which encourages pornography in order to fulfill its own present and future interests. We must demand a society which protects women from this exploitation and violence.

Theory and Practice:
Pornography and Rape

Robin Morgan

One of the first feminists to attack pornography back in the 1960's was Robin Morgan. She coined the phrase "Theory and Practice: Pornography and Rape." It has been used by feminists to point out the convergence of the two ever since. Says Robin, "The following article is based on what to my horror got termed in hard-boiled organizer's jargon 'The Rape Rap.' I must have communicated some version of it hundreds of times, with a ripening anger as women came forward with their own experiences of rape, and I realized how far-reaching and quintessentially patriarchal the crime was. There was a time when rape and pornography were embarrassing issues even in the Women's Movement: Such things were deplorable, to be sure, but they had to be deplored with a sophisticated snicker—not with outspoken fury. Today there are rape-crisis centers in major cities all over the nation, and feminist rape-prevention brigades. Many metropolitan police departments have special anti-rape squads run by women officers and new rape-reporting procedures devised by women; and self-defense classes for women are no longer seen as passing strange. . . . Feminists . . . sorties against the attendant issue—pornography—are still somewhat more awkwardly conducted, but women are every day becoming less concerned with being graceful and more bent on being free."

There is perhaps no subject relevant to women so deliberately distorted as that of rape. This is because rape is the perfected act of male sexuality in a patriarchal culture—it is the ultimate metaphor for domination, violence, subjugation, and possession.*

But the most insidious aspect of rape is the psychological fiction that accompanies it—with which all women are besieged until, for

* This does not mean that men in another cultural context would necessarily be the same, or that all men have acceded to the male sexual standards in this culture. Biological-determination theories will remain treacherous until we have enough feminist scientists to right the current imbalance and bias and create genuinely value-free research.

survival's sake, we even pretend to believe what we *know* is a lie. The fiction has many versions. We can look at a few representative examples.

There is the Pity the Poor Rapist approach. This version tells us that we must be sorry for our attacker. He is sick, he cannot help himself, he needs help.

He decidedly does need help (if he can be apprehended), but his victim needs it more—and first. She is not even supposed to defend herself for fear of being unwomanly. I find it educative that a woman who, for instance, notices her child being molested by a dirty old (or young) man on the playground, and who shampoos the man with a brick, is considered a proper mother, "the tigress defending her cubs." Yet should the same man molest her, she ought to, in society's view, welcome him and admit that she relishes being pawed, or if she must, plead winningly with him to stop. It is acceptable to defend one's child, but not one's self because it is considered the epitome of selfishness for the female to place her own concerns first. We are supposed to wipe the noses of all humanity before we dare think about ourselves. Well, we must learn to mother those selves and defend them at least as valiantly as we do our children.

The Spontaneity Lie is an offshoot of Pity the Poor Rapist. It informs us that he was just an average guy walking along the street (the lamb) who was positively seized with the urge to attack a woman. Sudden lust. In combating the spontaneity approach, one should remember that more than half of all rapes occur in breaking-and-entering situations—which do require, one would think, a modicum of premeditation.

There is always the basic Every Woman Loves a Rapist/All Women Want to Be Raped/Good Girls Never Get Raped/It's Always the Woman's Fault cliché. This is frequently carried to ludicrous extremes. Thus, if she wears slacks that's obviously meant as a challenge; if a skirt it's an incitement. If she glowers as she strides down the street, it's meant as an attention-getter; if she looks pleasant it's a come-on. Et cetera; *ad nauseam; ad infinitum.* And, besides, what was she doing out walking all alone by herself anyway at eleven o'clock in broad daylight? Doesn't she know her place?

Knowing our place is the message of rape—as it was for blacks the message of lynchings. Neither is an act of spontaneity or sexuality—they are both acts of political terrorism, designed consciously *and* unconsciously to keep an entire people in its place by continual reminders. For the attitudes of racism and sexism are twined together in the knot of rape in such a way as to constitute *the* symbolic ex-

pression of the worst in our culture.* These "reminders" are perpetrated on victims selected sometimes at random, sometimes with
particular reason. So we have the senseless rape murders of children
and of seventy-year-old women—whom no one can salaciously claim
were enticing the rapist—and we also have the deliberate "lesson-
rapes" that feminist students have been prey to on their campuses for
the past four years—acts based on the theory that all these frustrated
feminists need is a good rape to show 'em the light.

Thus, the woman is rarely unknown to her attacker, nor need the
rapist be a stranger to his victim—although goddess help her deal
with the more-than-usual scorn of the police if she reports rape by
a former jealous boyfriend, or an ex-husband, or her faculty advisor
or boss or psychiatrist. Many policemen already delight in asking the
victim such sadistic and illegal questions as, "Did you enjoy it?"
Consequently, any admission on her part, whether elicited or volunteered, that the rapist was actually an acquaintance seems to invite
open season on *her* morals.

But radical feminists see the issue of rape as even more pervasive
than these examples. For instance, I would define rape not only as
the violation taking place in the dark alley or after breaking into and
entering a woman's home. I claim that rape exists any time sexual
intercourse occurs when it has not been initiated by the woman out
of her own genuine affection and desire. This last qualifier is important because we are familiar with the cigarette commercial of the
"Liberated Woman," she who is the nonexistent product of the so-
called sexual revolution: a Madison Avenue-spawned male fantasy of
what the liberated woman should be—a glamorous lady slavering
with lust for his paunchy body. We also know that many women, in
responding to this new pressure to be "liberated initiators," have done
so *not* out of their own desire but for the same old reasons—fear of
losing the guy, fear of being a prude, fear of hurting his fragile feelings, *fear*. So it is vital to emphasize that when we say she must be
the initiator (in tone if not in actuality) we mean because *she* wants
to be. Anything short of that is, in a radical feminist definition, rape.
Because *the pressure is there*, and it need not be a knife blade against
the throat; it's in his body language, his threat of sulking, his clenched
or trembling hands, his self-deprecating humor or angry put-down or
silent self-pity at being rejected. How many millions of times have
women had sex "willingly" with men they didn't want to have sex

* Susan Brownmiller has since demonstrated this point in depth, with courage
and clarity, in her book *Against Our Will: Men, Women and Rape* (Simon &
Schuster, New York, 1975).

with? Even men they loved? How many times have women wished just to sleep instead or read or watch "The Late Show"? It must be clear that, under this definition, most of the decently married bedrooms across America are settings for nightly rape.

This normal, corn-fed kind of rape is less shocking if it can be realized and admitted that the act of rape is merely the expression of the standard, "healthy" even encouraged male fantasy in patriarchal culture—that of aggressive sex. And the articulation of that fantasy into a billion-dollar industry is pornography.

Civil libertarians recoil from linking the issues of rape and pornography, dredging out their yellowing statistics from the Scandinavian countries which appear to show that acts of rape decline where pornography is more easily procured. This actually ought to prove the connection. I am not suggesting that censorship should rule the day here—I abhor censorship in any form (although there was a time when I felt it was a justifiable means to an end—which is always the devil's argument behind thought control, isn't it?). I'm aware, too, that a phallocentric culture is more likely to begin its censorship purges with books on pelvic self-examination for women, or books containing lyrical paeans to lesbianism than with *"See Him Tear and Kill Her"* or similar Spillane-esque titles. Nor do I place much trust in a male-run judiciary, and I am less than reassured by the character of those who would pretend to judge what is fit for the public to read or view. On the contrary, I feel that censorship often boils down to some male judges sitting up on their benches, getting to read a lot of dirty books with one hand. This hardly appears to me to be the solution. Some feminists have suggested that a Cabinet-level woman in charge of Women's Affairs (in itself a controversial idea) might take pornography regulation into her portfolio. Others hark back to the idea of community control. Both approaches give me unease, the first because of the unlikeliness that a Cabinet-level woman appointee these days would have genuine feminist consciousness, or, if she did, have the power and autonomy from the administration to act upon it; the second because communities can be as ignorant and totalitarian in censorship as individual tyrants. A lot of education would have to precede community-controlled regulation to win that proposal my paranoid support. Certainly this is one problem to which simple solutions are just nonexistent, rhetoric to the contrary.

But women seem to be moving on the issue with a different strategy, one that circumvents censorship and instead is aimed at hurting the purveyors themselves, at making the business less lucrative by making the clients less comfortable. In one Southern town, women planned their action with considerable wit; they took up positions on their local porn strip and politely photographed each man as he entered or left the bookstores and movie houses. They used a very obvious camera—the large, newspaper-photographer type—sometimes chasing the man for a block as he fled in chagrin. One group of women who used this tactic deliberately worked with cameras that had no film—scaring and embarrassing the men was their aim. Another group, however, did use film and developed the shots. They then made up Wanted Posters of the men, which they plastered all over town—to the acute humiliation of the porn-purchasers, some of whom turned out to be influential and upstanding citizens of the community. In Seattle women's anti-pornography squads have stink-bombed smut bookstores—and the local papers were filled with approving letters to the editors. In New York three porn movie houses have been fire-bombed.

The massive porn industry grinds on, of course. In a replay of the liberated-woman shill, we are now being sold so-called female-oriented pornography, as if our sexuality were as imitative of patriarchal man's as *Playgirl* is of *Playboy*. It must be frustrating to the pushers of such tacky trash to realize that for most women *Wuthering Heights* is still a *real* turn-on, or that there are quite a few of us who remained loyal to Ashley Wilkes (especially as portrayed by Leslie Howard) and never were fooled by that gross Rhett Butler. Yet pornography today is becoming chic—serious movie houses, which usually run art films, are now cashing in on so-called art-porn. The Mick Jagger/sadism fad, the popularity of transvestite entertainers, and the resurgence of "Camp" all seem to me part of an unmistakable backlash against what feminists have been demanding. It is no coincidence that FBI statistics indicate the incidence of rape *increased 93 percent* in the 1960's. When people refuse to stay in their place, the message must be repeated in a louder tone.

And what is this doing to us? We are somewhat educated now as to the effects of rape on women, but we know much less about the effects of pornography. Some obvious trends can be noted: the market for go-go girls, nude models, and porno-film "actresses," which in turn affects women's employment (why be a secretary when you can make more money taking off your clothes?); the overlapping boundaries of the porn and prostitution industries; the erosion of the virgin/whore stereotypes to a new "all woman are really whores" attitude, thus erasing the last vestige of (even corrupted) respect for women; the promotion of infidelity and betrayal as a swinging alternative to committed relationships. But how to chart the pressure sensed by women from their boyfriends or husbands to perform sexually in ever more objectified and objectifying fashion as urged by porn movies and magazines? How to connect the rise of articles in journals aimed at educated, liberal audiences—articles extolling the virtues of anal intercourse, "fist-fucking," and other "kinky freedoms"? †

But how far-reaching is the effect, how individual, how universal? Individual in terms of the specific humiliation felt by the woman whose husband hides *Penthouse* or some harder-core version of it in the bathroom and then forces himself on her at night—or on other women when she fends him off—and then blames her for her frigidity and his inconstancy? Individual and universal enough to explain the recent horrifying rise in the rate of marital violence? (See Del Martin's definitive book *Battered Wives*, San Francisco: Glide Urban Center Publications, 1976.) Universal enough to have influenced all of twentieth-century theology?

Yet this has happened, through the work of that intellectual giant, the Christian theologian Paul Tillich—he who is revealed to us with such compassionate but uncompromising honesty by his widow in her brilliant, controversial book *From Time to Time* (New York: Stein & Day, 1973). After his death, Hannah Tillich tells us, she "unlocked the drawers. All the girls' photos fell out, letters and poems, passionate appeal and disgust." There was the pornographic letter hidden under his blotter; the knowledge of his favorite fantasy of naked women, crucified, being whipped; the discovery of all the affairs, the mistresses, the sexual secretaries, the one-night stands, the abuse of the worshipful female students who had sat at his feet, his "houris . . . tinkling their chains." She writes: "I was tempted to place between the sacred pages of his highly esteemed lifework these obscene signs of the real life that he had transformed into the gold of abstraction—King Midas of the spirit." Instead, Hannah Tillich dared write a book about herself, alchemizing her own integrity out of "the piece of bleeding, tortured womanhood" she says she had become.

So we can admit that pornography is sexist propaganda, no more and no less. [There is no comparison here with genuine erotic art—such as *The Tale of Genji* by Lady Shikibu Murasaki (c. 978–1031 A.D.), the great Japanese novelist of the Heian period.]

Pornography is the theory, and rape the practice. And what a

† Surely the currently (1976) popular "Punk Image" of the half-gangster, half-fifties-high-school-dropout male is related to these themes, an image described in *The Village Voice* as bringing back "masculine chic."

practice. The violation of an individual woman is *the* metaphor for man's forcing himself on whole nations (rape as the crux of war), on nonhuman creatures (rape as the lust behind hunting and related carnage), and on the planet itself (reflected even in our language—carving up "virgin territory," with strip-mining often referred to as a "rape of the land"). Elaine Morgan, in her book *The Descent of Woman* (New York: Stein & Day, 1972), posits that rape was the initial crime, not murder, as the Bible would have it. She builds an interesting scientific argument for her theory. In *The Mothers* (1927; New York: Grosset & Dunlap Universal Library edition, 1963), Robert Briffault puts forward much the same hypothesis for an evolutionary "fall" from the comparable grace of the animal realm; his evidence is anthropological and mythohistoric. In more than one book, Claude Lévi-Strauss has pursued his complex theory of how men use women as the verbs by which they communicate with one another (they themselves are the nouns, of course), rape being the means for communicating defeat to the men of a conquered tribe, so overpowered that they cannot even defend "their" woman from the victors. That theory, too, seems relevant here. The woman may serve as a vehicle for the rapist expressing his rage against a world which gives him pain—because he is poor, or oppressed, or mad, or simply human. Then what of *her*? We have waded in the swamp of compassion for him long enough. It is past time we stopped him.

The conflict is escalating now because we won't cast our glances down any more to avoid seeing the degrading signs and marquees. We won't shuffle past the vulgarity of the sidewalk verbal hassler, who is not harmless but who is broadcasting the rapist's theory and who is backed up by *the threat of the capacity to carry out the practice* itself. We will no longer be guilty about being victims of ghastly violations on our spirits and bodies merely because we are female. Whatever their age and origin, the propaganda and act which transform that most intimate, vulnerable, and tender of physical exchanges into one of conquest and humiliation is surely the worse example patriarchy has to offer women of the way it truly regards us.

Sadism and Catharsis: The Treatment Is the Disease

Susan Griffin

This article is an excerpt from a forthcoming book by Susan Griffin entitled *Pornography and Silence*. Griffin says she began by thinking about how women are made to disappear. "Our invisibility in history. The manuscripts of Sappho burned, the writing of women never published, lives of genius and speech spent obscurely, or in domestic labor and child-rearing (this labor neither spoken of nor paid for) . . . The testimony of a woman in court held suspect by virtue of her gender, her body, her self. The denigration of women, and our bodies, pervades every expression of this culture, no less in 'great' art and literature than in what is sold as pornography, and our outrage against pornography must reach for this clarity: that the very way patriarchy has of seeing is a crime against our lives."

In this article, Griffin speaks of catharsis, a model used by social scientists which hypothesizes that pornography is merely a device which allows men safely to get rid of antisocial behavior like rape, aggression against women, assault.

Catharsis, Catharsis, it is grimly implied, is the true role of pornography. There would be *more* rape, I hear the threat under the reasoning tone, were there not pornography. Be grateful. Be grateful. Oh, but what a depressing picture of the world believing this voice gives me. I imagine men filled with the desire for violence, the need for violence growing in them every day, as natural as hunger or thirst, controlled only by small, placating attention, bits of nourishment. I imagine the average male in the corner of a cage growling with menace. Here, his tenders say, let us give him these photographs of men beating women, of men holding knives up to women's throats, breasts, vulvas, of women's mouths gagged, their legs chained. This will appease him, they say, these images will bring him peace.

Drawn here in a woman's hand, this outline of male nature as essentially rapacious and brutal appears less glamorous than usual. But this is not my image. I have only copied the self-portraits of men;

it is the same picture of male nature that can be found, for instance, in the work of Norman Mailer.

His hero in *The American Dream* is far more violent than the man I have imagined. He goes beyond appeasement, past metaphorical catharsis. Only the real act can save him from the forces inside him; he murders his wife. As if this murder were what he had always wanted (the failure to murder his failure to be) the murder itself becomes a healing.

With his hands around his wife's throat, on the point of killing her, Mailer's hero envisions a door and on the other side of the door, "heaven was there, some quiver of jeweled cities shining in the glow of a tropical dusk. . . ." Yet he does not move toward this shining glow consciously. Rather, a kind of primal force in him takes to murder, and he likens this force to the power of his sexual feelings, "some black-biled lust, some desire to go ahead not unlike the instant one comes in a woman against her cry that she is without protection. . . ." Her death proceeds from him as if it were an inexorable historical process confirmed in its justice by the good it does him. . . .

> and *crack* I choked her harder, and *crack* I choked her again, and *crack* I gave her payment—never halt now—and *crack* the door flew open and the wire tore in her throat, and I was through the door, hatred passing from me in wave after wave, illness as well, rot and pestilence, nausea, a bleak string of salts. I was floating. I was as far into myself as I had ever been and universes wheeled in a dream. . . . I opened my eyes, I was weary, with a most honorable fatigue, and my flesh seemed new.

And this imagining of Mailer is in its turn not his own because it comes from a long tradition of heroes who are violent to women: Raskolnikov, Bigger Thomas, in fantasy; Eldridge Cleaver, Caryl Chessman, in fact. And the theme of male violence appears everywhere, the strange yet not surprising narcissism of the Hell's Angels, the rapaciousness and the threat of rapaciousness of armies; it creeps into one's consciousness when one pulls the curtains closed at night, or locks the door. And yes, it is true, men are violent. I have read the statistics. But still, I begin to doubt. An uncanny feeling comes to me after I see the image projected again and again on different screens. Perhaps this image is in itself precious; perhaps the violence itself takes place in the service of this image. Perhaps underneath violence is the desire to appear violent.

Even science labors to keep this image of man as a menace alive;

to prove it. The words of Robert Ardrey: "The territorial imperative is as blind as a cave fish, as consuming as a furnace, and it commands beyond logic, opposes all reason, suborns all moralities, strives for no goal more sublime than survival. . . ." Lionel Tiger's descriptions of the aggressiveness and dominance of male masques, Darwin's theories of the struggle for existence, Herbert Spencer's social Darwinism, all part of a large work of defense. Man is violent, they protest, almost hysterically, man will always be violent.

Be grateful, I hear them telling us, look what we sacrifice to you, our true nature, our redemption. But the imperative to violence in us (as blind as a cave fish) must be fed something, some tidbit, or else even we, with our good intentions, will be able to do nothing against it. And so pornography in the light of these protestations becomes almost an act of mercy. For just as it prevents terrible actual violence, we are told, it is a kindness to those men who wage war against their own natures, a sop to their own mighty urges.

Like much of the thought of this male civilization, the story ends in tragedy. What an abysmal bitterness. A civilization of discontent. A nature forever held back, to be satisfied simply with appeasement, the transcendence, the shining glow of tropical dusk behind the door of real rape and murder, to be forever denied. And what is more, this old story implies that this denial has taken place for the sake of women. Somehow it is because we like to have our kitchen floors clean, because we are fussily gentle and given to soft fabrics, if not a kind of softness in the head, men have to contain the grandness of their true natures. (Lionel Tiger writes that the equivalent of childbirth for the male includes "perhaps even the violent mastery and destruction of others.")

Underneath the argument that pornography is cathartic, then, is a terrible nostalgia and a grief from the imagined loss of this primal violence. And so the double message. The speaker who utters opposite truths out of each side of his mouth. The Janus head. Gemini. The twin love of violence and fear of violence in the warning, don't take away pornography or the beast will be unleashed.

I do not believe what this head is saying to me. In the first place, the head is severed. And it is not Salome who holds it up for admiration. The head has detached itself from the body and blames the body now for its own beastliness. For it is the head, the intellect, which has imagined this violence to be part of male nature and then must speak and protest and defend and prove because the head needs this violence as the body does not. What leads me to feel this, to sense it out?

The hysteria. The hysteria of these arguments, which I must now move through delicately and slowly, unwrapping a tangled and distorted web: this hysteria is a sign to me that the violence is unreal, has been fabricated by the severed head. And of course the head is hysterical. Without the body, it must feed on images alone.

What if we imagined our true natures, male and female, as undeniably tender?

Tenderness as deaf as moss, as enveloping as fog, it lives past words, opposes nothing, feeds all perception, cares for no concern past feeling . . . That laced through our profoundest stories are moments of confrontation when the soul of the heroine is overwhelmed because she perceives the depths of her ability to love and this takes the greatest courage, tests her being. Oh, but this is softminded. This in the culture of pornography, which is the culture of sadism, is the height of softmindedness.

Hysteria. For instance, the head claims out of one side of its mouth that pornography leads to nothing. Produces no behavior, they would say in the social science texts. That pornography does not make or encourage men to rape women, nor in any way to reproduce the acts of cruelty they see. But out of the other side of its mouth, the head tells us that pornography allows many men to achieve (and this in itself is an interesting word, "achieve") sexual release. This is not logical. Yet, in working through the knots of this hysteria, let me attempt to make it logical.

Perhaps what is being said by the two sides of the mouth is that pornography excites some behavior but not all behavior. That, to be precise, a pornographic magazine, with a drawing of a nude woman whose face is enclosed in a horse's bit, whose body is roped and suspended, will excite a man to sexual pleasure, but not to the desire to bind and bridle a woman.

Let us forget for a moment that the article which this drawing accompanies suggests that, "The world of restraint devices with its treasure trove of straps, harnesses and buckles, provides an acceptable way to act out their dream with a minimal risk of injury." Let us forget that these words surround the illustration in this case because here the argument is different. Here the argument is not for any acting out as "an acceptable way" to fulfill fantasy (leading, of course, to minimal injury). Here the argument is that simply to see a photograph or read a story about "restraint devices" (oh, how the language domesticates these horrors) is acceptable and leads to only minimal injury, if any injury at all.

And so that image, of the body of a woman unclothed and bound and in pain, which excites feeling in the body, the head says, introduces no corresponding idea of violence.

But this is the head speaking. And, of course, the image of violence does not make the body feel violent. A body feels violent only when physically frightened, threatened in its being. It is the head that requires images of violence, that is excited by them, that *wants* them. And this same male head convinces the body that it needs these images, pictures of women's bodies, and tyrannizes its own body, restrains and misshapes the bodily responses to these ends, to its far more complicated purposes. The head exploits the body's simple desire for pleasure and uses this for its own unsimple desires.

And the head that requires this violence will push the body further and further, for its demands, like the limitless world of images, can be inexorable. And so the head, while deftly constructing an ineffable association between the undeniable ways of the body and the tortuous binding of a woman, at the same time, out of the other side of its mouth, denies that such a thing as association exists. Says that a man may look at a picture of a woman bound and gagged and feel sexually, but feel no desire to bind or gag or cause pain.

In fact, the argument is that her body and the binding around her body have opposite effects on the same man. By her body, he is moved to action. He can "achieve" sexual pleasure. But her binding has an opposite effect. This does not stir him to action. This ends in the image, purges him of any striving toward action, placates him in his primal desire for violence.

What a tangle this head with its mouth speaking from two sides has created. It has obscured the perfectly obvious; that to put any two images together is to create an association. That to put violence and women's bodies together, to associate sexuality and violence fabricates a need. (But, of course, the head must conceal simple observations because it is the head which fabricates need, and in order to make a need felt, it is important that the need be believed, and, therefore, it must never be known that the need is fabricated.) Advertisers in the last decades have spent millions of dollars to create associations between their products and sexual pleasure in order to fabricate a need for those products. In this case the product is brutality toward women.

But I come back to the idea of catharsis. Because I have experienced catharsis. I have had catharsis pass through my mind and enter my body and have seen my body be sick and then be well as my mind was healed of what I held too long within myself without seeing.

And so why should it not be true that seeing pornographic photographs could purge a man of his need for violence, even if the mind has created the need? If it is a mental need, born of fantasy, fantasy should be able to answer that need.

But this has not been my experience, nor is this the shape of catharsis, for catharsis is not an end in itself. That deep experiencing of old, sometimes long-buried emotions bears a fruit, and the fruit is knowledge. If there were really to be a catharsis experienced regarding sexual violence toward women, the need for that violence would disappear or if it reappeared, be only a shadow of itself and renamed, linked to its source, its origin.

How I wish that Freud had begun his practice on young men, treating their hysteria, their fatal attraction to war, rape, dominance. How I wish he had treated the fathers who were accused of raping their daughters for whatever illness brought them to these acts. But this is the central problem, and why I write these pages and why our lives as men and women have taken the shape they have in this civilization. Such behavior as war and rapaciousness has not been seen as proceeding from illness. Such behavior has been termed normal, if not "animal," wild, untrammeled, uncivilized perhaps but not pathological. But this behavior is not seen as illness. Who sees. The severed heads are seeing. Freud himself was a severed head. He would not see himself.

And, of course, this behavior is normal in the sense that it is practiced by most men. As has been widely documented, first in Phyllis Chesler's *Women and Madness*, but now in many other places, male healers of the mind are themselves very often rapists and they rape their clients in the name of wellness. There is such a phenomenon as an illness which is created by and sustained by a culture; and one of those illnesses accounts for a great deal of the range of masculine behavior, including rape and sadism and the enjoyment of images of brutality toward women and the apologia for that brutality which constitutes much of our culture. Freud was not above this illness. What he saw, he saw through the lens of this cultural madness.

So how understandable it is that he treated mostly women, that he *saw* hysteria in women, so that the very term hysteria has come to connote a young female patient. When I think of catharsis, naturally the cases of the young women whom Freud treated come to mind. A woman who had fits of choking; one who had a morbid fear of snakes, whose arms were paralyzed; a woman who had attacks of dizziness and fear of heights. A young woman who would not eat or drink. In order to make them well, the doctor brought these women to their own memories. The death of a friend who was never mourned, the death of a father who was hated, a mother who forced her daughter to eat food which had sat for two hours and was cold. Feelings which could not be recognized or lived to their full extent and *never named* living on in the head, finally expressed by the body as distortions.

In all these cases it was not the mere experiencing of choking or dizziness or fear or paralysis or nausea or revulsion that healed illness. In each case the origin of these symptoms themselves could be revealed as unreal and the real source of illness be precisely named. Knowledge, ultimately, is what healed. Had these women gone on experiencing nausea or dizziness or fear or paralysis, moreover accompanied by the belief that these symptoms were somehow causes or accumulated passions which would subside with some indulgence, one might presume that the symptoms would have gotten worse, for the continual indulgence in them would strengthen a belief in them and thus take each psyche farther away from a real knowledge of herself.

But this is precisely what pornography, which the severed heads claim is cathartic, does. It is dangerous to confuse the therapeutic experience with the experiencing of the symptoms of one's illness. But such is an old habit, an old trick of systems of oppression, whether they be psychic or social. What George Orwell called the politics of language; to name peace war or war peace. This is what Mary Daly calls reversal. The truth only hidden in what is said. The wolf in sheep's clothing. Language itself, which can be the healing agent, takes us farther away from what we know to be true, and we are severed from our own knowledge and so obsessed with the distorted ghost of truth.

And then once possessing this knowledge, one desires to be free. This is the first emotion. I have felt it. In *Tribute to Freud*, H. D. wrote of her investigations of dream states and memories, "I am drifting out to sea. But I know I am safe, can return at any moment to Terra Firma." This is the clarity one wants, not the freedom to be ill to the extremity of one's illness, but the freedom which comes from being free of illness, free of an obsession with the past.

Why So-Called Radical Men Love and Need Pornography

Andrea Dworkin

This article is a result of Andrea Dworkin's long history of activism in the left, particularly in the anti-Vietnam war protest during the 1960's. Later, she says, "I began to question why the men who were my peers in terms of age and personal and political history had such a tremendous interest in pornography." "Why So-Called Radical Men Love and Need Pornography" was written to answer that question.

I.

> When they arrived at the place God had pointed out to him, Abraham built an altar there, and arranged the wood. Then he bound his son Isaac and put him on the altar on top of the wood. Abraham stretched out his hand and seized the knife to kill his son.
>
> —GENESIS 22:9–10

Men love death. In everything they make, they hollow out a central place for death, let its rancid smell contaminate every dimension of whatever still survives. Men especially love murder. In art they celebrate it, and in life they commit it. They embrace murder as if life without it would be devoid of passion, meaning, and action, as if murder were solace, stilling their sobs as they mourn the emptiness and alienation of their lives.

Male history, romance, and adventure are stories of murder, literal or mythic. Men of the right justify murder as the instrument of establishing or maintaining order, and men of the left justify murder as the instrument of effecting insurrection, after which they justify it in the same terms as men on the right. In male culture, slow murder

148

is the heart of eros, fast murder is the heart of action, and systematized murder is the heart of history. It is as if, long, long ago, men
made a covenant with murder: I will worship and serve you if you
will spare *me*; I will murder so as not to be murdered; I will not betray you, no matter what else I must betray. Murder promised: to
the victor go the spoils. This covenant, sealed in blood, has been re-
newed in every generation.

Among men, the fear of being murdered causes men to murder.
The fathers, who wanted their own likeness lifted from the thighs of
laboring women, who wanted sons, not daughters, at some point
recognize that, like wretched King Midas, they have gotten their way.
There before them are the sons who are the same as they, sons who
will kill for power, sons who will take everything from them, sons
who will replace them. The sons, clay sculpted but not yet fired in
the kiln, must kill or be killed, depose the tyrant or be ground to
dust, on a battlefield or under his feet. The fathers are the divine
architects of war and business; the sons are a sacrifice of flesh, bodies
slaughtered to redeem the diminishing virility of the aging owners of
the earth.

In Amerika, the most recent sacrifice of the sons was called Viet
Nam. As Abraham obeyed the God created to serve his own deepest
psychosexual needs, raised the knife to kill Isaac with his own hand,
so the fathers of Amerika, in obedience to the State created to serve
them, sated themselves on a blood feast of male young.

The sons who went were obedient apprentices to the fathers. War
had for them its most ancient meaning: it would initiate them into
the covenant with murder. They would appease their terrible fathers
by substituting the dead bodies of other sons for their own. Each son
of another race that they killed would strengthen their alliance with
the fathers of their own. And if they could also murder without being
murdered and kill in themselves whatever still shunned murder, then
they might have the father's blessing, be heir to his dominion, change
in mid-life from son to father, become one of the powerful ones who
choreograph war and manipulate death.

The sons who did not go declared outright a war of rebellion. They
would rout the father, vanquish him, humiliate him, destroy him.
Over the grave of the fresh-killed father, feeding on the new cadaver,
would flower a brotherhood of young virility, sensual, without con-
straint, and there would be war no more.

Still, this innocence knew terror. These rebels had terror marked
indelibly in their flesh—terror at the treachery of the father, who had
had them sanctified, adored, and fattened, not to crown them king of

the world, but instead to make them ripe for slaughter. These rebels had seen themselves bound on the altar, knife in the father's hand coming toward them. The father's cruelty was awesome, as was his mammoth power.

II.

> Noah, a tiller of the soil, was the first to plant the vine. He drank some of the wine, and while he was drunk he uncovered himself inside his tent. Ham, Canaan's ancestor, saw his father's nakedness, and told his two brothers outside. Shem and Japheth took a cloak and they both put it over their shoulders, and walking backwards, covered their father's nakedness; they kept their faces turned away, and did not see their father's nakedness. When Noah awoke from his stupor he learned what his youngest son had done to him. And he said: "Accursed be Canaan. He shall be his brothers' meanest slave."
>
> —GENESIS 9:20–25

The fathers hoard power. They use power to amass more power. They are not sentimental about power. In every area of life, they act to take or to consolidate power.

The rebellious sons, born in the image of the father, are born to power, but they do not value it in terms the father can recognize. These sons renounce the fathers' cold love of power. These sons claim that the purpose of power is pleasure. These sons want power to keep them warm between the thighs.

The fathers know that taboo is the essence of power: keep the source of power hidden, mysterious, sacred, so that those without power can never find it, understand it, or take it away.

The rebellious sons think that power is like youth—theirs forever. They think that power can never be used up, thrown away, or taken away. They think that power can be spent in the pursuit of pleasure without being diminished, that pleasure replenishes power.

The fathers know that either power is used to make more power, or it is lost forever.

In Amerika, during the Viet Nam war, the argument took this form: the fathers maintained, as they always have, that the power of manhood is in the phallus; keep it covered, hidden; shroud it in religious taboo; use it in secret; on it build an empire, but never expose it to the powerless, those who do not have it, those who would, if they could but see its true, naked, unarmed dimensions, have contempt for it, grind it to nothing under their thumbs. The fathers wanted to maintain the *sacred character* of the phallus; as Yahweh's name must not be pronounced, so the phallus must be omnipresent in its power, but in itself concealed, never profaned.

The rebel sons wanted phallic power to be secular and "democratic" in the male sense of the word; that is, they wanted to fuck at will, as a birthright. With a princely arrogance that belied their egalitarian pretensions, they wanted to wield penises, not guns, as emblems of manhood. They did not repudiate the illegitimate power of the phallus; they repudiated the authority of the father that put limits of law and convention on their lust. They did not argue against the power of the phallus; they argued for pleasure as the purest use to which it could be put.

The fathers used the institutions of their authority—law, religion, etc.—to forbid the hedonism of the rebel sons because they understood that these sons, in their reckless promiscuity, would undermine male hegemony: not the power of the fathers over the sons, exercised with raw malice in Viet Nam, but the power of all men over all women. In vulgarizing the penis, the rebels would uncover it; in uncovering it, they would expose it to women, from whom it had been hidden by carefully cultivated and enforced ignorance, myth, and taboo for hundreds of centuries. The fathers knew that the romance of boys enchanted by their own virility could not take the place of taboo in protecting the penis from the wrath, buried but festering, of those who had been colonialized by it.

III.

You must not uncover the nakedness of your father or mother.
                                                —LEVITICUS 18:7
You must not uncover the nakedness of your father's wife; it is your father's nakedness.
                                                —LEVITICUS 18:8
You must not uncover the nakedness of your father's sister; for it is your father's flesh.
                                                —LEVITICUS 18:12

According to the editors of *The Jerusalem Bible*, "uncovering nakedness" is a "pejorative phrase for sexual intercourse." The above prohibitions in Leviticus, written to delineate lawful male behavior, all forbid incest—incest with the father. In vulgar English, they might all read: you must not fuck your father.

Abraham binds Isaac on the altar, to penetrate him with a phallic substitute, a knife. In male mythology, knife or sword is a primary metaphor for the penis; the word vagina literally means sheath. The scenario itself, devoid of any symbolism, is stark homoerotic sado-masochism.

Noah is violated when Ham sees him naked. The offense of the youngest son is so vile to Noah that he exiles that son's descendants into eternal slavery.

Father-son incest, repressed, veiled in a thousand veils, too secret even to be denied, is an invisible specter that haunts men, stalks them, shames them. This erotic repression is the silent pulse of institution-alized phallic power. The fathers, wombless perpetuators of their own image, know themselves; that is, they know that they are dangerous, purveyors of raw violence and constant death. They know that male desire is the stuff of murder, not love. They know that male eroticism, atrophied in the mummified penis, is sadistic; that the penis itself is as they have named it, a knife, a sword, a weapon. They know too that the sexual aggression of men against each other, especially sons against fathers, once let loose would destroy them.

The fathers do not fuck the sons, not because they have never wanted to, but because they know the necessity of subordinating eroti-cism to the purposes of power: they know that this desire, above all others, must be buried, left to rot under the ground of male experi-ence to feed the vermin that crawl there. To take the son would sug-gest to the son another possibility—that he might turn on the aging father, subdue him through sexual assault.

The fathers must destroy in the sons the very capacity to violate them. They must turn this impulse to paralysis, impotence, dead nerve endings, memory numbed in ice. For if father and son were naked, face to face, the male weapon that is aggression mortified into what men call passion would rend the father, conquer and disgrace him.

In war, the fathers castrate the sons by killing them. In war, the fathers overwhelm the penises of the surviving sons by having ter-rorized them, having tried to drown them in blood.

But this is not enough, for the fathers truly fear the potency of the sons. Knowing fully the torture chambers of male imagination, they see themselves, legs splayed, rectum split, torn, shredded by the saber they have enshrined.

Do it to her, they whisper; do it to her, they command.

IV.

In Amerika, after the Viet Nam war, this happened.

The rebellious sons were no longer carefree boys, wildly flushed by the discovery of their penises as instruments of pleasure. They had seen the murder spawned by the fathers coming toward them, pursuing them, encompassing them. They had been chastened and hardened, stunned and fixed in the memory of a single horror: the father had bound them on the altar; the father's hand, clutching the knife, was coming toward them.

The rebellious sons had gotten older. Their penises too had aged, experienced impotence, failure. The capacity of the nineteen-year-old boy to fuck at will was no longer theirs.

The rebellious sons, as the fathers might have prophesied, had experienced another loss, a consequence of their prideful sacrilege: they had profaned the penis by uncovering it, ripping from it the effective protection of mystery and taboo; those colonialized by it had seen it without mystification, experienced it raw, and they had organized to destroy its power over them. The sons, vain and narcissistic, did not recognize or respect the revolutionary militance of the women: they knew only that the women had left them, abandoned them, and that without the supine bodies of women to firm up the earth under them, they had nowhere to put their feet. The very earth beneath them betrayed them, turned to quicksand or dust.

The sons, dispossessed, did have a choice: to bond with the fathers to crush the women or to ally themselves with the women against the tyranny of all phallic power, including their own.

The sons, faithful to the penis, bonded with the fathers who had tried to kill them. Only in this alliance could they make certain that they would not again be bound on the altar for sacrifice. Only in this alliance could they find the social and political power that could compensate them for their waning virility. Only in this alliance could they gain access to the institutionalized brute force necessary to revenge themselves on the women who had left them.

The perfect vehicle for forging this alliance was pornography.

The fathers, no strangers to pornography, used it as secret ritual. In it they intoned chants of worship to their own virility, sometimes only a memory. These chants conjured up a promised land where male virility never waned, where the penis in and of itself embodied pure power. The fathers also used pornography to make money. In their system, secret vice was the alchemist's gold.

Using the rhetoric of the youths they no longer were, the sons claimed that pornography was pleasure, all the while turning it to profit. Proclaiming a creed of freedom, the sons made and sold images of women bound and shackled. Proclaiming the necessity and dignity of freedom, the sons made and sold images of women humiliated and mutilated. Proclaiming the urgent honor of free speech, the sons used images of rape and torture to terrorize women into silence. Proclaiming the absolute integrity of the First Amendment, the sons used it to browbeat women into silence.

The sons want their share of the father's empire. In return, they offer the father this: new avenues of making money; new means of terrorizing women into submission; new masks to protect the penis. This time, the sons will make the masks. The cloth will be liberal jargon about censorship; the thread will be such pure violence that women will avert their eyes.

The sons have already allied themselves with one sector of fathers —organized crime. Still spouting anticapitalist, liberationist platitudes, they have not hesitated to become the filth they denounce.

The other fathers will follow suit. The secret fear of incestuous rape is still with them, and it is intensified by the recognition that these sons have learned to turn pleasure to profit, profligacy to power.

In pornography, the rebellious sons have discovered the keys to the kingdom. Soon they will be sitting on the throne.

Men and Pornography: Why They Use It

Phyllis Chesler

This excerpt from Phyllis Chesler's book *About Men*, published in 1978, draws on her interviews with hundreds of men, and from the literature and mythology which have produced the male image. Chesler examines father/ son sexual competition, male menopause, mother/son incest taboos, power problems, and finally the question of male violence, and gives us important new insights into the psychological motivations for the male creation and maintenance of pornography.

Upon being asked about their sexual fantasies, many men describe pornographic scenes of disembodied, faceless, impersonal body parts: breasts, legs, vaginas, buttocks. Men of all ages fantasize, voyeuristically, scenes of whorehouses and male gang rapes; scenes of rape and mutilation; scenes of seduction and strangling; scenes of "clever" or omnipotent sexual control of extremely young and innocent children.

These are all typical sexual fantasies found in pornographic magazines and films; these are the images that men masturbate to; these are the scenes that men try to act out in whorehouses; these are the images behind closed or opened male eyes, when men have sex.

Is there any connection between such rape fantasies and the real, violent crime of rape? It may be that the actual pain and horror which women experience when raped is more easily minimized or misunderstood by men who find idealized rape fantasies sexually "pleasurable."

Some men told me about unique sexual fantasies—at least they were fantasies previously unknown to me. Several heterosexual men had sexual "sports" fantasies. One man imagined that he was "up to bat, with the bases loaded, and when I hit a home run, I came."

Another man fantasized winning a yacht race; a third swore that imagining a football game—the smell of male sweat, the excitement of the crowd, the thrill of a touchdown—made him come faster or in a more exciting way.

Many heterosexual men reported masochistic sexual fantasies involving either men or women, but apparently such fantasies are less common, less vivid, and less compulsively used than sadistic fantasies. Based on my own experience and on talking to many women, it seems that few women of any sexual persuasion enjoy sadistic sexual fantasies with men as the masochistic objects. Only men do—usually homosexual men. Most heterosexual men cannot bear imagining themselves in the devalued, female sexual role: at the mercy of other men.

Upon being questioned about their sexual fantasies, some men insisted they had none—and definitely not during intercourse. But they insisted with such vehemence, such pride, that it seemed they thought it was more "manly" or more "normal" not to need the leftover images of childhood masturbation.

The male need to renounce and disidentify with their mothers; the sons' need to resolve sexual competition and other rivalries initiated by fathers; the inevitable fact of male sexual "aging"; and the long period of male masturbation in childhood. Looked at together, these needs and facts partially explain both the function and the pornographic or sadistic content of male sexual fantasies.

What can be considered a male version of menopause probably begins quite early—at age twenty-one or twenty-two. Its chief symptom, Don Juanism, or compulsive sexual "conquesting," is an attempt to return to, or deny the loss of, male childhood and adolescent physiological sexual prowess as well as to flee from heterosexual intimacy. Pornographic scenarios often feature older men, even "old" men, as ever-potent and forever capable of competing sexually with their own lost adolescent selves or with their own sons. Fathers are extremely threatened by or ambivalent toward the ease and constancy of their sons' or younger men's erections. Their rage is eased by pornographic sexual fantasies and by the realities they reflect, such as the continued access to many women or increasingly younger women than many men can expect, even though they age.

These same sexual fantasies also prepare impatient sons to "wait" their turn, since they are assured of having their "turn" for the rest of their lives. In this sense such sexual fantasies are like legacies, inheritances, legal promises of acquisition. Paternal property, paternal ownership of women, belongs to sons just because they have penises:

If only they will wait a little while longer; if only they will do what their fathers expect of them.

Often the sons of powerless fathers do not "wait," since they are not promised a great inheritance, nor are they as clear about what is expected of them. The sons of powerless men are denied the emotion of father respect as well as the inheritance of property. Therefore, their rebellion and their rage are not just against their fathers; they are also against father culture, which will not resolve things for them by settling something desirable on them in the future. The anger or sorrow of disinherited or powerless sons is analogous to what most economically poor people feel about the rich. Poor people are not usually against rich people, or against the meaning of being rich. They are just bitter about not being rich themselves.

Pornographic sexual fantasies also ward off the submerged, reactive, and rejected desire for heterosexual incest or intimacy. Few pornographic fantasies involve "older" women as the desirable sexual objects. By obeying the incest taboo—in reality as well as fantasy— boys are fleeing from their own (demeaned) infancy, dependence, and similarity to their mothers. Boys are also fleeing from what they have repressed: their father's jealousy or competition for maternal attention, a rivalry that ended in some kind of truce between men.

For such reasons most pornographic, fantasied sex objects are younger than oneself—not older. Only young boys and unruly male adolescents are genuinely and even romantically "turned on" by images of older women. It is a European and not an American tradition that favors both the sexual initiation of young men by older women, and the taking of "older" women as lovers by men in their twenties and thirties. But when men begin to practice sexuality in reality, they usually practice on the easiest and most "attractive" women to get at: younger females and those of obvious childbearing capacity.

Pornographic sexual fantasies serve two other major purposes. First, the image of pleasurably active or satisfied men—an image that whorehouses try to resurrect—helps men overcome or deny outright any feelings of passivity, fear, disgust, or inadequacy. Male physical fatigue or sexual awkwardness or mysteriously failing sexual "interest" is denied in such "inspirational" sexual images. Rape fantasies —or sometimes real rape—reinforce men in the belief that they are superior to women and so can "have" a woman whenever they choose to.

Second, pornographic sexual fantasies are a major way of denying, absorbing, or containing male violence toward other men. Andrea Dworkin analyzes this phenomenon:

The pornography of male sadism almost always contains an idealized, or unreal, view of male fellowship. . . . Each man, knowing his own deep-rooted impulse to savagery, can presuppose this same impulse in other men and seeks to protect himself from it. The rituals of male sexual sadism over and against the bodies of women are the means by which male aggression is socialized so that a man can associate with other men without the imminent danger of male aggression against his own person. . . . In other words, women absorb male aggression (sexually) so that men are safe from each other.[1]

In fantasy, then, no man has to be more "pleasing" than another man to merit sexual attention: No man has to be very sexually, economically, or socially powerful to fantasize that many kinds of women are at his disposal.

In fact, of course, economically richer and more powerful men do command more sexual attention, more easily and for a longer period of time, than do economically poorer men. But as long as the economically poorest of men has some sexual property and some illusion of male sexual equality—as long as men share the belief that every man is at least sexually (and therefore in every other way) superior to all women—the sharp and bitter edge of male rivalry is dulled, if not sweetened, by such shared patriarchal illusions—and by the opiate of pornographically induced male sexual orgasm.

Male emotions of rage, outrage, jealousy, and shame—toward more powerful men—are laid to rest, or acted out, in women's beds or in pornographic sexual fantasies. Pacifying sexual orgasms help men avoid the even greater excesses—of fratricide or patricide—that would otherwise surely occur in the "dark Satanic mills" of male employment or on the male battlefields of war.

Pornography and the Dread of Women: The Male Sexual Dilemma

Susan Lurie

Writer Susan Lurie claims that pornography is one of the "stories men tell" to combat a complex dread of women and of female sexuality. Her analysis of the origins of that dread began with her study of psychoanalytic approaches to literature. Freud's misogynistic notions of female nature and sexuality seemed to her not only inaccurate but also slanderous. Equation of the phallus with the powerful seemed far more a wish-fulfillment fantasy than a reflection of human reality. Here Lurie investigates the fantasy of the powerful penis and its necessary complement of the powerless female, and unravels the lie about women which is articulated in pornography, in male theories, and in social institutions. In the course of her study, she offers a new reading of the Oedipus myth which suggests a more accurate interpretation of the Oedipus complex in men.

Pornography consists of stories, in words and in images, that men formulate, read, and/or watch for their sexual pleasure. In these stories the nature of woman is very specifically characterized. Always she regards male sexual wishes as her command. Frequently and even more alarmingly, she appears to regard these commands as her own desire; there is no hint of a female sexuality that does not jibe precisely with male needs, even when the pornographic drama requires her personal suffering, humiliation, harm. Pornographers literally attempt to shape female sexuality in the image of male sexual fantasies. A famous example is *Deep Throat*, in which a woman is conjured up whose sexual feeling is conveniently located in her throat. In pornography woman's body (and especially her genitals) is displayed as a dehumanized object to be exposed, manipulated, and, often enough, mutilated. Her eyes and mouth, which

159

would both indicate and *allow* her to indicate her humanity, are often sealed; in the most violent versions she endures rape, and even murder, for the sake of male orgasm. The pornographers have her report a need to be "filled with male desire," and sign female pen names to their misogynistic fantasies in an effort to convince their public that pornography is simply "explicit sexuality" and reflects what is sexually fulfilling to men and women alike.

Women recognize this fabrication as an insidious lie, perpetrated in the interests of male sexual functioning. We recognize it as a lie not only about our sexuality but also about our very humanity. For the implication that women are merely the receptacles for male will and desire in sex also implies our willing availability for male manipulation in other realms. We see the reflection of this attitude in the culture at large, in the most acceptable, most "moral" manifestations of that culture: in family and work roles, in literature, in romantic love, in religion. The male fantasy that lies about, as it attempts to repress, the true nature of female sexuality and capability permeates all our institutions.

Pornography takes this fantasy to its extreme. It is significant that this extreme occurs in relationship to, and for the purpose of, exciting male sexual pleasure. This indicates, it seems to me, that male sexual functioning is at the crux of the dilemma. We know from psychology that fantasies that give pleasure are formed to combat a disappointing, hostile reality. What is it about the sexual organization of men that inspires pornographic fantasies about sexual intercourse with women? What do men fear has been or could be done to them by women? What are the characteristics of the hostility they perceive in women which must be combated, especially as regards sexual intercourse, with such fantasies?

I believe the answers lie in an investigation of male psychosexual development, the dilemmas peculiar to male sexual organization that permeate their personal development in a social environment which not only nurtures and magnifies these dilemmas but also forges additional ones. The evidence of these male dilemmas abounds in every cultural articulation of the patriarchy, but perhaps most comprehensively in the stories men tell. Accordingly, my inquiry here will refer to a variety of male tales, citing male-authored psychosexual theories of men and women, mythology and literature, in addition to pornography, as evidence of the hopes and fears that motivate male lies about women. In the light of this inquiry, I believe it will be possible to unravel the male fantasy that is pornography and to expose the lies it involves as a desperate attempt for self and sexual preservation.

Psychologists have emphasized over and over again how traumatic the separation from the narcissistic world of infancy is. Prenatally and in infancy, all humans feel that the world (a world made up of themselves and their mothers) exists for their own best interests, is a very part of themselves. With the gradual discovery of individuality, of vulnerability to other things and other people (and with the recog nition that Mother is one of these other people, complete with her own subjective will) comes a feeling of abandonment, of grief, and a longing for the security, the utter accommodation that was the first knowledge of life.

Yet, even as the grievous nature of individuality emerges, the special capacities that will compensate for it are developing. New physical abilities reveal and provide access to a large and delightful world not apparent during infancy. But again obstacles arise that limit access to the world: other people (including Mother), other things, the limitations of physical capability. So now the supreme individual compensatory power comes to the rescue: *the imagination that can transform all the world to what one would like it to be,* that can contrive wish-fulfillment fantasies and schemes to outwit an unaccommodating reality. Because nothing is invulnerable to imaginative conception, the imagination feels like the most powerful, most essential aspect of individual identity.

Another individual capacity that develops and intensifies after the traumatic separation from Mother is sexuality—which in the young child is autoerotic. Autoeroticism, like the imagination, is experienced as a crucial and special compensation that individuality offers; it is deeply pleasurable, satisfies an urgent need, and is literally in the child's own hands. And, as with the imagination, the child will often resort to autoerotic pleasure in the face of disappointment; in fact, she or he will resort to both at the same time, infusing the autoerotic pleasure with fantasies of mastery in the world. Imagination and autoeroticism become vitally linked as the most reliable, the most powerfully pleasurable modes of self-satisfaction the child "gets" to compensate for the loss of Mother and infancy; they are perceived as the essence of individual existence, as they are used in service of each other in the attempt to re-create a secure, accommodating, controllable world.

But this vital linkup raises crucial contradictions for the little boy. For while his imagination lets him transcend and transform all that disappoints or threatens him, the very source of his powerful sexual feelings, his penis, is physically and objectively vulnerable, a vulnerability that is experienced as threatening to the existence his sexuality crowns. Despite the intense pleasure that his penis affords him, he finds its other characteristics disturbing: It changes shape, it seems somewhat precariously attached, it sometimes "acts up" against his will. His penis feels vulnerable not only to physical harm but also, like all external, perceivable things, to the kind of "magical transformation" that he knows the imagination can effect. To combat this fearful situation, the little boy fervently resorts to the positive side of the identification he senses between his imagination and his sexuality, trying to invest the latter with all the invulnerable powers of the former. He may want to regard his penis as the "magic wand" that can make the world reflect the shape of his desire. Yet this fantasy will always rest uneasily on the fear which generated it: That all the capacities which dignify his individuality (i.e., his very existence) are as vulnerable as he senses his sexuality to be.

In case his own sense that his individual capability (his post-infancy mode of personal survival) is tied to the fate of a paradoxically powerful/vulnerable penis (sexuality) isn't strong enough, the little boy has a whole system of socialization to convince him of it. Much more is made of his sex and of his penis than of the little girl's sexuality; in fact, he probably notices that precious little is indicated about her sexuality. This delightful but problematic sexual/individual existence appears to be his province alone and very much involved with the fact that he has a penis. He is weaned from his mother's nurturance much more vigorously than the little girl because, as he is told, he is a "little man"—he has a penis. Simone de Beauvoir notes that "the penis' high valuation . . . appears as a compensation, ardently accepted by the child for the hardships of . . . weaning. . . . Later on he will incarnate his transcendence and his proud sovereignty in his sex." [1]

And in the little boy's ardent acceptance of his penis as the symbol of the individuality that compensates for the loss of the nurturing oneness with his mother, that early union is perceived as a time when he *didn't have* this special awareness of his penis, didn't have this prized phallic sexuality. *Union with his mother, however blissful, means to be penisless*; and because it turns out that she doesn't even have a penis, and because she has already demonstrated the distressing fact of her subjectivity, her possession of a will that can counter and preside over his, he fantasizes that *union with*

Mother is to be what she is, not what he is.* That is, he fantasizes that this union is one in which Mother's superior will presides to so great an extent that he is formed in her likeness. And while this seems to have been a satisfactory, indeed delightful, arrangement during infancy, his present individual/sexual self, symbolized in his penis, clearly could not survive such an arrangement. The whole situation runs dangerously counter to the urgings of the constellation of individual capabilities he experiences as compensation for the separation from his mother: to manipulate the world from his "individual center" and to prize his penis (sexuality) like his life. What he is taught (that his survival boasts the importance of his penis, but requires him to relinquish his mother's nurturing care), and what he infers from this teaching (that infancy/union with his mother is a "penisless state" where she possesses him and makes him like her) complicate and foil his longing for his mother's nurturance. A perfect tautology has emerged: he can't have Mother because he has a penis, and can't have a penis if he has Mother.

Which brings us to castration fear. Freud noticed that the little boy learns early that "to be a woman is to be without a penis," and the fact that women don't have penises sparks the boy's conjecture that a "penisless state" may be possible for himself. Freud also noticed that men and boys have fantasies, usually unconscious, of being castrated as the result of wanting their mothers.[4] All these Freudian observations are very compatible with and actually support the above argument. Freud, however, continued his analysis by interpreting the little boy's desire for his mother as a sexual desire, and characterized the feared castration as forthcoming from the rival father. Freud labeled this constellation of desire and fear the Oedipus complex because in the myth, Oedipus kills his father and marries his mother.[5]

However, I believe, a stronger argument can be made that the little boy's desire for his mother is a longing not for sexual intercourse, but

---

* Dorothy Dinnerstein astutely emphasizes how disturbing the realization of Mother's independent will is, especially as it has the power to prevail over the child. Dinnerstein notes that "Woman is the will's first, overwhelming adversary. She teaches us that our intentions can be thwarted . . . by the opposed intentions of other living creatures. In our first real contests of will, we find ourselves more often than not defeated. The defeat is always intimately carnal, and the victor is always female."[2] Dinnerstein also points out that a sense of mysterious, vast power surrounds this female will: ". . . the intentionality that resides in female sentience comes . . . to carry an atmosphere of the rampant and limitless, the alien and unknowable."[3]

for the well-being of infancy. At this point he greatly prizes the individual nature of his autoeroticism; he wants to keep it for himself. In fact, his sexuality and his longing for his mother are opposed; he believes one is the price he pays for the other. That his nonetheless powerful yearning for his mother may include the fantasy of eliminating his father is not only because he wants her all to himself but also because the father is the "model" and the advocate of the little boy's "phallic" individuality. If the child opts for his mother, he fears he must eliminate both his phallus and its symbol-advocate, his father. As Freud noted, the little boy turns from this longing for his mother because he fears it involves castration; but he fears this castration will come from the mother (not from the father, as Freud theorizes), by a union with her in which her superior will presides and he becomes "what she is" (meaning he becomes "castrated"), and in which he senses he does not possess her (as he felt he did in infancy) but rather she possesses him. Accordingly, in his later relationships with women, he will insist that his will presides, that women become an extension of "what he is."

Despite the configuration of the Oedipus complex, Freud did recognize that the child could fear castration as a result of somehow being turned into the likeness of a woman. In his negative Oedipal configuration, Freud claims that this kind of castration fear is experienced when the little boy seeks his father's love and figures out he would have to be a woman to qualify for that love.[6] In this way Freud keeps the power of inspiring castration fear centered in the male; the child simply calculates what his father wants. But it seems to me that it is precisely because of this castration fear that the child develops a longing for his father (and not vice versa). The child wants his father, the symbol-advocate of his phallic individuality, to safely provide the "mother love" that inspires just such a castration fear: being transformed into the likeness of a woman. That this castration fear persists in the presence of a "safer" longing is because little boys seldom get the "mother nurturance" they are seeking from their fathers. Without the evidence that fathers can come through with this nurturance, the persistent longing for it will continue to inspire the castration feared from the mothers, no matter who is the target of that longing.

It is significant to note that some modern male theorists recognize that castration fear is generated by the mother and not the father, yet go to great lengths to conclude that this fear results from the perception of the mother as "mutilated"—a priori castrated—herself the essence of a helplessness the little boy fears he will "catch." While

Norman O. Brown asserts that castration is feared in relation to the mother, he nonetheless holds fast to the conviction that it is "horror at the mutilated creature" that generates this fear even if—as Brown does acknowledge—this horror is a fantasy of the child's own invention.[7] Brown is on the right track yet veers away, as all male theorists do, from broaching the idea that the fantasy the child invents is not that the mother is mutilated but that she has a terrible power and is capable of mutilating *him,* despite the fact that she has no penis (which for him is the necessary representative of individual intention and power).* The fantasy of the "mutilated mother/woman" is not a terrifying one, nor is it an early one; it is, as we shall see, a comforting fantasy, one that the male absorbs from his acculturation as he grows to adulthood, and one which his reliable imagination embraces with great enthusiasm. The concept of the "mutilated creature" is a wish-fulfillment fantasy intended to combat the early imagined dread of what his mother's intentional power, very much intact, might have in store for him.

Ernest Becker gets somewhat closer to the real issue with his observations that castration fear is less the result of the child's comprehension that one set of genital features is more complete than another than it is the result of existential considerations. Becker claims, quite reasonably, that Mother's "no penis" demonstrates to the boy child that his shape is arbitrary, that his penis does not necessarily equal individual existence. Yet Becker continues his analysis in a way that effectively equates the significance of women with that of dogs and cats. He says that the child discovers:

> He could just as well have been born male or female, even dog, cat, or fish—for all that it seems to matter as regards power and control. . . .[9]

Yet if this were the case, it would seem castration fear should be triggered by cats and dogs as well as by Mother. It is not only a matter of the child's discovery that his shape is not so special but also that he fears his very specialness (that his individual existence is

* While the "rational" speculation of male psychological theorists does not permit the notion that males can fantasize a castrating power in women, the irrational speculation of fifteenth-century witch-hunters went wild with this notion. Mary Daly notes that these demonologists were concerned with "whether witches may work some Prestidigitatory Illusion so that the Male Organ appears to be entirely removed and separate from the Body?"[8] The conclusion is that witches most certainly do have the power to make penises disappear.

identified with his penis) is somehow vulnerable to his mother and her love; he fears, in fact, "as regards power and control," that Mother is his threatening superior.

The terrifying problem, of course, is not that Mother is "castrated," but that she isn't. *Males would be castrated, mutilated, if they had no penises,* and the idea that women possess the whole range of individual powers that the male identifies with his penis and yet have "no penis," is what is so terrible. Eventually men embrace the project their socialization meticulously designs for them: To convince themselves and all the world that women are what men would be if men had no penises—bereft of sexuality, helpless, incapable. And this project permeates the range of male cultural articulation—from pornography to learned discourse. The very effort that goes into castrating women* (both literally and metaphorically) is very convincing evidence that males do not, in their heart of hearts (or whatever place real terror is banished to), regard women as a priori castrated, despite an elaborated socialization that would persuade them otherwise.

Yet this socialization is vigorous and effective. The tremendous importance with which the little boy's penis is invested, as regards his sexuality and his individual capacities, encourages him to believe with all his might that women and girls are afflicted with an absolute lack in these departments. And the acculturation that triggers these ideas also reinforces them. Girls are represented as cute but not very good at the things boys take pride in; about the worst thing a little boy can be called is a "girl." That the little girl is nurtured, babied, much longer than he (it may very well look to him as if she enjoys this nurturing all her life), reinforces this lack he projects on her. He traded Mother and nurturance for his penis: his sexuality and his talents. She made no such exchange. Later on when he discovers sexual intercourse, he will simply extend his autoerotic world view to the conviction that female sexual parts (parts? just a hole in his view) exist to receive and accommodate his sexuality, which he wants to believe is the only sexuality. Freud's version of the male fantasy of "penis as the only sexuality" takes the truly fantastic shape of

---

* As Diana Russell and Nicole Van de Ven observe in *Crimes Against Women,* ". . . anxious as men appear to be about it, females are much more widely subject to castration." [10] Women in several cultures are forced to suffer clitoridectomy (the removal of the entire clitoris), excision (the removal of the clitoris and the adjacent parts of the labia minora, or all the exterior genitalia except the labia majora), and infibulation (excision followed by the sewing of the genitals to obliterate the entrance to the vagina except for a tiny opening). [11]

"penis envy" in young girls. He claims that the mere sight of the boy's penis causes girls to renounce their sexual feelings (vague as Freud supposed they must be) in despair at being penisless.[12]

Armed with his anxiety about the vulnerability of his prized organ, his fear of union with a woman, and his need to believe that female sexuality exists to accommodate his own, the mature male confronts sexual intercourse. And here the plot thickens in ways that sorely threaten his capacity to function sexually without anxiety. The very ability of women to arouse him is at once delightful and capable of inspiring the childhood fear of female power over his penis. In the act of coitus he not only joins with the woman but his penis "disappears" inside her. With ejaculation the very substance of his penis is given over to her, and what he "gets back" is soft, depleted.

Sexual intercourse with women, which the male senses should be the crowning moment of his phallic/individual career, turns out to have characteristics that make it the closest most men will ever come to "castration." * The old fear of losing his power/sexuality through union with a woman is reactivated (however unconsciously). But now this fear is complicated by its inextricable attachment to the object of his "individual" drive for sexual pleasure (whereas his childhood longing for his mother was opposed to his sexuality). He cannot renounce his desire for a lover without renouncing his sexuality, so he tries to renounce the fear by denying that women have power, will, autonomous sexuality—especially during sexual intercourse.

Maturation and the experience of coitus complicate the issue in yet another crucial way. While the little boy prides himself on the fact that he has a penis and the little girl does not, the mature male discovers that behind the "no penis" lurks a vagina. Unlike his penis, this vagina is not easily vulnerable to sight and grasp, does not seem

---

* Freud recognized that the act of coitus is to men both fearful in itself and representative of the fear of women generally. Yet, predictably, he interpreted his observations as indicative of woman's inherent weakness and inferiority. Freud claimed that

> Man fears that his strength will be taken from him by woman, dreads becoming infected with her femininity and then proving himself a weakling. The effect of coitus in discharging tensions and inducing flaccidity may be a prototype of what these fears represent.[13]

Freud's interpretation participates in that general male "phallic fabrication" which insists male fear is never generated by a fantasy of female power, but always involved with the astute cognizance that women are inherently diseased with weakness, inferiority.

"precariously attached," does not change shape, and cannot be hacked off. Moreover, the vagina seems to have characteristics analogous to human functions that take in (the penis), transform (the penis and semen in conception), and "eliminate" (the penis that "slips out" after coitus, depleted). These are the kinds of activities the male associates with the individual, willful project of shaping the world in one's own best interests, a project that he has always identified with (his) sexuality. The vagina reminds him of a mouth that devours and swallows; the fear becomes that of the "vagina dentata," the vagina with teeth which devours with gusto, with intention. More alarmingly, the vagina reminds him of the characteristics of the imagination, that supreme and magical individual capacity that functions more than any other to transform the world according to individual desire.

Because his sexuality has always been linked to all his individual capacities and especially to his imagination, he imagines that female sexuality (now that he must contemplate its reality) must be similarly aligned. Yet the physical nature of the vagina does not seem to raise the contradictions for woman between the all-powerful imagination and a vulnerable, objective sexuality which the male has faced since childhood. On the contrary, he has already noticed the vagina is "like" the imagination; not only does it take in and transform, it is internal; and, most awesomely, the womb, to which it leads, "creates" real, live babies (like, in fact, he once was).

Female sexuality seems naturally equipped to be what he needs to insist (because he fears it is *not* the case) his sexuality is: invulnerable and aligned with (identified with and so an extension of) that creative imaginative power which enables one to regain sovereignty over the world. When these observations are combined with his castration fears, the whole gestalt generates the fearful fantasy (however conscious or unconscious) that women are better equipped to obtain that sovereignty which includes control over him—a control he associates with castration and, symbolically, his utter ruination. This terrifying female power can now be fantasized as centered in her sexuality. Accordingly, the occasion which seems ripest for the kill is one which his own "will to power" drives him toward: sexual intercourse. So, here especially, he must convince himself that it is his will, his power, his sexuality that prevails over the female's.

And men come to identify what they fear from this mysterious female power with what all humans fear from the mysterious forces of destiny that are hostile to, and eventually triumph over, all life: the forces that lie behind aging, misfortune, death. In classical mythology the Fates are women who hold the "phallic thread" of a man's life in their hands, a thread they weave into a fabric of their own choosing; the thread either runs out in their hands, or they snip it off when the fabric of life is completed (female power = castration = death).[14] Unlike the later patriarchal deity (who was invented to take care of the problem), these ladies do not shape males in their image. But the human males that are their prophets, who by "knowing what she knows" are aligned with the Fateful female, come close to this image in a way that manifests what men fear from union with the female. The classical wise men and prophets are metaphorically castrated, divested of their capacities, through old age and/or physical handicaps (most notably blindness).

In fact, Tiresias, the most venerable of the classical prophets, comes by his gift in a manner that articulates the male's fearful conception of the power inherent in a female sexuality autonomous from his own. Because he has lived as both a man and a woman, Tiresias is asked to decide an argument between Zeus and Hera as to who has more sexual pleasure in intercourse: men or women. He declares that female sexuality is more pleasurable (read intense, powerful) than male sexuality,[15] and, with this proclamation, becomes the last male in western history to venture such a "learned" opinion. And for good reasons; what happens to Tiresias symbolizes what men fear is bound up with the acknowledgment of a female sexuality, intense and powerful in its own right. As soon as he claims a superior sexual experience for women, Tiresias comes under the power of women; he is blinded (metaphorically castrated) by Hera, and the best Zeus can do for him is to press him into the service of the female Fates. Tiresias' story demonstrates both the male fear that female sexuality is somehow more powerful than his own, and that the very acknowledgment of female sexuality entails the renunciation of his own "phallic capabilities." In fact, Tiresias reverses the exchange the little boy senses that he makes in obtaining his sexuality/capability in place of his mother's nurturance; Tiresias gets security (long life) and alignment with female power for a metaphorical castration.

An even more famous mythological character who ends up wise to Fate, but blind, old, and dependent on a female, is Oedipus— whose legend Freud cited to substantiate the theory that males want to eliminate their fathers in a sexual rivalry for their mothers (a rivalry that generates a fear of retaliatory castration by the fathers). But while Oedipus does indeed kill his father and marry his mother, the other events and characters in the myth (according to Sophocles' dramatic version, *Oedipus Rex* [16]) seem to indicate that Oedipus' central conflict is not a sexual rivalry with his father but rather a fight for survival against a fate that returns him to a union with his mother and the incapacitation (castration) and ultimate dependence on a woman that this union implies.

It is important to note that Oedipus emphatically does *not* want to kill his father and marry his mother as the oracle decrees he will. He gathers all his capacities to combat the loathsome decree, and flees what he mistakenly thinks are his real parents in an attempt to avoid it. In the course of his flight, he easily knocks off several men who get in his way, one of whom is his real father. His father does not pose a very great challenge, nor does the patricide directly yield him his mother, nor, more importantly, does it eliminate the metaphorical castration that Oedipus eventually suffers. What the patricide does accomplish is the direct clearing of the way to the Sphinx, the mysterious female monster who is a much more dangerous character than his father. The female monster not only possesses a secret (which represents that unfathomable female power men fear can annihilate their sexuality/existence) but also has the capacity and the propensity to kill men because they don't know that secret. And although Oedipus answers the riddle, his triumph is a temporary, illusory one; for while knowledge (which implies acknowledgment) of the "monstrous female mystery" yields him the love of a woman and the kingdom that goes with that love, what he finally reaps is incapacitation and dependence on a woman (Antigone). What he gets is the dreaded union with his mother and all that it implies.

Just what is this "monstrous female mystery" that spells disaster for men whether or not they know the gory particulars? The Sphinx asks, "What has four legs, and two legs, and three legs?" The answer is "Man" and refers to the "three ages of human life"—infancy (when one crawls on all fours), maturity (when one stands upright), and old age (when one leans on a cane).[17] To know the answer to the riddle is to acknowledge the mortal progress of life, a dreadful insult to the phallic fantasy of individual omnipotence. What the Sphinx knows—that life is changeable, fragile, mortal—is the human dilemma, yet men locate the source of that dilemma, for all the reasons discussed above, in a hostile female power/knowledge. Accordingly, it is not surprising that the Sphinx's images of life's mortal progress are in terms of the transformation of man's extremities; a change in legs is a polite way of referring to a change in "extremity number one"—the Sphinx's images are a metaphor for castration, a castration that she has in mind.

Like Tiresias, Oedipus suffers for his knowledge and acknowledgment of the female by becoming "infected" with the portent of that knowledge (his inevitable incapacitation and mortality). Yet the vanquishing of the Sphinx before his marriage may very well symbolize the male fantasy that if the hostile female principle is somehow subdued by his wits or by force (in some versions of the myth, Oedipus kills the Sphinx), adult sexual/loving unions with women will not carry the anticipated dangers that trace back to his early fear of the castration that reunion with his mother implies. Yet despite his best efforts, Oedipus' wife turns out to be his mother. Although he has used all his phallic capacities to avoid doing so, Oedipus has returned to the union with his mother, has realized the female-authored fate that he has attempted to foil since childhood. He seems to know the price he has to pay, and dramatically enacts the exchange the little boy fears he has to make if he gets back his mother and the "kingdom" she provided during infancy: He puts out his eyes, metaphorically castrating himself, and gives himself up to the care of the female, Antigone, for the rest of the his life.

Because men are afraid that their lovers, being women, may harbor the castrating power they fear from their mothers, and because the experience of sexual intercourse complicates matters with its physical analogs to "castration" and the revelation of a female sexuality less vulnerable than the male's, the Sphinx (the hostile female principle) enters the picture most dangerously in the context of male adult loving/sexual unions with women. For sexual intercourse is the paradoxical occasion that both promises to celebrate male phallic individuality and threatens to annihilate it.

Pornographic fantasies are attempts to resolve this paradox, to get rid of the threatening Sphinx, by embracing the promise and vigorously, often violently, denying the threat. Because the threat is always forthcoming from a mysterious female sexuality and capability, pornography asserts that women have neither, that women are (often literally) castrated, helpless, incapable. Pornography articulates the fantasy that in coitus, a male's will and desire always and easily preside, that his sexual wishes, complicated as they are by his fearful fantasies, always inspire an obedient and/or enthusiastic accommodation from women.

Pornographic images point specifically to the fears they are meant to combat. Exposure and manipulation of female sexual parts is meant to indicate that female sexuality is vulnerable and utterly available, unconnected to subjective will (though he fearfully fantasizes that it is invulnerable and aligned with a will that threatens his sexuality). Female sexual mutilation, often self-inflicted, indicates that she is, should be, can be castrated—even that she desires that castration (though he fears she desires and can accomplish *his* castration). Women are portrayed as naturally helpless or easily rendered so, because men fear a female power that can render them helpless. No evidence of the true requirements of female sexuality are allowed to surface because that sexuality threatens the supremacy of the penis, and is evidence that women are not castrated although they have no penises. Women are given "deep throats" instead of vaginas so that men can not only deny female nature but also shut women up, keep them from refuting that interpretation. The torture, rape, mutilation, and killing of women in pornography reverses the death threat associated with the castration men fear from women. That men sign female names to misogynistic sexual dramas helps them demonstrate that there is only one source of sexual will in the world—that women want only what men desire in sex (though they suspect this is not the case), and reflect the fear that they are lying about her sexual and human nature (which they are).

But just as Oedipus' apparent victory over the Sphinx leads him to, rather than protects him from, the dreadful fate he has feared since childhood, so pornographic fantasies perpetuate and intensify, rather than eliminate, the male dread of women. For trapped in the web of their own fearful fabrications, a web that acculturation wraps around each new generation of males, there is no way out of that fear. The male dilemma is truly the dilemma of Oedipus: He fears that he will either be annihilated by a mysterious female power or that he will make a good show of getting rid of this power yet still end up being destroyed by it. The only way out is indeed to get rid of the Sphinx—but this can only be accomplished by realizing that the Sphinx is not an incarnation of the "female principle" but rather the incarnation of male fantasized fears. Yet it is not these fears that make their way to the surface articulations of the culture but the wish-fulfillment lies intended to allay those fears. Accordingly, it is the lies, specifically about female sexuality and capability, that must be eradicated; without the lies that justify and reinforce the fears, the fears themselves can be unmasked and dissolved. For a terrible female power that is the enemy of individual survival, that feeds on the penises of little boys and even men, can only adhere in a culture in which women's own individual capabilities (and the vulnerability they imply) are ardently repressed. Likewise, a terrible female sexuality, full of a dark and hostile intent, can only be fantasized in a social environment that ardently mystifies and denies female sexuality.

The "oracle" of mortality is a universal human dilemma, bound up with the early human discovery of the paradox of powerful/vulnerable individuality. That boys and men associate mortal fear with "castration" may be somewhat inevitable, but the fantasy that women are the source of the dilemma is largely a matter of socialization. Fantasized dread can give way before a reality that proves that dread erroneous. And women are the only ones capable of providing this particular segment of reality—a women's version, the real version, of female sexuality and capability. For, as we have seen, even the most learned of male theorists are trapped in male fabrications about women.

Women must continue to counter these fabrications by insisting that the images and institutions of the culture reflect the reality of women. Yet the male fantasy, and the social institutions that perpetuate it, are powerful and long-rooted; Oedipus is about 2,500 years old. A good deal of resistance has been, and will be, encountered: Oedipus fights his "enlightenment" with every outrageous lie and accusation he can think of. He knows that the "revelation of the truth" means the end of his reign. And, clearly, the enormous male resistance to women's version of women (which includes women's understanding of how men need to regard women and why) stems from male fears that a "women's version" will spell the end of male cultural dominance—not to mention male dominance of women. However, such a cultural transformation is the male's only hope of salvation from his frantic and fatal lifetime war with the Sphinx, the only means of purging the dreadful fears that motivate pornography and all male lies about women.

The Propaganda of Misogyny

Beverly LaBelle

After studying, talking, meeting, and marching, women concluded that pornography was indeed used by men to keep women in sexually stereotyped boxes, to make it impossible for us to feel safe alone, day or night, on the street or in our homes. We were then able to look at pornographic material not as entertainment in any sense of the word but rather as a kind of political media published by men and for men to perpetuate male authority and female submission. This was a revelation, for it meant that pornography was a kind of propaganda and as such a central and undeniable feminist political issue. Here Beverly LaBelle demonstrates that pornography is a form of indoctrination.

In order to understand how pornography functions as a type of propaganda for male-supremacist attitudes, it is necessary to define propaganda and elaborate on its main techniques. Propaganda, most simply defined, is *psychological manipulation of the public by powerful, often invisible elites for the purpose of the furthering of a particular ideology*. As explained in the book *Public Opinion and Propaganda*, it is ". . . a systematic attempt by an interested individual or group of individuals to control the attitudes of groups of individuals through the use of suggestion and consequently to control their actions." [1]

Propaganda always seeks to present its viewpoint on a subject as the only viable one, and to discredit its opponents by portraying them as evil, stupid, or inferior. The glorification of one ethnic, religious, or ideological group at the expense of an opposing group is one of the prime functions of cultural or governmental propaganda. Propaganda encourages fear of and anger toward groups that are different from the mainstream or dominant group of the society. It discourages the ideals of equality and mutual respect.

Genuine arguments are not used in propaganda because the answers are predetermined. A closed mind, not a questioning one, is the aim of all propaganda no matter how sincerely the propagandist may state that he is merely trying to present an unbiased opinion on a topic.

Simplified, easily assimilated opinions masked as truths and aimed at the least intellectual segment of the population form the bulk of the propaganda message. Fast results and mass effects are the desired aims. The easiest way to accomplish these ends is to convince people that they are being threatened in some way by a scapegoat group. The propagandist must create or augment this mood of fearful dissatisfaction in order for his ideas to be readily absorbed.

Rarely are all the ideas in any propaganda complete fabrications. Usually a mixture of lies and verifiable facts is the favored approach. Sometimes the impression of listening to the arguments of the opponents and even of granting their ideas some credence is given in order to boost the image of the propagandist. An example of this technique is the quasi-acceptance of certain aspects of the Women's Movement, such as abortion-on-demand and "sexual self-determination," by *Playboy* and other pornographic magazines.

In his book *Techniques of Persuasion,* J.A.C. Brown lists eight techniques which are universally employed in propaganda campaigns.[2] They are:

1. Use of stereotypes
2. Name substitution
3. Selection
4. Lying
5. Repetition
6. Assertion
7. Pinpointing the enemy
8. Appeal to authority

We will demonstrate that pornography makes extensive use of all of them.

The first technique is the use of *stereotypes* to create a fixed, unfavorable idea of the chosen scapegoat group. The images of human beings in pornography are blatant examples of stereotyping. Men and women are portrayed as diametrical opposites, as different species, very often as enemies. Women are invariably portrayed as carnal, submissive, promiscuous, whore-victims, perennially and repeatedly subdued and conquered by the eternally worshipped phallus. Their only needed credentials are bare breasts and exposed genitalia. The color of their skin or hair is varied merely to provide an illusion of variety. The personality of the pornographic model is never well developed in any of the X-rated books or films because her mind is completely unimportant. In short, pornography propagates a view of women as nothing but "tits and ass"—silly creatures who exist only to be fucked, sexually used, and forgotten.

The second technique, *name substitution*, helps create a biased reaction to the "victimized" group by referring to them with pejorative terms such as "nigger," "kike," "commie," etc. These terms, invented especially for the group in question, allow people to remove them from the context of "human being" and place them in a subhuman category. Pornography rarely uses anything but derogatory words to describe women and women's sexuality. "Cunt," "scumbag," "twat," "hot tube," "tramp," etc., are just a tiny sampling of the unpleasant terms routinely used in pornography to define women.

Technique number three is *selection*, a process whereby only certain facts are presented to the public. These facts are always those which are favorable to the propagandist and unfavorable to his opponent. Two major forms of *selection* are noticeable in pornography: First, pornographers present only one vision of women's sexuality to their readers and viewers. This vision, contrary to the findings of studies on women's sexuality by Shere Hite [3] and other researchers, portrays women as sexually subservient to men, turned on by every sexual move they make. A good example is the common theme of the rape victim who finds that she "loves it" once she "relaxes" and allows herself to "enjoy the experience." Real rapes, of course, are physically and emotionally destructive, as most research and many interviews reveal. The second major form of the *selection* technique used by pornographers is in their editorial content. Pornographers (and apologists for pornography) exclusively report the supposedly "good" effects of the pornography and refuse to admit or to print the possible adverse consequences that unrestrained access to such material may engender.

Downright lying is the fourth technique. It requires little explanation to realize that pornography is nothing but a downright lie about women. An example:

"Columbine Cuts Up," a feature in a recent issue of *Chic* magazine, published by Larry Flynt. The photo essay portrays a young blond woman thrusting a large kitchen knife into her vagina. Blood is spurting from the wounds, but the look on her face is one of sexual ecstasy, almost glee. Obviously any real woman who had hurt herself like this would be in severe pain—she would not be smiling.

Repetition is a necessary technique because it helps the public become accustomed to whatever ideas the propagandist is attempting to inculcate. The more a concept is reiterated, the more persuasive and influential it becomes. As Adolf Hitler declared in *Mein Kampf*, only after the simplest ideas are repeated thousands of times will the masses finally remember them. People begin to accept such ideas as the truth because they are pervasive. Slogans and maxims are often used advantageously in this particular technique, e.g., "Heil Hitler," American television advertising jingles, the phrase "all women secretly want to be raped," etc. Pornography is one of the most boringly repetitious types of media. A few seduction plots are endlessly repeated, with minor variations added for spice and stimulation: The old myth that women are inferior and that the male should do whatever he pleases with these easily available "pieces of meat" forms the main theme.

An element of urgency is also emphasized in pornography at this point in order to increase the strength of the idea and thus promote action. An action is needed for the reduction of anxiety or desire induced by the propaganda campaign. Such an action could take the guise of a purchase, a vote, a rape (in pornographic propaganda), or even tacit agreement with the goals of a "Final Solution," as in the case of the Nazi propaganda machine.

Assertion is similar to the selection technique, but it differs in that it entails not merely pointing out the pertinent idea but also boldly asserting and promoting the idea. Pornography is by its very nature an aggressively assertive philosophy. Its producers proclaim its ideas loudly and forcefully in two main ways. The first is by the inescapable, lurid presence of pornography everywhere in our society (large, gaudy posters on X-rated theaters, and magazines flaunting naked women in drugstores, in corner stores, and even in public buildings where the business of government is carried on). The second is the pornographers' campaign to silence their opponents by invoking the First Amendment and thereby securing for themselves the right to peddle their anti-woman ideas everywhere in the name of free speech.

The seventh technique, *pinpointing the enemy*, is self-explanatory. An enemy or scapegoat is of prime importance in any propaganda campaign because it serves to direct aggression away from the propagandist and to strengthen feelings of solidarity within the group that the propagandist is seeking to influence. Hatred is one of the most powerful unifying emotions, since it permits feelings which are usually suppressed to be brought to the surface and expressed stridently. Women are the enemy in pornography—they are the group to be subdued and vanquished. A good example of this targeting of women is *Hustler* magazine's continued attack on major feminist thinkers in the country. Gloria Steinem, Susan Brownmiller, Shere Hite, and other women have repeatedly been subject to ridicule, name-calling, and slander.

The last technique, *appeal to authority*, is a vital step in proving that the ideas of the propaganda are respectable and intelligent. This approach often incorporates references to the past, testimonials from famous people, and quotations from so-called "experts." Pornography uses all these methods to justify its content. First, there is the underlying assumption that sex as portrayed in pornography is the natural, time-proven way of obtaining satisfaction. "The best propaganda is that which works invisibly, penetrates the whole of life without the public having any knowledge at all of the propagandist initiative," said Joseph Goebbels. Second, famous people are often featured in the more serious articles in soft-core magazines, implicitly expressing their support for the "liberating joys" of pornography. The *Playboy* interview has played a major role in this appeal to authority. Simply featuring United States presidents,* stars, great authors, artists, and major sports figures builds credibility. Third, psychological and sociological studies describing the beneficial effects of pornography are often quoted in pornographic magazines as "proof" that such publications are not harmful. Pornography successfully wraps a cloak of respectability around itself via these techniques.

Concealed under its facade of sexually liberating entertainment, pornography propagates the philosophy of male supremacy. It establishes ideologically that women exist solely for the sexual gratification of men. Because such dehumanized ideas about women are so widely accepted, pornography is often not recognized as a system of propaganda designed to exploit and misrepresent the sexual differences between men and women. Beneath the surface of badly written prose and lurid pictures lie millennia of institutionalized female bondage.

Pornography is the propaganda of misogyny. In order to dissipate its power, we must expose and reevaluate not only pornography but the culture it reinforces. The battle against pornography is a reeducative process whose end result must be an essential change in our cultural mores. As women we must destroy the pornographic image in order to be seen and treated as full human beings.

* Ed. Note: United States President Jimmy Carter gave an interview in *Playboy* magazine a few years ago.

A Little Knowledge

Ann Jones

"I became interested in pornography (which has always repelled me) while I was interviewing battered women who had killed their batterers," says Ann Jones. "Pornography kept coming up over and over again. One woman had shot her husband through his pornographic tattoo. Alerted, I began asking questions specifically about pornography."

Jones discovered that when asked directly, most women denied any connection between pornography and the beatings they suffered at the hands of husbands, lovers, boyfriends. But later in the conversation, it would emerge that the men read *Playboy* or *Hustler*. When she pointed out that this was the material about which she was asking questions, the women replied, "But that's not pornography; that's just a magazine." By the time she finished the research on her book (*Women Who Kill: An American Social History*) she was convinced that the connection between pornography and violence against women was "real and vital." This paper is a result of that conviction.

Every few seconds in America a woman or girl is slapped, slugged, punched, chopped, slashed, choked, kicked, raped, sodomized, mutilated, or murdered. She loses an eye, a kidney, a baby, a life. That's a fact. And if the statistics are anywhere near right, at least one of every four women reading this paragraph will feel that fact through firsthand experience.

It takes very little mental equipment to figure out that a genre depicting the physical exploitation, humiliation, wounding, and killing of women encourages (in fact, teaches) the behavior that produces these female casualties.

We hear, of course, that it is natural for men to be aggressive: It comes with the genes or the territory. But that "natural" aggression seems limited to violence and acquisitiveness—by an odd coincidence the two hearty masculine values that contribute most to our American way of life. We hear too that men may become violent because of unemployment, stress, inflation, women's liberation—anything but

179

men themselves and their own ideals. The cure for male violence acted out in wife-abuse, rape, incest is thought to lie in full employment or psychiatric counseling or home-cooked meals. But even the "experts" can't be sure. They agree only that there should be more money available for research, that apparently innocuous activity which has replaced prayer in our time as an excuse for inactivity.

Do not get me wrong. I do not have anything against scholarship. I just like to know who is doing it and why because studies of the effects of pornography, like other social science studies, so often confirm the presuppositions of the researcher. And so-called "raw data" can be cooked to different tastes. For example, take the work of writer Gladys Denny Shultz, who is not a social scientist. She naïvely went into a couple of prisons, sat down with the sex offenders, and asked them what they thought about pornography. Half the men Shultz interviewed told her that pornography played a definite part in their crimes either by arousing them or by actually teaching them what to do, or both. Many men told her that they believed they would not have committed their crimes had they had any other source of information about sex except pornography. She announced these findings in answer to *The Report of the Commission on Obscenity and Pornography* ("What Sex Offenders Say About Pornography," *Reader's Digest*, July 1971, pp. 53–57), and concluded that it would be wise to "hold off breaking down any more barriers [with regard to pornography] until we can get a clearer idea." However, the experts, in this case the treatment directors of the two prisons, told Shultz that her conclusion was wrong. The proper inference to be drawn from her data, they said, is that offenders tend to blame others for their crimes.

It is likely that there is some truth in both of these views, but folks who buy one or the other wind up playing in different ballparks. Agree with the experts that the offenders have a psychological problem, and you end up paying the experts to treat them. Agree with Shultz and half the offenders, and you go after pornography itself.

To be fair-minded and reasonable, we discuss the findings of the so-called experts, pointing out the shortcomings of this study, the irrelevance of that. Men continue to examine how pornography affects men and to publish their research on the topic, while women are stuck with only bruises, shame, anger, and a certain knowledge of the truth.

Very well. Let us do our own studies of ourselves. Let us ask, as Diana Russell did, "Did he ever attempt to act out something he had seen in pornography?" And let us hear the answers: "He whipped me, he tied me up and sodomized me, he beat me up."

A group of women from Rochester, New York, called on a theater owner to protest his showing of *The Story of O*. But he asked them for their evidence that the film was demeaning to women, and they didn't have any. They spoke only from their own conviction, and they were not social scientists. With women, outrage is not enough. We have to tally our wounds in keeping with the best social science practice.

Very well, then. Let us count. Ask battered women what their husbands "read." And ask those much maligned authorities: the cops. Ask the police chiefs (something like 60 percent of them) who agree that pornography leads to crimes of violence against women. Ask the cops who saw all the pornographic pictures papering the walls of the shack where Melvin Rees tortured Mildred Jackson and her five-year-old daughter, Susan. Ask the cops who cataloged the pornographic magazines retrieved from the bedside of David "Son of Sam" Berkowitz. Ask battered Jennifer Patri, who finally shot her husband, a man who played pornographic tapes for his daughters and who made at least one of those daughters, as well as his wife, "monkeys" in his sexual circus. Ask battered Bernadette Powell, who finally was forced to shoot her ex-husband in self-defense—right through his pornographic tattoo.

What gives these people—experienced police and victims—less authority than social scientists? In its day so-called hard science has been used to verify everything from the geocentric universe to Aryan supremacy. And next to the physical sciences, the social sciences are shaky indeed; as bodies of knowledge, they are much less ancient and credible than pornography itself. At best, they are designed to measure very limited behaviors; they cannot assess complex social trends. Responsible social scientists should be among the first to admit the limits of possible experimentation and the absurdity that the felt experience of over half the population should await verification at their hands.

Jews would not stand for it; nor Blacks. They have had their holocaust, their lynch mobs. They know that the last violation is implicit in the first, that the jokes and insults and grotesque public images may be only the warm-up for annihilation. And they act to protect themselves from defamation.

Is it really too much for reasonable women and men to recognize hate when they see it? If I were to see the picture of a Jew tied, spread-eagled, stripped, whipped, sucking cock, I think I would conclude rather quickly that the person who made the picture did not hold Jews in high esteem. But put a woman in that picture, and men chuckle while women turn away. Many women, deliberately excluded from a man's world, know nothing of pornography beyond the anti-septic, apparently "harmless," *Playboy* centerfold. Others of us get lost in the smoke of "civil liberties" or "sexual liberation" and never see that the fire is burning under our identity, our safety, our lives.

While other maligned groups develop political consciousness and power at the ballot box and cashbox, we are still persuaded, flattered, cajoled, and shamed into collaboration. So the cycle continues: De-meaned by pornography, we lose the self-respect it takes to say, "Enough!" We consent to our own destruction.

In 1960 one white woman and eleven Black women in every 100,000 American women became murder victims. Today it is three white women and sixteen Black. There are some statistics for you.

While studies progress and "good men" hem and haw, the violence against women goes on—and not in the streets only. Denied relief from anti-woman propaganda, refused police and court protection, a surprising number of would-be victims recently have struck back. Rape victims have turned the attacker's weapon upon himself, and battered women have defended themselves with deadly force. The law has been brought to admit that in some circumstances rape victims may act in justifiable self-defense, but the case of battered wives is by no means clear. Certainly it is possible to argue that a state which denies a women legal protection from physical harm has breached the social contract and forfeited the right to punish her for protecting her-self. So far as I know, nobody has advanced this argument; to do so in a patriarchal state is a lot like spitting into the wind.

Occasionally a battered woman who kills and pleads self-defense is acquitted, and her story is publicized with sympathy in *Family Circle*, with alarm in *Newsweek* and *Time*. But look at the record: Roberta Shaffer, convicted and sentenced to five years; Judy Sturm, ten years; Gloria Timmons, indeterminate to twenty years; Elsie Monick, four to fifteen years; Patricia Evans, two to six years; Cynthia Denny, five to ten years and three to five years; Sharon Crigler, ten years; Claudia Thacker, five to twenty years; Carol Ann Wilds, fifteen to twenty-five years; Hazel Kontos, life; Jenna Kelsie, fifteen to twenty-five years; Jennifer Patri, ten years; Lillian Quarles, ten years; Patricia Hale, fifteen to twenty-five years; Kathy Thomas, fifteen years; Barbara Jean Gilbert, eight years; Patricia Hamilton, six years; Ruth Childers, five years; Shirley Martin, three to seven years; Bernadette Powell, fifteen years to life; Carolyn McKendrick, five to ten years; Martha Hutchinson, fifteen years. Why, despite all the evidence of repeated assault and self-defense, were these women convicted?

Mostly it is a question of public attitudes—of who believes what about women. And generally what the general public believes about abused women is that they ask to be battered, get their kicks from it, and in a profound way deserve it. Battery, that fecund source of sexual thrills and good times for good ol' boys, is an all-American pastime. It is almost never seen by the male-oriented legal system as sufficient grounds for homicide in self-defense.

Bernadette Powell, on trial for murder in Ithaca, New York, patiently and with an effort to control herself, catalogs years of abuse: She was slapped, punched, kicked, burned with cigarettes, tied up to a post in the basement. The district attorney (aptly named Joe Joch and himself recently divorced by his wife on grounds that he beat her and their child) cross-examined Powell: "Isn't it a fact that you liked it?" he asked, although it was not a question. "Do you know what a masochist is?" "When he tied you up, did you have sex?" "Was his penis out?" Some of the male jurors (nine out of twelve were men) openly snickered at the questions. In the end they convicted her of murder, and the judge sentenced her to fifteen years to life.

The attitudes of the district attorney probably were shared by most jurors. And why? "Pornography," says Kathleen Ridolfi of the Woen's Self-Defense Law Project, "is one of the most important ways of transmitting those attitudes. It is anti-woman propaganda. It shapes public opinion. And that means that when a woman goes on trial she faces the bias of the jurors, the judge, and even her own attorney, who probably reads *Playboy* at least."

I cannot offer any studies to show a correlation between jurors' decisions and subscriptions to *Penthouse*. I only assume, in a most unscientific manner, that there is a connection. It is this: Pornography demeans women. It spreads an attitude which large numbers of men share. Among these men are rapists, wife-abusers, police, prosecuting attorneys, defense lawyers, judges, and jurors. Police do not arrest assailants; they tend to blame women for rape and to regard female victims of "family quarrels" as hysterical people to be calmed by mediation. District attorneys, for a variety of equivocations, decline to prosecute these offenses. Judges may regard them as trivial, and jurors as everyday domestic matters, although often reflecting a certain foolhardy vindictiveness on the part of the woman. It adds up to conviction.

So pornography teaches the violent abuse of women and fosters it. At the same time it provides the ideological basis for juries to condemn women who fight back. It promotes violence in the streets and bedrooms, and it reaffirms violence in the courtroom.

Meanwhile men go on getting high on their canned fantasies. And the record books fill up with one bizarre case after another. They do not add up to anything as significant as social science research, you understand, for they are merely random examples—anecdotes really —the sort of thing that happens all the time. Take, for example, the classic case of Donald Fearn, who abducted seventeen-year-old Alice Porter in Pueblo, Colorado. Fearn drove Alice Porter to an abandoned church, tied her up on the altar, tortured her all night with instruments, including hot wires and an awl, mutilated her while she still lived in ways so horrible that they have never been publicly reported, beat her to death with a hammer, and threw her broken body down a well. After his arrest he explained: "Ever since I was a young boy I have wanted to torture a beautiful young girl." Now where do you suppose he got an idea like that?

SECTION IV.

Research on the Effects of Pornography

But standing alone we learned our power, we repudiated man's counsels forevermore; and solemnly vowed that there should never be another season of silence until we had the same rights everywhere on this green earth, as man.
*——*ELIZABETH CADY STANTON
History of Women's Suffrage
Volume I, 1881

Pornography and Repression: A Reconsideration of "Who" and "What"

Irene Diamond

In 1973, when the United States Supreme Court handed down the famous Miller decision, which permitted states and cities to establish their own "community standards" regarding the definition of obscenity, Irene Diamond suddenly found herself somewhat at odds with her liberal friends who were aghast at the decision. Before that time she had not thought much about pornography; liberal reaction to the court decision made her realize that feminists had our own point of view to develop on the issue. Except for a conversation with a female friend who thought *Playboy* was great, her feelings and thoughts on the subject remained tucked away for several years until a *Playboy* photographer came to Purdue University in 1977 in search of undergraduates for an upcoming spread on "Girls of the Big Ten." Women at Purdue organized a protest demonstration.* Diamond, an instructor in political science, participated in the demonstration and was shocked at the angry response the demonstrators received from students on campus. She realized then that work on pornography was necessary.

In this paper, first delivered in 1978 at the annual meeting of the Western Social Sciences Association, Diamond takes a critical look at some of the studies and experiments which shaped *The Report of the Commission on Obscenity and Pornography*, and examines the assumptions on which that data is built.

"Porn Is Here to Stay," asserts the headline of an article by sociologist Amitai Etzioni in *The New York Times*.[1] Yet if pornography does have such staying power, it is not because of the "naturalness" of sexuality, as Etzioni suggests, but because of the resiliency of certain historic and economic institutions which structure and shape sex-

* Ed. Note: In fact, Purdue women were the only "Big Ten" women who protested *Playboy*'s presence on campus that year.

ual expression. My purpose here is to reexamine the assumptions and data on which prevailing liberal views of pornography rest, and to suggest that pornography is primarily a medium for expressing norms about male power and domination, thereby functioning as a social control mechanism for keeping women in a subordinate status.

Historically efforts to control pornography have been made by people interested in suppressing matters relating to sex—from birth control to sex education to scientific studies. Opposing arguments typically have come from those promoting openness in sexual matters.

Since John Wilkes's *An Essay on Women* in the eighteenth century, pornography has sometimes been used to criticize the prevailing social order. Consequently, the contemporary wisdom within the social science community and among "progressive" intellectuals says that all attempts to control pornography are in fact efforts by persons of unenlightened and unhealthy sexual views to repress sexuality and to maintain the established order. Predictably, Etzioni dismisses a 1976 poll indicating that most Americans approve of cracking down on pornography by declaring that most of these people

> have difficulty accepting their own sexuality and feel that unless the authorities keep the lid on, their urges may erupt. A democratic society requires holding at bay these sexual anxieties and their repressive political expressions.[2]

About the "true motivations" of such people neither Etzioni nor I have any relevant evidence, but his is the conventional liberal approach to the question of pornography and repression. According to this view, the "what" or content of pornography is sex, and consequently any curbs on it strike at the sexual freedom of consumers and the creative freedom of artists. The "who" of concern are the male consumers and artists and not the women degraded or abused in the films, photographs, or shows; nor the women who might become the "accidental" real-life victims of nonfantasy acts; nor the women whose oppression is reinforced by the dissemination of distorted views of women's nature.

Women are invisible in this conventional liberal approach because (1) patriarchal society tends to define reality in terms of men's activities; (2) liberal society discusses pornography in terms of abstract rights and principles disconnected from the grim reality in actual communities; and (3) traditional moralists and liberationists alike believe that human sexuality has a fixed, "naturally" given shape. (For the former that unchanging force is an unmitigated evil, whereas for the latter it is an unmitigated good.) Each of these factors has shaped the basic assumption that pornography is nothing more than a medium for sexual expression. H. Montgomery Hyde in his history of pornography writes:

> It is generally agreed that the essential characteristic of pornography is its sexuality. In order to come within the category of pornography, material must have the power to excite sexual passions.[3]

Since free, unfettered sexual expression is viewed as an unquestionable good leading to complete human liberation, pornography itself has often become associated with all that is progressive and good. For instance, Al Goldstein, editor of *Screw*, one of the many 1960's tabloids designed to expose the hypocrisies of society by shocking its sensibilities, described pornography as "one of the most sane manifestations of the human condition." [4] And Paul Goodman, though not a "porn-pusher" à la Goldstein, called on the Supreme Court in 1961 to "set aside the definition of pornography as obscenity—just as it set aside the doctrine of separate but equal facilities—and to clarify and further the best tendency of the sexual revolution." [5] Amid all the controversy the subject has generated, both among scholars and the public, the single generally held assumption is that the content of the "genre" is sexuality. What has been at issue is whether the open expression of sexual feelings promotes or destroys the health of society.

One explanation of pornography's place in history argues that it is a uniquely modern phenomenon, emerging for the first time during the seventeenth century in response to the strains of modernization.[6] Steven Marcus elaborates on this position, arguing that industrialization and urbanization split sexuality off from the rest of life. In response to this increasingly repressive situation, pornography emerged and flourished. Pornography for Marcus is "nothing more than a representation of the fantasies of infantile sexual life." [7] The "newness" of pornography is by no means accepted by either pornography or sexual historians; but it is an article of faith in the conventional wisdom that the so-called "excesses" of pornography—its tendency toward what has been euphemistically termed the "unaesthetic"—are solely attributable to the repression of sexuality in the modern society at large.

Recognition of the primacy of patriarchal power and violence in pornography began with *Sexual Politics*, published in 1969, wherein

Kate Millett dramatically demonstrated the centrality of male domination and female subjugation in literary descriptions of sexual activity. Others before her may have noted the sadistic aspects of
pornography, but no one had linked sexuality and cruelty to the
maintenance of patriarchy. Moreover, Millett argued that growing
sexual permissiveness during the twentieth century gave greater lati-
tude to the expression of male hostility.[8]

Millett exposed the woman-hatred of the avant-garde pornographic
literary artists of the twentieth century, while Robin Morgan in her
commemorative essay, "Goodbye to All That," written in 1970 in
response to the women's take-over of the underground newspaper *Rat*
(a take-over prompted in part by *Rat*'s pornographic character), exposed the woman-hatred of the left/hippie underground newspapers.
She wrote:

> It's the liberal co-optative masks on the face of sexist hate and
> fear worn by real nice guys we all know and like, right? We have
> met the enemy, he's our friend. And dangerous . . . A genuine
> left doesn't consider anyone's suffering irrelevant or titillating.[9]

In 1974 Andrea Dworkin expanded on this critique of pornographic avant-garde literature and underground newspapers. She argued:

> *Suck* is a typical counter-culture sex paper. Any analysis of it
> reveals that the sexism is all-pervasive, expressed primarily as
> sadomasochism, absolutely the same as, and not counter to, the
> parent cultural values.[10]

This pattern was certainly not unique to the anti-establishment literature of the sixties, for as Sheila Rowbotham observed with regard to
the pornography of the eighteenth century:

> It challenged the hypocrisy of the bourgeois in regarding selfish-
> ness and the power to dominate others as the most essential
> features of manhood while taming them in the service of indus-
> try and family stability. But it never challenged selfishness or
> domination as the basis of sexual relations.[11]

A year later, in her exhaustive examination of the history of rape,
Susan Brownmiller made the connection between pornography and
violent repression against women. For Brownmiller "pornography is
the undiluted essence of anti-female propaganda." She argued that the
philosophy of pornography is one and the same as that of rape, and

that the open display of pornography promotes a climate in which acts of sexual hostility are not only tolerated but ideologically encouraged. Brownmiller analyzed misogyny not only in the arts and literature but also in the systematized, commercially successful propaganda machines currently found on the Forty-second Streets of the nation's cities.[12]

With the appearance in this country in late 1975 of *Snuff*, a pornographic film which purported to show the actual sexual assault, murder, and dismemberment of a woman, feminist activities began to be directed against the portrayal of sexual violence. Arguments were raised as to the relationship between the increase of violence in pornography and the media and the increasing rate of rape. And it was also during this period that feminists began to argue that the increasing violence itself was accounted for by men's response to feminism. Ellen Willis wrote:

> The aggressive proliferation of pornography is . . . a particularly obnoxious form of sexual backlash. The ubiquitous public display of dehumanized images of the female body is a sexist, misogynist society's answer to women's demand to be respected as people rather than exploited as objects. All such images express hatred and contempt, and it is no accident that they have become more and more overtly sadomasochistic . . . their function is to harass and intimidate, and their ultimate implications are fascistic.[13]

Pornography, it is thus argued, is a political phenomenon.

For feminists the "what" of pornography is power and violence, and the "who" of concern is women. Women as a class are victimized ideologically, and this has a real carry-over in terms of the actual physical victimization and repression of individual women. Feminists do not hold with the "traditional moralist" perspective that pornography is primarily about sex and is therefore evil, but they agree with the moralistic argument that the effects of pornography are harmful. In terms of public policy, the two normally disparate positions may fall on the same side of the fence, but the potential harms that motivate the moralist to act are not those that motivate feminists. Charles B. Keating, Jr., head of one of the most active, national anti-pornography organizations writes:

> The traditional Judeo-Christian ethic does not condemn pleasure as an evil in itself; it does condemn the pursuit of pleasure for

its own sake, *as an end* rather *than a means*, deliberately excluding the higher purposes and values to which pleasure is attached. . . . (the sex drive) serves the individual and the common good of the human race, only when it is creative, productive, when it ministers to love and life. When, however, it serves only itself, it becomes a perversion. . . . Every word by which the organs of sex are designated bears out this statement: genital, generative, reproductive, procreative.[14]

The wrongness of pornography in this view stems from the fact that it is a pleasure which may be substituted for other "higher" pleasures, thus destroying the "virtue" of the viewer. It is wrong because of what it does *not* lead to. The possibility that pornography may have consequences for victims other than the viewer is of less concern. This emphasis is understandable because according to the patriarchal religious view, the victims of concern to feminists—the abused wives, rape victims, and brutalized actresses—are in fact fallen women responsible for their fate.

From a feminist perspective, on the other hand, the crucial proposition concerns the impact of pornography on potential victims other than the consumer: The presence of pornography is related to actual violence against women. Pornography is not merely the reflection of men's sexual fantasies, unrelated to larger structures, but is in fact one of the mechanisms that has sustained the systematic domination of women by men throughout history. Pornography then is not unique to any particular historical period, but because it serves political purposes, its use will intensify when that domination is challenged. Pornography's "excesses" are best explained as manifestations of this backlash, not—as the traditional liberal view would have it—as responses to the "repression of sexuality." Pornography, both in its quantity and violent nature, proliferates in response to efforts to alter the sexual status quo. These are the propositions suggested by a feminist interpretation of pornography. What is the available evidence?

Pornography and Violent Behavior

The President's Commission on the Causes and Prevention of Violence concluded in 1969 that on the basis of its research, media violence can induce persons to act aggressively, and yet the Commission on Obscenity and Pornography concluded a year later that exposure to pornography does not seriously promote antisocial behavior.

The latter report has been widely and continually acclaimed in the liberal social science community. It contends that at worst pornography is merely harmless, and at best it provides for "more agreeable and 'increased openness' in marital communication." [15] * How was it possible for two huge government-sponsored research projects, staffed by many of the leading social scientists of the day, to arrive at seemingly contradictory conclusions? The violence commission's report confirmed the accepted liberal credo that environment is an important determinant of human behavior, while this relationship was rejected by the Commission on Obscenity and Pornography. A social-learning (imitation) model was deemed appropriate in explaining the impact of violence in the media, but was not applicable to the impact of pornography. These disparate conclusions can only be understood in the light of prevailing liberal ideology of the late 1960's. Violence on the part of ordinary citizens in the midst of civil disorders was viewed unfavorably, while sex in the midst of the so-called "sexual revolution" was viewed as an unmitigated good; the respective commissions framed their research questions accordingly.

As we might expect, the Commission on Obscenity and Pornography in carrying on the long tradition described earlier assumed that its subject of concern involved nothing more than "explicit sexual materials." In fact, the commission chose not to use the term "pornography" in its report because it felt that the term denoted subjective disapproval of the materials in question.[16] Use of the scientifically neutral term "sexual materials" also permitted the commission more readily to use its investigations as a vehicle for raising the subject of sex education. The commission, being a product of its time, reflected both the best and worst of the liberal ideology. Unfortunately, its seemingly genuine concern with documenting the need for sex education in a society which had often frowned on such education became hopelessly confused with its primary goal of proving that anything associated with the expression of sexuality was good. These "biases" influenced the final report in several respects: the choice of research

* Ed. Note: The members of the Commission on Obscenity and Pornography were William B. Lockhart, Frederick H. Wagman, Edward E. Elson, Thomas D. Gill, Edward D. Greenwood, Morton A. Hill, G. William Jones, Charles H. Keating, Jr., Kenneth Keating (resigned June 1969 before the commission inquiry was over), Joseph T. Klapper, Otto N. Larsen, Irving Lehrman, Freeman Lewis, Winfrey C. Link, Morris A. Lipton, Thomas C. Lynch, Barbara Scott, Cathryn A. Spelts, and Marvin E. Wolfgang. They were appointed by President Lyndon B. Johnson.

designs employed by the various investigators, the interpretation of the individual data sets, and the integration of the various studies into the actual report.

Attitude Surveys

The commission's investigators undertook a wide variety of surveys designed to discover different populations' *attitudes* toward pornography and its effects. These studies suggested that persons who had greater experience with sexual materials were less fearful of their effects. All the "good" people—educated persons, young persons, men —tended to view pornography as harmless and as providing information about sex. We have no reason to doubt the accuracy of the commission's description of these attitudes, but placing this information first suggests that they may have been playing some variant of "if enough of the right people believe it to be so, then it is so." Not included were data indicating that sex offenders more often than nonoffenders reported agreement with pornography's socially desirable or neutral effects.[17] Regardless of intent, the point is that opinion data, however interesting, do not address the question of effects.

It is perhaps noteworthy that the violence commission did not undertake opinion polls of who did or didn't believe that the effects of violence in the media were harmful. The final report chose not to explore some of the fascinating material the surveys did uncover with regard to the politics of pornographic usage. (For instance, Alan Berger and his colleagues in their survey of high school students observed, "this data suggests that it is the boys who introduce the girls to these movies, and this suggests that dating may be one of the major mechanisms by which boys *manage* [emphasis mine] the introduction." [18]

Retrospective Studies *

Due to the ethical problems involved in human experimentation, retrospective studies are often used in social research, although it is

* Ed. Note: Retrospective studies, in contrast with "pure" experiments, do not directly manipulate subjects. In such studies persons with a particular characteristic that is of interest to the researcher (in this case persons who have committed sex offenses) are identified and then compared with other persons who have similar social and economic characteristics but do not have the characteristic being studied. The object is to determine, through interviews or available records, whether the two groups differ in their usage of a product which is thought to produce the particular characteristic under study.

difficult if not impossible to establish causal relationships through the use of such designs. Here again it is worth noting that the violence commission did not undertake a single study that attempted to identify violent offenders and then trace their usage of violent materials. The pornography commission, however, conducted several retrospective studies of sex offenders, some with appropriate control groups and some without. These studies provided part of the commission's supporting evidence for its conclusion:

> Empirical research . . . has found no reliable evidence to date that exposure to explicit sexual materials plays a significant role in the causation of delinquent or criminal sexual behavior among youth or adults.[19]

This conclusion relied on the findings that sex offenders and "sex deviants" reported less exposure to erotica during adolescence than other adults, whereas during adulthood sex offenders were not significantly different in degree of exposure to such materials, or in reported likelihood of engaging in "sociosexual" behavior following exposure.[20] In fact, the available evidence in the technical reports is contradictory because the term "sex offender" is used inconsistently. In two of the four studies in which controlled comparisons were made between offenders and other groups, rapists were a minority. A variety of different persons formed the majority of offenders—exhibitionists, pedophiles, persons convicted of "taking indecent liberties," and homosexuals.* It is only in these studies that the data indicate fairly conclusively that "sex offenders" had less exposure to pornography during adolescence.

In the two studies in which "sex offenders" referred only to rapists, we find the following: In one study (C. E. Walker) made of a group of sixty incarcerated rapists, usage of pornographic materials during adolescence was not examined other than to determine at what age the subjects first saw various kinds of pornography. The investigators indicate that there were no statistically significant differences in the age of first exposure, but then note: "Visual inspection of the means

---

* In R. F. Cook and R. H. Fosen, "Pornography and the Sex Offender: Patterns of Exposure and Immediate Arousal Effects of Pornographic Stimuli," *Technical Reports of the Commission on Obscenity and Pornography,* Vol. 7, p. 149 the group of sixty-three sex offenders included sixteen rapists and ten attempted rapists; in W. T. Johnson, L. Kupperstein, and J. Peters, "Sex Offenders' Experience with Erotica," *Technical Reports of the Commission on Obscenity and Pornography,* Vol. 7, p. 163, the forty-seven sex offenders included twelve rapists.

revealed a tendency . . . for the comparison groups to be exposed to pornography at an earlier age." [21] Rapists indicated less frequent usage during adulthood, but, as we might expect, these *incarcerated* subjects also reported that "pornography was not easy to obtain." Rapists did report *collecting* pornography for a significantly longer time than did other men, but no data are presented as to whether the collector's habit is more common among one group or another. The investigators conclude, oddly enough, that "sex offenders, if anything, tend to have less experience with pornography than other groups." [22]

Another study (Goldstein et al.), which isolated sex-offender rapists, attempts a more sophisticated analysis of pornography usage through the life cycle. Twenty rapists, plus a variety of different control groups, were questioned about their use of pornographic materials during the past year, the rapists being asked to report on the year prior to their incarceration. On the basis of data derived in this manner, the investigators conclude that rapists had less exposure to all stimuli and media. During adolescence there were few significant differences; however, the investigators report what they term "dramatic" differences during preadolescence (six to ten)*: Thirty percent of the rapists, as opposed to two percent of the control subjects, reported exposure to hard-core pornographic photos. This study also reports that "only rapists stand out in reporting a significantly *earlier age* of *peak experience*. [emphasis mine]." † The study adds that "the rapists only report *more frequent exposure* than controls for the most *vivid experience* [emphasis mine]." [23]

On the question of behavioral impact there is a tendency in both these studies for data to be interpreted away. In the Walker study the data indicate that rapists "reported more frequently than the control group that pornography had led them to commit a sexual crime." It is suggested that this response is perhaps just a "convenient, ready-made explanation" for their current situation (the control group here is a group of similarly incarcerated non-sex offenders), and, moreover,

---

* Ed. Note: This section of the study was not included in *The Report of the Commission on Obscenity and Pornography*, but it is available in the investigators' own book, *Pornography and Sexual Deviance* (see reference 25).

† M. J. Goldstein, H. S. Kant, L. L. Judd, C. J. Rice, and R. Green, "Exposure to Pornography and Sexual Behavior in Deviant and Normal Groups," *Technical Reports of the Commission on Obscenity and Pornography*, Vol. 7, p. 1. The authors indicated that the data in the report were not completely analyzed, which presumably accounts for the preadolescence material appearing only in their 1973 book.

expert clinical judges did not rate the fantasy productions of the sex offenders in response to projective stimuli as indicating significantly more pathological sexual thought, sexual arousal, or aggressive sexual inclinations.

This conclusion is striking, when in the preceding paragraph Walker notes that these ratings "were only minimally reliable and demonstrated essentially no validity." [24] Somewhat similarly the Goldstein study notes that "only the rapists stand out from all other groups in containing a higher percentage who wished to imitate the portrayed activity." Yet because only 57 percent of the rapists, as opposed to 85 percent of the controls, actually attempted to imitate some feature of their peak erotic stimulus, the rapists are then characterized as having "low-beam performance" in contrast with their statements of high interest.[25] The crucial question of under what circumstances "performance" is carried out is not dealt with. In sum, when only rapists are categorized as sex offenders, the actual data do not suggest that rapists have been deprived of pornography, nor is there firm evidence that rapists do not imitate portrayed behaviors.

Some of the data problems are attributable to the restrictive categorizations of rapists. This was the case in a survey by M. M. Propper of young (sixteen to twenty-one) male reformatory inmates. The data that show these inmates reporting considerable experience with sexual materials are footnoted in the report with the comment, "*only* 3% of the sample had been *incarcerated* for assault, and *only* 2% for sex offenses [emphasis mine]." [26] Not included in the report itself are data indicating that 62 percent of these "juveniles" scored high on a "peer sex behavior index," which included such items as "gang bangs" and "intentionally getting a girl drunk." Scores on this index were positively related to exposure to "erotic materials." Propper himself concluded that "contrary to the opinion that high exposure may inhibit sexual practices, the data suggest a greater amount of activity among those who are more highly exposed." [27]

Experimental Laboratory Studies

Unlike the various commissions that have studied the impact of violence, the Pornography Commission did not undertake a single controlled laboratory study involving children. In its call for "Needed Additional Research," the commission noted this gap and indicated that fears about the consequences of such studies had precluded them. Gary Wills has recently noted the irony of this situation:

The group first deferred to a social instinct that childhood exposure to "pornography" would have a powerful effect, before going on to argue on the basis of tests invalidated by that first deference to the view that it has such an effect! [28]

The fourteen laboratory studies used either male college students or married couples as subjects, and only three of these studies were designed in a way that permitted the examination of the possible relationship between pornography and aggressive behaviors. Most studies examined the impact of viewing pornography on attitudes, or reported feelings of sexual arousal or sexual behavior outside the laboratory. In one study of married couples, 11 percent of the women reported that they sought therapy after viewing hard-core pornography films with their husbands; however, these studies were not designed to consider aggressive sexual behavior.[29] In many of the experiments most of the materials the subjects were shown might be more properly classified as sex education materials, rather than the amalgam of sex, violence, and woman-hatred which typifies pornography in the real world.

Of the three experiments that did deal with aggression, two were conducted by Donald L. Mosher and lacked the most elemental feature of standard laboratory research—a control group. His designs were clearly derived from the popularly held theory that if men are provided with a "safety outlet" for expressing "normal" feelings of hostility and aggression toward women, they will be less inclined to act on those feelings. On the basis of his finding that males who exhibited highly "sex-calloused" attitudes showed a decline in such attitudes after viewing pornography, the commission concluded that "fears" about learning such attitudes from the medium were "unwarranted." That these subjects would probably have shown the same decline after watching *Mr. Rogers' Neighborhood* was simply ignored.[30]

Only one study was modeled on the extensively used experiments which had enabled violence researchers to conclude that aggressive behaviors were learned from media representations of aggression. P. H. Tannenbaum found that subjects delivered stronger electrical shocks to other participants after viewing an "erotic" film sequence than did subjects who viewed neutral or aggressive films. And, perhaps most significantly, when aggressiveness and eroticism were joined in the same presentation, subjects delivered the most intense shocks.[31] The commission's brief reference to this study was counterbalanced with a reference to the findings from Mosher's other "experiment," [32] a study which purported to show that subjects were less inclined to be verbally aggressive toward females after viewing pornography. The commission made this comparison between the two studies despite the fact that Mosher's work lacked controls, the most basic ingredient of experimental design.

In concluding our discussion of the commission's use of experimental studies, we should mention the now-famous satiation study conducted by J. L. Howard et al. This study, though it did not deal with the issue of aggressive behaviors, was extensively cited in the commission report and has often been offered in the popular media as proof of the catharsis theory. Howard found that college students exhibited a decreased interest in pornographic materials after being fed large amounts in a short period of time.[33] Presumably after getting a proper "dosage," interest is satisfied. The commission never dealt with the contradiction between this experiment and its own surveys which indicated that in the real world, pornography consumers are habitual consumers.

Social Indicator Statistics

The final type of evidence upon which the commission relied was longitudinal data on the availability of pornography and reported sex offenses in both the United States and Denmark. For the United States the commission argued that the number of rapes known to the police was a "crude" measure, and felt that the more "refined" measure of arrests for rape was more appropriate.[34] Rape and pornography had both increased over the decade, but the conclusion was that if availability were related to the incidence of rape, "one would have expected an increase of much greater magnitude than the available figures indicate." It must be said that the commission also noted that the data did not disprove a causal connection. The big piece of evidence, however, which in the intervening years has often been put forth as positive proof for catharsis or "safety-outlet" theories, was the quasi-experiment presented by the Danish data. The Danes had gradually removed all legal restrictions on pornography during the 1960's, and the data appeared to indicate that sex crimes had in turn taken a dramatic turn downward. It was presumed that this decline was not attributable to changes in legislation, law enforcement procedures, or people's readiness to report sex crimes. Further research has proven otherwise. Certain crimes such as homosexual prostitution were no longer being included in the statistics, thus artificially deflating the overall sex crime figures, but, most crucially, rape did not decline, and the more likely possibility is that a real increase occurred.* The report of the commission demonstrated a decline in rape by combining the statistics for "rape" and those for "attempted rape." These data were "adapted" from the statistics in the technical report by R. Ben-Veniste.[35] His raw data indicated a decline in "attempted rape," but Ben-Veniste himself did not discuss the issue of a decline in rape.[36] Berl Kutchinsky's study reported slightly different figures for "rape," and concluded that the overall decline in sex crimes *had not* occurred in the area of rape.[37] In 1976 both J. H. Court of Australia and Victor Bachy of Belgium published papers that reported new rape statistics released by the Copenhagen police, and these figures are considerably higher than those originally reported by Kutchinsky. According to Court, "the trend since 1969 indicates that there has been a rise to a new level higher than anything experienced in the previous decade." [38]

The Danish experiment then, has *not* proved that the proliferation of pornography leads to a decline in sexual assaults against women.

Conclusion

In summary, the conclusions of the Commission on Pornography and Obscenity as to the harmlessness of pornography are not warranted on the basis of the actual data that were *available to the commission* itself. I wish to stress that point, because in my discussion I referred to both the Goldstein and Kant data that are reported only in their published book and to the recent corrections of the Copenhagen rape statistics. One might well wonder why the Goldstein report to the commission was made on the basis of partially analyzed data or why the rape statistics were gathered so hastily, but from my analysis it should be clear that the commission's conclusions cannot be attributed to the fact that it was not afforded the advantage of these newer data.

Social scientists such as Etzioni who adhere to the conventional model of pornography and repression have argued that the commission's data provided incontrovertible support for their position that pornography is harmless. In fact, a better case can be made for a model hypothesizing a relationship between pornography and the repression of women. If we take into account the commission data and emendations noted above, as well as the extensive data on the learn-

* J. H. Court notes these changes in "Pornography and Sex Crimes: A Reevaluation in the Light of Recent Trends Around the World," *International Journal of Criminology and Penology*, Vol. 5, 1977, pp. 129–57.

ing of violent behaviors via the media, the evidence supports this proposition. Other data worthy of more careful examination in the future include reports from some cities that tracts with large numbers of pornographic outlets tend to have disproportionately high rape rates, reports from police officers that rapists are often found with pornographic materials in their possession, as well as reports that wife-batterers are often devotees of pornographic literature.*

At this point I do not have systematic quantitative data to support my second proposition that pornography proliferates in response to efforts to alter the sexual status quo: I would argue however that the relationship between pornography and actual violence against women cannot be understood unless we accept the reasoning of this proposition. If we do not recognize the existence of an institutionalized sexual hierarchy in which men are dominant, then we are left with no explanation for why women are so often selected out as victims of violence. Liberal social science has tended not to document these patterns because its models do not acknowledge the existence of patriarchy. This crucial theoretical gap also leaves liberals at a loss to explain why the legitimizing of pornography in the 1970's has not resulted in the predicted loss of interest and sales. However, when we take account of the power relationships between men and women, we can begin to understand the role of pornography in the real world. Pornography is one of the routine mechanisms for sustaining these relationships. We must also consider that as women take on new economic roles, tremendous stress is put on the "old" relationships between the sexes. Just as all dominant segments in power relationships (e.g., the ruling class in a state system and the ruling race in a slave system) increase the use of violence and repression in periods of stress, we can expect men to respond accordingly. When we begin

* Data on the tracts are cited in Captain Carl I. Delau, Cleveland, Ohio, Police Department memo, August 1977; and in "Study of the Effects of the Concentration of Adult Entertainment Establishments in the City of Los Angeles," mimeographed, Los Angeles City Planning Department, June 1977. Mildred Daley Pagelow reported on wife-batterers as devotees of pornographic literature in *Women Against Violence in Pornography and Media Newspage*, Vol. 1, No. 7, December 1977. And, in response to my question during a public talk on wife abuse, Commander James Bannon of the Detroit Police Department (Commander Bannon also holds a Ph.D. in sociology with a specialization in sex roles) responded that "often we find that the man is trying to enact a scene in some pornographic pictures." Liberals have tended not to believe the opinions of police officers, which may explain why the commission ignored the police department reports about rape and pornography that were available to it.

to recognize these dynamics, we can understand why pornography appears to grow both in quantity and in degree of violence in certain historical periods. A British psychiatrist, F. E. Kenyon, writes:

> The considerable output of pornography in Victorian times may have resulted not only from the repressive, puritanical and hypocritical society, but also as a reaction to emerging female emancipation. Similarly today the further threat of "Women's Liberation" could be partly responsible for another outpouring of pornography.[39]

The contemporary proliferation of pornography must also be understood as forming part and parcel of the "commoditization" of sexuality in the capitalistic economy at large. And pornography may serve the interests of capitalism in yet another way. Pamela Hansford Johnson observes:

> When the Nazis took on the government of Poland, they flooded the Polish bookstalls with pornography. This is a fact. Why did they do so? They did so on the theory that to make the individual conscious only of the need for personal sensation would make the social combination of forces more difficult . . . The Nazi scheme was the deliberate use of pornography to the ends of social castration. The theory was, and it is worth considering that—permit all things for self-gratification and you are likely to encourage withdrawal from any sort of corporate responsibility.[40]

Although Johnson calls attention to the consequences of self-indulgence, her analysis also suggests that the reaffirmation of male power and control promoted by pornography, and the behaviors thereby encouraged, serve to deflect attention from the total absence of control that is the lot of most men in their economic roles within a capitalistic society.

One might acknowledge that violence is endemic to pornography, and that men often act on these fantasies, but view these connections as a "natural" expression of human sexuality. Robert Stoller, a psychoanalyst, writes:

> An essential dynamic in pornography is hostility. Perhaps the most important differences between more perverse and less perverse ("normal") pornography, as between perversion and "normality," is the degree of hostility (hatred and revenge fantasies) bound or released in the sexual activity. One can raise the pos-

sibly controversial question whether in humans (especially males) powerful sexual excitement can ever exist without brutality also being present.[41]

Stoller has recognized the complexity of the prevailing pattern of male "sexual" behavior in patriarchal society, but he has not acknowledged the possibility that this "natural" dynamic may in fact be structured by patriarchy. Admittedly this is a difficult proposition to test because patriarchy has been so universally dominant. In the laboratory it is difficult to distinguish sexual from violent arousal, a seeming confirmation of the "nature" argument; but experimental studies have never considered how these arousal mechanisms are themselves conditioned by sexist attitudes. Toward clarifying these issues, I propose a test of my hypothesis. My proposal is a laboratory study akin to the Tannenbaum experiment mentioned in this paper, with the crucial addition of a measure for subjects' adherence to patriarchal values. The question is whether there is any variability in the apparent physiological interconnection between violent and sexual arousal, and if so, whether attitudinal predispositions can account for the way the two co-vary. Such a study, no matter how imaginative and sensitive its design, would still be a very crude approximation of complex biological and historical processes, so careful historical study in combination with field studies of nonpatriarchal systems might provide a more appropriate test. These possibilities are just meant to be suggestive. New concepts and modes of scientific practice will present themselves as feminists begin to theorize. We must begin to consider that sexuality is a product of social existence and as such is subject to human will.

Dirty Books, Dirty Films, and Dirty Data

Pauline B. Bart and Margaret Jozsa

"When I came to the Medical School of the University of Illinois," says Dr. Pauline Bart, "medical students, almost all of whom were male, were shown pornographic movies as part of their sex education training. These films were to 'desensitize' the students so that they would not express shock, horror, disgust, and disbelief when their patients brought them sexual problems. (This was before sex education complete with audiovisual aids became big business.) The psychiatrist teaching the class apologized to the male students for the large size of the actor's penis, and assured them that the actors were chosen for this reason and that men were perfectly normal if their penises were not as large as those on the screen. There was no apology for the way females were treated in the film.

"In 1977 at a conference on rape, Dr. Diana Russell showed me some 'comic' books depicting incest, rape, and woman-torturing. In the first two instances, the girl and woman were portrayed as enjoying the violence, of course. In the latter case, caustic substances were shown being poured into the vagina of a woman tied into the lithotomy (gynecological) position.

"Finally, on my last trip to the Bay Area, City Lights Bookstore (which I have always associated with revolutionary beat poets) had a comic-book version of *The Story of O* on its counter so everyone walking in would see it. I had read the book years ago, but the impact of the comic-strip form was much different—I felt as if I were being successively slapped in the face."

These recollections about pornography formed the basis for further research and thought by Dr. Bart, and in 1978 at the Feminist Perspectives on Pornography conference, she presented this paper (written in collaboration with Margaret Jozsa), which reviews the research on pornography in the last decade.

It is difficult to demonstrate the real-world effect of pornography (or even that of violence in pornography) through research because we do not know the relationship among any of the following: what people believe and what they tell researchers they believe; what

kinds of things they think they will do and what they *actually* will do
and under what circumstances they will do it; e.g., if they do it in an
experimental laboratory situation in a psychology department, will
they do it in the outside world and, conversely, if they do it outside,
will they do it for the psychologist? And material that is not pornographic in one context may be in another. These factors are important
to keep in mind as we examine the research that men have gathered
on the effect of pornography on society.

In addition, we need to keep in mind the climate in which the
research was conducted. The intellectual and social climate of the
sixties and seventies brought us the "sexual revolution." To most
liberal and radical men, the sexual revolution meant that all women
were put on earth for their sexual gratification, that "good girls" were
no longer off limits (in fact, they were labeled "neurotic"), and that
any kind of sex between consenting adults was not only permissible
but desirable.

Women such as Joan Baez urged us to use our bodies for the
"Cause" (against the Vietnam War) with the famous slogan "Girls
say yes to boys who say no." Not being sexually available was the
equivalent of original sin, and guilt was a taboo feeling, much as sex
and aggression (particularly for women) used to be taboo. A "liberated" woman contaminated her body with the Pill, and if she got
pregnant she obtained an abortion—no fuss, no muss, no responsibility for the men. The concept of a "consenting adult" was broadly
defined, since power differentials between men and women were not
addressed and women saying no were not taken seriously. This world
view is epitomized in the famous Fritz Perls prayer "I do my thing,
and you do your thing. I am not in this world to live up to your expectations. And you are not in this world to live up to mine."

This climate was ideal for the proliferation of pornography: How
could women object? They would be uncool, unhip, neurotic, frigid,
or whatever pejorative was popular. With knowledge of this climate,
we will examine some of the research on pornography in the last two
decades in order to expose the inadequacies and the inherent biases,
and to comment on how this research pertains to women.

*   *   *

There are two working models which researchers have traditionally used to study pornography and aggression: the catharsis model
and the imitation model. The catharsis model, when applied to pornography, assumes that the more you see the less you do. In contrast,
the imitation model states that the more you see the more you do.
In her recent work, "Machismo in Media Research: A Critical Re-

view of Research on Violence and Pornography," Thelma McCormack discusses both models.[1] The catharsis model, derived from psychoanalytic theory, is primarily used in pornography research; the imitation model, grounded in learning theory, is primarily used in aggression research. Depending upon the researcher and the type of experiment, one or the other model is used in the research we will be reviewing in this paper. So it is important to have a basic knowledge of how each model works.

The catharsis model states that art, literature, religion, and other symbolic systems serve as "safety valves," reducing the tension created by sublimating "antisocial" forces in the psyche.[2] It assumes that fantasy, dreams, and jokes reveal our tabooed wishes and are based on instincts which are sublimated for the sake of peace and social order. This model also assumes that "antisocial behavior" has its origin in human nature, and that the reduction of one's drives is socially desirable. Moreover, it supposes that men have a different sexual nature from women; that sex and aggression are linked for men and that they have more difficulty than women in controlling such behavior.[3] Indeed, Freud believed "the sexuality of most men shows an admixture of aggression, of a desire to subdue. . . ."

This model predicts pornographic movies and books serve society by allowing men to release, in a harmless way, their sexual aggressions against women by viewing pornography. Much research on pornography has been conducted using this model. Most of it purportedly demonstrated the lack of harm—and, in some cases, the benefits—that flowed from pornography, and has been widely cited in defense of pornography.

According to McCormack, most researchers have been content to use the catharsis model for research on pornography. But recent researchers are questioning the assumptions underlying this model, particularly the sexist premises of the model. McCormack points out that biases include the "use of (mainly) male subjects, a logic dictated by a notion that for any theory of aggression or sexuality, men are the active group, men have the responsibility, and men confront the consequences of their own behaviors." [4]

It is this research, based on the cathartic model, which we will examine in the first part of our paper. We will discuss each article and point out the difficulties, biases, and inadequacies inherent in the experiments, surveys, and research.

The imitation model differs from the catharsis model because it suggests that people learn patterns of violence from role models. Anger, frustrations, and aggression are behaviors which are acquired like any other social habits—from the examples around us. Thus, aggressive behavior is learned; therefore, it is cultural rather than instinctive. Some recent researchers have used this model to suggest that the rapist, so pervasive in recent pornography, functions as a role model for male readers and viewers.[5] Toward the end of this paper, we will summarize their findings, which we believe point to the conclusion that violent pornography is harmful.

We begin by critiquing the research that was reported in *The Journal of Social Issues* "Pornography: Attitudes, Use and Effects." (Volume 29, No. 3, 1973). This journal is a standard reference on pornography (together with *The Report of the Commission on Obscenity and Pornography*). In fact, many of the experiments reported in the journal were conducted by independent researchers under the auspices of the commission, which funded the work and donated staff members for the research.

Experience with and Attitudes Toward Explicit Sexual Materials
(W. Cody Wilson and Herbert I. Abelson)

According to W. Cody Wilson and Herbert I. Abelson,[6] an overwhelming majority of adults report having been exposed at some time to "explicit sexual materials." This conclusion is based on data derived from 2,486 face-to-face interviews of adults in the United States. The survey was presented as an "opinion survey on current social issues." The researchers designed the questionnaire so that it approached the subject in what they felt was a "natural and non-threatening way." It asked general questions on books and magazines, then questions on involvement in social issues, next questions on "sex education," and finally, "explicit questions regarding sexual depictions." The creators of the survey sought to avoid biases and distortions by eliminating words and phrases like "pornography" (substituting "sexual materials") and "oral-genital activity" (using "mouth-sex contact" instead). However, there is no community consensus on what are "sexual materials." In much of the research done to date, the terms "pornography," "erotica," and "explicit sexual materials" are used interchangeably. This is an important variable, as a film showing two people making love is much different from one portraying the rape and murder of women for male sexual stimulation. Distinctions between these terms must be at the basis of any valid work in pornography research.

Obscenity and Contemporary Community
Standards: A Survey
(Douglas H. Wallace)

In a survey of 1,083 adults which attempted to determine a "single standard" for evaluating "erotic pictures," Douglas H. Wallace considered only what he termed "pictorial erotica." [7] The images ranged from "fully clothed male and female models to coital activities to oral-genital relations." However, he omitted the themes of sadomasochism, bondage, and fetishism because of what he calls "their relatively low frequency in adult magazine stores." But new research has shown that the barriers have been pushed back each time former taboos became acceptable. Today we are faced with sadomasochism, incest, and violence in pornography rather than "mere" objectification such as is found in much of the milder pornography of the late sixties and early seventies (see Malamuth and Spinner below). Research on pornography must deal with both forms of the material.

The Effect of Easy Availability of Pornography
on the Incidence of Sex Crimes: The Danish Experience
(Berl Kutchinsky)

In his widely cited review of the "Danish Experience," Berl Kutchinsky found that with the increased availability of pornography in Denmark there were marked decreases in the number of "sex offenses" committed there.[8] He believes that making pornography readily available gave the public a safety outlet for their psyches (i.e., the catharsis model). However, rape was *not* one of the sex offenses that decreased in Denmark following the liberalization of pornography laws. A close look shows that Kutchinsky lumped rape with flashers, Peeping Toms, and other milder "sex offenses" when he drew his conclusions.

In addition to this serious shortcoming in his research, there is also the fact that some sex offenses (such as voyeurism) were decriminalized in Denmark in the interim between the liberalization of pornography laws and the study by Kutchinsky. This would account for some of the "marked decrease" in sex offenses he reports.

Furthermore, Kutchinsky himself states that after the laws were liberalized, there were "changes in attitudes" toward sex offenses. Thus he states that fewer young women tended to report sex crimes. He attributes this factor to the development of a more "tolerant view of minor sexual interferences" on the part of the young women, and states that the "new generation (is) . . . less concerned about these things than the old generation."

It does not seem to occur to Kutchinsky that young females may be unwilling or unable to report such sex crimes anymore because of the changing societal attitudes. Although he remarks that the police may have a "reduced tendency to register reports" on certain kinds of sexual offenses, he does not deal with the fact that this would undoubtedly affect young females' attitudes about reporting such offenses to the authorities.

Sex Differences, Sex Experiences, Sex Guilt and Explicitly Sexual Films
(*Donald L. Mosher*)

In his study of 377 individuals, Donald L. Mosher showed two pornography films which portrayed "face-to-face intercourse and oral-genital sex" to 194 single males and 183 single females.[9] This experiment attempted to answer a number of questions: (1) How sexually arousing is the viewing of explicitly sexual films? (2) What sort of affective states accompany the viewing of such films? (3) Are there changes in sexual behavior in the twenty-four hours following viewing? (4) Are there changes in emotions in the twenty-four hours following or changes in opinions in the two weeks following the viewing of the films? (5) Are there different reactions to the films? And, finally, (6) what sort of differences in reactions exist between the sexes?

He used as a test film a "better-than-average" pornographic film because, as he himself stated, it showed more affection and fewer genital close-ups. Thus, it would "have appeal to sexually uninhibited, experienced adults of both sexes" more than most pornography, which is "kinky" and "oriented toward a male audience."

He concluded that the study "provides no evidence that explicit sexual films had untoward consequences on those who viewed them." He stated that the subjects "remained calm" and that none had any "visible negative reactions at the time." In addition, he found that women "can indeed be responsive to explicitly sexual stimuli," but that they were "more disgusted" by oral-genital sex than the "more sexually experienced, less guilty men," and he suggested that women may have a "personality disposition of sex guilt" which explains this reaction to pornography.

Mosher does wonder in passing, "What is the nature of disgust and its relation to female personality?" but there is no effort in this experiment to look at the treatment of women in pornographic films and books. Their objectification is so taken for granted that the issue is not even discussed. Mosher's data is often cited as evidence for a pro-pornography position, but it tells us little about women's responses to pornography.

One of Mosher's recommendations is that a massive sex education effort take place.[10] A noble statement, but one that does not follow from his data unless he is referring to the fact that people who scored high on "sex guilt" and low on "sexual experience," particularly females, were less likely than the others to enjoy pornography. Presumably the benefit to be obtained by increased sex education is enabling women to enjoy pornography.

Is Pornography a Problem?
(James L. Howard, Myron B. Liptzin, and Clifford B. Reifler)

In their research conclusions, James L. Howard, Myron B. Liptzin, and Clifford B. Reifler restate the cliché based on the catharsis model: that continued "exposure to pornography leads to a steadily decreasing interest" in the material; but they quickly admit that many questions still need answering.[11]

They exposed twenty-three subjects to pornographic materials for ninety minutes per day for fifteen days. The behavior and attitudes of the subjects were tested extensively before and after exposure to the materials. The researchers concluded that exposure to pornography had no "detrimental effect on the subjects." But they noted that their experiment was not "representative of the general population," as it used only twenty-one to twenty-three-year-old subjects, all of whom were white and male, with some college background. Further, the subjects were all from families with above-average incomes, they were all judged "psychologically stable," and they were all volunteers. These are the only researchers represented in *The Journal of Social Issues* who recognize that perhaps one should study the effect of pornography on women. Thus, their title could be changed from "Is Pornography a Problem?" to "For Whom Is Pornography a Problem?"

Exposure to Pornography, Character, and Sexual Deviance: A Retrospective Survey
(Keith E. Davis and G. Nicholas Braucht)

In a study of 365 subjects from different social groups (jail inmates, college students, people of three ethnic backgrounds, and members of Catholic and Protestant organizations) Keith E. Davis and G. Nicholas Braucht showed that there is a possibility that early exposure to pornography may have some impact on later-life deviance (or, conversely, that exposure to pornography is a product of a sexually deviant life-style),[12] a finding in the tradition of the imitation model. They found that there was a positive relationship between "sexual deviance" and exposure to pornography at all age levels. They felt more study was needed to show a concrete causal relationship between deviant sexual behavior and pornography, but they also felt that they could not reject the view that exposure to pornography at early ages plays a role in the development of sexually deviant life-styles.

In this retrospective study on exposure to pornography, the terms "character" and "sexual deviance" are so value-laden as to be almost useless. The authors list homosexuality and "sex without love" in the same deviant category as rape, prostitution, exhibitionism, and transvestism. They then find a relationship between each kind of behavior and the reading of pornography.

Their conclusion attempts to minimize their findings. They state that "a key to the reasoning that pornography could have a causal impact on sexual deviance is a judgment about the content and message of the materials," and assert that a better view looks at the individual's "attitude toward the body, toward sexual relations, and toward persons." [13] In other words, they prefer to assume the neutrality of pornographic material and to blame any negative effect instead on the untoward character of the individual reader. It obviously did not cross their minds that sadomasochistic pornography contributes to the development of an individual's "attitude toward the body, toward sexual relations, and toward persons."

Exposure to Erotic Stimuli and Sexual Deviance
(Michael J. Goldstein)

Michael J. Goldstein studied convicted male rapists, homosexuals, transsexuals, pedophiles, and heavy pornography users (the latter were obtained from flyers left in "adult book stores"), and a control group from the community.[14] Generally he found that the institutionalized sex offenders, homosexuals, transsexuals, and heavy users of pornography had less frequent exposure to pornography during adolescence than did the control group. This is not necessarily surprising if one is aware that the sex offenders are not much different from the general male population and therefore not much different from the control group. Goldstein also states: "Rapists had no greater likelihood of encountering material combining sexuality and aggression (sadomasochistic theme) than the controls, so that the idea for the aggressive sexual act does not appear to derive from pornography." [15]

The assumption that the control group does not contain rapists is untenable given the data that the majority of women do not report rape to the police, particularly if the victim knows the rapist. A 1978 study found that of 635 rape complaints received only ten men were found guilty of rape and ten of other offenses, and we do not know how many of these actually served time in prison.[16]

Pornography, Sexuality, and Social Psychology
(*Paula Johnson and Jacqueline D. Goodchilds*)

In a section entitled "Comment" in *The Journal of Social Issues*, researchers Paula Johnson and Jacqueline D. Goodchilds point out that the nature of pornography is changing. "The last 10 years have seen a change from pulp books describing foreplay in great detail and from "beaver" films with an emphasis on static display to very explicit depictions of sexual acts in both books and film format." [17] We can now add: "to very violent sexual acts of aggression" (see Smith, 1976; Feshbach and Malamuth, 1978).

It is clear that many researchers set out to prove that sex is not obscene, and therefore pornography/erotica (and the distinction was not made) should not be censored. We would agree that sex per se is not obscene, but the objectification of women is part of our oppression. More important, these research findings, though universally quoted on the subject, do not apply to the kind of explicit, visually depicted sadomasochistic pornography available on newsstands everywhere.

Also it is very important to recognize that all the researchers in *The Journal of Social Issues* are male and the subjects are mainly male. One study did use married women looking at pornographic films in the presence of their husbands,[18] but the obvious bias that entailed was not addressed. The English common-law precept that the husband and wife are one, and that one is the husband, seemed to have been assumed. Nor did the study take into account any conflict of interest between those with structural power—i.e., husbands—and those without—i.e., wives. One can only guess, as McCormack states, what the results would have been if experiments had been conducted by females (ideally, feminists using female subjects) not in the presence of males.[19]

Johnson and Goodchilds state:

> We think that a feminist would ask questions and form hypotheses based on a sensitivity to sex roles and an interest and concern for female as well as male sexuality. The anthropologists' caveat against a majority dominant group's studying its own culture suggests, too, that the female researcher's involvement in the study of the "male problem," pornography, might have unexpected but significant benefits.[20]

*   *   *

Robin Morgan has written that "Pornography is the theory and rape the practice." [21] In research experiments by Smith and by Feshbach and Malamuth, this relationship is explored, demonstrating that currently some males are engaging in pornography research that is useful to women.

Don Smith, in his work "Sexual Aggression in American Pornography: The Stereotype of Rape" (1976), studied 428 "adults only" paperbacks that were published between 1968 and 1974 and readily available in stores other than "adults only stores." [22] He found in these books 4,588 sex episodes, of which one fifth involve an act of rape. Some of his more important findings are:

1. Ninety-one percent portray rape of a female by a male, mainly of one female by one male.
2. Eighty-six percent of the rapists depicted are known to the victim, and no brutality is used (e.g., choking, kicking).
3. Twenty-one percent involve raping a virgin; e.g., more commonly, the plot involves "innocents" performing or being forced to perform an act or acts which they never have before. Married housewives also are frequently depicted, since their rape represents not only dominance over the woman but also over her husband.
4. The average number of acts in books depicting rape have increased from two in 1968 to three in 1970–1973 to four in 1974. The ratio of explicit sexual content to other content has increased from about one third to about two thirds. This finding is particularly important, given the research we will describe later in this paper.
5. In virtually all cases the female's terror of what she knows

is about to happen to her (particularly when she sees the large size of the attacker's genitals) is described in great detail, and considerable attention is given to her physical resistance and pleas for mercy. Yet, before the act is over her sexual desires will have been stirred to the point that she is physically cooperating—filled, at the same time, with shame and humiliation at the "betrayal of her mind by her body." Much is made during the act of reducing the female to begging the male verbally (in words she's never uttered before) for sex from him.

a. A prominent theme is that the victim really wants to be subjugated—wants to be forced to submit.
b. Shamed by her own physical gratification and her recognition that she actually liked what was done to her, the victim reports the act (to the authorities, her husband, or anyone else) in less than 3 percent of the episodes.
c. Less than 3 percent of the attackers meet with any negative consequences in the plot of the books; indeed, the attacker is usually rewarded with the sexual devotion of the victim (except in the case of unknown assailants). Neither the victim nor the attacker is portrayed as having any reason for regrets, and the victim usually goes on to a richer, fuller sex life as a result of her now-awakened sex potential.

Smith notes that rape is presented in pornography as being a part of normal female-male sexual relations—with benefits for both victim and attacker—that rape is a pact of sexual mastery in addition to being a crime of power (e.g., the victim enjoys the act), and states that his research findings support much of what Brownmiller says. He concludes that "the world depicted in these rape acts is one of machismo, an anti-female world—with a contempt, not just for females, but for other males as well." [23]

Neal M. Malamuth and Barry Spinner's longitudinal content analysis of sexual violence in the pictorials and cartoons of *Playboy* and *Penthouse* magazines from 1973–1977 supports Smith's contention that the amount of violence in pornography is increasing. While they found that amount relatively small, it increased significantly over the time span analyzed, primarily as a result of a sharp increase in the frequency of sexually violent pictorials, particularly in *Penthouse*. They are concerned because the coupling of sex and violence may so condition readers that violent acts become associated with sexual pleasure. In addition, readers may believe that women in general, like the women depicted in these magazines, are basically masochistic and in need of male domination.[24]

Research conducted by Seymour Feshbach and Neal M. Malamuth in "Sex and Aggression: Proving the Link" used an imitation or learning model.[25] They found that college men who viewed pornography that fused sex and violence tended to be more sexually aroused by the idea of rape and less sympathetic to the victims than a control group.

In a further study, college students read two versions of a mildly sadomasochistic story from *Penthouse*. One group read the original, and another group read a similar but nonviolent version. After completing a questionnaire assessing their level of sexual arousal, the students were given a story about rape to read in which pain cues were moderate and the "terrified victim, compelled to yield at knife point, was not portrayed as sexually excited." A second questionnaire demonstrated that males who read the violent story were more sexually aroused by the account of rape than the others who read the non-violent version. It was as if the men who had read about a woman's pleasure at being mistreated had then interpreted the victim's pain in the rape scene as a "sign of sexual excitement," and the greater their judgment of the victim's pain, the greater their sexual excitement. By contrast, in the case of the males who had read the non-violent version, the greater their perception of the victim's pain, "the lower their sexual response."

Thus, Feshbach and Malamuth state that "one exposure to violence in pornography can significantly influence erotic reactions to the portrayal of rape."[26]

In addition, both groups of men not only identified with the rapist, but 51 percent said that they might commit rape if they were assured they would not be caught. Because this finding might seem startling to those not familiar with the feminist analysis of rape, we wrote Malamuth asking for further information. Malamuth replied that indeed 51 percent of the men did so answer the question "How likely are you to behave as this man did if you could be assured of not being caught and punished?"[27] Moreover, he referred to similar results obtained by T. Tieger of Stanford University, and to replications of the above findings reported by Malamuth and his colleagues at the meetings of the Canadian Psychological Association[28] and the American Psychological Association.[29]

The authors conclude that erotic violence has indeed become the theme in pornographic literature. "The juxtaposition of violence with sexual excitement and satisfaction provides an unusual opportunity for conditioning of violent responses to erotic stimuli." [30] The message that pain and humiliation can be fun encourages the relaxation of inhibitions against rape. They believe that psychologists should therefore support "community efforts to restrict violence in erotica to adults who are fully cognizant of the nature of the material and choose knowingly to buy it"—an inadequate policy recommendation, given their findings. They are opposed to the fad of sadomasochistic fashion ads (such as those in *Vogue*) as well as "the practice of some therapists who try to help their patients overcome sexual inhibitions by showing them films of rape or by encouraging them to indulge in rape fantasies. . . . Psychologists . . . ought not to support, implicitly or explicitly, the use and dissemination of violent erotic materials." They suggest that we sharply discriminate between sexual and aggressive feelings by accepting children's sexual interests while discouraging "violent or habitually aggressive behavior." [31] And, having found differences between female and male responses to the same stimuli (i.e., pornography) as well as having discovered that more than half the latter's self-reports bear a "striking similarity to the callous attitudes often held by convicted rapists," [32] they call for further empirical research to analyze the reactions to sexually violent stimuli and effects of these exposures on beliefs, as well as for additional research on portrayals of sexual violence that will inhibit or disinhibit the sexual responsiveness of "normal subjects." [33] Similarly, social psychologist Edward Donnerstein, using a learning-theory approach, found that "films of both an erotic and aggressive nature can be a mediator of aggression toward women." [34,35]

Conclusion

Much of the current research on pornography is inadequate. The terms "erotica," "pornography," and "explicit sexual materials" are used interchangeably. Most of the research on pornography was done before violence pervaded pornography. Most researchers were male, as were most subjects. The effect of pornography on women has not been sufficiently studied; particularly not on women in society, since experimental groups are not the same as the real world. We suggest that there is an elective affinity or compatibility between the "do-your-own-thing" (male) ethic reflected in the so-called sexual revolution, which pervaded the sixties and seventies, and the increasing presence of and blatant content of pornography.

We have demonstrated that the catharsis model is inadequate; i.e., the model that says pornography drains off tensions so that men do less if they read or see more. If this model were correct, then as the amount of pornography increased, the rate of rape should have decreased. In fact, both have been increasing. The imitation model provides us (in the more recent research) with data demonstrating the pervasiveness and distorted view of rape in pornography (i.e., the woman enjoys it; this makes men more sympathetic to the rapist and less so to the victim. He interprets her pain as pleasure and reports he is more likely to engage in rape). However, the imitation model is also inadequate. It assumes that people are made of unimprinted wax and stamped with whatever messages role models present. If that were true, we would all have turned out exactly like our parents.

We need an alternative feminist model—a conflict model, which would assume that men's interests and women's interests are not always the same and, in fact, may be largely *in conflict*. The speedy dissemination and incorporation into textbooks and other publications of the findings of the Commission on Obscenity and Pornography—findings which have been shown to be patently biased and based on shockingly sloppy research (and certainly not relevant to the violent pornography of today, although it is referred to to allay our concern about such pornography)—should warn us to examine carefully what is presented as "scientific truth." The history of science demonstrates that science is not value-free. Neither are scientists. The accepted paradigms frequently serve the interest of the status quo. In this case, sexism is the status quo, and pornography is one of the factors maintaining and reinforcing a sexist society. The conflict model suggested by McCormack [30] and the authors of this paper does not assume that men and women have the same interests: Pornography is not in the interest of women.

Pornography and Violence:
What Does the New Research Say?

Diana E. H. Russell

As feminist social scientists examine past research (most of it done by the Commission on Obscenity and Pornography), it becomes clearer and clearer that the commission did not do a thorough job of exploring the effects of pornography on human beings. New research conducted in the last decade indicates that exposure to pornography *does* result in more aggressive, violent, and sexist behaviors on the part of the viewers. Dr. Diana E. H. Russell, Associate Professor of Social Sciences at Mills College in California, reports on this recent research.

Evaluating existing research on the effects of pornography is fraught with difficulties. First, distinctions are rarely made between "explicit sexual materials," "erotica," and "pornography." Second, precise descriptions of the films, pictures, or stories used in experiments are usually lacking, so that it is often impossible to know whether the findings are relevant to an evaluation of the effects of pornography or not. Third, many researchers have focused on the effects of "erotica" on sexual behavior, but a distinction is rarely made between destructive, sexist sexual behavior and healthy nonsexist sexual behavior. Another major focus has been on the relationship between sexual arousal and aggression, whereas my major concern in this article is with the relationship between pornography —regardless of arousal—and violence against women.

It is crucial to differentiate between pornography, erotica, and sexually explicit educational materials. By *pornography*, I mean *explicit representations of sexual behavior, verbal or pictorial, that have as a distinguishing characteristic the degrading or demeaning portrayal of human beings, especially women.** *Erotica* differs from pornography *by virtue of its not degrading or demeaning women, men,*

* This is a simplified version of a definition formulated by Helen Longino in Section I of this book.

or children. Like pornography, it is often intended to turn people on sexually. And like pornography, erotica may also be sexually explicit —though it often tends to be more subtle and/or artistic than is usual for sexually explicit materials. *Sex education materials* differ from erotica in that they are not designed to excite people but to educate them. Of course, they may also be sexually stimulating to some people, and are usually sexually explicit as well. Sex education materials are not supposed to be sexist; when they are they would meet my definition of pornography.

These distinctions are exceedingly important. As a feminist sociologist, I am in favor of erotica and sex education but against pornography. I will try to make these distinctions more real by referring to a particular experiment.

Pauline Bart and Margaret Jozsa, and Irene Diamond mention the research of Donald L. Mosher, who sought to ascertain the effects of two erotic movies on students. A measure of "sex calloused" attitudes toward women was administered to the 256 male students involved. This scale focused on attitudes approving of the sexual exploitation of women. Some examples follow, with the percentage of subjects who agreed shown in parentheses:

> Most women like to be dominated and sometimes humiliated (58%);
> When a woman gets uppity, it's time to _____ her (24%);
> _____ teasers should be raped (51%);
> A woman doesn't mean "No" unless she slaps you (39%).*

Not surprisingly, Mosher reports that "sex calloused males were more liable to use force to obtain coital access and to believe that force was justified (26%)." [1] Mosher found that these men were also more liable to use other exploitive techniques in order to try to obtain intercourse: attempting to get the woman drunk (39%), falsely professing love (25%), or showing a woman pornography or taking her to a "sexy" movie (16%). [2]

Contrary to expectation, after viewing the erotic movies, there was some decrease in these sex calloused attitudes. [3]

In trying to understand these results the description of the two films is particularly helpful. [4] As Bart and Jozsa point out, Mosher admitted using "better-than-average" films that showed "more affection than is typical of much pornography," and fewer genital closeups so that they might appeal more to women than would pornography,

---

* I assume the blanks were filled in for the students. However, they were not completed for the readers of the published article.

"which is oriented toward a male audience and more 'kinky' sex." [5] Although this description of the films is rather spare, it does seem they may well qualify as erotica rather than pornography. My own viewing of pornography films certainly confirms Mosher's observation that it is very rare to see affection combined with sex. In this context it is interesting to note that G. Schmidt and his colleagues similarly found that increased feelings of aggression were evident only after the subject's reading of "erotic" stories devoid of affection and love.[6]

I believe that movies portraying respect, affection, tenderness, and caring along with sex—including totally explicit sex free of sex-role stereotypes—would be educative, erotic, and therapeutic, particularly for men with sex calloused attitudes. However, as the well-known psychologist H. J. Eysenck and his colleague D.K.B. Nias point out, most pornographic films are not like this:

> Even when they do not overtly depict scenes of violence and degradation of women at the hands of men, such as rape, beatings, and subordination, the tone is consistently anti-feminist, with women only serving to act as sexual slaves to men, being made use of, and ultimately being deprived of their right to a sexual climax—in the majority of such films, the portrayal ends with the men spraying their semen over the faces and breasts of the women.[7]

To bring my discussion of research on pornography down to the level of pornography, I will cite an example: An article entitled "Rape: Agony or Ecstasy?" was published in 1971 in a magazine called *Response: The Photo Magazine of Sexual Awareness*, described as "Educational Material for Adults Only." [8] This was just one year after the Commission on Obscenity and Pornography had declared pornography to be harmless. While reading the following extracts from the article, consider the likelihood that readers would realize that the "study" cited is a pornographer's invention. The article is accompanied by seven graphic photo illustrations.

> Nearly one-half of all women who are forcibly raped experience orgasm during the assault, according to a report recently released by researchers from the University of Michigan.
>
> Dr. Coin was immediately impressed by the number of women who had actually found the coital stage pleasurable, as 73% did, and the 47% who had been stimulated to orgasm. . . .
>
> A number had been forced to perform or submit to activities which were not usual to their sex lives, such as anal intercourse,

fellatio, cunnilingus, rear entry, etc. Most found these new acts highly erotic within the context of rape. . . .

"I felt like an animal," interviewers were told repeatedly, or "I lost control of myself." Nearly all reported that their physical actions, after arousal, were much more violent than usual. Many recalled biting and scratching their assailants, and cooperating with exaggerated coital motions of their own. . . .

The physical struggle which typically preceded intromission also was undoubtedly of erotic significance. During man's origins, the report points out, the most physical and brutish of males were also the best equipped to defend and provide for offspring and mates. Thus they were the most sought-after sex partners. As psychologists have long known, we are not so far removed from the jungle but that such characteristics still contribute to erotic response in the female.

Fear, too, has a sexually exciting quality for most women . . . The fear rape victims feel certainly adds to their responsiveness. . . .

When one allows for the many cases of rape where intercourse was of very short duration, even less than one minute, it appears that virtually every woman who became aroused achieved orgasm if given a reasonable chance. . . .

The emotional impact of forced intercourse is also an aid to orgasm, the researchers have concluded. The situation in which the victim finds herself is so unique, the sensations so unfamiliar, that they command all of her attention. . . .

"Only about one woman in twenty whom we contacted had trouble resuming her regular pattern of sex response," the doctor reports. "And most of these had been sexually unstable *before* being raped" . . .

For the most part, American women can perhaps take some comfort in the fact that if they should ever become the victim of a rapist, neither the actual assault nor the aftereffects may be as traumatic as had been feared.

Do we really need research to tell us that such material reinforces or even fosters dangerous myths about rape? Material such as this not only can encourage men to rape, but it also serves to undercut the credibility of the victims, thereby contributing to their isolation and victimization by society.

In attempting to measure the effects of pornography, no research to date has used a stimulus such as the article above, even though the research design would be much easier to execute than much of that which has already been done. For example, people's attitudes toward rape, including the degree to which they subscribe to the myths about it, could be assessed before and after reading materials about rape published in pornographic magazines. Such an experiment would be much more relevant to the question of how pornography relates to rape and other violence against women than most research published until now. But neither women nor feminists have been given money to do this research. So at present we shall have to look with a feminist sensibility at what *has* been done.

Before reviewing some of the relevant work that has been done it is important to examine some of the characteristics of the population pornography caters to. For if men had no propensity to rape and beat women, or even if only a tiny minority of them have it, then pornography would have less violence-promoting potential.

Many feminist students of rape have pointed to the connection between rape and normative sex-role behavior. In *The Politics of Rape*, I suggested that if one were to see sexual behavior as a continuum, with rape at one end and sex liberated from sex-role stereotyping at the other, much of what passes as normal heterosexual intercourse would be seen as close to rape.[9] Lorenne Clark and Debra Lewis articulate the same idea, arguing that given the unequal power relationship between men and women, coercive sexuality is the norm.[10] In their chapter on "rapists and other normal men," they point out that "men are unwilling to acknowledge that there is anything abnormal about wanting sexual relations with an unwilling partner, because they fear that if full, consensual sexuality were to become the standard of acceptable sexual relations, they would be deprived of many . . . of the sexual acts they now enjoy."[11] Out of this perspective comes their rhetorical question: "If misogyny and sexual aggression are the rule rather than the exception, then why are not all men seen as real or potential rapists?"[12] Clark and Lewis conclude that "all men are shaped by the same social conditioning . . . , and they are all sexually coercive to some degree—at least, at some point in their lives."[13]

Eugene J. Kanin's research over the past two decades on male sexual aggression and the victimization of females supports the notion that forced sex in the high school and college age population is widespread. Approximately 62 percent of a group of female first-year university students reported "experiencing offensive male sexual aggression during the year prior to university entrance," 21 percent reported forceful attempts at intercourse, and 9 percent reported "more violent attempts at sexual intercourse accompanied by 'menacing threats or coercive infliction of physical pain.' " [14] Similar figures were obtained for a more varied group of students.[15]

More recently, Neal Malamuth, Scott Haber, and Seymour Feshbach asked a sample of ninety-one students (fifty-three males and thirty-eight females) to read a "rape story." As is customary in much psychological research, the students were not drawn in any random sampling process; they volunteered to participate in the research as part of a requirement of introductory psychology courses. After the male students had read the rape story, they were asked whether they personally would be likely to act as the rapist did in the same circumstances.[16] The identical question was then repeated, this time with an assurance that they would not be punished. The results:

> On a response scale ranging from 1 to 5 (with 1 denoting "none at all" and 5 "very likely"), 17 percent of the men specified 2 or above when asked if they would emulate such behavior "under the same circumstances"; but a total of 51 percent responded that they might do it if they were assured that they would not be caught! [17]

Malamuth, Haber, and Feshbach further point out that "these men also found the rape story more sexually arousing, believed that the victim enjoyed it, and were more likely to try to justify the act." [18] In interpreting these results, it is helpful to know the content of the rape story. The following is all that is reported:

> An approximately 500 word passage was written depicting a male student raping a female student:

> "Bill soon caught up with Susan and offered to escort her to her car. Susan politely refused him. Bill was enraged by the rejection. 'Who the hell does this bitch think she is, turning me down,' Bill thought to himself as he reached into his pocket and took out a Swiss army knife. With his left hand he placed the knife at her throat. 'If you try to get away, I'll cut you,' said Bill. Susan nodded her head, her eyes wild with terror."

> The story then depicted the rape. There was a description of sexual acts with the victim continuously portrayed as clearly opposing the assault.[19]

If 51 percent of this sample of male college students might be willing to act out such a violent rape on someone who had merely rebuffed a mild advance, one wonders how much the percentage might increase if the story were about a man who forced intercourse on his wife after she had declined his sexual advances for over a week. Or consider the following story: A man invites out a very attractive woman, known to be promiscuous, wines and dines her in anticipation of sexual intercourse, proceeds to neck and pet with her at his home later in the evening, and then gets turned down in a rude and abrupt fashion. What percentage of men might be willing to rape a woman in such a situation? Alfred Kinsey allegedly said that the difference between rape and a good time may hinge on whether the girl's parents were awake when she finally came home.[20] It would be truer to say that the difference between rape and a bad time is often that the woman goes ahead and agrees to have intercourse.

Research on how women experience the impact of pornography has so far been of little interest to male researchers. I would therefore like to present some preliminary results from my own research.*

Nine hundred thirty-three women 18 years and older, who were living in San Francisco during the summer of 1978, were interviewed to ascertain the prevalence of sexual assault in that city. These women were drawn from a random-household sample obtained by a San Francisco public-opinion polling firm—Field Research Associates. The women in the study were asked the following question: "Have you ever been upset by anyone trying to get you to do what they'd seen in pornographic pictures, movies, or books?" Of the 929 women who answered this question, 89 (10 percent) said they had been upset by such an experience at least once, while 840 (90 percent) said they had no such experience. Since the sample is a representative one, one can predict from this finding that 10 percent of the adult female population in San Francisco would say that they have been upset by men having seen something in pornography and then trying to get the women to do what they'd seen. Of course, it is possible that the women may be wrong in thinking that the men were inspired by what they had seen in the pornographic pictures, movies, or books. On the other hand, there are apt to be many instances of upsetting sexual contact in which the woman was unaware that the man's idea came from having viewed pornography; these instances would not get picked up by this question.

Those who answered "Yes" to the question were then asked to

* This research was supported by Grant RO1 MH2890 from the National Institute of Mental Health, Rockville, Md.

describe the experience that upset them the most. As will be noted in some of the replies quoted below, although many of the women were able to avoid doing what was asked or demanded of them, others were not so fortunate. And even in cases where the behavior was avoided, the woman often ended up feeling harassed and/or humiliated.

Selected Answers to Pornography Questions:

Have you ever been upset by anyone trying to get you to do what they'd seen in pornographic pictures, movies, or books? IF YES: Could you tell me briefly about the experience that upset you the most?

Ms. A: Urinating in someone's mouth.

Ms. B: It was a three-girls-and-him situation. We had sex. I was really young—like fourteen.

Ms. C: He was a lover. He'd go to porno movies, then he'd come home and say, "I saw this in a movie. Let's try it." I felt really exploited, like I was being put in a mold.

Ms. D: I was staying at this guy's house. He tried to make me have oral sex with him. He said he'd seen far-out stuff in movies, and that it would be fun to mentally and physically torture a woman.

Ms. E.:   It was physical slapping and hitting. It wasn't a turn-on; it was more a feeling of being used as an object. What was most upsetting was that he thought it would be a turn-on.

Ms. F: He'd read something in a pornographic book, and then he wanted to live it out. It was too violent for me to do something like that. It was basically getting dressed up and spanking. Him spanking me. I refused to do it.

Ms. G: He forced me to have oral sex with him when I had no desire to do it.

Ms. H: This couple who had just read a porno book wanted to try the groupie number with four people. They tried to persuade my boyfriend to persuade me. They were running around naked, and I felt really uncomfortable.

Ms. I: It was S & M stuff. I was asked if I would participate in being beaten up. It was a proposition, it never happened. I didn't like the idea of it.

Interviewer: Did anything else upset you?

Ms. I: Anal intercourse. I have been asked to do that, but I don't enjoy it at all. I have *had* to do it, *very* occasionally.

Ms. J: My husband enjoys pornographic movies. He tries to get me to do things he finds exciting in movies. They include twosomes and threesomes. I always refuse.

Also, I was always upset with his ideas about putting objects in my vagina, until I learned this is not as deviant as I used to think. He used to force me or put whatever he enjoyed into me.

Ms. K: He forced me to go down on him. He said he'd been going to porno movies. He'd seen this and wanted me to do it. He also wanted to pour champagne on my vagina. I got beat up because I didn't want to do it. He pulled my hair and slapped me around. After that I went ahead and did it, but there was no feeling in it.

Ms. L: I was newly divorced when this date talked about S & M and I said, "You've got to be nuts. Learning to experience pleasure through pain! But it's your pleasure and my pain!" I was very upset. The whole idea that someone thought I would want to sacrifice myself and have pain and bruises. It's a sick mentality. This was when I first realized there were many men out there who believe this.

Ms. M: Anal sex. First he attempted gentle persuasion, I guess. He was somebody I'd been dating a while and we'd gone to bed a few times. Once he tried to persuade me to go along with anal sex, first verbally, then by touching me. When I said "No," he did it anyway—much to my pain. It hurt like hell.

Ms. N: This guy had seen a movie where a woman was being made love to by dogs. He suggested that some of his friends had a dog and we should have a party and set the dog loose on the women. He wanted me to put a muzzle on the dog and put some sort of stuff on my vagina so that the dog would lick there.

Ms. O: My old man and I went to a show that had lots of tying up and anal intercourse. We came home and proceeded to make love. He went out and got two belts. He tied my feet together with one, and with the other he kinda beat me. I was in the spirit, I went along with it. But when he tried to penetrate me anally, I couldn't take it, it was too painful. I managed to convey to him verbally to quit it. He did stop, but not soon enough to suit me.

Then one time, he branded me. I still have a scar on my butt. He put a little wax initial thing on a hot plate and then stuck it on my ass when I was unaware.

Ms. P: My boyfriend and I saw a movie in which there was masochism. After that he wanted to gag me and tie me up. He was stoned. I was not. I was really shocked at his behavior. I was nervous and uptight. He literally tried to force me, after gagging me first. He snuck up behind me with a scarf. He was hurting me with it and I started getting upset. Then I realized it wasn't a joke. He grabbed me and shook me by my shoulders and brought out some ropes, and told me to relax, and that I would enjoy it. Then he started putting me down about my feelings about sex, and my inhibitedness. I started crying and struggling with him, got loose, and kicked him in the testicles, which forced him down on the couch. I ran out of the house. Next day he called and apologized, but that was the end of him.

As may be clear from some of the quotations cited, there was often insufficient probing by the interviewers to determine the exact nature of the unwanted sexual experience. This means that the number of clear-cut cases of forced intercourse (i.e., rapes) reported in answer to this question is likely to be a considerable underestimate (see Table 1).

Table 1.   SEXUAL ASSAULTS REPORTED IN ANSWER TO QUESTION: *Have you ever been upset by anyone trying to get you to do what they'd seen in pornographic pictures, movies or books?*

Sexual Assault	*Number*
Completed vaginal intercourse with force	4
Completed oral, anal, or vaginal intercourse with foreign object, with force	10
Attempted oral, anal, vaginal intercourse with foreign object, with force	1
Total	15

While it cannot be concluded from these data that pornography is *causing* the behavior described, I think one can conclude that at minimum it *does* have some effect. The most notable is that 10 percent of the women interviewed felt they had been personally victimized by pornography. Regarding the men's behavior, at the very least it appears that some attempt to use pornography to get women to do what they want.* It also seems likely that some pornography may have reinforced and legitimized these acts, including the assaultive behavior, in those men's minds. In some cases the actual *idea* of doing certain acts appears to have come from viewing pornography—as in the suggestion that a dog be used on a woman, and in some of the S & M proposals.

Millions of dollars were spent on the research conducted by the Commission on Obscenity and Pornography, which came up with the false conclusion that pornography is harmless. Just the few questions cited here, included in a survey on another topic, are sufficient to refute their irresponsible conclusion.

In recent years several researchers have been exploring the effects of sexual arousal by "erotic" stimuli upon aggressive behavior. Seymour Feshbach and Neal Malamuth write:

> The typical procedure is to expose some subjects to a sexually arousing stimulus—an erotic film or written passage—and then provide them with an opportunity to act aggressively against someone else, usually a confederate of the experimenter who makes a preset number of errors in a guessing game. For each error, the subject may administer an electric shock to the confederate that ranges in intensity from the barely perceptible to the quite strong. (Unknown to the subject the shock leads to the confederate are disconnected.) The average level of shock the subject administers over the series of error trials provides researchers with an index of the level of aggression.[21]

Some of this research shows that exposure to "erotic" stimuli (we don't know if they are pornographic or erotic) can facilitate aggressive behavior,[22] while other research shows an inhibiting effect.[23] Various theories have been developed to try to explain the discrepancies. Some studies have also attempted to determine whether or not "erotica" has a differential effect on aggression toward women and

* Donald Mosher's finding that 16 percent of a sample of 256 male college students had "shown a girl pornography, or taken a girl to a sexy movie to induce her to have intercourse" was noted earlier in this section: "Sex Callousness toward Women," op. cit., p. 318.

men. According to Edward Donnerstein, "The general conclusion has been that no differential sex effects occur." [24] Donnerstein goes on to point out a number of problems with this research:

> First, there is strong evidence that prior or subsequent anger instigation is critically important in facilitating aggression following erotic exposure . . . Second, previous researchers have found that only under conditions of high sexual arousal [does] a facilitative effect on aggression seem to occur.[25]

Donnerstein also emphasizes that even now, the kind of research that would be most relevant to our concerns as women—i.e., the effects of aggressive cues juxtaposed with "erotica"—is almost non-existent.[26] Except for the study by P. H. Tannenbaum described by Irene Diamond, the Commission on Obscenity and Pornography neglected this issue, as have subsequent researchers. Happily, Donnerstein is one of the exceptions. He used two neutral, two "erotic," and two "aggressive-erotic" films, each of four minutes' duration. The neutral films were of a talk-show interview, the "erotic" films "depicted a young couple in various stages of sexual intercourse. . . . The aggressive-erotic films contained scenes in which an individual with a gun forces himself into the home of a woman and forces her into sexual intercourse." [27] The subjects were 120 male undergraduates, and aggressive behavior was measured by the "typical procedure" described by Feshbach and Malamuth above. Some of the students in the study were also subjected to insults which were designed to arouse their anger in order to test the impact of anger on their behavior prior to viewing "erotic" movies.

Donnerstein reported that an important difference emerged, depending on whether the "victim" of aggression was male or female:

> When angered subjects were paired with a male, the aggressive-erotic film produced no more aggression than exposure to the erotic film. Those subjects paired with a female, however, *only* displayed an increase in aggression after viewing the aggressive-erotic film. In fact, this increase occurred even if subjects were not angered, although the combination of anger and film exposure produced the highest level of aggressive behavior.[28]

Donnerstein's explanation is that "the female's association with observed violence was an important contributor to the aggressive responses toward her." [29] In other words, the male subjects associated the victimized woman in the film with the woman in the experiment, making her "an aggressive stimulus which could elicit aggressive responses." [30] Donnerstein concludes that if his interpretation is correct, "it would be expected that films which depict violence against women, even without sexual content, could act as a stimulus for aggressive acts toward women." [31] Later Donnerstein goes a step further. "There is ample evidence," he maintains, "that the observation of violent forms of media can facilitate aggressive responses, yet to assume that the depiction of sexual-aggression could not have a similar effect, particularly against females, would be misleading." [32] "Misleading" is quite an understatement, judging from the data from my own study. It would be inconsistent and dangerous!

Bart and Jozsa describe in some detail the very important experiment done by Feshbach and Malamuth which demonstrates that "one exposure to violence in pornography can significantly influence erotic reactions to the portrayal of rape." [33] Bart also quotes their interpretation of the fact that men who had read a mild S & M story adapted from *Penthouse* were more sexually aroused in response to a subsequent violent rape story than were others who had read a nonviolent story. In explanation, Feshbach and Malamuth write: "It is as if men who had read about a woman's pleasure at being mistreated had then interpreted the victim's pain in the rape scene as a 'sign of sexual excitement.' " [34] To me, a more likely interpretation is that if men can see women as masochistic—i.e., *enjoying* pain—this alleviates their consciences and disinhibits their misogynistic enjoyment of hurting women, or at the least, of conquering them.

I believe that Neal Malamuth and his colleagues are doing the most significant work on the relationship between pornography and violence. However, while recognizing that useful information does emerge from some of their questions to the women respondents, I am appalled by their insensitivity. After reading the violent rape story described earlier (see page 223), women students were asked whether they were likely to enjoy being victimized under the same circumstances described in the story, if they were assured no one would ever know.[35] On the one hand, these questions are the exact equivalent of those asked of the male students in the study by Malamuth et al. On the other hand, I can well imagine what the reaction would be if Black people were asked if they'd like to be beaten up by white people if they were assured no one would know about it! Or imagine an average man's reaction to a question about whether he would enjoy another man forcefully sodomizing him. It is a reflection of how oppressed we are as women that such questions can still be asked and answered.

The answers? "Subjects revealed considerable fear of rape and a clear belief that they personally would not enjoy being victimized" in the same [36] or in different circumstances.[37] "Females as well as males, however, seemed to believe . . . that over 25% of the female population would derive some pleasure from being victimized." [38] How sad it is to learn that college women and men today are still not immune to this rape myth.

Another important finding reported by Feshbach and Malamuth is that after reading the rape story, "female subjects were most aroused when the rape victim was portrayed as experiencing an orgasm and no pain, males were most aroused when the victim experienced an orgasm and pain." [39] However, to simply report such findings without analyzing their meaning and implications seems irresponsible. For the same reason I am very critical of Nancy Friday's publication of women's masochistic fantasies in *My Secret Garden*.[40] It is true that many women have masochistic fantasies and can be sexually aroused by pornography, even violent pornography, according to the study just cited. This does not make it harmless. It does not mean it is healthy. It does not mean that women's and men's responses to pornography are equatable. Nor does it mean that women like or want to be raped.

Rape and other masochistic female fantasies are a reflection of women's powerless role in society, the intense socialization they receive to accept that role, and their sexual repression.* To quote what I wrote in *The Politics of Rape* five years ago:

> It cannot be overstressed that having voluntary fantasies of being raped, and wanting to be raped in actuality, are two entirely different things. First, people are in complete control of their fantasies, even if the fantasy involves a situation in which they are out of control . . . Second, a person is rarely likely to feel fear in a fantasy which *she* has constructed. But in a real rape or attempted rape situation, unlike the fantasy version, women are usually afraid and often terrified.[41]

It is interesting to know that in some instances the sexual responses of males and females are similar. But this should not allow us to lose sight of the fact that outside of the laboratory, large numbers of males are not being raped, beaten up, or murdered by large numbers of females. Nor are masochistic women accosting unwilling men and

* In a study of women's fantasies during sexual intercourse, Barbara Hariton and Jerome Singer report that "older Catholic women, presumably reared in situations more focused on sexual repression and a traditional feminine role, relied somewhat more on submissive fantasies to enhance their sexual arousal." See *Journal of Consulting and Clinical Psychology*, Vol. 42, 1974, p. 321.

demanding to be raped. Violence is primarily a male problem in this and other patriarchal societies.* And even masochists who act out cannot, by definition, force their fantasies on an unwilling person. Masochists may be as sick as sadists, but they are *not* as dangerous to others!

In fairness to Neal Malamuth and his colleagues, I should clarify that *they* certainly are not suggesting that women want to be raped. They emphasize that there is not "a simple relationship between fantasies and sexual behavior," [42] and that their research has been more focused on males. In another of their studies, twenty-nine male students were classified as sexually force-oriented or nonforce-oriented on the basis of their responses on a questionnaire.[43] These students "were randomly assigned to be exposed to rape or mutually consenting versions of a slide show. All subjects were then exposed to the same audio description of a rape read by a female. They were later asked to create their own fantasies." [44] Malamuth regarded the most significant finding to be that "those exposed to the rape version, irrespective of their sexual classification, created significantly more sexually violent fantasies than those exposed to the mutually-consenting version." [45] He concluded that:

> In keeping with the possibility that violent sexual fantasies may have undesirable effects is the consistent finding that sexual responsiveness to sexual violence is associated in college students with a callous attitude towards rape and rape victims and with a self reported possibility of raping.[46]

Gene Abel and his associates have undertaken interesting research on the sexual response of rapists and "nonrapists" (i.e., men not convicted of rape) to pornography. Their research seems at first glance to show a marked difference between men convicted of rape and those not convicted of rape. Abel et al. measured the erections of thirteen rapists and seven "nonrapists" during what they describe as "vivid, two-minute descriptions" of rape and nonrape sexual scenes.[47] The vivid audiotape descriptions were presented in the following order: mutually enjoyable intercourse, rape, mutually enjoyable intercourse (a repeat of the earlier description), and rape (a repeat of the earlier description). The results: The average percentages of erection responses for the rapists were 60 percent, 69 percent, 65 percent, and 54

---

* There is a 9 to 1 ratio of male to female arrests for violent crimes in the United States. For a fuller discussion of the statistics and sources to substantiate the assertion that violence is primarily a male problem, see Diana E. H. Russell, "Fay Stender and the Politics of Murder," *Chrysalis*, No. 9, 1979.

percent, respectively; and for the "nonrapists," 62 percent, 17 percent, 60 percent, and 14 percent, respectively.[48] While this does establish a considerable difference in the responses of the rapists and "nonrapists," it is important to note that turn-ons of 17 percent and 14 percent to a story of rape on the part of the "nonrapists" is not insignificant, particularly as these same investigators consider that "excessive" sexual arousal to rape themes is a measure of the "proclivity to rape." In addition, the rape incident described involved the use of a knife and slapping on the part of the rapist, and crying and screaming by the victim. Once again, one wonders if the amount of sexual arousal by the "nonrapists" would have increased had the story involved a woman with a "bad reputation" who was perceived as an exploitive tease. In addition, the research of D. Briddell et al. suggests that the responses of the "nonrapists" might have changed considerably had they believed they had drunk alcohol.

Briddell et al. designed an ingenious experiment to test the effects of alcohol and cognitive set on sexual arousal to the same audiotaped descriptions used by Abel et al.[49] They found that alcohol did not significantly influence levels of sexual arousal. However,

> Subjects who *believed* [emphasis mine] they had consumed an alcoholic beverage evidenced significantly more arousal to the forcible rape recording and to the sadistic stimuli than subjects who believed that they had consumed a nonalcoholic beverage, regardless of the actual contents of the beverage.[50]

Briddell et al. conclude that "these findings . . . suggest that normal heterosexual males who have been drinking (or believe they have been drinking) may exhibit sexual arousal patterns indistinguishable from those patterns reported for identified rapists." [51]

To recapitulate: It appears that a large percentage of the male population has a propensity to rape. Important inhibitors to the acting out of this propensity are, first of all, *social controls*—e.g., the possibility of being caught and apprehended. *Social norms* that define rape as unacceptable behavior constitute a second source of inhibition. When social norms do not so define rape—as during times of war, or in certain subcultures (for example, the Hell's Angels), or where group rape is seen as an acceptable way to punish deviant women—one would anticipate a greater percentage of men willing to rape. The third and crucial factor is *conscience*. Some men clearly abhor the idea of rape because they see it as immoral and brutal behavior.

For consumers of the violent pornography so prevalent today, men's inhibitions against rape may be undermined on all three levels. In Bart and Jozsa's "Dirty Books, Dirty Films, and Dirty Data," the results of Don Smith's content analysis of 428 "adults only" paperbacks published between 1968 and 1974 are reported in some detail. The most relevant points are:

1. The amount of rape—one fifth of all the sex episodes involved completed rape; [52]
2. The fact that the number of rapes increased with each year's output of newly published books; [53]
3. That 6 percent of the episodes involved consisted of incestuous rape; [54]
4. The focus on the victim's fear and terror, which became transformed by the rape into sexual passion (over 97 percent of the rapes resulted in orgasm for the victims, in three-quarters of these instances, multiple orgasm was experienced); [55]
5. The fact that less than 3 percent of the rapists experience any negative consequences, and many are rewarded.[56]

Furthermore, Neal Malamuth and Barry Spinner also report that "By 1977 an individual examining the two best-selling erotica magazines (sic) will have been exposed in about 10% of the cartoons and close to 5% of the pictorial stimuli to sexual violence." [57] Later they point out that "the information conveyed in much of the sexually violent materials is that women are basically masochistic and in need of male domination." [58]

First, such pornography makes it seem that a lot of ordinary men commit rape, and that they often suffer no remorse but instead gain sexual, ego, and other gratifications. Hence, men may begin to believe that rape is not a breach of norms. Second, it can make rape appear easy to accomplish and easy to get away with—thus possibly affecting inhibitions due to fears of being caught. Third, and most important, it can inhibit the conscience. If a man can persuade himself that women really *like* being raped, that they don't really mean "no," then what reason is there for guilt?

In this context it is disturbing that even such important and sometimes sensitive research as that done by Neal Malamuth, Seymour Feshbach, and Yoram Jaffe is marred by such thinking. For example, these researchers refer to a depiction of rape that results in orgasm for the woman as a "benign rape." [59] They argue that "if a pleasurable outcome for the victim is a highly potent factor affecting subjects' sexual arousal, then it would seem inappropriate to consider fantasy rape stories as necessarily reflecting hostile aggression . . ." [60] This is a very frightening perspective for researchers to have. We must remember that prior to the "pleasurable outcome" the victim was violently attacked and terrified. Malamuth, Heim, and Feshbach describe the rape-story stimulus as follows:

> The rape versions of the passage began with a description of the woman fighting the advances of the male and trying unsuccessfully to get free. Interspersed throughout the passage were depictions of her being "forcefully crushed," "terrified," "paralyzed," and "forced." Her reactions consisted of "screaming," "panic," "paralysis," and a "frenzy of tears." [61]

How can this be interpreted as a benign or a nonhostile fantasy? The effect of the orgasm at the end of the story is likely to free the rapist (or the person identifying with him) from guilt, to show how powerful he is and how animal-like women are underneath their "pure facades."

Another approach to the question of the effects of pornography is simply to point out that the imitative models that have been established after decades of research apply to pornography too. As Victor Cline writes with some exasperation, after citing several studies in which children and adults imitate "sexual" behaviors after watching another person perform such activities,[62] "Are the laws of learning somehow repealed or inoperative here but not in the rest of life?" [63]

In 1974 Cline, a psychologist, edited a book on pornography entitled *Where Do You Draw the Line?* He deserves to be commended for his strenuous and informed critique of the Commission on Obscenity and Pornography. However, it is as difficult to sift through his biases to find a valid argument or a well-described piece of research as it is to read and evaluate the ten volumes of the commission reports. Whereas the commission's reasoning was that sex is good, sex and pornography are synonymous, therefore pornography is harmless, Cline's reasoning is that sex is bad, sex and pornography are synonymous, therefore pornography is bad. In addition, he is homophobic.

Aside from the application of imitative or observational learning to viewers of pornography, Cline points out that laws of learning referred to as "classical" and "instrumental conditioning" are also highly relevant. For example, he cites work by S. Rachman of the Institute of Psychiatry, Maudsley Hospital, London, who has demonstrated repeatedly that sexual fetishism can be created in the laboratory, using sexually explicit pictures. Rachman

> exposed male subjects to colored photographic slides of nude females in sexually arousing positions along with a picture of female boots. Eventually, through simple conditioning, the male subjects were sexually aroused at merely seeing only the picture of the female boot.[64]

The point is not that such a fetish is necessarily harmful. Ethical considerations constrain researchers from creating more socially harmful sexual behavior in the laboratory. However, a simple application of these same laws of conditioning suggests that when men are sexually aroused by watching pornographic movies or pictures which depict rape, they can come to associate rape with sexual arousal.

Even if men are not sexually excited during the movie, subsequent masturbation to movie images which have included rape reinforces the association, constituting what McGuire and his colleagues refer to as "masturbatory conditioning." [65] The pleasurable experience of masturbation can thereby make the image as well as the act of rape more sexually exciting.

The movie *A Clockwork Orange* dramatized the use of aversive conditioning by the association of electric shocks with pictures of rape. These techniques have been used more frequently to try to get homosexuals to become heterosexual than to change the behavior of rapists. After citing many such studies, Cline concludes that "this literature suggests that erotic materials have great potential power to assist in the shift of sexual orientation when used under certain prescribed conditions. The possibility of deliberate or accidental real-life conditionings in the reverse direction has to be given due consideration here." [66] It seems obvious that if either erotica or pornography can be effectively used to elicit behavioral changes of any kind in a doctor's office, its potential to effect change in other circumstances is thereby also proven.

More recently, Hans Eysenck and D. K. B. Nias have made similar arguments in their book *Sex, Violence and the Media*. After reviewing Rachman's research cited above, they suggest that "the theory of conditioning, combined with the evidence from the above studies, indicates that it might be possible to create a rapist or sadist in the laboratory by presenting scenes of rape or sadism immediately prior to normally arousing scenes." [67]

After an extensive review of the literature on TV violence as well as pornography, Eysenck and Nias conclude that:

> It seems clear to us that there are certain areas of sexual behavior which should be completely excluded from the list of permitted activities [for depiction on film]; sex involving children is one such area, rape and other forms of sexual violence, vividly and explicitly presented, are others. Sex involving animals would probably also come into this category. . . . Torture, bondage and sado-masochistic acts involving sex may also be mentioned here. Such films may perhaps be shown on psychiatric prescription to patients addicted to such perversions, but they are not safe for public showing.[68]

Another justification offered by Eysenck and Nias for their proposal of limited censorship is as follows:

> Where the context is hostile to women, as most pornographic films are, we feel that such films should fall under the category of "incitement to violence towards minority groups"—even though women are not a minority group. Nevertheless such films do constitute a clear case of incitement to maltreat women, downgrade them to a lower status, regard them as mere sex objects, and elevate male *machismo* to a superior position in the scale of values. Evaluative conditioning, modeling, and desensitization all point to the same conclusion, namely that such presentations have effects on men's attitudes which are detrimental to women; in fairness to more than one half of the population, such incitements should be proscribed.[69]

Marvin Wolfgang, a well-known sociologist and one of the authors of *The Report of the Commission on Obscenity and Pornography*, appears to have changed his assessment of pornography's effects. Wolfgang has recently said that "the weight of the evidence (now) suggests that the portrayal of violence tends to encourage the use of physical aggression among people who are exposed to it."[70] At the rally following the march organized by Women Against Pornography in New York, October 20, 1979, Lynn Campbell called for a new government commission which would fund nonsexist research on the effects of pornography, and which could draw up workable proposals for dealing with this serious and growing problem.[71] I believe that a new *Feminist* Commission would help to further substantiate and reaffirm Wolfgang's totally revised assessment, and thereby help to support our campaign against pornography.*

* I would like to express my appreciation to Pat Loomes for her helpful feedback and suggestions on an earlier draft of this paper.

I would also like to thank Women Against Pornography in New York for sending me copies of many important unpublished papers they have gathered for their library.

SECTION V.

Pornography and the First Amendment

Thus far women have been the mere echoes of men. Our laws and constitutions, our creeds and codes, and the customs of social life are all of masculine origin. The true woman is as yet a dream of the future.

—ELIZABETH CADY STANTON
Speech at The International
Council of Women, 1888

Pornography and the First Amendment: Prior Restraints and Private Action

Wendy Kaminer

Wendy Kaminer wrote this article because she found that very few people understand the complex legal process involved in First Amendment cases. A practicing attorney with experience in criminal law and the First Amendment, she was a member of Women Against Pornography and helped draft their position paper on freedom of speech and pornography.

Feminist protests against pornography often seem to posit a choice between the First Amendment rights of a few pornographers and the safety, dignity, and independence of all women. Pornography is speech that legitimizes and fosters the physical abuse and sexual repression of women, and censorship appeals to some as a simple matter of self-preservation. A battle line has been drawn between "feminists" and "First Amendment absolutists," and the Women's Liberation Movement, which has been a struggle for civil rights and freedom of choice, has suddenly become tainted, in the popular view, with a streak of antilibertarianism.

None of this has been necessary. The bitter debate over pornography and free speech derives from misconceptions on both sides about the methods and goals of the anti-pornography movement and the practical meaning of First Amendment guarantees of free speech. Feminists need not and should not advocate censorship, but we have every right to organize politically and to protest material that is degrading and dangerous to women.

There are two basic constitutional principles that must be understood in formulating a position against pornography:

1. Public v. private action. The First Amendment guarantees freedom of speech against government interference and repression. It does not restrict or even apply to private actions.
2. Prior restraint. The government cannot impose restraints

on the publication of speech that has not first been proven illegal. It can only act after the fact to punish someone for saying something illegal; it cannot stop her from saying it.

The First Amendment is a restriction of the power of the government to restrain or repress speech; it establishes a right to free speech in the individual in relation with her government. It does not affect or apply to private relationships; it does not restrict private actions.

Women can protest pornography with impunity under the First Amendment as long as they do not invoke or advocate the exercise of government authority. Only the government, by definition, can violate a First Amendment right. A woman who goes as far as "trashing" a porn shop could be convicted of a variety of offenses under the state criminal law and would probably be liable to the target business in a civil-damage action, but she would not have violated any rights to free speech.

We have our own First Amendment right to protest pornography, to engage in consciousness-raising and political organizing. The First Amendment is designed to maintain an open "marketplace of ideas," an arena in which competing private-interest groups can assert their views free of government repression. Women speaking out against pornography are fulfilling a classic First Amendment role.

The First Amendment applies to government action at the state or federal level. Generally the control of obscenity or pornography in practice is a matter of state law, although there are federal statutes prohibiting interstate, international, or postal traffic in obscene materials.[1] But official regulation of speech at any level is governed by constitutionally mandated rules of legal procedure designed to protect the basic right *to* speak.

The heart of the First Amendment is its procedural safeguards against the imposition of prior restraints on any form of speech. It protects the act of expression, although it may not always protect the substance of what is said. Obscenity may, in principle, be prohibited under state law and is generally treated as a criminal offense. But the government may not restrain or prohibit any material before a judicial determination that it is, in fact, obscene. The government may not, in practice, take any general action, either civil or criminal, against a class of speech; it may only act against an individual utterance *after* it has been proven to fall within an unprotected class or to present an immediate threat to the national security.

Freedom of speech is largely a matter of procedure; the First

Amendment works by narrowly proscribing the power of the government to enforce speech-related prohibitions. Its enforcement process is borrowed from criminal law. All speech is presumed protected until proven otherwise, just as all defendants in criminal cases are presumed innocent until proven guilty. In each case the government bears a heavy burden of proof, and a conviction of guilt or a finding of obscenity depends on the weight of the evidence. Every instance of speech must be judged individually on its own merits before it may be prohibited, just as every criminal defendant must be tried before he may be sentenced.

Obscenity is not, in theory, protected by the First Amendment. In 1957 in *Roth* v. *United States*, 354 U.S. 476, the Supreme Court held that obscenity (like libel) was simply not speech and could be prohibited. But the practical problems of defining obscenity and separating it from protected speech are overwhelming. The current definition of obscenity was enunciated by the Supreme Court in 1973, in *Miller* v. *California*, 413 U.S. 15. It is material "that the average person, applying community standards, would find . . . as a whole, appeals to the prurient interest," material that "depicts or describes, in a patently offensive way, sexual conduct specifically defined by the applicable state law," and material that "taken as a whole, lacks serious artistic, political, or scientific value."

Most hard core pornography would probably be found legally obscene under *Miller* and could therefore be prohibited. But effective, generalized enforcement of obscenity laws is not possible without violating the very basic prohibition of prior restraints.

Every single book, magazine, or film must be proven to be obscene in an individualized judicial proceeding before it may be enjoined. This makes it almost impossible for the government to take any generalized action against businesses that regularly deal in pornography. A bookstore selling allegedly obscene material cannot be closed by the state until every book in it has been found obscene—in court. A store with an inventory of 1,000 books cannot be closed because of 50 or 100 or even 500 obscenity convictions. The state cannot restrain the sale of remaining or future stock that has not been proven obscene and must all be presumed to be protected speech. Broad civil-injunctive relief against pornography-related businesses is barred by the prohibition of prior restraints, regardless of the number of underlying obscenity convictions.*

Even individual convictions for obscenity are difficult to obtain,

* Several jurisdictions have enacted nuisance or "padlock" statutes that provide for the closing of an entire business on the basis of individual obscenity

and the process in each case is complicated by First Amendment procedures. The seizure of any allegedly obscene material for use in a pending trial must be based on a narrowly drawn judicial warrant and cannot completely cut off access to the material. Thus, a district attorney may seize one copy of a book as evidence in a given case, but he cannot prohibit its sale or distribution before a hearing or judicial determination of obscenity. Seizures of material for evidence in obscenity cases must comport with due-process requirements under the First Amendment as well as with Fourth Amendment standards for search and seizure. Obscenity prosecutions are long, costly, and unpredictable and are, necessarily, a piecemeal approach to the problem of pornography.

The attempt to define and control obscenity simply hasn't worked for feminists or First Amendment lawyers. The Court has been struggling with a legal definition for the past twenty years since the current obscenity doctrine was formulated in *Roth*. The definition has undergone relatively minor changes since then, the most important being the shift to local standards of "prurience." In addition, the courts changed the requirement that the work in question be "entirely without redeeming value" to an evaluation of the work "as a whole." These changes have apparently not increased the general number of obscenity prosecutions or the rate of convictions.[2]

Moreover, the current definition of obscenity is conceptually unsound, for it does not set forth a predictable, objective test even for hard-core, sexually explicit material. Instead, it involves a balancing of the social and cultural utility of the material at issue with community standards of prurience. This belies the principle on which it is based: that obscenity can be identified and prohibited.

There is, of course, a good deal of frustration among feminists about ineffective obscenity laws, and a natural concern for developing feasible legal alternatives. It has been suggested that pornography could be readily prohibited because it is dangerous and incites violence against women, based on the "clear and present danger" standard of review traditionally invoked by the Court in free-speech cases. The perception that pornography is dangerous is basic and must be impressed upon the public consciousness, but it does not translate so simply into First Amendment law.

---

violations. These ordinances are unconstitutional under prevailing law because they impose prior restraints on speech, *Universal Amusements* v. *Vance*, 587 F2d. 159 (5th Cir., 1978); aff. 48 LW 4273.

The clear and present danger standard would actually afford greater legal protection to pornography than current obscenity laws. It is a strict standard of review, governing the regulation or prohibition of *protected* speech. It is, arguably, sounder constitutional law than the formulation of obscenity as "nonspeech," and it more accurately reflects a feminist view of pornography as dangerous propaganda, but it would substantially restrict government control over obscene material. The clear and present danger standard is more logically invoked in *defense* of pornography. It was, in fact, unsuccessfully advocated by the defendant in *Roth* v. *United States*, 354 U.S. 476, in which the Court, instead, carved out an obscenity exception to the First Amendment. Feminists who urge the adoption of this standard should understand its legal and political implications. Otherwise they may find themselves unwittingly on the side of the pornographers and First Amendment absolutists.

The clear and present danger standard describes a very narrow exception to the general restriction of government power over protected First Amendment activity. It was formulated to review instances of official repression of political speech: Clear and present danger essentially means an immediate threat to the national security. The standard was first enunciated by the Supreme Court in 1919 after the First World War, to allow for prosecutions for anti-draft pamphleteering under the Espionage Act; it was used in the early 1950's to uphold convictions for allegedly "subversive" speech under the Smith Act; it has recently been invoked unsuccessfully by the government in an attempt to restrain the publication of the Pentagon Papers.[3] It is applied in cases in which the government appears as the "aggrieved party," i.e., in its role as guardian of the national security. Its use in a pornography case would raise an initial problem of identifying a plaintiff; pornography may be a crime against women, but it is not necessarily a crime against the state.

Adoption of a clear and present danger standard to prohibit pornography would be an implicit recognition that it is protected political speech, which would considerably heighten practical problems of proof and enforcement. It is probably easier to prove that a given instance of speech is "obscene" than to prove that it presents "an immediate danger," and the clear and present danger standard imposes a particularly heavy burden of proof on the government. It must demonstrate in every case, with direct factual evidence, a compelling, even overwhelming threat to the national security. This does not mean that the speech at issue might be or could be dangerous, and it does not refer to the cumulative effect of a certain kind of speech. It means a tangible, immediate, and individualized danger that can only be avoided by suppressing publication.

Sociological studies and expert testimony pointing to a connection between pornography generally and violence against women would not establish a clear and present danger in an individual case, as a matter of law. It might not even be properly admissible as evidence. Use of this sort of generalized evidence to demonstrate that a given instance of speech is dangerous would be like trying a defendant in a criminal case with evidence of "similar" crimes committed by "similar" people. Every instance of speech must always be tried on its own merits; restraints could still only be imposed on specific utterances actually found to present an immediate danger. Moreover, a retreat to a clear and present danger standard and the acceptance of pornography as protected speech would actually strengthen these prohibitions against prior restraints.

The final irony is that in politicizing pornography, feminists are unintentionally signaling a need for a return to a more "permissive," clear and present danger standard in obscenity cases. Pornography is being redefined by women in terms of power instead of sex and "prurience"; it is being characterized as dangerous political speech. The courts are being asked to weigh the argued connection of pornography with violence against the underlying right of speech. This is the kind of balancing involved in a clear and present danger case, but again this is the standard applied to protected speech and the strongest restriction of government authority under the First Amendment. By framing pornography as political speech, feminists are, in some respects, legitimizing it in ways that First Amendment absolutists never could.

This does not mean that pornography protests are necessarily counterproductive, but it underscores the need fully to understand the legal process while shaping an effective anti-pornography movement. It makes little sense for feminists to focus on a legal "war" against pornography or to direct much energy to reformulating obscenity prohibitions.

The primary obstacles to effective legal control of pornography are procedural not definitional; it's not so much a matter of the standard that is used to identify unprotected speech in each case (which may change) but the procedures by which they are applied, which must remain constant. We cannot point to a dearth of women judges, prosecutors, or jurors to explain the failure of the system to enforce obscenity laws, because the problem is not in the way in which pornography is perceived but in the ways in which laws must be enforced. We must understand that procedural safeguards cannot be suspended simply to deal with pornography or any other single class of speech. These procedures are meaningless if not applied in every instance, because they are specifically designed to insure a consistent legal process; in First Amendment cases they provide additionally for the narrow enforcement of speech-related regulations, so as not to infringe upon or deter protected activities. The underlying principle of the First Amendment is that the power of the government to regulate speech and political dissent that would derive from a system of prior restraints would be more dangerous than any given instance of unprotected speech.

We simply cannot look to the government to rid us of pornography; legally there are no "final solutions." The feminist movement against pornography must remain an anti-defamation movement, involved in education, consciousness-raising, and the development of private strategies against the industry. We have a crucial role of our own to play in a marketplace in which pornography is flourishing.

But it is essential for us to maintain a larger political perspective and a sense of ourselves as one of many competing private-interest groups. We can and should speak out, and take action against pornographers because they comprise a hostile group with interests antithetical to our own, that threatens our independence and well-being; but we cannot ask the government to speak for us. The Women's Movement is a civil rights movement, and we should appreciate the importance of individual freedom of choice and the danger of turning popular sentiment into law in areas affecting individual privacy.

Legislative or judicial control of pornography is simply not possible without breaking down the legal principles and procedures that are essential to our own right to speak and, ultimately, our freedom to control our own lives. We must continue to organize against pornography and the degradation and abuse of women, but we must not ask the government to take up our struggle for us. The power it will assume to do so will be far more dangerous to us all than the "power" of pornography.

A Political-Legal Analysis of Pornography

Robin Yeamans

One of the major problems feminists confront in attacking pornography is the decision of how, if at all, to use the law. Here, attorney Robin Yeamans gives her view of the way laws are made, and how we should go about getting court action to stop violent pornography. This paper was first delivered at a symposium on pornography in San Jose, California.

The pornography problem arises at a precarious point in our country's history. The far right is delighted to have feminists line up with them to suppress pornography (and by association be identified as opposing sex education, reproductive rights, and other "obscenity" causes of the conservative forces). Yet at the same time, Nazis and other right-wingers are strongly proclaiming their free-speech "rights" (and many liberals are supporting them in this claim). Feminists see an epidemic of violence against women and are determined to stop it, yet we do not want to strengthen the hand of the conservatives by working for legal precedents which may assist them in their goals.

In this complex social context, I define pornography, all of which I believe should be suppressed, as *any use of the media which equates sex and violence*. This is a narrow definition. It would not cover material which is simply degrading to women, but it would ban much "hard-core" material, and it does focus attention on the fact that women want to ban pornography because it promotes violence aganist women.

There are two traditional legal views of pornography: the liberal and the conservative. Greatly simplified, they are as follows: Liberals say that pornography is part of "free speech" and thus is protected by the First Amendment to the United States Constitution.

Conservatives say that the First Amendment does not protect

media expression having to do with sex (which they term "obscene"). Thus, they believe the government can take action against such media without threatening the Bill of Rights.

Neither of these traditional views is acceptable. We must fashion a third approach to the problem. I suggest that we stress the intimate connection between violence and pornography. We are not opposed to sex in the media, but we must stem the tide of violence against women. To do so we must also stem media encouragement of that violence.

Although liberals refuse to control pornography because they believe it to be a form of expression, the truth is that there are many forms of speech which are not allowed or which are closely regulated. For example, libelous speech is not permitted. During wartime, certain kinds of speech are held in close check. Advertising is thoroughly regulated. It is clear that political, legal, and social factors play a large part in decisions made concerning the control of speech. Here is an example with which I am personally familiar:

On October 8, 1977, the Nazis had a demonstration in St. James Park in San Jose, California. I went to the city council and obtained a permit for the Equal Rights Congress to hold a counter-demonstration in the same park in opposition to the Nazis. Although I represented many people who were against the Nazis' right to hold a rally, the city council gave them a permit, arguing that they had to protect their right to "free speech." At the rally some people approached the Nazis (evidently to try to stop them from conducting their activities). The police not only protected the Nazis by standing between them and their opponents, but also by providing a police van to hustle them to safety. This police concern for Nazi safety is in stark contrast to their concern for battered women. It is common knowledge that women who go to the police and the courts and say, "This man is going to hurt me—will you protect me?" get the response, "No. *Until he hurts or kills you,* we cannot do anything."

Until the Nazi rally I believed that the police could not protect battered women. But apparently they can furnish protection to life and limb prior to injury *if they care to do so.* In other words, the police decision not to protect battered women and to protect Nazis is a *political* one.

Indeed, one could say that the wife is often being beaten because of her "free speech." Many wives are beaten while they argue with their husbands. But woman's exercise of speech is not regarded as "free speech," and it is not protected by the police before injury.

Not only is the Nazis' free speech (or more accurately, their right to prepare to commit mass murder) protected, but the rights of the media to show material that encourages violence against women are also protected. The privately owned media are creating and exacerbating a social problem. The rights of the media owners are in direct conflict with the rights of the battered and abused women and children in this country. It is my firm conviction that the rights of media owners are going to have to give way because the right to life and limb is sacred above any other.

There *is* legal precedent to permit lawyers and courts to take the position that pornography—the media equation of sex with violence which directly and indirectly encourages violence against women and children—must stop. Speech soliciting people to commit crimes is not permitted. Pornography is virtually soliciting men to commit crimes of violence (though the solicitation may be termed implicit and not explicit). This is basically the "subliminal sell," and the end product is violence.*

So far the effect of pornography *on all portions* of our society has been impossible to measure. For one thing, social scientists cannot find a control group in the United States which has not been raised on some sort of violence portrayed in the media.

But this problem is a false one. When the courts (which are political bodies) are ready to hear a message, they will hear it. That is why in 1896 the United States Supreme Court could decide in *Plessy* v. *Ferguson* that "separate but equal" facilities for minority persons were constitutionally acceptable, and then fifty-eight years later, in *Brown* v. *Board* (1954), decide that "separate educational facilities are inherently unequal." First the Court found segregation acceptable. Later when the political climate had changed, they did not require *evidence* that segregation hurts. They just said segregation is *"inherently* unequal."

Just as the Court was convinced in the education area, it can and must be convinced in the pornography area. At present the

---

* Ed. Note: A few of the most important cases which set the precedent that soliciting people to commit crimes is not permitted are: California Penal Code 653 Statute 653f: "Every person who solicits another . . . to join in the commission of robbery, burglary, grand theft, receiving stolen property, extortion, rape by force or violence, perjury . . ." Another case to examine is *Silva* v. *Municipal Court for Oakland-Piedmont* (App. 11S, Cal. Rptr. 479) which concerns the statute prohibiting solicitation of another to engage in lewd and dissolute conduct. Although there are no direct legal precedents yet for determining that pornography is speech that solicits criminal acts from men, lawyers can begin to fashion the legal tools to deal with such cases and the accompanying problems, such as definition of the implicit message, etc.

political climate for women's rights is bad and becoming worse. Right now we may not be able to "prove" that pornography is harmful to women. Nevertheless, our undying efforts to do just that will help the courts to see that women's rights must be protected. It is a long process, and education and organization are important parts of that process, as they were in the segregation cases. But when the courts finally make that political decision, we will prevail.

Let's Put Pornography
Back in the Closet

Susan Brownmiller

Susan Brownmiller has been speaking about the censorship of pornography since 1975 when she called for a ban on it in her book *Against Our Will: Men, Women and Rape*. In 1978 she participated in a panel discussion entitled "Pornography and the First Amendment," in which she spoke with conviction about eliminating pornography. In 1979, while organizing a March on Times Square with Women Against Pornography, she put her thoughts on paper in an article that was subsequently published in *Newsday Magazine*. This is a reprint of that article.

Free speech is one of the great foundations on which our democracy rests. I am old enough to remember the Hollywood Ten, the screenwriters who went to jail in the late 1940's because they refused to testify before a congressional committee about their political affiliations. They tried to use the First Amendment as a defense, but they went to jail because in those days there were few civil liberties lawyers around who cared to champion the First Amendment right to free speech, when the speech concerned the Communist Party.

The Hollywood Ten were correct in claiming the First Amendment. Its high purpose is the protection of unpopular ideas and political dissent. In the dark, cold days of the 1950's, few civil libertarians were willing to declare themselves First Amendment absolutists. But in the brighter, though frantic, days of the 1960's, the principle of protecting unpopular political speech was gradually strengthened.

It is fair to say now that the battle has largely been won. Even the American Nazi Party has found itself the beneficiary of the dedicated, tireless work of the American Civil Liberties Union. But—and please notice the quotation marks coming up—"To equate the free and robust exchange of ideas and political debate with commercial exploitation of obscene material demeans the grand conception of the First

Amendment and its high purposes in the historic struggle for freedom. It is a misuse of the great guarantees of free speech and free press."

I didn't say that, although I wish I had, for I think the words are thrilling. Chief Justice Warren Burger said it in 1973, in the United States Supreme Court's majority opinion in *Miller* v. *California*. During the same decades that the right to political free speech was being strengthened in the courts, the nation's obscenity laws also were undergoing extensive revision.

It's amazing to recall that in 1934 the question of whether James Joyce's *Ulysses* should be banned as pornographic actually went before the Court. The battle to protect *Ulysses* as a work of literature with redeeming social value was won. In later decades, Henry Miller's *Tropic* books, *Lady Chatterley's Lover* and the *Memoirs of Fanny Hill* also were adjudged not obscene. These decisions have been important to me. As the author of *Against Our Will*, a study of the history of rape that does contain explicit sexual material, I shudder to think how my book would have fared if James Joyce, D. H. Lawrence and Henry Miller hadn't gone before me.

I am not a fan of *Chatterley* or the *Tropic* books, I should quickly mention. They are not to my literary taste, nor do I think they represent female sexuality with any degree of accuracy. But I would hardly suggest that we ban them. Such a suggestion wouldn't get very far anyway. The battle to protect these books is ancient history. Time does march on, quite methodically. What, then, is unlawfully obscene, and what does the First Amendment have to do with it?

In the Miller case of 1973 (not Henry Miller, by the way, but a porn distributor who sent unsolicited stuff through the mails), the Court came up with new guidelines that it hoped would strengthen obscenity laws by giving more power to the states. What it did in actuality was throw everything into confusion. It set up a three-part test by which materials can be adjudged obscene. The materials are obscene if they depict patently offensive, hard-core sexual conduct; lack serious scientific, literary, artistic or political value; and appeal to the prurient interest of an average person—as measured by contemporary community standards.

"Patently offensive," "prurient interest" and "hard-core" are indeed words to conjure with. "Contemporary community standards" are what we're trying to redefine. The feminist objection to pornography is not based on prurience, which the dictionary defines as lustful, itching desire. We are not opposed to sex and desire, with or without the itch, and we certainly believe that explicit sexual material has its place in literature, art, science and education. Here we part company rather swiftly with old-line conservatives who don't want sex education in the high schools, for example.

No, the feminist objection to pornography is based on our belief that pornography represents hatred of women, that pornography's intent is to humiliate, degrade and dehumanize the female body for the purpose of erotic stimulation and pleasure. We are unalterably opposed to the presentation of the female body being stripped, bound, raped, tortured, mutilated and murdered in the name of commercial entertainment and free speech.

These images, which are standard pornographic fare, have nothing to do with the hallowed right of political dissent. They have everything to do with the creation of a cultural climate in which a rapist feels he is merely giving in to a normal urge and a woman is encouraged to believe that sexual masochism is healthy, liberated fun. Justice Potter Stewart once said about hard-core pornography, "You know it when you see it," and that certainly used to be true. In the good old days, pornography looked awful. It was cheap and sleazy, and there was no mistaking it for art.

Nowadays, since the porn industry has become a multimillion-dollar business, visual technology has been employed in its service. Pornographic movies are skillfully filmed and edited, pornographic still shots using the newest tenets of good design artfully grace the covers of *Hustler*, *Penthouse* and *Playboy*, and the public—and the courts—are sadly confused.

The Supreme Court neglected to define "hard-core" in the Miller decision. This was a mistake. If "hard-core" refers only to explicit sexual intercourse, then that isn't good enough. When women or children or men—no matter how artfully—are shown tortured or terrorized in the service of sex, that's obscene. And "patently offensive," I would hope, to our "contemporary community standards."

Justice William O. Douglas wrote in his dissent to the Miller case that no one is "compelled to look." This is hardly true. To buy a paper at the corner newsstand is to subject oneself to a forcible immersion in pornography, to be demeaned by an array of dehumanized, chopped-up parts of the female anatomy, packaged like cuts of meat at the supermarket. I happen to like my body and I work hard at the gym to keep it in good shape, but I am embarrassed for my body and for the bodies of all women when I see the fragmented parts of us so frivolously, and so flagrantly, displayed.

Some constitutional theorists (Justice Douglas was one) have maintained that any obscenity law is a serious abridgement of free speech. Others (and Justice Earl Warren was one) have maintained that the

First Amendment was never intended to protect obscenity. We live quite compatibly with a host of free-speech abridgements. There are restraints against false and misleading advertising or statements— shouting "fire" without cause in a crowded movie theater, etc.—that do not threaten, but strengthen, our societal values. Restrictions on the public display of pornography belong in this category.

The distinction between permission to publish and permission to display publicly is an essential one and one which I think consonant with First Amendment principles. Justice Burger's words which I quoted above support this without question. We are not saying "Smash the presses" or "Ban the bad ones," but simply "Get the stuff out of our sight." Let the legislatures decide—using realistic and humane contemporary community standards—what can be displayed and what cannot. The courts, after all, will be the final arbiters.

For Men, Freedom of Speech;
for Women, Silence Please

Andrea Dworkin

Shortly after Andrea Dworkin spoke on pornography at a New York University Law School conference in December 1978, *The New York Times* published two editorials (both of which quoted from Dworkin's speech) which characterized feminists as "overwrought" and "strident" and which underlined the First Amendment's protection of offensive expression. Dworkin submitted the following response, but the *Times* refused to publish it. So did *The Washington Post, Newsweek, Mother Jones, The Village Voice, The Nation, The Real Paper*, the *Los Angeles Times* Syndicate, the *New York Times* Syndicate. . . .

A great many men, no small number of them leftist lawyers, are apparently afraid that feminists are going to take their dirty pictures away from them. Anticipating the distress of forced withdrawal, they argue that feminists really must shut up about pornography—what it is, what it means, what to do about it—to protect what they call "freedom of speech." Our "strident" and "overwrought" antagonism to pictures that show women sexually violated and humiliated, bound, gagged, sliced up, tortured in a multiplicity of ways, "offends" the First Amendment. The enforced silence of women through the centuries has not. Some elementary observations are in order.

The Constitution of the United States was written exclusively by white men who owned land. Some owned black slaves, male and female. Many more owned white women who were also chattel.

The Bill of Rights was never intended to protect the civil or sexual rights of women and it has not, except occasionally by accident.

The Equal Rights Amendment, which would, as a polite after-thought, extend equal protection under the law such as it is to women, is not yet part of the Constitution. There is good reason to doubt that it will be in the foreseeable future.

The government in all its aspects—legislative, executive, judicial, enforcement—has been composed almost exclusively of men. Even juries, until very recently, were composed almost entirely of men. Women have had virtually nothing to do with either formulating or

256

applying laws on obscenity or anything else. In the arena of political power, women have been effectively silenced.

Both law and pornography express male contempt for women: they have in the past and they do now. Both express enduring male social and sexual values; each attempts to fix male behavior so that the supremacy of the male over the female will be maintained. The social and sexual values of women are barely discernible in the culture in which we live. In most instances, women have been deprived of the opportunity even to formulate, let alone articulate or spread, values that contradict those of the male. The attempts that we make are both punished and ridiculed. Women of supreme strength who have lived in creative opposition to the male cultural values of their day have been written out of history—silenced.

Rape is widespread. One characteristic of rape is that it silences women. Laws against rape have not functioned to protect the bodily integrity of women; instead, they have punished some men for using women who belong to some other men.

Battery is widespread. One characteristic of battery is that it silences women. Laws against battery have been, in their application, a malicious joke.

There is not a feminist alive who could possibly look to the male legal system for real protection from the systematized sadism of men. Women fight to reform male law, in the areas of rape and battery for instance, because something is better than nothing. In general, we fight to force the law to recognize *us* as the victims of the crimes committed against us, but the results so far have been paltry and pathetic. Meanwhile, the men are there to counsel us. We must not demand the conviction of rapists or turn to the police when raped because then we are "prosecutorial" and racist. Since white men have used the rape laws to imprison black men, we are on the side of the racist when we (women of any color) turn to the law. The fact that most rape is intraracial, and more prosecution will inevitably mean the greater prosecution of white men for the crimes they commit, is supposedly irrelevant. (It is, of course, suddenly very relevant when one recognizes that this argument was invented and is being promoted by white men, significantly endangered for perhaps the first time by the anti-rape militancy of women.) We are also counseled that it is wrong to demand that the police enforce already existing laws against battery because then we "sanction" police entry into the home, which the police can then use for other purposes. Better that rape and battery should continue unchallenged, and the law be used by some men against other men with no reference to the rightful protection of women. The counsel of men is consistent: maintain a proper—and respectful—silence.

Male counsel on pornography, especially from leftist lawyers, has also been abundant. We have been told that pornography is a trivial issue and that we must stop wasting the valuable time of those guarding "freedom of speech" by talking about it. We have been accused of trivializing feminism by our fury at the hatred of women expressed in pornography. We have been told that we must not use existing laws even where they might serve us or invent new ones because we will inevitably erode "freedom of speech"—but that the use of violence against purveyors of pornography or property would not involve the same hazards. Others, less hypocritical, have explained that we must not use law; we must not use secondary boycotts, a civil liberties No-No (since women do not consume pornography, women cannot boycott it by not buying it; other strategies, constituting secondary boycotts, would have to be used); we must not, of course, damage property, nor do we have the right to insult or harass. We have even been criticized for picketing, the logic being that an exhibitor of pornography might cave in under the pressure, which would constitute a dangerous precedent. The men have counseled us to be silent so that "freedom of speech" will survive. The only limitation on it will be that women simply will not have it—no loss, since women have not had it. Such a limitation does not "offend" the First Amendment or male civil libertarians.

The First Amendment, it should be noted, belongs to those who can buy it. Men have the economic clout. Pornographers have empires. Women are economically disadvantaged and barely have token access to the media. A defense of pornography is a defense of the brute use of money to encourage violence against a class of persons who do not have—and have never had—the civil rights vouchsafed to men as a class. The growing power of the pornographers significantly diminishes the likelihood that women will ever experience freedom of anything—certainly not sexual self-determination, certainly not freedom of speech.

The fact of the matter is that if the First Amendment does not work for women, it does not work. With that premise as principle, perhaps the good lawyers might voluntarily put away the dirty pictures (pictures that do dirt to women) and figure out a way to make freedom of speech the reality for women that it already is for the literary and visual pimps. Yes, they might, they could; but they will not. They have their priorities set. They know who counts and who does not. They know, too, what attracts and what really offends.

SECTION VI.

Taking Action

Why is it that men's blood-shedding militancy is applauded and women's symbolic militancy is punished with a prison cell and the forcible feeding horror? It means simply this, that men's double standard of sexual morals, whereby the victims of their lust are counted us outcasts while the men themselves escape all social censure, really applies to morals in all departments of life. Men make the moral code and they expect women to accept it.

—EMMELINE PANKHURST
My Own Story, 1914

"We Sisters Join Together..."

Megan Boler, Robin Lake, and Bridget Wynne

Although the Miss America pageant is not usually thought of as pornographic, it has been a major platform for the reduction of women from full human beings into sexual objects. The pageant epitomizes the all-pervasive sexism in our society. As one of the first anti-Miss America documents stated, "Women [are] forced daily to compete for male approval, enslaved by ludicrous 'beauty' standards we ourselves are conditioned to take seriously. The Pageant . . . attempts to . . . enslave us all the more in high-heeled, low-status roles, to inculcate false values in young girls . . . to seduce us to prostitute ourselves before our own oppression."[1] Furthermore, says the document, Miss America and *Playboy* magazine's centerfold are two of a kind: To win approval, women must have the "Unbeatable Madonna-Whore Combination—we must be sexy but wholesome, delicate yet strong enough to cope, demure yet titillatingly bitchy."[2]

The Miss America pageant is one of our country's biggest celebrations. It is supported by the largest corporations in the nation. It is aired every year on television. The contest has been so successful that dozens of spin-off pageants have been created—Miss Junior America, Miss Universe, Miss World, Miss Farm USA—the list goes on and on. Today females are contestants in new and even more "daring" exposures of the body: Miss Nude America and Miss Wet T-Shirt are two examples. These competitions are so much a way of life that we rarely stop to challenge the concept of a woman walking down a platform nude or in a bathing suit, parading in front of a group of male judges who look over her legs, her breasts, her waist; who compare her bodily measurements with those of other contestants; and who make a choice of the "best" female based primarily on these exterior qualities, just as judges at cat or dog or livestock shows do.

Years ago, before any real objection had been raised to pornography, feminists correctly identified and targeted both the Miss America pageant and *Playboy* magazine as enemies of the true liberation of women. As we mounted the anti-rape movement and launched reproductive-rights campaigns, we also accused both these institutions of generating and perpetuating sexist attitudes toward women. It is fitting that this section begins with a description of the earliest actions by feminists to call attention to media exploitation of women's bodies.

> Men cannot see or accept women as human beings. Sexploitation
> is the turning of women's bodies into *objects* for male satisfac-
> tion. Men exploit women's bodies by rape, pornography, making
> them into bunnies or topless go-goes. . . . Men see women as
> cunts, broads, chicks, bitches, babes, girls, dolls—anything but
> real human beings.[3]

Thus WITCH (Women's International Terrorist Conspiracy From
Hell) expressed their anger at the *Playboy* empire's objectification of
women. During this same era, an *ad hoc* group of feminists were also
launching protests against the exploitation of women inherent in the
Miss America pageants.

> Every day in a woman's life is a walking Miss America contest.
> . . . This mockery of womanhood will be celebrating its 50th
> anniversary September 7–13 [1969] in Atlantic City. . . . This
> year, let's close it down. Women are not cattle. . . .[4]

These expressions of anger were voiced by pioneers in the feminist
struggle against the sexist images of women which continue to assault
us today. The *Playboy* empire and the Miss America pageants were
the two early targets of these protests.

The 1968 Miss America protest was a dramatic exercise of women's
growing power, as well as an impetus for the *Playboy* protests which
followed. Organizers considered their Atlantic City demonstration a
"zap" action to promote awareness of women's oppression as a social
issue. They picketed the pageant in protest of the sexism, racism, and
ageism inherent in the contest, using surprise "guerilla" tactics to dis-
rupt the event. News media across the country reported the feminists'
draping of a Women's Liberation banner over the balcony inside the
pageant auditorium.

The promoters of the 1968 pageant had not been prepared for this
first feminist protest; but the next year found the pageant promoters
wary and defensive. Atlantic City officials and contest sponsors undertook elaborate measures to protect their business investments.
Prepared for a myriad of disruptive maneuvers, police served an in-
junction on each demonstrator as she stepped on the boardwalk to
picket. Buses chartered to bring women to the demonstration suddenly
and mysteriously canceled travel agreements, alluding to unnamed
mechanical failures. Double police barricades were set up.

But the pageant promoters' tactics did not deter the 200 protesters,
who arrived from various eastern cities. Demonstrators put up posters, distributed leaflets, and held a news conference.

The exuberance of the 1968 protest had evolved into more sophisticated organizing techniques. Feminists were now clearly identifying their opponents: "Our enemies are not the women, but those men who make us into 'bunnies' and 'beauty queens,' symbols of a deliberate campaign to denigrate women. Destruction of these institutions of our oppression will be an important step for every woman in this society." [5]

Protesters who were unable to come to Atlantic City during the pageant week of September 7–13 were urged to organize protests at their local *Playboy* Clubs and to write to pageant sponsors and *Playboy* magazine to protest the dehumanizing objectification of women.

Other consciousness-raising tactics erupted across the country. On February 7, 1969, the manager of *Playboy*'s College Promotion Department was expounding the magazine's philosophy to about seventy-five Grinnell College students, when ten people suddenly invaded the room, distributed literature, proclaimed "*Playboy* is the money changer in the temple of the body," and removed their clothes. This "nude-in" received national coverage.

On Easter Eve, 1970, more than fifty demonstrators with banners and toy bunnies appeared at the Boston *Playboy* Club. Several weeks later in March, twenty men marched into an MIT fraternity conference held at the Boston *Playboy* Club, chanting, "Free our sisters, free ourselves!" New Yorkers protested in May with an all-day demonstration against the New York *Playboy* Club, and San Francisco feminists joined the nationwide movement with a demonstration at the local *Playboy* Club, protesting *Playboy*'s control over the lives of women and men.

Women expressed their anger in other, quieter ways as well. In December the Michigan Women's Liberation Coalition exhibited the "Mr. April" centerfold from *off our backs* (a Women's Liberation newspaper) as part of a Women's Week shopping-mall display. The Oakland Mall's public relations manager demanded that "Mr. April" be removed immediately, but "Mr. April" was absent only until a sister replaced the modest photographs, not having heard about the request. The manager then threatened to dispose of the entire "lib" display if "Mr. April" was not permanently removed. The December issue of the Women's Liberation Coalition newsletter pointed out that "apparently the Oakland Mall management finds nothing wrong in the use of women's bodies in various stages of nudity to sell items and entice the public, but finds the similar use of a man extremely distasteful." [6]

As women protested their objectification by the advertising industry, others accelerated the war against *Playboy*. Chicago, the national headquarters of *Playboy* Clubs and home of empire-builder Hugh Hefner, was the target of an April 15, 1970, protest launched by the Chicago Women's Liberation Union. A vigorous, chanting picket line, maintained by 200 to 300 Women's Liberation Union members and supporters, protested outside the *Playboy* mansion throughout the night. The date was chosen because the mansion was being used that evening by the Vietnam War Moratorium Committee for a benefit. The benefit attendees, most of whom were liberal and affluent, did not see the absurd contradiction between opposing oppression in Southeast Asia and supporting sexism at home. Although many dismissed the pickets as "cute" or seemed to feel personally affronted by the protesters, several guests honored the picket line and departed amidst loud cheers from picketers. One notable incident was the appearance of a platinum-blond *Playboy* bunny in an upstairs window flashing a clenched-fist salute. She was filmed by television cameras before being whisked away by *Playboy* staffers.

Hefner himself was confronted by vocal feminists within his slick organization, as well as by protesters chanting in the streets. Trouble for Hefner began brewing in September 1969, when journalist Susan Braudy was commissioned to write an account of the emerging Women's Liberation Movement for *Playboy* magazine. As outlined by *Playboy*'s editor, the article was to be a fair, objective, nonjudgmental description "in a tone that is amused but never snide." [7] But Hefner had something quite different in mind. In a confidential memo distributed to his staff, he delineated *his* objectives for the Women's Liberation article. The infamous memo read:

> These chicks are our natural enemy. . . . It is time we do battle with them. . . . What I want is a devastating piece that takes the militant feminists apart. They are unalterably opposed to the romantic boy-girl society that *Playboy* promotes. . . . Let's get to it and make it a real winner. [8]

But Braudy refused to make the corrections demanded by the Hefner-controlled staff, and her article was never published. What *Playboy* did publish was a story entitled "Up Against the Wall, Male Chauvinist Pig" about the most radical members of the Women's Liberation Movement. The article's author, Morton Hunt, gallantly relegated the Women's Liberation Movement to the "discard pile of history."

Braudy later related her frustration with the *Playboy* editorial staff in a May 1979 issue of *Glamour* magazine:

> Lehrman [the editor] wanted me to agree to describe only the radical feminists as representing the movement. I wouldn't. He kept saying, "I told them they shouldn't have gotten a writer with ideological hang-ups. You have hang-ups." [9]

Playboy's journalistic attempt to discredit and undermine the Women's Liberation Movement backfired when the above memo from Hefner was reprinted by news publications throughout the nation. This episode did much to stimulate feminist rage and publicly validate feminist contentions. The memo was discovered and disclosed by Shelley Schlicker, a *Playboy* Club secretary and a bold contributor to the Women's Liberation Movement. Not surprisingly, she was fired shortly after her disclosure of Hefner's memo. She immediately joined her sisters in their demonstration. Interviewed while picketing outside her former place of employment, she told reporters: "Hefner has made millions selling this air-brushed image of women to insecure men who are taught to want a playful pet rather than a person. But it won't work. We will no longer sell ourselves in return for a pair of ears and a tail and a condescending pat on the behind." [10] She added that two other secretaries had previously been fired for refusing to type the anti-Women's Liberation article.

In April 1970 Dick Cavett held a "get together" on his television show for Hugh Hefner, psychiatrist Rollo May, and feminists Sally Kempton and Susan Brownmiller. Liberation News Service printed an article on April 29 about this debate, in which Claudia Dreifus wrote:

> At last . . . the exotic specimens were brought forth: two liberated women. . . . When Cavett naïvely asked Susan why she thinks Hefner is her enemy, Susan responded that the man exploits and degrades women for a profit. Hef was offended. Susan asked him if he would like to walk around girdled into an absurd costume with a cotton tail stuck to his ass! The necessity for an answer was averted, because just about then the show ran out of time. [11]

The reality of women's exploitation is perpetually evaded, overlooked, and ignored by male exploiters, not the least of whom is Hugh Hefner. If he had answered truthfully, he would have been admitting that this painful degradation is so oppressive that of course he wants no part of the other end of it—the women's end. But he didn't answer the question.

Looking back on these events from the present when we are faced with magazines like *Hustler*, movies like *The Story of O*, and "snuff" films, Hefner and his *Playboy* empire seem comparatively mild. Current pornography is so violent it understandably has distracted us from our war against *Playboy*. But we must remember that it was exploitive images of women such as those promoted by Hefner that laid the groundwork for today's atrocities in pornography and media. Hefner still represents our essential opponent, oppressor, and enemy. We must continue to fight the objectification of women. Women are not "cunts, broads, bunnies, chicks, bitches, babes, girls, dolls." We are human beings and must not allow ourselves to be oppressed and exploited in any way, for any purpose. Indeed,

> We sisters join together to fight you, your *Playboy* Empire, and everything you represent, and we shall build instead a society in which women and men are free to relate to each other as equal human beings of dignity and worth.[12] *

---

* Special thanks to Kathleen Barry for the use of her personal files on the *Playboy* demonstration and the Miss America protests. Thanks also to the University of Wyoming History Archives for the use of their file on the protest against *Playboy*.

"Women Have Seized the Executive Offices of Grove Press Because..."

Laura Lederer

While women in Atlantic City picketed the Miss America pageant and women in Chicago targeted the *Playboy* empire, feminists in New York City were fighting another battle against pornography, this time on the left.

During a unionization struggle against Grove Press bosses, feminists attacked the publishing house for the pornographic literature it was turning out alongside its more radical titles. The sit-in that evolved out of this action is important because it was a manifestation of the growing split between the male radical movement and feminists, and the beginning of a new "second wave" of feminism. Women's recognition that our energies were being used for typing and secretarial work while we were denied the more serious decision-making jobs in the movement dovetailed with our recognition that our bodies were also being used by the self-styled "radical" media to sell books and make money. As usual, those making the profits were white males.

"I had been working at Grove Press as an editor for two and a half years when, in the spring of 1970, four other employees and I were summarily fired," says Robin Morgan. "The reason officially given was 'reorganization needs,' but the real motive for the firings was punishment for the sin of trying to organize a union. Grove Press had built a facade reputation as a left-liberal, avant-garde publisher, but much of its output consisted of sexist paperbacks which objectified women. I had refused to work on these, restricting my editorial duties to the political books, but I could not ignore the unequal treatment of women employees (from editor to janitor) all around (and including) me."

Many feminists had been angry about the sexism of the books published at Grove Press, but, in deference to the women who worked there, had held off taking any action. When Robin and several other women were fired, they moved in and joined forces with the union organizers. While union activists agitated for a union in Grove Press, feminist activists attacked the slick pornography which had been passing for leftist-intellectual coffee-table material. Books like *I Am Curious Yellow* and *Crimson Hairs: An Erotic Mystery Story* had cover illustrations of nude women's bodies à la *Playboy* magazine, and were published alongside *The Autobiography of Malcolm X* and *Che Guevara in Bolivia*.

Morgan says that the 1970 action against Grove Press was "the first . . . militant move taken in the current feminist wave. It was . . . the first time since the days of the suffrage fight that women were arrested in a purely feminist cause. It was the first time the liberal realm of publishing had been attacked by women, and it was the first time feminists openly declared pornography as an enemy."

It happened like this: In the midst of the organizing efforts concerning jobs, salaries, editorial decision-making power, and other issues, Barney Rosset, owner of Grove Press and its *Evergreen Review* subsidiary, waved an article from the *San Francisco Chronicle* in a woman editor's face. The article was entitled "A Feminist Takes on the Evergreen," and was written by West Coast feminist Ellen Smith Mendocino. It began:

> *Evergreen Review*, the slick magazine for New Left intellectuals, has one thing in common with *Playboy*, it seems to me: it exploits women in order to sell copy. While putting down the ethos of middle class commercialism in its articles and fiction, *Evergreen* turns around and sells itself by the worst sort of pandering to that ethos.

Rosset was enraged by the article. "Robin Morgan was behind this article, wasn't she?" he demanded of the woman editor. In fact, Morgan had never before heard of or seen the article. But Rosset believed that the union organizing at Grove Press was a front for the Women's Liberation Movement. That Friday, six Grove Press employees (including Morgan) received telegrams enclosing checks of severance pay that stated: "Because of reorganization in the editorial department, we have found it necessary to terminate your employment."

On Monday, April 13, Robin Morgan and over thirty women walked into Grove Press and occupied the executive office. Union organizers held a rally outside. The women inside held a press conference and issued a set of demands which included reparations from

Grove Press for the damage it did to women by publishing porno-graphic books. The feminist occupiers intended to stay put until Barney Rosset spoke with them, but the police were called, and that afternoon the women were arrested.. They were driven to the station, fingerprinted and booked, and (because night court was over) thrown into jail for the night. There they were searched, stripped, and given internal examinations under the pretext of search-ing for drugs.

Morgan says that in strategic terms the feminist occupation of Grove Press was a success. "The punishment was comparatively light, the results rewardingly vengeful. Not only the Women's Movement, but much of the left supported the feminist action." Boycotts of Grove Press books, both by individuals and by radical bookstores, became commonplace. "Many leading left journalists and theorists severed their publishing associations with Grove Press. Ultimately, this action was the fuse that ignited, years later, the feminist move-ment against pornography." The following is an abridged reprint of the demands feminists made when they occupied Grove Press.

Women Have Seized the Executive Offices of Grove Press Because:

Grove Press and its subsidiaries, *Evergreen Review*, Grove Films, and other corporate enterprises, have earned millions off the basic theme of humiliating, degrading, and dehumanizing women through sadomasochistic literature, pornographic films, and oppressive and ex-ploitive practices against its own female employees. (For example, women employees are fired for their political beliefs and are denied medical benefits for their children.)

WE CHARGE GROVE PRESS WITH THE ABOVE CRIMES AGAINST WOMEN

In self-defense, we women are holding the Grove offices in trust until we are guaranteed the following just conditions:

1. All publication of books and magazines, and all distribution of films that degrade women must be stopped immediately.

2. Barney Rosset must open *all* his personal and corporate finan-cial books and records to our examination and that of our women lawyers—and to Grove Press authors and stockholders—to effect complete disclosure of Rosset's financial arrangements. And, on the basis of this disclosure, we demand that the profits go to the following:

—twenty-four-hour-a-day free child-care centers to be controlled by the women who use them.

—a training program for Black, brown, and poor white women controlled by these same groups to prepare themselves as they see fit for jobs other than the kind they now hold at Grove Press; for example, cleaning women and secretaries.

—a fund for recently divorced and widowed women to help them get back on their feet.

—a fund to establish free abortion and birth-control clinics which would be controlled by women in their own communities.

Furthermore:

—the millions of dollars of profits from *The Autobiography of Malcolm X* must go to the Black community to be distributed by the Black women of that community. The shockingly small royalties now paid to Betty Shabazz and her children must be quadrupled.

— the millions of dollars of profits on books written by Latin and South American revolutionaries, such as Guevara, Castro, and Debray, must go to the people of the Spanish-speaking community to be distributed by the women in that community.

3. The profits from Venus Books, Zebra Books, and Black Cat Books (the hard core of Grove's pornographic subsidiaries) must *all* go to those women who are the *special* victims of this propaganda, by the following means:

—a bail fund to free each month a minimum of one hundred political prisoners (most of whom are prostitutes) from the Women's House of Detention.

—a fund to meet the needs, medical and otherwise, of those women who have been raped and/or assaulted.

4. A company-wide cooperative must be established to end "one-dirty-old-man-rule" at Grove Press. Women must control 51 percent of all decisions, editorial and otherwise.

WE WOMEN INTEND TO HOLD THE GROVE PRESS OFFICES UNTIL THESE FEMINIST DEMANDS ARE MET!

Barney Rosset must negotiate with the employees' union.

No more business-as-usual for Grove Press and *Evergreen* magazine!

No more using of women's bodies as filth-objects (both Black and white) to sell a phony radicalism-for-profit to the middle-American-white-male!

No more using of women's bodies to rip off enormous profits for a few wealthy capitalist dirty old straight white men, such as Barney Rosset!

No more using of women as shit-workers to produce material that degrades them; no more underpaid, demeaning, degrading work for anyone!

No more scapegoating of women for daring to demand the rights and respect that are—for any human being—inalienable!

No more wearing of a radical mask by these exploiters to cover the sexist leer, the racist smirk, the boss-man's frown!

No more peddling of Grove movies that offer nudity as "sexual liberation," but present women as "hung up" and men as "liberated," and that force women to act out their bestialized oppression while the whole world is watching!

No more financing of male-left radicals in cushy life-styles by selling their hypocritical radicalism to *Evergreen* for lots of money—a magazine that with *Playboy* is one of the heaviest anti-woman propaganda machines in the country.

No more male radicals who can ignore the oppression of women— as sex objects, as workers, as union organizers, as feminists, as radicals, as revolutionaries, as socialists—and continue to reap profits based on the degradation of women.

Snuff—*The Ultimate in Woman-Hating*

Beverly LaBelle

Following the first feminist anti-pornography actions in the early seventies, organizing ceased. More serious and crucial battles (or so it seemed at the time) were being fought in the arenas of reproductive rights (birth control, abortion, self-help health care) and crisis intervention (against crimes of sexual violence such as rape and woman-battery). During this five-year period the pornography industry grew, unchallenged by women. Slowly the so-called "pretty porn" of the earlier *Playboy* days changed, became more anti-woman, more exploitive, and finally more violent. New magazines like *Hustler* and *Penthouse* appeared on the racks; X-rated movies like *Deep Throat* and *Emanuelle* were released to "legitimate" theaters, with some small murmurs of upset here and there but generally without protest.

In 1976 a film surfaced which was to change all that: *Snuff*. Billed as a movie which recorded the real murder of an actress for male sexual stimulation, it attracted hundreds of eager men at X-rated and neighborhood theaters around the country. As word of the movie spread, feminists were shocked into action. *Snuff* was the powder keg that moved women seriously to confront the issue of pornography. This important article recounts the plot of *Snuff* and relates some of the main battles fought by *ad hoc* feminist groups across the country. Its author, Beverly LaBelle, attended the film and later helped to organize against it.

Snuff is the name of a highly publicized movie which purports to show the actual murder and dismemberment of a young woman. It achieved notoriety because of the carnage of its final five-minute sequence.

The film first surfaced in 1975 shortly after the New York City Police Department announced that they had confiscated several "underground" South American pornographic films containing actual murder footage. These films were given the name "snuff" films because the actresses were murdered (snuffed out) in front of the

cameras in order to excite the jaded sexual palates of a select pornography audience that requires death rather than mere sex as an
aphrodisiac. The curiosity of the regular pornography market was
whetted by this police discovery, and the idea of a commercialized
"snuff" film was born.

The scenario revolves around a South American cult that is dominated by a man named Satan. All his followers are lovely young
women who are willing to rob, beat, and murder at his command.
Before joining this select cult, each woman must undergo an initiation
of torture in order to seal her commitment to Satan. There is a small
amount of rhetoric about killing the rich in revenge for the sufferings
of the poor, but this minor theme never achieves prominence and was
obviously added in an attempt to justify the violence of the film. The
cult also holds some confusing occult beliefs similar to those depicted
in Saturday afternoon "horror" films. However, the producer did hope
to draw a parallel between Satan's devotees and Charles Manson's
"family." The similarities between these two groups are too numerous
and too obvious to be mere coincidences. Undoubtedly the image of
Charles Manson as a new prototype of sex and violence was deliberately emulated in *Snuff*.

The plot is fuzzy, but eventually it becomes clear that the cult is
planning a ritual slaughter to avenge both the suffering poor and the
demon god of their "religion." The band of mystics proceeds to murder a number of random people, none of whom appear to be members
of the elite classes. In one scene a cult member revenges herself upon
her ex-lover by castrating him with a razor. The actual cutting is not
shown—just scenes of his face contorted by agony. Perhaps the director felt that this scene of a man being destroyed by a woman would
be too repellent for his male audience to depict graphically. After that
gruesome scene, the blood-crazed devotees prepare for the long-
awaited sacrifice of their "perfect victim," an unborn child ready to
burst forth from the womb of a beautiful, blond woman (the reincar-
nation of Sharon Tate, no doubt). First they shoot her wealthy lover,
and then they surround the bed where she lies, cowering in fear, with
her enormous stomach protruding beneath the satin sheets. The dagger is held high in an invocation to the "powers of evil" and then
plunged savagely into her stomach, which explodes with the sounds
of gushing blood and gurgling amniotic fluid.

Then silence for a moment before the camera pulls back, and we
see the production crew of the film talking about the success of that
final scene. A pretty young blond woman who appears to be a production assistant tells the director how sexually aroused she was by

the stabbing finale. The attractive director asks her if she would like to go to bed with him and act out her fantasies. They start fumbling around in bed until she realizes that the crew is still filming. She protests and tries to get up. The director picks up a dagger that is lying on the bed and says, "Bitch, now you're going to get what you want." What happens next goes beyond the realm of language. He butchers her slowly, deeply, and thoroughly. The observer's gut re-vulison is overwhelming at the amount of blood, chopped-up fingers, flying arms, sawed-off legs, and yet more blood oozing like a river out of her mouth before she dies. But the climax is still at hand. In a moment of undiluted evil, he cuts open her abdomen and brandishes her very insides high above his head in a scream of orgasmic conquest. The End . . . Fade into blackness. There are no credits listed in the final moments of the film.

Snuff was one of the very first pornographic films to elicit strong protest from the feminist sector of the population. It marked the turning point in our consciousness about the meaning behind the countless movies and magazines devoted to the naked female body. *Snuff* forced us to stop turning the other way each time we passed an X-rated movie house. It compelled us to take a long, hard look at the pornography industry. The graphic bloodletting in *Snuff* finally made the misogyny of pornography a major feminist concern.

Across the country wherever the movie appeared, feminists mobi-lized to protest the showing. In San Diego at the end of September 1977, a feminist noticed *Snuff* playing in a local theater. An im-promptu telephone tree notified women from feminist groups, com-munity groups, and church groups, and a meeting was called that night at The Women's Store. There women discussed tactics and decided to picket the movie house the following night. Here is what happened, excerpted from a letter written to *New Woman's Times*:

> About forty women showed up the next night ½ hour before the first showing of the film. We made a circle and walked in front of the theater chanting "Stop *Snuff* Now!" and "This is violence to women." We passed out flyers (which we had printed up that day) to people coming out of the supermarket and other nearby stores. In addition, we were able to get our point across to many people in the city because several TV stations arrived to cover the picket. One of the stations, Channel 8, sensationalized the movie and interviewed the theater owners and moviegoers much longer than they did us; but the other stations gave good

balanced coverage which brought home the issue of violence to women.

Two hours after we began picketing, our action was proving successful: no one was entering the theater. We marched for five hours. Before we left the theater we talked with the manager to see if they were going to stop showing *Snuff*. He said they were getting so much publicity that it would be held over for another week. We said we would be back the next night.

When we returned the following night, the movie had been changed. We assume this was a direct result of the community pressure we brought to bear in our ad hoc organizing against *Snuff*. Our last action was a trip to *The San Diego Union*, the city newspaper. We received assurance from the publisher that they would not advertise *Snuff* if it came to another San Diego theater.[1]

Denver, Colorado, was the scene of another *Snuff* protest:

The women's community of Denver, Colorado protested the attempted showing of *Snuff*. Two of us organized a mass telephone campaign to the theater chain, constantly harassing the owner. We distributed leaflets throughout the community and the neighborhood where the theater was located. Then we made a plea to the Denver district attorney, Dale Tooley, who (because it was near election time) banned the movie and took all the credit for it.

We showed up at the theater before we knew the movie had been banned, prepared to protest the film or interrupt the showing, but we did not have to—our pressure on the D.A. had brought results.[2]

In New York City when *Snuff* was first screened at a movie house off Times Square, it came at a time when there was considerable publicity being given to privately released pornographic films showing actual rape and murder. The films were being offered at private screenings reportedly for prices ranging from $100 to $500 a person.[3] Here *Snuff* attracted daily picketing by feminists, which touched off a lengthy dispute over constitutional rights of freedom of expression. Here is an excerpt from the leaflets which feminists distributed in New York City:

Why Are We Here? We are opposed to the filming, distribution, and mass marketing of the film *Snuff* currently showing around the clock at the National Theater in New York City. The term "snuff" has been used in the underground film circle to label those pornographic films depicting actual, cold-blooded murder of women. Purportedly a film of this type was produced in Buenos Aires, Argentina and in this film a real woman was murdered. It is implied in advertisements of the film currently showing that this may be the same film.

Whether or not the death depicted in the current film *Snuff* is real or simulated is not the issue.* That sexual violence is presented as sexual entertainment, that the murder and dismemberment of a woman's body is commercial film material is an outrage to our sense of justice as women, as human beings.

Women and other persons of conscience will demonstrate at Manhattan District Attorney Robert Morgenthau's offices to protest his refusal to recognize the clear and present danger of a film in this borough which purports to be a photographic recording of a woman's actual torture and murder.

A telegram signed by many prominent citizens in the arts, the clergy, and social services to petition the removal of this film has received no response from the D.A. Neither has he responded to the continuous demonstrations in front of the National Theater nor the hundreds of phone calls received by numerous city officials.†

"Pickets sell tickets" said Allan Shackleton, the man who did the distribution and advertising for *Snuff*. Shackleton told reporters that he was "out to make money, and to be noticed by the motion picture industry." He also said that he had several offers to make sequels to *Snuff*.[4]

Pickets, phone calls, and demonstrations at the district attorney's office in New York City brought no action against the movie, but in other cities around the country, such as Buffalo, Los Angeles, and San Jose, *Snuff* left town early after mobilization by women's groups.

One last series of events in Monticello, New York, is worth reporting. When *Snuff* came to Monticello, a protest was organized by NOW and the local chapter of WAVAW (Women Against Violence Against Women). More than 150 people attended the first perfor-

* Ed. Note: Women were very concerned about the possible real death of a female in the filming of *Snuff*, but when film distributors denied it was a "real" woman who was murdered, feminists quickly moved to state that the murder of one woman was only the first of many concerns we had about "snuff" films.
† Leaflet distributed by a New York City *ad hoc* feminist group against *Snuff*. The contact was Leah Fritz, the well-known feminist writer and journalist.

mance of the movie. The audience was a mixed group of all ages (the minimum legal age was eighteen for an X-rated film).

Three women, led by Jane Verlaine of Monticello, made a complaint to the police after the first performance, based on the fact that the film's promotion of the murder of women was sexually stimulating. Here are the events that followed this showing of *Snuff*, taken from the daily accounts by *The Times Herald Record*, a Monticello daily newspaper:

> THURSDAY, MARCH 11, 1976:
> About 40 demonstrators peacefully protested here against the showing of *Snuff*, a motion picture depicting the disembowelment of women. The protestors, including a handful of men, marched in front of the Rialto Theatre. They carried placards including the inscriptions, "Snuff kills women—zap it" . . . Jane Verlaine . . . one of the protest leaders . . . made a complaint to Monticello police after the first performance. The complaint was based on grounds (that) the film's promotion "advertises and advocates murder of women as sexually stimulating." They related portions of the film to police. Sgt. Walter Ramsay, while recording the complaint, said D.A. Emanuel Gellman advised him, "As it stands now, there is no basis for a complaint." Gellman explained that he cannot take action against theatre owner Richard Dames because "There is no place we can go if violence is the only complaint." The only time he can act, he said, is if the complaint is based on pornography. He said he does not believe pornography is involved in this instance.[5]

On Friday, March 12, the women took their complaint to District Attorney Emanuel Gellman, and on Sunday they filed a criminal information. Richard Dames, owner of the theater in question, was charged with second-degree obscenity and ordered to appear in court. Women Against Violence Against Women hired a lawyer, and both sides squared off for a fight.

What followed was a series of delays and court misunderstandings. The defense submitted a motion for dismissal, and the court was adjourned for three weeks; the court required that WAVAW subpoena the film for court viewing. When WAVAW lawyer Andrea Moran did so, the subpoena was quashed the night before the trial. The next day the judge dismissed the case for insufficient evidence: WAVAW did not have a copy of the film. Moran protested this "Catch-22," and the case was appealed. In the meantime ten months passed, but finally in late December 1977, this news clipping appeared in the local paper:

Wednesday, December 16, 1977:
County Court Judge Louis B. Scheinman has reversed a Village Court decision and ordered a trial on obscenity charges for theatre owner Richard Dames in connection with the showing of the film *Snuff* in Monticello in March 1976.

The decision was a victory for the feminist group, Women Against Violence Against Women, which has been seeking prosecution on the grounds that the film, which shows the simulated murder and dismemberment of women, is an incitement to acts of violence against women. . . .

Attorney Moran said Tuesday she was very happy with Scheinman's decision, calling it a "real victory for decency." [6] *

* Ed. Note: After this decision the attorney for Richard Dames contacted Andrea Moran. An agreement was made that Dames would publicly apologize to all women for showing *Snuff*, and that the women would then drop charges. Following this agreement, Richard Dames disappeared. At this printing the case has not yet been concluded.

Fighting Pornography

Martha Gever and Marg Hall

In Rochester, New York, women came together to fight *Snuff* and other pornographic movies in their communities, but found that *ad hoc* organizing efforts were not enough. They discovered that if they forced one movie out of town, another appeared at a theater down the street. If they succeeded in closing down that theater, they still had to face the magazine racks filled with pornography at their local grocery stores. When they opened their daily papers to the entertainment section, they were confronted with ads for pornographic movies, live sex shows, exploitive magazines. It was clear that continuing action was needed.

"Fighting Pornography" was written for this book by two members of Rochester Women Against Violence Against Women, a group of women who met at an *ad hoc* demonstration and stayed together to become one of the most effective anti-pornography organizations in the country.

Playing Soon: **Penetration.** *Unbelievably violent . . . graphic . . . a double turn-on. He always hurts the one he loves. Some women deserve it.*

A group of about ten women, many of them strangers, met one summer afternoon in 1976 to discuss possible strategies to stop a local movie theater from showing *Penetration*. We decided to create our own poster with our own message—to alert the community to the true meaning of the advertisement for the movie. Our message read: "The Monroe Theater's movie promotes rape. *No* women deserve it." Their obscene poster was removed; the movie was never shown.

This action against a pornographic movie marked the beginning of an active feminist group in Rochester—a group committed to exposing rapist culture and to identifying pornography as another weapon used to perpetuate women's slavery. Many of us had avoided confronting this cornerstone of male culture, and, like most women, we were virtually ignorant about pornography. When we looked more closely, we noticed the direct verbal and visual threats and the theme of violence common in pornographic movies and magazines. As a result of political actions and extensive discussion with women we have learned a great deal—about the meaning and function of pornography and about women's need to destroy it. And we are still learning.

After our almost instantaneous success against *Penetration*, our informal group disbanded. Many of the same women came together the following spring, however, for a spontaneous feminist media campaign. We redecorated Rochester with large, colorful, silk-screened posters produced for various holidays: "Smash Patriarchy" for International Women's Day, "Child Bearing Is Slave Labor" for Mother's Day, "Lesbian Pride" to mark Gay Pride Week (during the height of Anita Bryant's crusade in Dade County), "Smash Patriarchy" again for Father's Day. That summer we also printed signs reading, "Woman Hating Propaganda Sold Here," which were pasted on stores and movie theaters selling "men's entertainment." Seeking to stir public consciousness, we saw these posters as provocative, and hoped to generate awareness and discussion of feminist concerns. Word of our nocturnal postering expeditions spread; women drawn to unorthodox feminist activity met each other.

The public display of radical feminist messages encouraged extended conversations about women, media, propaganda, censorship, violence against women—and our legal rights. We had always regarded freedom of speech as a given and unquestionable right, and we found ourselves contradicting this freedom for pornographers. Our thinking was clarified somewhat when we considered the denial of free speech to women and the exclusion of women's voices in practically all popular culture. Furthermore, these thoughts were confirmed by our experience. In 1977 *A Boy and His Dog*, a film which concludes with the cannibalization of a woman by the boy and dog referred to in the title, played at the University of Rochester. When women distributed leaflets pointing to the misogyny of the movie, especially in the final scene, men at the university declared this a case of "censorship," and the debate began. The effects of this controversy extended far beyond the university campus—the brutalization of women would not be silently tolerated; the fact of feminist resistance became known in Rochester.

When a movie called *Nazi Love Camp* came to Rochester in June 1977, the radio ads promised "Women beaten, women tortured, and more . . . Come see *Nazi Love Camp*." Again women met and discussed strategy. We decided to picket one theater, a drive-in, that evening. Within five minutes of our arrival, sheriff's deputies informed us that we would have to leave—for our own safety. Since there was no sidewalk, they told us, we might be hit by a passing car and be injured. When we questioned this order, we were threatened with arrest. Although our action was legal, we realized that our civil rights were irrelevant to the police. Persistence would lead to jail. In spite of our outrage, most of the women who went to the drive-in that night were not willing to risk arrest. Several women had children, and many had commitments which could not be postponed or ignored. Also, underlying our decision to obey orders was a fear of the unknown— we did not know if our protests against this movie would be defended by other women or if, instead, we would appear ridiculous. The police effectively intimidated us. We left.

The next day, a smaller group—five women—formed a picket line outside another theater showing *Nazi Love Camp*, one housed in a Holiday Inn in downtown Rochester. Before we arrived, someone had painted, "Their Profit, Our Blood. This Movie is a CRIME Against Women" on the side of the building. Again the police were called and our names, addresses, and ages dutifully written down, but we refused to leave. One woman was searched illegally. Another woman was threatened by a theater employee while a police officer listened. Our cynicism and our militancy grew.

Through feminist newspapers we learned about *Snuff* and its extreme brutality; we also learned that feminists in other cities had protested this movie. In October 1977 *Snuff* came to Rochester and played at the Holiday Cine theater, and we quickly organized a picket line there. A few of us felt discouraged when the demonstration ended, and no one had made plans to continue the protest. We also doubted that mere picketing would be effective. While carrying signs and chanting slogans in public was a new experience for some, as well as a departure from traditionally female, "ladylike" behavior, this action seemed too mild, almost passive, considering the violent and threatening nature of *Snuff*. Our instinct with this film, as in the past, was to use a direct approach. We never seriously considered appealing to men in power to intervene on our behalf (for example, asking the district attorney to ban the movie). We preferred tactics which might undermine rather than reinforce the legitimacy of their authority. Also, established methods worked too slowly. The situation was urgent—the theater held "continuous showings daily" of a movie that was characteristically different from other pornography in that it went farther than ever before.

We read on the poster: "The Bloodiest Thing that Ever Happened in Front of a Camera." We saw displayed on Main Street a woman's body cut into pieces by a pair of bloody scissors. This was how they advertised *Snuff*. It seemed appropriate to destroy that poster; it was the least we could do. The next morning four of us went to the theater, spray-painted the doors and chained them shut, put glue in the locks, broke the display window, and ripped up the poster. We were then arrested by plainclothes police, who had been told by a "confidential informant" that some kind of "overt action" was going to happen at the theater. (We learned this months later when our lawyers obtained access to the file in the district attorney's office.) During our brief stay in jail, many more women learned of *Snuff*. The protests intensified. A large sit-in was planned but never carried out, since the movie left town ten days early. We had acted in desperation, had not planned our arrest, and did not foresee the consequences of this action. The apathy that preceded our militant action disappeared after our arrest. Rather than alienating women, our dramatic and direct action inspired others to demonstrate against *Snuff*.

Now four of us were facing prosecution; the initial charge was a felony—criminal mischief. A defense committee formed to support us. We chose a name for ourselves: Rochester Women Against Violence Against Women (RWAVAW). We had serious doubts about the value of participating in the judicial system, which is run by men to serve male interests. As feminists we wanted to bring our views inside the courtroom and do things on our own terms as much as possible. The assistance of a lawyer who shared our politics and respected our goals was crucial. A feminist attorney from nearby Buffalo enthusiastically offered her help.

Refusing to accept the system's definition of guilt, we rejected plea-bargaining offers. We sensed that many women would support us and realized the political advantages of a trial: It could be a valuable opportunity for feminists to organize. What happened outside the courtroom was perhaps more important than anything that happened inside.

Not everyone in Rochester was comfortable with illegal tactics, especially when they involved the destruction of property. Some people described our behavior as violent. The defense committee responded by emphasizing that the real crime was *Snuff*. We claimed that breaking a window to stop this crime was justified—in this culture women are terrorized every day; we are treated as the property of men, and our freedom to live without being the victims of male violence is limited. Our punishment for fighting back against *Snuff* pointed out how pervasive such violence is, and the part that the legal system plays in it. When we talked to women about these issues, it seemed we had hit a nerve. Large numbers of women attended a series of benefits held to raise a defense fund. The discussions which had begun in two's and three's and small groups widened and deepened and grew more public. Women began to identify themselves as political activists.

The defense committee met regularly to prepare for the trial. We grew closer and stronger; working collectively we learned necessary skills. The defense committee spoke in public, produced literature, distributed posters, organized meetings, communicated with the mass media, helped develop a legal strategy for the trial, mobilized women to come to court, and even arranged for child care in the Rochester Hall of Justice. We were ready; we were in a strong position.

At the beginning of the trial, the judge suddenly realized he knew the family of one of us and disqualified himself. Months dragged by as we waited for a new judge. No judge would take the case, and the theater owner would not let the district attorney drop the charges. We grew weary of waiting, so we demanded a trial. The original judge then requalified himself and planned to try only three of us. We feared procedural issues would obscure the real reasons for our trial. Also, many of our political goals had already been accomplished. So we accepted a plea bargain that had been offered earlier. Pleading guilty to disorderly conduct (a violation) a year after our arrest allowed us to move on to other projects. This also gave us the freedom to take credit publicly for destroying the *Snuff* poster. Many women came to our sentencing and, violating prescribed courtroom behavior, applauded our statements to the judge. Our sentence was $100 restitution to be paid to the owner of the Holiday Cine theater. We never paid. The defense committee was dissolved.

Rochester Women Against Violence Against Women still exists. It continues to work to increase public awareness about the anti-woman messages in pornography and other media, and to initiate direct action against the public display of cruelty to women. We have developed a slide program which relates pornography, especially violent pornography, to the mainstream of American culture by placing images from *Hustler* and *Penthouse* and "hard-core" pornography next to fashion photographs, general advertisements, and fine art. In discussions following the slide presentation, we urge women to develop strategies to discourage this view of women-as-commodities and women-as-victims; for example, by confronting sons, husbands, or other male relatives who buy pornography, or by joining in demonstrations against local pornography merchants.

In addition to speaking at various meetings and in classrooms, etc., we collect and distribute feminist literature on pornography. We have reprinted numerous articles, and we periodically produce leaflets which explain why pornography is misogyny and describe our group's activities.

While education on pornography and its meaning for women is essential, such a program is incomplete—discussion should inspire action. In Rochester, RWAVAW provides a base for organizing women to take direct action against pornographers and their accomplices. For example, after one slide presentation, about thirty of us decided to visit a local pornographic bookstore, thereby disturbing business as usual. Another evening a group of women loudly and rudely disrupted a screening at the University of Rochester of the sadistic movie *The Story of O*; the showing was discontinued. In addition to creating financial problems for men who choose to sell women's bodies as entertainment, these kinds of actions have enabled women to ally ourselves with other women to oppose our common victimization. Furthermore, our actions inevitably have led to more discussions.

We are continually learning and refining our thinking when we engage in these discussions and actions. Most women immediately make connections with the issues we raise. Men, on the other hand, often feel threatened as they see women becoming stronger and more vocal; maybe this is because we are challenging their identity as privileged males. Connecting pornography to all forms of woman-hating, we demand its elimination. At the same time we recognize the deeper, long-term transformation that must occur in order to abolish misogyny. Legislative solutions will not do. We advocate militant and direct action by feminists. Our methods have proved successful; our numbers are growing. This organizing on the local level is the foundation for a serious challenge to the tradition of male rule.*

* Ed. Note: Martha Gever has recently produced a documentary videotape entitled "A Crime Against Women," which deals with her arrest and the issues that are raised when women confront men about violent pornography. The tape is available for rental or purchase by writing 668 South Ave., Rochester, N.Y. 14620.

Rochester WAVAW is not the only group which has concluded that direct, militant action is the best way to combat the spread of pornography. In 1977, in Denver, Colorado, a group called The Bluebird Five used cans of spray paint to deface a pornography theater showing violent pornographic movies. More recently (1979) and more well-known, feminist Marsha Womongold shot a bullet through the window of a store in Cambridge which sold pornography. Womongold later told reporters that she believes that educating the whole society to understand how pornography hurts women is too slow a process. She reached the "lamentable conclusion that feminists must also act outside the law to effectively confront this abuse." She has written a pamphlet entitled *Pornography: A License to Kill*. See the Bibliography for information on how to obtain it.

Pornography and Grief

Andrea Dworkin

This paper was originally a speech presented in 1978 at the Feminist Perspectives on Pornography conference in San Francisco. Embodying a sweeping vision of the problem, it was delivered directly before a Take Back the Night March. The march was held as a way of demonstrating our commitment to stopping the tide of violence against women, whether by rapists or batterers or imagemakers in the mass media.

As night fell, 3,000 marchers gathered to hear Andrea Dworkin's "Exhortation to March." Then we wound our way toward Broadway, which was crowded with tourists, neon signs advertising live sex shows, adult bookstores, and pornographic theaters. Chanting slogans such as "No More Profit Off Women's Bodies," we filled the street entirely, blocking off traffic and completely occupying the Broadway strip for three blocks. For an hour, and for the first time ever, Broadway belonged not to the barkers, pimps, or pornographers, but instead to the songs, voices, rage, and vision of thousands of women.

I searched for something to say here today quite different from what I am going to say. I wanted to come here militant and proud and angry as hell. But more and more, I find that anger is a pale shadow next to the grief I feel. If a woman has any sense of her own intrinsic worth, seeing pornography in small bits and pieces can bring her to a useful rage. Studying pornography in quantity and depth, as I have been doing for more months than I care to remember, will turn that same woman into a mourner.

The pornography itself is vile. To characterize it any other way would be to lie. No plague of male intellectualisms and sophistries can change or hide that simple fact. Georges Bataille, a philosopher of pornography (which he calls "eroticism"), puts it clearly: "In essence, the domain of eroticism is the domain of violence, of violation." [1] Mr. Bataille, unlike so many of his peers, is good enough to make explicit that the whole idea is to violate the female. Using the language of grand euphemism so popular with male intellectuals who write on the subject of pornography, Bataille informs us that "[t]he passive, female side is essentially the one that is dissolved as a separate entity." [2] To be "dissolved"—by any means necessary—is the role of women in pornography. The great male scientists and philosophers of sexuality, including Kinsey, Havelock Ellis, Wilhelm Reich, and Freud, uphold this view of our purpose and destiny. The great male writers use language more or less beautifully to create us in self-serving fragments, half-"dissolved" as it were, and then proceed to "dissolve" us all the way, by any means necessary. The biographers of the great male artists celebrate the real-life atrocities those men have committed against us, as if those atrocities are central to the making of art. And in history, as men have lived it, they have "dissolved" us—by any means necessary. The slicing of our skins and the rattling of our bones are the energizing sources of male-defined art and science, as they are the essential content of pornography. The visceral experience of a hatred of women that literally knows no bounds has put me beyond anger and beyond tears; I can only speak to you from grief.

We all expected the world to be different than it is, didn't we? No matter what material or emotional deprivation we have experienced as children or as adults, no matter what we understood from history or from the testimonies of living persons about how people suffer and why, we all believed, however privately, in human possibility. Some of us believed in art, or literature, or music, or religion, or revolution, or in children, or in the redeeming potential of eroticism or affection. No matter what we knew of cruelty, we all believed in kindness; and no matter what we knew of hatred, we all believed in friendship or love. Not one of us could have imagined or would have believed the simple facts of life as we have come to know them: the rapacity of male greed for dominance; the malignancy of male supremacy; the virulent contempt for women that is the very foundation of the culture in which we live. The Women's Movement has forced us all to face the facts, but no matter how brave and clear-sighted we are, no matter how far we are willing to go or are forced to go in viewing reality without romance or illusion, we are simply overwhelmed by the male hatred of our kind, its morbidity, its compulsiveness, its obsessiveness, its celebration of itself in every detail of life and culture. We think that we have grasped this hatred once and for all, seen it in its spectacular cruelty, learned its every secret, got used to it or risen above it or organized against it so as to be protected from its worst excesses. We think that we know all there is to know about what men do to women, even if we cannot imagine why they do what they do, when something happens that simply drives us mad, out of our minds, so that we are again imprisoned like caged animals in the numbing reality of male control, male revenge against no one knows what, male hatred of our very being.

One can know everything and still not imagine snuff films. One can know everything and still be shocked and terrified when a man who attempted to make snuff films is released, despite the testimony of the women undercover agents whom he wanted to torture, murder, and, of course, film. One can know everything and still be stunned and paralyzed when one meets a child who is being continually raped by her father or some close male relative. One can know everything and still be reduced to sputtering like an idiot when a woman is prosecuted for attempting to abort herself with knitting needles or when a woman is imprisoned for killing a man who has raped or tortured her or is raping or torturing her. One can know everything and still want to kill and be dead simultaneously when one sees a celebratory picture of a woman being ground up in a meat grinder on the cover of a national magazine, no matter how putrid the magazine. One can know everything and still somewhere inside refuse to believe that the personal, social, culturally sanctioned violence against women is unlimited, unpredictable, pervasive, constant, ruthless, and happily and unselfconsciously sadistic. One can know everything and still be unable to accept the fact that sex and murder are fused in the male consciousness, so that the one without the imminent possibility of the other is unthinkable and impossible. One can know everything and still, at bottom, refuse to accept that the annihilation of women is the source of meaning and identity for men. One can know everything and still want desperately to know nothing because to face what we know is to question whether life is worth anything at all.

The pornographers, modern and ancient, visual and literary, vulgar and aristocratic, put forth one consistent proposition: erotic pleasure for men is derived from and predicated on the savage destruction of women. As the world's most honored pornographer, the Marquis de Sade (called by male scholars "The Divine Marquis"), wrote in one of his more restrained and civil moments: "There's not a woman on earth who'd ever have had cause to complain of my services if I'd been sure of being able to kill her afterward." [3] The eroticization of murder is the essence of pornography, as it is the essence of life. The torturer may be a policeman tearing the fingernails off a victim in a prison cell or a so-called normal man engaged in the project of attempting to fuck a woman to death. The fact is that the process of killing—and both rape and battery are steps in that process—is the prime sexual act for men in reality and/ or in imagination. Women as a class must remain in bondage, subject to the sexual will of men, because the knowledge of an imperial right to kill, whether exercised to the fullest extent or just partway, is necessary to fuel sexual appetite and behavior. Without women as potential or actual victims, men are, in the current sanitized jargon, "sexually dysfunctional." This same motif also operates among male homosexuals, where force and/or convention designate some males as female or feminized. The plethora of leather and chains among male homosexuals, and the newly fashionable defenses of organized rings of boy prostitution by supposedly radical gay men, are testimony to the fixedness of the male compulsion to dominate and destroy that is the source of sexual pleasure for men.

The most terrible thing about pornography is that it tells male truth. The most insidious thing about pornography is that it tells male truth as if it were universal truth. Those depictions of women in chains being tortured are supposed to represent our deepest erotic aspirations. And some of us believe it, don't we? The most important thing about pornography is that the values in it are the common values of men. This is the crucial fact that both the male Right and the male Left, in their differing but mutually reinforcing ways, want to keep hidden from women. The male Right wants to hide the pornography, and the male Left wants to hide its meaning. Both want access to pornography so that men can be encouraged and energized by it. The Right wants secret access; the Left wants public access. But whether we see the pornography or not, the values expressed in it are the values expressed in the acts of rape and wife-beating, in the legal system, in religion, in art and in literature, in systematic economic discrimination against women, in the moribund academies, and by the good and wise and kind and enlightened in all of these fields and areas. Pornography is not a genre of expression separate and different from the rest of life; it is a genre of expression fully in harmony with any culture in which it flourishes. This is so whether it is legal or illegal. And, in either case, pornography functions to perpetuate male supremacy and crimes of violence against women because it conditions, trains, educates, and inspires men to despise women, to use women, to hurt women. Pornography exists because men despise women, and men despise women in part because pornography exists.

For myself, pornography has defeated me in a way that, at least so far, life has not. Whatever struggles and difficulties I have had in my life, I have always wanted to find a way to go on even if I did not know how, to live through one more day, to learn one more thing, to take one more walk, to read one more book, to write one more paragraph, to see one more friend, to love one more time. When I read or see pornography, I want everything to stop. Why, I ask, why are they so damned cruel and so damned proud of it? Sometimes, a detail drives me mad. There is a series of photographs: a woman slicing her breasts with a knife, smearing her own blood on her own body, sticking a sword up her vagina. *And she is smiling.* And it is the smile that drives me mad. There is a record album plastered all over a huge display window. The picture on the album is a profile view of a woman's thighs. Her crotch is suggested because we know it is there; it is not shown. The title of the album is *Plug Me to Death.* And it is the use of the first person that drives me mad. "Plug Me to Death." The arrogance. The cold-blooded arrogance. And how can it go on like this, senseless, entirely brutal, inane, day after day and year after year, these images and ideas and values pouring out, packaged, bought and sold, promoted, enduring on and on, and no one stops it, and our darling boy intellectuals defend it, and elegant radical lawyers argue for it, and men of every sort cannot and will not live without it. And life, which means everything to me, becomes meaningless, because these celebrations of cruelty destroy my very capacity to feel and to care and to hope. I hate the pornographers most of all for depriving me of hope.

The psychic violence in pornography is unbearable in and of itself. It acts on one like a bludgeon until one's sensibility is pummeled flat and one's heart goes dead. One becomes numb. Everything stops, and one looks at the pages or pictures and knows: this is what men want, and this is what men have had, and this is what men will not give up. As lesbian-feminist Karla Jay pointed out in an article called "Pot, Porn, and the Politics of Pleasure," men will give up grapes and lettuce and orange juice and Portuguese wine and tuna fish, but men will not give up pornography. And yes, one wants to take it from them, to burn it, to rip it up, bomb it, raze their theaters and publishing houses to the ground. One can be part of a revolutionary movement or one can mourn. Perhaps I have found the real source of my grief: we have not yet become a revolutionary movement.

Tonight we are going to walk together, all of us, to take back the night, as women have in cities all over the world, because in every sense none of us can walk alone. Every woman walking alone is a target. Every woman walking alone is hunted, harassed, time after time harmed by psychic or physical violence. Only by walking together can we walk at all with any sense of safety, dignity, or freedom. Tonight, walking together, we will proclaim to the rapists and pornographers and woman-batterers that their days are numbered and our time has come. And tomorrow, what will we do tomorrow? Because, sisters, the truth is that we have to take back the night every night, or the night will never be ours. And once we have conquered the dark, we have to reach for the light, to take the day and make it ours. This is our choice, and this is our necessity. It is a revolutionary choice, and it is a revolutionary necessity. For us, the two are indivisible, as we must be indivisible in our fight for freedom. Many of us have walked many miles already—brave, hard miles— but we have not gone far enough. Tonight, with every breath and every step, we must commit ourselves to going the distance: to transforming this earth on which we walk from prison and tomb into our rightful and joyous home. This we must do and this we will do, for our own sakes and for the sake of every woman who has ever lived.

SECTION VII.

Looking Ahead

The fact is, women are in chains, and their servitude is all the more debasing because they do not realize it. O to compel them to see and feel and to give them courage and the conscience to speak and act for their own freedom, though they face the scorn and contempt of all the world for doing it.

—SUSAN B. ANTHONY

Uses of the Erotic:
The Erotic as Power

Audre Lorde

This speech was first presented at the Berkshire Conference on the History of Women, and six months later was the concluding speech at the Feminist Perspectives on Pornography conference. It is also published in a pamphlet edition by Out and Out Books.

There are many kinds of power, used and unused, acknowledged or otherwise. The erotic is a resource within each of us that lies in a deeply female and spiritual plane, firmly rooted in the power of our unexpressed or unrecognized feeling. In order to perpetuate itself, every oppression must corrupt or distort those various sources of power within the culture of the oppressed that can provide energy for change. For women, this has meant a suppression of the erotic as a considered source of power and information within our lives.

We have been taught to suspect this resource, vilified, abused, and devalued within western society. On one hand the superficially erotic has been encouraged as a sign of female inferiority—on the other hand women have been made to suffer and to feel both contemptible and suspect by virtue of its existence.

It is a short step from there to the false belief that only by the suppression of the erotic within our lives and consciousness can women be truly strong. But that strength is illusory, for it is fashioned within the context of male models of power.

As women, we have come to distrust that power which rises from our deepest and non-rational knowledge. We have been warned against it all our lives by the male world, which values this depth of feeling enough to keep women around in order to exercise it in the service of men, but which fears this same depth too much to examine the possibilities of it within themselves. So women are maintained at a distant/inferior position to be psychically milked, much the same way ants maintain colonies of aphids to provide a life-giving substance for their masters.

But the erotic offers a well of replenishing and provocative force to the woman who does not fear its revelation, nor succumb to the belief that sensation is enough.

The erotic has often been misnamed by men and used against women. It has been made into the confused, the trivial, the psychotic, the plasticized sensation. For this reason, we have often turned away from the exploration and consideration of the erotic as a source of power and information, confusing it with its opposite, the pornographic. But pornography is a direct denial of the power of the erotic, for it represents the suppression of true feeling. Pornography emphasizes sensation without feeling.

The erotic is a measure between the beginnings of our sense of self, and the chaos of our strongest feelings. It is an internal sense of satisfaction to which, once we have experienced it, we know we can aspire. For once having experienced the fullness of this depth of feeling and recognizing its power, in honor and self-respect we can require no less of ourselves.

It is never easy to demand the most from ourselves, and from our lives, and from our work. To go beyond the encouraged mediocrity of our society is to encourage excellence. But giving in to the fear of feeling and working to capacity is a luxury only the unintentional can afford, and the unintentional are those who do not wish to guide their own destinies.

This internal requirement toward excellence which we learn from the erotic must not be misconstrued as demanding the impossible from ourselves nor from others. Such a demand incapacitates everyone in the process, for the erotic is not a question only of what we do. It is a question of how acutely and fully we can feel in the doing. For once we know the extent to which we are capable of feeling that sense of satisfaction and fullness and completion, we can then observe which of our various life endeavors bring us closest to that fullness.

The aim of each thing which we do is to make our lives and the lives of our children more possible and more rich. Within the celebration of the erotic in all our endeavors, my work becomes a conscious decision—a longed-for bed which I enter gratefully and from which I rise up empowered.

Of course, women so empowered are dangerous. So we are taught to separate the erotic demand from most vital areas of our lives other than sex. And the lack of concern for the erotic root and satisfactions of our work is felt in our disaffection from so much of what we do. For instance, how often do we truly love our work?

The principal horror of any system which defines the good in terms of profit rather than in terms of human need, or which defines human need to the exclusion of the psychic and emotional components of that need—the principal horror of such a system is that it robs our work of its erotic value, its erotic power and life appeal and fulfillment. Such a system reduces work to a travesty of necessities, a duty by which we earn bread or oblivion for ourselves and those we love. But this is tantamount to blinding a painter and then telling her to improve her work and to enjoy the act of painting. It is not only next to impossible, it is also profoundly cruel.

As women, we need to examine the ways in which our world can be truly different. I am speaking here of the necessity for reassessing the very quality of all the aspects of our lives and of our work.

The very word "erotic" comes from the Greek word *eros,* the personification of love in all its aspects—born of Chaos—and personifying creative power and harmony. When I speak of the erotic, then, I speak of it as an assertion of the life force of women; of that creative energy empowered, the knowledge and use of which we are now reclaiming in our language, our history, our dancing, our loving, our work, our lives.

There are frequent attempts to equate pornography and eroticism, two diametrically opposed uses of the sexual. Because of these attempts, it has become fashionable to separate the spiritual (psychic and emotional) away from the political, to see them as contradictory or antithetical. "What do you mean, a poetic revolutionary, a meditating gunrunner?" In the same way, we have attempted to separate the spiritual and the erotic, reducing the spiritual thereby to a world of flattened affect—a world of the ascetic who aspires to feel nothing. But nothing is farther from the truth. For the ascetic position is one of the highest fear; the gravest immobility. The severe abstinence of the ascetic becomes the ruling obsession. And it is one, not of self-discipline, but of self-abnegation.

The dichotomy between the spiritual and the political is also false, resulting from an incomplete attention to our erotic knowledge. For the bridge which connects them is formed by the erotic—the sensual—those physical, emotional, and psychic expressions of what is deepest and strongest and richest within each of us, being shared: the passions of love in its deepest meanings.

The considered phrase, "it feels right to me," acknowledges the strength of the erotic into a true knowledge, for what that means and feels is the first and most powerful guiding light toward any understanding. And understanding is a handmaiden which can only wait upon, or clarify, that knowledge, deeply born. The erotic is the nurturer or nursemaid of all our deepest knowledge.

The erotic functions for me in several ways, and the first is in the power which comes from sharing deeply any pursuit with another person. The sharing of joy, whether physical, emotional, psychic or intellectual, forms a bridge between the sharers which can be the basis for understanding much of what is not shared between them, and lessens the threat of their difference.

Another important way in which the erotic connection functions is the open and fearless underlining of my capacity for joy. In the way my body stretches to music and opens into response, hearkening to its deepest rhythms, so every level upon which I sense also opens to the erotically satisfying experience, whether it is dancing, building a bookcase, writing a poem, examining an idea.

That self-connection shared is a measure of the joy which I know myself to be capable of feeling, a reminder of my capacity for feeling. And that deep and irreplaceable knowledge of my capacity for joy comes to demand from all of my life that it be lived within the knowledge that such satisfaction is possible, and does not have to be called marriage, nor god, nor an afterlife.

This is one reason why the erotic is so feared, and so often relegated to the bedroom alone, when it is recognized at all. For once we begin to feel deeply all the aspects of our lives, we begin to demand from ourselves and from our lives' pursuits that they feel in accordance with that joy which we know ourselves to be capable of. Our erotic knowledge empowers us, becomes a lens through which we scrutinize all aspects of our existence, forcing ourselves to evaluate those aspects honestly in terms of their relative meaning within our lives. And this is a grave responsibility, projected from within each of us, not to settle for the convenient, the shoddy, the conventionally expected, nor the merely safe.

During World War II, we bought sealed plastic packets of white, uncolored margarine, with a tiny, intense pellet of yellow coloring perched like a topaz just inside the clear skin of the bag. We would leave the margarine out for a while to soften, and then we would pinch the little pellet to break it inside the bag, releasing the rich yellowness into the soft pale mass of margarine. Then taking it carefully between our fingers, we would knead it gently back and forth, over and over, until the color had spread throughout the whole pound bag of margarine, leaving it thoroughly colored.

I find the erotic such a kernel within myself. When released from its intense and constrained pellet, it flows through and colors my life with a kind of energy that heightens and sensitizes and strengthens all my experience.

We have been raised to fear the yes within ourselves, our deepest cravings. For the demands of our released expectations lead us inevitably into actions which will help bring our lives into accordance with our needs, our knowledge, our desires. And the fear of our deepest cravings keeps them suspect, keeps us docile and loyal and obedient, and leads us to settle for or accept many facets of our oppression as women.

When we live outside ourselves, and by that I mean on external directives only, rather than from our internal knowledge and needs, when we live away from those erotic guides from within ourselves, then our lives are limited by external and alien forms, and we conform to the needs of a structure that is not based on human need, let alone an individual's. But when we begin to live from within outward, in touch with the power of the erotic within ourselves, and allowing that power to inform and illuminate our actions upon the world around us, then we begin to be responsible to ourselves in the deepest sense. For as we begin to recognize our deepest feelings, we begin to give up, of necessity, being satisfied with suffering and self-negation, and with the numbness which so often seems like the only alternative in our society. Our acts against oppression become integral with self, motivated and empowered from within.

In touch with the erotic, I become less willing to accept powerlessness, or those other supplied states of being which are not native to me, such as resignation, despair, self-effacement, depression, self-denial.

And yes, there is a hierarchy. There is a difference between painting a back fence and writing a poem, but only one of quantity. And there is, for me, no difference between writing a good poem and moving into sunlight against the body of a woman I love.

This brings me to the last consideration of the erotic. To share the power of each other's feelings is different from using another's feelings as we would use a Kleenex. And when we look the other way from our experience, erotic or otherwise, we use rather than share the feelings of those others who participate in the experience with us. And use without consent of the used is abuse.

In order to be utilized, our erotic feelings must be recognized. The need for sharing deep feeling is a human need. But within the European-American tradition, this need is satisfied by certain proscribed erotic comings together, and these occasions are almost always characterized by a simultaneous looking away, a pretense of calling them something else, whether a religion, a fit, mob violence, or even playing doctor. And this misnaming of the need and the deed gives rise to that distortion which results in pornography and obscenity—the abuse of feeling.

When we look away from the importance of the erotic in the development and sustenance of our power, or when we look away from ourselves as we satisfy our erotic needs in concert with others, we use each other as objects of satisfaction rather than share our joy in the satisfying, rather than make connection with our similarities and our differences. To refuse to be conscious of what we are feeling at any time, however comfortable that might seem, is to deny a large part of the experience, and to allow ourselves to be reduced to the pornographic, the abused, and the absurd.

The erotic cannot be felt secondhand. As a Black Lesbian Feminist, I have a particular feeling, knowledge, and understanding for those sisters with whom I have danced hard, played, or even fought. This deep participation has often been the forerunner for joint concerted actions not possible before.

But this erotic charge is not easily shared by women who continue to operate under an exclusively European-American, male tradition. I know it was not available to me when I was trying to adapt my consciousness to this mode of living and sensation.

Only now, I find more and more woman-identified women brave enough to risk sharing the erotic's electrical charge without having to look away, and without distorting the enormously powerful and creative nature of that exchange. Recognizing the power of the erotic within our lives can give us the energy to pursue genuine change within our world, rather than merely settling for a shift of characters in the same weary drama.

For not only do we touch our most profoundly creative source, but we do that which is female and self-affirming in the face of a racist, patriarchal, and anti-erotic society.

Pornography and the Women's Liberation Movement

Diana E. H. Russell

This article was first presented as the concluding speech at the Feminist Perspectives on Pornography conference in 1978, where Diana E. H. Russell, a founding member of Women Against Violence in Pornography and Media, gave her views on how the Women's Movement should proceed to fight pornography.

Why have most women in the Women's Movement shied away from pornography as a woman's issue for so long? This is an important question. Until a greater portion of the Women's Movement is with us on this, we aren't going to get very far. The fact is that an incredible, scary, hate campaign against women has been escalating in the last eight years with scarcely a peep of protest from most feminists. Only with the "snuff" movies can we talk of the movement taking action. But after the "snuff" movies left town—temporarily—so did most of the action.

Why?

I believe there are many reasons. First, because we have observed that the anti-pornography forces have almost always been conservative, homophobic, antisex, and pro the traditional family. They have equated nudity and explicit sex with pornography. They are often against abortion, the Equal Rights Amendment, and the Women's Liberation Movement. We have been so put off by the politics of these people, that our knee-jerk response is that we must be *for* whatever they are *against*.

But we don't have to ally ourselves with them. We haven't yet. And we won't! The women amongst them can relate to our focus on the abuse of women by pornography better than we can relate to the "sin" approach. They can come to us if they can accept the rest of our politics too.

The second reason why most feminists have so far ignored the issue of pornography is that most of us bought the male liberal and radical line that being against any aspect of the so-called sexual revolution meant being a reactionary, unliberated prude. Men were seen as the sexually liberated sex, women the sexually repressed sex. To be liberated, women at least had to tolerate and accept male sex trips, including pornography, and sometimes try to imitate them, as in *Playgirl* magazine. But all this assumes that there can be a sexual revolution without a sex-*role* revolution too, and that change means women changing to be more like men. No thank you!

The third reason for neglecting this issue is that most of us have refused to look at pornography ourselves. It is painful to face the hatred of women so evident in it. While we resent what we are *forced* to see in our newspaper ads, in the grocery stores, in the red-light-district posters and neon signs, few of us follow through and say, "My Goddess! This stuff is hateful. I need to check out what is going on *inside* some of these places!" Like some Jews in Germany early on in the Nazi period who didn't want to read the writing on the wall, many women prefer not to know the depth and dangerousness of misogyny. Heterosexual women in particular have a hard time facing this aspect of male culture, since they don't want to see this side of the men they relate to. But most lesbians haven't made an issue out of it either, and a few have even confused male abuse of lesbians in pornography with lesbian pornography. Far more disturbing yet, some actually argue that sadomasochistic sex is fun and healthy for lesbians. Sadly, few of us have been immune to the liberal-radical line on pornography.

A fourth reason is that we have been deceived like everybody else by the male scientists and so-called experts who claim that there is no evidence showing that pornography is harmful. We are told that pornography helped diminish the problem of rape and other sex crimes in Denmark, that this is a fact, and that any feelings we may have to the contrary about pornography are irrational. But new research and a more thorough analysis of the existing research has revealed that this was an irresponsible conclusion of the Commission on Obscenity and Pornography, as well as of many other almost exclusively male scientists who have done similar research.

A fifth reason why so few feminists have confronted pornography is that we have often, for practical and strategic reasons, taken a piecemeal approach to problems. We focus on battered women, or rape, or the molestation of female children, or whatever. But all these crimes against women are linked. How can we stop rape and woman-battering by staffing rape-crisis centers and refuges when there are thousands of movie houses, millions of publications, a multibillion-dollar business that promote the idea that violence and the rape of women is sexually exciting to men, and that *we* like it too?

Sixth, as with prostitution, many of us get confused by the argument that it is an issue of survival (money) for some women. This is true, and I think it's important to recognize that women's role in pornography is not the primary problem. It is the men who profit most from it, and who are its consumers, who must be attacked and exposed. But beyond that, we cannot automatically support every institution which happens to provide some money for some women. The German concentration camps did that too. We *have* to consider whether the institution is operating in such a way as to be destructive to women as a *class*. Money aside, many women including ex-pornography models, have made a strong case for the destructive effect on the women involved.

Seventh, there is a fear that being anti-pornography means we are necessarily pro-censorship. For people who have worked through all the other reasons, this one often still bothers them. So I'd like to spend a little more time on it.

With few exceptions, most feminists, as well as liberal and radical nonfeminists, have been so hung up on the censorship issue that they have refused to allow themselves to recognize pornography as a problem for women, refused to analyze what is going on in pornography and why, and refused even to allow themselves to *feel* outraged by it. We have largely remained silent while this ever more conspicuous and vicious campaign against us has been mounted—even though it is impossible to open our newspapers to the entertainment section and not see something of what is going on, at least in this city.

I wish we could end this short-circuiting in our thinking and feeling. It seems to me there are four distinct and important steps in dealing with a social problem.

1. First, we need to *recognize* it. Many problems are never recognized as such. The murder of women, for example, is still hidden by the word homicide. There are very few murders of women by women —when we are murdered it is almost always by men. We have to recognize *fem*icide before we can consider why the problem exists and what can be done about it.

2. The second step involves *feeling* about the problem once it is recognized. To simply acknowledge rape, woman-battering, woman-hatred in pornography, and not *feel* outraged is another kind of unhealthy short-circuiting that goes on.

3. Third, we need to try to understand the *cause* of the problem, to

analyze it, before we can take action. If, for example, our analysis of rape is that it happens rarely and a few crazy men are responsible, clearly it has very different implications than if we see rape as an extreme acting out of the socially sanctioned male role.

4. And, finally, there is the question of what to do about it. In the case of pornography it is only at step four that the issue of the pros and cons of censorship or banning comes up, and it is only one of many, many questions. Equally important are questions on the pros and cons of civil disobedience, demonstrations, boycotts, education, petitions, legal suits, or the use of more militant tactics.

In the case of pornography many people, including feminists, don't allow themselves to contemplate the first three steps—is pornography a problem, is it a woman's problem, and if so, what do I *feel* about this problem? Why does this problem exist? They simply say, "I'm against censorship of any kind!" And the meaning of the First Amendment becomes the topic of discussion. In this way the freedom of speech issue has been used, not always consciously, to freeze us into saying and doing nothing against pornography.

I would hope that whatever your particular view is on the First Amendment in relation to pornography, *you* will avoid this short-circuiting process, and you will point out to others when they are doing it. I believe that to act together we have to be in agreement regarding the first steps of recognition, feeling, and analysis. We also have to be able to agree on some actions we think are worth doing. But we don't have to agree on the banning issue.

I personally believe that portraying women being bound, raped, beaten, tortured, and killed for so-called sexual stimulation and pleasure should be banned, because I believe these portrayals encourage and condone these crimes against women in the real world. People seem to have forgotten that many individual liberties are curtailed by all societies for the perceived welfare of the whole society. Examples in the United States are polygamy, marriage or sex with individuals below a certain age, incest, cannibalism, slavery, rape, homicide, assault, and, absurdly, homosexuality. The point is that all societies have found it necessary to outlaw many forms of violent and exploitive behavior, and thereby deny individuals the right to act out certain impulses. Sometimes, of course, prejudice and ignorance are behind these restrictions, as in the case of homosexuality. But it is clear that pornography is not such a case. I do not see myself as unconcerned about free speech and the First Amendment. And I am quite happy to work with other feminists who disagree with my position on banning pornography.

However, working to obtain laws to bar violent pornography does not seem to me to be a *priority* strategy at this time. Not that I believe in any one strategy to the exclusion of others. I think a multistrategy approach is appropriate, with women choosing tactics in keeping with their politics, their skills, and their circumstances. However I do believe action is necessary—lots of it—and soon! Change is not brought about by magic spells or ardent wishes.

I want to say more about civil disobedience, a strategy that I believe would be particularly effective for women in this country at this time.

I believe this strategy has lost some of its appeal as an effective tool because its victories for Black people in this country seemed very short-lived and insufficient. But women as a caste are obviously in a very different situation from Blacks as a caste, and I believe some of these differences would make civil disobedience much more effective for women.

The depth of concern about an issue is sometimes measured by willingness to pay a price of some kind, e.g., the inconvenience and indignity of arrest. The suffragette's fight is a case in point. But if the tactics used scare and threaten the public, as happened with the Weathermen or the SLA (Symbionese Liberation Army), for example, then they are likely to backfire. Civil disobedience shows commitment and concern in a very dramatic way without making people feel so threatened.

When a minority group engages in civil disobedience, it ultimately depends on the often nonexistent goodwill of the majority whether demands are met or not. Women are not only a majority but are so integrated into the male world, particularly in the family, that we cannot be isolated and ghettoized in the same way that members of minority groups have been. If wives and girl friends are being arrested for actions against pornography, husbands and lovers are going to have to deal with it. First, they will have to take care of children and/or the household—itself a consciousness-raiser. They will be *made* to care about pornography, at least in this indirect way, because it will affect them negatively in a way they can recognize.

Another way in which civil disobedience is a particularly suitable tactic is that most of us don't relish being violent. Civil disobedience is therefore much easier for us to practice than for men.

Hence, a factor that is often a *strategic* weakness for us—our integration with the male population—becomes a strength. A factor that is often a *tactical* weakness for us—a common unwillingness to meet violence with violence—becomes a strength. And to the extent that we are badly treated by the police in this situation, we will gain all the more support for our cause. This is not to say that those of us who are less integrated into the male world—particularly lesbians— don't have an important place in this struggle. We have the advantage of not having to deal with male resistance in our homes, which is why we have played and continue to play such a key role in the Women's Movement. This also means we would probably be among the first to take the risks necessary to show how powerful civil disobedience can be as a strategy for women on this and other issues.

Women have been taking life-and-death risks for centuries. Simply by being women, we risk being raped. Many of us are hassled at work or beaten at home because we are women. Some of these risks we cannot avoid. Some risks perhaps we can. Continuing to live with a violent husband or lover, for example, is very, very risky. Indeed, marrying someone we barely know, or even someone we know very well, can be very risky in a society that does not recognize rape within marriage, and in which the interests of males are so entrenched both legally and socially. I would like to urge all of us to examine our lives and see if there isn't a way to take fewer personal risks and more political risks.

The time has surely come for us to face the viciously sexist nature of pornography; to confront this form of the male backlash; and to spread the word to other women that we will have to organize to take action, to stop this dangerous anti-women propaganda. By taking more political risks where necessary, women may need to take fewer personal risks later on.

Beyond Pornography:
From Defensive Politics
to Creating a Vision

Kathleen Barry

———————————————————————————————————————

Feminist author and organizer Kathleen Barry was active in Women's Movement demonstrations against *Playboy* magazine in the early seventies. She has worked this past year on a book entitled *Female Sexual Slavery* (Englewood Cliffs, N.J.: Prentice-Hall, 1979), in which she discusses the interconnection of pornography, the enslavement of women, and other forms of sexual violence. This paper was the opening speech at the 1978 Feminist Perspectives on Pornography conference in San Francisco.

———————————————————————————————————————

Pornography is a logical and necessary issue for feminists. It is the media of sexual objectification and violence against women. It abstracts those practices to a level of symbolic representation and presents them to the society at large as entertainment in books, pictures, and movies. As a *collective* representation of sexual objectification and violence against women, pornography differs from other feminist issues like rape or wife-battery, which are specific acts against *individual* women. The feminist response to pornography calls for some different solutions and some new strategies and actions.

Pornography is both more visible and less tangible than the individual acts of sexual violence perpetrated by rapists, wife-beaters, incest aggressors, or pimps. While feminists can respond to wife-battery and rape with legal action and by opening crisis centers and refuge shelters, we cannot rely on self-help measures in confronting pornography, whose victims are not only individual women but all women. The public support we slowly cultivated against rape was the result of making visible the individual acts of sexual violence. But pornography is already highly visible—on stands in neighborhood grocery stores as well as on marquees of movie theaters. Its visibility is an indication of its social acceptance. Pornography has become a valid, legitimate institution, neither condemned nor supported by

307

the law. The use of women as sexual objects is so pervasive as to be generally accepted as a normal representation of women. Such conditions constitute what I have called the ideology of cultural sadism (see *Female Sexual Slavery*), an ideology that permeates thinking and attitudes so deeply that its consequences (in the practice of sadism or masochism, for example) are assumed to be to some degree normal if not biologically determined.

For feminists, taking on the issue of pornography means challenging the very ideals of a sexually exploitive society. Our challenges threaten the sexual values promoted by masculinist ideology. In so doing, we are confronting the sexist double standard which, while legally condemning acts of sexual violence, in fact ideologically validates them in media such as pornography.

The challenge we face with the issue of pornography is compounded by the fact that unlike specific acts of violence to women (like rape) pornography is a $4-billion-a-year industry protected, as it is controlled in part, by organized crime. The feminist challenge that demands redefining sexual values is also a direct threat to that economic vested interest.

As women's consciousness is raised as to the content and intent of pornography, we see a mounting rage that cannot and will not be controlled. That rage began to erupt ten years ago when, in the beginning of this wave of feminism, we first began to confront pornography and the media of sexual objectification and violence. Those early demonstrations against *Playboy* and other sexually exploitive empires sparked considerable energy among feminists. But the tide of opinion was organized against us. The Commission on Obscenity and Pornography was but one of many groups to insist that there was no relationship between pornography and behavior, and to assert that trying to control pornography would only result in threatening freedom of speech. Liberal tactics were effective then, and we withdrew from the issue. But our rage has been seething ever since.

In the last ten years we have acquired considerable knowledge about the strategies of anti-feminists. We now recognize that, in one feminist issue after another, the attempts to silence us follow a very definite pattern. Our own recent history: How we began to address the issues, the opposition we faced, and how we responded are important to recall and can be instructive now.

Ten years ago abortion and rape were words that were rarely used. They were considered private problems, invisible as issues and silenced in women. But as feminism has addressed each of these issues, we have moved beyond immobilizing silence into action, beyond our original defensiveness to burning issues of sexual politics. (The fact that we are still fighting for freedom from forced motherhood and freedom from rape is a testimonial not to our failure but to the deep entrenchment of those practices in society.)

We introduced abortion as a feminist issue while it was still illegal across the country. We educated the public as to the urgency of that issue through the personal testimony of women who had been victims of butcher-abortionists; we took our cause to the public, to the streets, to the legislatures, to the courts. As we documented the loss of women's lives through desperate attempts to self-abort or at the hands of butcher-abortionists, we were told, as we are now told, that *we* are the ones who are trying to destroy life. *We* were called murderers and were asked just where do *we* draw the line. (It is interesting that that question was being asked by the very people who were giving us a right-to-life argument while they were also campaigning for the death penalty—not a minor contradiction.) *

In those early abortion campaigns, the issue was not our opposition's concern over the right to life any more than it is now. They charged us then with destroying the right to life, using this as a tactic to intimidate us. Their goal was to send us back home, to silence us. Our campaign for women's control over our own bodies, for our right to live free from forced motherhood, was and continues to be what the "friends of the fetus" wanted to destroy. I think that as a movement they are sometimes more aware than we of the potential female power that would be unleashed if we acheived self-determination.

Our opposition's strategies were the same some years later when we took on the issue of rape. Feminists are continuing to demand recognition of rape victims by the courts and the general public as victims of sexual assault. In demanding that the courts treat victims as victims and not as criminals, we campaigned for laws that would prohibit extensive probing into the sexual lives and characters of the victims. Again we are accused of trespassing on someone else's rights, this time the rights of the defendant.

Every time we fight for a basic human right for ourselves, a right that should be ours simply because we exist, we are told that we are

* Ed. Note: At the June 1978 National Right-to-Life convention, a few dissenters tried to get the "right-to-life" people to adopt antinuclear and antideath-penalty platforms. They were rebuffed on the grounds that "unborn life is perfect, whereas born life is imperfect"—according to the Women's Action Alliance.

infringing on someone else's rights—that *we* are morally corrupt for wanting a decent life, control over our own destinies, and freedom from exploitation and violence. We must recognize this as a patriarchal tactic to keep us on the defensive—to intimidate us, to send us home, to silence us.

Through it all we have not given up; our rage has not been suppressed. Our passion for our own liberation has always overcome intimidation. The increasing numbers of women who are pouring into the streets for Take Back the Night demonstrations across the country and the increasing reports of feminist disruptions of pornography movies or harassment of pornography bookstores indicate that our opposition's tactics have failed.

Some cautions and strategies in addressing the pornography issue are suggested from our experience with other issues. The male vested interest that is mobilized to protect both the economic profits and sexual power derived from pornography is never expressed directly in their tactics. Pornography perpetrators do not tell us to back off because we will hurt their profits or destroy their power. Instead, they hire batteries of lawyers and charge us with eroding constitutional guarantees to freedom of speech. The ideology of cultural sadism has convinced many that the Constitution should be used to protect the vile misogynistic hatred of women perpetuated in pornography, and that we should not inhibit pornographers' "freedom of speech." We are now warned that should we demand the elimination of pornography and attempt to use legal power to accomplish this, we will be giving our oppressors the power to oppress us further by setting legal precedents which will be used to inhibit *our* freedom of speech.

Looking at this argument, we should recognize two things: (1) They oppress us already, and (2) *our* freedom of speech has already been effectively curtailed. Our voices are silenced through the sexual terrorism that dominates our lives, a terrorism that stems directly from pornography. But, most important, we must challenge abuses of power in every instance of their occurrence and not expect that those who hold power over us will deal with us generously or even equitably in terms of the rights they assume for themselves.

Each time we achieve some gain for our sex, we experience a resurgence of anti-feminism. Shortly after the Supreme Court decision removing legal prohibition of abortion, we were faced with an escalation in the forced sterilization of poor and ethnic minority women as well as denial of abortion to the poor. Those reactionary practices mean that the backlash forces us to deeper levels of challenge and confrontation; they do not mean that we should not have challenged state abortion laws. We have learned in one issue after another that one victory usually leads to a backlash and therefore requires continued uncompromised confrontation. *There are no easy roads to liberation.*

In addition to our opposition's attempt to redefine the issue of pornography to one of freedom of speech, the burden of proof has been placed on us to come up with the evidence that pornography affects behavior or causes sexual violence. There have been volumes and volumes of research on pornography that attempt to deny any causal connection between pornography and rape or other forms of sexual violence. While I have analyzed the ideological bias that guided and directed that research in my book, I submit that the causal connections between pornography and sexual violence are perfectly evident. We do not need to follow individual men out of specific pornographic theaters and witness them raping the first woman they see to realize as women what impact pornography has on our lives. We need only appeal to our own common sense.

The fact that it took the Commission on Obscenity and Pornography several million dollars, several years, and several volumes of research to try to disprove what is self-evident and can be derived from common sense is a testimonial to its ideological bias, sexist research, masculinist values. In the end the commission's work has little to do with the study of the relationship between pornography and behavior, and everything to do with its own protection of male vested interests.

It is said in radical circles that liberals are the ones who will hang you only a half inch from the ground. With that in mind, recall that sociologist Marvin Wolfgang was one of the two commissioners who issued a minority statement in *The Report of the Commission on Obscenity and Pornography* indicating that it *did not go far enough* in recommending the removal of any restrictions of adults' access to pornography. The commission called for the removal of all restrictions, noting that there was no evidence that pornography would be harmful to juveniles.

Now, almost ten years later, after a drastic escalation in pornography, an increase in rape, a proliferation of rings that buy and sell children for pornography—in short, after thousands of women and children have suffered the assault of sexual terrorism and violence as a result (in part) of the legitimization that Wolfgang and his colleagues gave to pornography—after all that, *Time* magazine

(August 27, 1979) reports that Marvin Wolfgang may have had a change of heart and that he may find a causal connection between pornography and sexual violence. It is our lives, our bodies, and those of our children that have paid the expense of that earlier liberal rhetoric.

It is costly for us to be diverted to false issues like freedom of speech or busy work (such as trying to prove through research what we already know through common sense). While we research, discuss, and debate the merits of each issue, pornography proliferates. The pornography empire will not be affected by our discussions. It will be altered by our actions.

Recently the *Bay Guardian* referred to Women Against Violence in Pornography and Media as "Laura Lederer and her humorless gang of women against everything." Resorting to ridicule when other strategies fail, our opposition ultimately reveals a deep fear, a fear of what would happen to male power and what kind of society would result if we could establish a social order free from sexual exploitation and violence. They are not afraid of what we are *against*. They are afraid of what we are *for*. What we are for is so much more powerful than what we are against.

While hiking last summer, I had been thinking about why we've been so restrained in confronting the issue of pornography. One morning after hiking up from a deep canyon that was very beautiful but dark and overhung with trees, I came out onto open rock. Feeling the warmth and glow of the sun, I turned to look behind me and saw an incredible expanse of mountains. The sun was coming up over them, gilding their edges. I was overwhelmed with their majesty. At that moment I realized that if we are going to destroy the effects of pornography on our lives and in our society we must start thinking bigger. We must each be able to visualize on a grand scale what it is that we want for ourselves and for our society. As we bring our visions together, we will coalesce our battle with a vision that is beyond the negation of what is.

Would you try now to think of what it would be like to live in a society in which we are not daily, every minute, bombarded with sexual violence? Would you try to visualize what it would be like to go to the movies and not see it, to be able to walk home and not be afraid of it, to be able to walk through the drugstore and not view it? We have a right to that kind of society, to that kind of life. But we can only achieve it by creating a vision of what we want and fighting for it. If we set that as our goal and demand nothing less, we will not stop fighting until we've achieved it.

Afterword

Adrienne Rich

This book is in some ways a microcosm of the American feminist movement as it stands at the beginning of the 1980's. It is a gathering of testimonies very different from each other in focus and style: a collection of position papers, analyses, meditations, critiques, journalism, narratives both personal and collective, exhortations, research studies, documentary and oral history, programs for action. This is a movement with a decade or more of its own contemporary history-making to look back upon, and a still earlier generation of activism and rhetoric to consult and criticize—not only the abolitionist and suffrage movements but the nineteenth-century American social reform and temperance movements, with their recognizably feminist underpinnings, their reputation for puritanism and their later co-option by conservatives—not to mention the nineteenth-century British antislavery movement led by Josephine Butler. It comes out of the only vital, growing, international political movement of the decade—a movement, to quote Ida Husted Harper in an earlier context, "greatly misrepresented in the public press" [1]—for reasons on which this book sheds considerable light.

When the manuscript of *Take Back the Night* arrived, I sat down to read it through in preparation for writing this afterword, convinced that much of the material would be familiar to me in substance if not in text. I had listened to most of the speeches when they were given, had heard participant accounts of many of the actions against pornography, was familiar with most of the arguments and research. But as I read on, I realized not only that new facts and insights are constantly accruing around this issue but also that the book is vastly more than the sum of its parts. It is in fact an immense peeling back of layer upon layer of false consciousness and of what Kathleen Barry has termed "denial-through-hiding," [2] a web of connections that leap into visibility, strand by strand, as we read.

The individual papers gathered here will be used, debated, and quoted for a long time to come. Brought together in this way they pierce to the core of a devastating human reality, as not even the most eloquent of them can do on their own. The process of reading the manuscript as a whole has deepened my perception not only of pornography itself and its omnipresence in our lives, but of the dynamics among racism, woman-hating, and compulsory heterosexuality; of the powerful economic interests which comprise the pornography empire and which are ranged against even the most moderate demands of women; of the institutional misogyny that underlies apparent permissiveness or tolerance toward feminism. I felt I was acquainted with these connections, but they come together in this book with an impact—a resonance—which if profoundly angering and disturbing also offers a fierce, clear shock of relief: *Yes, it is all of this, and more. And I need to know it all.*

For this collection traces a classic progression in political consciousness: from the acceptance of objectification and exploitation as "the way things are" to questioning, to anger, to *ad hoc* local activism, spontaneously emerging in many places at the same time, to further analysis, to a radical and encompassing skepticism which boldly and lucidly insists on examining every ethical, political, legal, aesthetic, and social question from a woman's point of view. It presents a diversity of approaches and viewpoints on a single theme, which becomes no longer singular but reveals itself as one knot in a tangle of issues that freedom-loving women are learning to address in multiple, sometimes divergent ways. What is singular, what is held in common by every writer in this book, whatever their differences, is the view that the true subject of pornography is not sex or eros but objectification, which increasingly includes cruelty, violence against women and children, the crushing out of the soul; that it does not speak for the erotic choices of women; and that the intensification and proliferation of pornography in our time can be associated with deeply repressive patterns of political violence, such as witch burning, lynching, pogroms, fascism.

Confronting pornography and the powerful institutions which promote and protect it can be radicalizing for all women, especially perhaps for white women who, by virtue of living white in a racist society, may be tempted to imagine that privilege is the same thing as freedom, or that accepting tokenism will purchase truly human status. For pornography is relentless in its message, which is the message of the master to the slave: *This is what you are; this is what I can do to you.* The Black lesbian/feminist writer and activist Barbara Smith has spoken of Black women having to perceive, for mere survival in a doubly negated identity, that "this is not a world for us"[3]— an early-acquired radical skepticism. Examining the images and issue of pornography within the particular time frame of American history, white women are also making connections which lead increasingly to the understanding that, delusions of white-skin privilege to the contrary, this is not a world for us either. The objectification of the "pure" white middle-class wife, mother, and daughter was always part of a skein of sexual fantasy and cruelty, an ideology of sexual violence which would become more "normal" and respectable as a result of its symbiosis with a socially condoned and respectable racism. Writing in this book of the correlation between the "carnal hatred" displayed by the white man against Black men and women in slavery and in lynchings, and the "increasingly obscene and inhuman treatment of white women by the white male in pornography and in real life," Tracey A. Gardner points toward the heart of a transaction that many white feminists, partly because of racism, have failed to understand. The first taste of total institutionalized license to sexual violence came to the white male in America as the legal, absolute master of Black slaves, or as the downtrodden white laborer to whom Black people were allowed as lawful prey. In the words of Lillian Smith, a white antiracist,

> Somehow much in the white woman that he could not come to terms with, the schizophrenic split he had made in her nature— the sacred madonna and the bitch he had made of her—could now be projected, in part, onto another female: under slavery, he could keep his pure white "madonna" and have his dark tempestuous "prostitute." [4]

But white violence against Black men was also sexual. Lura Beam, a white woman who taught in southern Black schools from 1908 to 1919, reports both the disemboweling of pregnant Black women in lynchings and the carving up of Black male sexual organs "for love powders"; castration was integral to the lynching ritual for men.[5] The lynching of Black men, justified by the "protection of white womanhood," had a pornography of its own. To quote Lillian Smith again:

> In the name of *sacred womanhood*, of *purity*, of *preserving the home*, lecherous old men and young ones . . . who had violated the home since they were sixteen years old, whipped up lynchings, organized Klans, burned crosses, aroused the poor and ignorant to wild excitement by an obscene, perverse imagery describing the "menace" of Negro men hiding behind every cypress waiting to rape "our" women.[6]

I want to understand the American female experience in terms of the specific, sexually bitter, morally problematic mutual history lived through by women of color and white women on this continent; but also I need to understand the sexually-based violence and enslavement of women built into cultures which are not western or white—and the methods by which women everywhere have survived or actively countered that violence.

Perhaps one of the most important statements in this book is made by Andrea Dworkin when she says that pornography is "not a genre of expression separate and different from the rest of life . . . it is . . . fully in harmony with any culture in which it flourishes." (Kathleen Barry, in her brilliant study *Female Sexual Slavery*, demonstrates this exhaustively.) This remark is consonant with what I have called the radical skepticism of feminist thought: a skepticism which insists on the connectedness of what we have been taught to keep separate. When we face the implications of the studies on pornography and media, pornography and social science, pornography and family life, pornography and the traffic in women, pornography and economic power, pornography and racism, we become aware that the glorification of violence against women is not a surface growth which can be deftly excised, leaving the anatomy around it untouched, it is systemic, and to question it is to question the entire society by which it thrives.

And so we cannot treat pornography—hard core or soft core, crude or sophisticated—as an isolated "social problem." If its message is a lie about women, that we exist to pleasure and service men and that our deepest pleasure lies in enslavement and subordination, it also affirms the enforcement of heterosexuality for women, the male right of sexual access. There is a continuum between the bridal mannequin, blank faced and sleepwalking in veil and train, in one store window, and the equally faceless mannequin in spike-heeled boots, chain jewelry, leather collar, and girdle, her body jerked awry as by the voltage of electric shock, in another. In Helen Longino's words: "To suggest, as pornography does, that the primary purpose of women is to provide sexual pleasure to men is to deny that women are independently human or have a status equal to that of men."

Kathleen Barry has analyzed the cross-cultural network of "sex colonization," which includes wife-battery; incest; marital rape; the Muslim code of "honor" regarding female chastity; marriage through seclusion, arrangement, and bride-price; genital mutilation; and enforced prostitution, of which pornography is the ideology. She includes in this system, and I would even more strongly emphasize,

taboos on and punishment for lesbian behavior, including the vogue
for pseudolesbian pornography (see the interview with "Jane Jones"
in this book) and the wipeout of actual lesbian history and expression.
Pornography needs to be understood as a statement about the restriction of fundamental choices for women, the enforcement of male
right of access—on male terms—which may include variations on
passivity, torture, rape, mutilation, humiliation, but always with the
requirement that we pretend to like it.

There is a continuum between the "soft-focus" objectification of
the pretty teenage model in the pages of "women's magazines,"
"fashion magazines," or the daily papers, and the pipelines transport-
ing young women runaways to sexual slavery. There is a continuum
between the pimp—white or Black—beating, drugging, imprisoning
the prostitute—Black or white—and the towers of metropolitan buildings, where white male entrepreneurs develop a multibillion-dollar
power complex based on images of women chained, battered, dis-
figured, raped. In between, there is the more elegant imagery pur-
veyed by Bloomingdale's or Saks Fifth Avenue, by *Vogue* or *The
New York Times Magazine*. Reinforcing all these is the assertion of
literary intellectuals that "the question is not *whether* pornography,
but the quality of the pornography." [7]

"Passionately humanistic!" a critic lauds a novel depicting the
hero's "witty" murder of his feminist wife and a series of her feminist
friends. The celebration of woman-degrading literary and graphic
propaganda; the silencing or jeering of the feminist claim to dignity,
integrity, and self-determination for women; the invisibility or grotesque caricaturing of lesbian existence. The Black woman (and the
Asian, the Hispanic, the Native American, the woman of color in
general) still represented—and often treated—as the presumed or
potential harlot, though in the blatancy of recent pornographic media,
the white woman—and the female child—have been visibly dumped
from the pedestal of purity to become part of this highly saleable
imagery.

There is a continuum along which we can trace the breakdown of
the masquerade of humanism: the "rational" Jeffersonian white male
who is free to rape the Black woman, have her whipped, stripped
naked on the auction block, and sold; free to lynch the Black man,
torture, strip, castrate, and hang him; still today killing or condoning
the killing of Black men, women, and children, but his "humanism"
now also unabashedly focused against the white woman—she also,
whatever her caste or privilege, *carnally hated*, meant to be not merely

dominated and humiliated in daily life but beaten in bondage, forced to eat feces, her nipples rubbed raw with pincers, her body fed into a meat grinder. *This is not a world for any of us.*

And, as Alice Walker acknowledges, Black men are buying into this also.

And I find myself connecting the genital cruelty and obsession imaged in pornography, not only with the genital cruelty and intentional terrorism of lynchings but also with customs such as clitoridectomy and infibulation practiced in Third World cultures, the *genital torturing of women* to make them more fit for marriage, more satisfying to the male organ. Woman as property, converted by ritual violence to nothing more than a hole to be sewn and unsewn, her clitoris excised, her genitals the focus of incalculable ingenuity (who could first have imagined such operations and how many women have died from them?)[8]; operations calculated to ensure male sexual ownership and control, just as lynchings helped to ensure the de facto enslavement of Black people after "Emancipation."

In 1967 when Susan Sontag wrote her essay "The Pornographic Imagination," she declared that pornography is not ultimately about sex but about death. ("It's toward the gratifications of death, surpassing those of eros, that every truly obscene quest tends.")[9] She may very well have changed her views by now. I think it as romantic to say that pornography is about death as that it is about eros. It is an abstract statement rendered in the world of literary criticism, not the world of necessary activism. It tells us nothing about what we might do, those of us who are experiencing its repercussions in our daily lives, not as art but as rape, assault, and the fear of walking out at night.

Pornography is about slavery. To oppose pornography requires that we connect culturally glorified violence against women with more traditionally recognized forms of political enslavement; that we ask: What is the meaning and function of the slave? For slavery too is in harmony with any culture in which it flourishes.* And the enslavement of women as women has traditionally gone almost unrecognized. It has been culturally rationalized, romanticized, or simply taken for granted.

What is the meaning and function of the slave in this culture? I am not talking here about the agreed-upon acting out by two indi-

---

* It can be argued metaphorically that slavery is a "living death," based on the power of one individual over another's life which makes the second completely subject to the will of the first. But slavery and death are in fact two different states, and people in life-and-death situations have made choices between them.

viduals of what is called "sadomasochism"—however impoverished I may consider this as a moral or political statement. I am talking about an enforced social condition, an institutionalized status. I do not think any purely psychological answer will suffice. And any true economic answer would mean exploding the meaning of economics itself, to take seriously the emotional economy which has always been the assigned burden of women and "inferior" groups. The slave—female or male—has been feminized—assigned the weakness, capriciousness, emotional instability, childishness of the female stereotype—on the way to being dehumanized. (And the backlash against women's politicization in the seventies began with a prescribed return to high heels, makeup, skirts, and other dysfunctional modes of "high fashion.") Yet, as Angela Davis noted, the system of Black slavery in America depended on the *defeminization* of the Black woman, who became, in Zora Neale Hurston's words, "de mule ob de world." [10] Animalization. (The contempt and fear of animals revealed in that! And: "She's really a splendid animal," a man said to me, years ago, about a mutual friend who was tall, Nordic, blond, and beautiful in the most acceptable style.)

The fact is that both the psychological and the economic answers heretofore given to such questions have been the products of a "humanism"—and a Marxism—which do not take female slavery seriously. A humanism which has defended *The Story of O* and the Marquis de Sade's ideas as radical art and political philosophy; which does not see how their repetitive themes—the reduction of women through violence to hated flesh, literally, to excrement—both foreshadow and flash back to the Holocaust, the Siberian slave camps, the atrocities of Vietnam, Iran, Chile, or wherever the crushing out of the soul has been attempted and often realized.

Pornography is the message of the master to the slave: *This is what you are; this is what I can do to you.* But freedom-loving women discern in it another message; it is the master's unwitting depiction of himself. *This is what I am.* The visible figures in pornography may be women, the men, when present, are masked, as in *Story of O*; but we know it is men who direct these movies, men who order these scenes, men who take the pictures, men who control their mass distribution, men who buy them and who self-righteously defend them. And this is the portrait of maleness that men are willing to tolerate, whether they claim it for their own or not. I confess that I cannot understand why men who think of themselves as seekers of a new sensitivity, as humanists, as nonviolent activists, as would-be transformers of the human condition—why such men are not actively and vocally appalled at pornography, not even for women's sake but for the portrayal of men that pornography exhibits. The most radical skepticism still does not make me understand.

When feminists a decade ago first began to protest pornography, their outcry was against the routine, soul-destroying objectification of women's faces and bodies, not simply the representation of sexual violence. In the ensuing decade, a rapid proliferation in the production and distribution of pornographic materials—ranging from slick magazines to videocassettes—and an acceleration of extreme violence in all media have drawn attention from mundane, everyday objectification, our reduction to one-dimensional meaninglessness. We need to keep the continuum always before us—from the creation of the white doll-woman to the present vogue for blond child-pornography models; between the pornography of racism and fascism and the pornography which portrays all women—bitches or dolls—as victims by nature. We need to be very clear as to how the aesthetics of enforced heterosexuality have both created and reflected those glazed, passive-seductive images of women that look forth from the most apparently innocuous advertising. And, finally, how all objectification is a prelude to and condition of slavery.

And if today a Black-Third World feminism is becoming increasingly articulate, a movement of women of color who have known all along that "this is not a world for us"; and if a white feminist consciousness is also emerging which can connect the politics of race and of enforced heterosexuality with the message of pornography; and if more and more women come to full understanding that it is and always has been suicidal for us to be lured into implementing slavery—our own or other people's—then I believe and hope that in the decades before us, in Andrea Dworkin's words, we will begin to take back not only the night but of necessity and choice the daylight as well.

References

Section I. What Is Pornography?

Questions We Get Asked Most Often

1. For a good summary of these experiments, see Urie Bronfenbrenner, *Two Worlds of Childhood: US and USSR* (New York: Russell Sage Foundation, 1970), pp. 109–115.

Pornography, Oppression, and Freedom: A Closer Look

1. *Women Against Violence in Pornography and Media Newspage*, Vol. II, No. 5, June 1978; and Judith Reisman in *Women Against Violence in Pornography and Media Proposal*.
2. American Law Institute *Model Penal Code*, sec. 251.4.
3. *Report of the Commission on Obscenity and Pornography* (New York: Bantam Books, 1979), p. 239. The Commission, of course, concluded that the demeaning content of pornography did not adversely affect male attitudes toward women.
4. Among recent feminist discussions are Diana Russell, "Pornography: A Feminist Perspective" and Susan Griffin, "On Pornography," *Chrysalis*, Vol. I, No. 4, 1978; and Ann Garry, "Pornography and Respect for Women," *Social Theory and Practice*, Vol. 4, Spring 1978, pp. 395–421.
5. *The Oxford English Dictionary*, Compact Edition (London: Oxford University Press, 1971), p. 2242.
6. Urie Bronfenbrenner, *Two Worlds of Childhood* (New York: Russell Sage Foundation, 1970); H. J. Eysenck and D.K.B. Nias, *Sex, Violence and the Media* (New York: St. Martin's Press, 1978); and Michael Goldstein, Harold Kant, and John Hartman, *Pornography and Sexual Deviance* (Berkeley: University of California Press, 1973); and the papers by Diana Russell, Pauline Bart, and Irene Diamond included in this volume.
7. Cf. Marshall Cohen, "The Case Against Censorship," *The Public Interest*, No. 22, Winter 1971, reprinted in John R. Burr and Milton Goldinger, *Philosophy and Contemporary Issues* (New York: Macmillan, 1976), and Justice William Brennan's dissenting opinion in *Paris Adult Theater I* v. *Slaton*, 431 U.S. 49.
8. Ronald Dworkin, *Taking Rights Seriously* (Cambridge: Harvard University Press, 1977), p. 262.

Section II. Pornography: Who Is Hurt

Child Pornography

1. Robert Sam Anson, *The San Francisco Chronicle*, October 25, 1977.

2. *The History of Childhood*, Lloyd de Mause, ed. (New York: Harper Torchbooks, 1974), passim.

3. Herant A. Katchadourian and Donald T. Lund, *Fundamentals of Human Sexuality* (New York: Holt, Rinehart & Winston, 1972), p. 439.

4. Samuel G. Kling, *Sexual Behavior and the Law* (New York: Bernard Geis Associates, 1965), p. 216.

5. Wilson Bryan Key, *Media Sexploitation* (Englewood Cliffs, N.J.: Prentice-Hall, 1976), pp. 56–58.

6. Advertisements: Underwear, "Little Miss Teenform, Eiderdown"; also "Caress Soap and Baby Soft Cosmetics" in *Seventeen*, August 1977. (Unfortunately, I do not have the names and dates of other publications in which these ads appear, but I do have pictures of all publications in my files.)

7. Rosemary Kent, "Clothes Conscious Kids," *Harper's Bazaar*, January 1977, p. 110.

8. William Burroughs, *Naked Lunch* (New York: Grove Press, 1959), p. 141.

9. Bob Williams, "Antoine Job Outlook Cool," *New York Post*, November 26, 1976.

10. Fyodor Dostoyevsky, *The Possessed*, trans. Constance Garnett (New York: Laurel Press, 1959, 1964), p. 711.

11. Fyodor Dostoyevsky, *Crime and Punishment* (New York: Laurel Press, 1959, 1962), p. 537.

12. Graham Ovenden, "On O. G. Rejlander," in *Victorian Children* (New York: St. Martin's Press and Robert Melville Academy editions, 1972), plates 111, 112.
    Edward Lucie Smith, "On Pascin," in *Eroticism in Western Art* (London: Thames and Hudson, 1972), p. 150.
    "On Balthus," ibid., p. 182.

13. David Hamilton, *Sisters* (New York: William Morrow & Co., 1973), p. 15.

14. Vincent Canby, "Film: 'Pretty Baby' by Louis Malle," *The New York Times*, April 5, 1978.

15. Judith Crist, "Beauty in Baby," *New York Post*, April 5, 1978.

16. Luticia Kent, "Malle: 'Pretty Baby' Could Be Called the Apprenticeship of Corruption," *The New York Times*, April 16, 1978.

17. Christina Rossetti, "In an Artist's Studio," in *The World Split Open*, Louise Bernikow, ed. (New York: Vintage Books, 1974), p. 125.

18. Aubrey Beardsley, *The Story of Venus and Tannhauser* (New York: Award Books, 1967), pp. 106–109.

19. "Memoirs of Josephine Mutzenbacher," Felix Salten, in *The Encyclopedia of Erotica*, Dr. Paul J. Gillette, ed. (New York: Award Books, 1967), p. 309.

20. Guy de Maupassant, *The Colonel's Nieces* (California: Brandon Books, 1972), p. 63.

21. Peter Quennell, *Casanova in London.* (New York: Stein & Day, 1971), p. 2.

22. Frank Harris, *My Lives and Loves* (New York: Castle Books, Inc.,

by arrangement with Grove Press, 1963), p. 877.

23. Anonymous, *My Secret Life* (New York: Grove Press, 1966), passim.

24. Walter Lenning, *Portrait of De Sade* (New York: Herder & Herder, 1971), pp. 35–63.

25. Pamela Hansford Johnson, *On Iniquity* (New York: Charles Scribner's Sons, 1967), p. 125.

26. George Steiner, "Night Words," *The Case Against Pornography*, ed. David Holbrook (La Salle, Ill.: Library Press, 1973), p. 234.

27. Neil Gallagher, *How to Stop the Porno Plague* (Minneapolis: Bethany Fellowship, Inc., 1977), p. 20.

28. Ibid., p. 21.

29. Ron Sproat, "Working Day in a Porno Factory," *New York Magazine*, March 11, 1974.

30. Robin Lloyd, *For Money or Love* (New York: Ballantine Books, 1977), p. 93.

31. Barbara Campbell, "Officials Consider Child Pornography Hard to Prosecute," *The New York Times*, January 15, 1977.

32. Vern and Bonnie Bullough, *Sin, Sickness and Sanity: A History of Sexual Attitudes* (New York: New American Library, 1977), pp. 109–111, 171.

33. Clive Barnes, "Introduction," in *The Report of the Commission on Obscenity and Pornography* (New York: Bantam Books, 1970), pp. ix–xvii.

34. Ibid., p. 147.

35. Ibid., p. 664.

36. Bullough, op. cit., p. 174.

37. Barbara Campbell, "Aid Asked in Blocking Use of Children in Pornography," *The New York Times*, November 14, 1977.

38. Mitchell Ditkoff, "Child Pornography," *American Humane Society Magazine*, Vol. 16, No. 4, Denver, Colorado (1978), p. 30.

Testimony Against Pornography: Witness from Denmark

1. Jean-Claude Lauret, *The Danish Sex Fairs* (London: Jasmine Press, 1970), quoted by David Holbrook in *The Case Against Pornography* (New York: The Library Press, 1973), p. 6.

2. Victor Bachy, "Danish 'Permissiveness' Revisited," *Journal of Communication*, Vol. 26, No. 1, 1976.

Pornography in Sweden: A Feminist's Perspective

1. "Pornography and Sex Crimes: A Re-evaluation in the Light of Recent Trends Around the World," in John H. Court, *The International Journal of Criminology & Penology*, Vol. 5, 1977, pp. 129–157.

Section III. Pornography: Who Benefits

Men and Pornography: Why They Use It

1. Andrea Dworkin, "The Root Cause," *Our Blood* (New York: Harper & Row, 1976).

Pornography and the Dread of Women:
The Male Sexual Dilemma

1. Simone de Beauvoir, *The Second Sex*, trans. H. M. Parshley (New York: Alfred A. Knopf, 1968), p. 253.
2. Dorothy Dinnerstein, *The Mermaid and the Minotaur* (New York: Harper & Row, 1977), p. 166.
3. Ibid., p. 164.
4. Charles Brenner, *An Elementary Textbook of Psychoanalysis* (New York: Doubleday & Co., 1957), pp. 117–121.
5. Ibid., p. 117.
6. Ibid., p. 121.
7. Norman O. Brown, *Life Against Death* (Middletown, Conn.: Wesleyan University Press, 1959), p. 124.
8. Mary Daly, *Gyn/Ecology* (Boston: Beacon Press, 1978), p. 188.
9. Ernest Becker, *The Denial of Death* (New York: The Free Press, 1973), p. 41.
10. *Crimes Against Women*, Diana E. H. Russell and Nicole Van de Ven, eds. (Millbrae, Calif.: Les Femmes, 1976), p. 150.
11. Ibid., pp. 150–151.
12. Brenner, op. cit., p. 122.
13. Sigmund Freud, *Sexuality and the Psychology of Love* (New York: Basic Books, 1963), p. 76.
14. "Fate," *The Oxford Classical Dictionary* (Oxford, England: Oxford University Press, 1970), p. 430.
15. "Tiresias," ibid., p. 1070.
16. Sophocles, *The Oedipus Plays of Sophocles*, trans. Paul Roche (New York: New American Library, 1958).
17. "Riddles," *The Oxford Classical Dictionary*, 1970, p. 924.

The Propaganda of Misogyny

1. Leonard William Doob, *Public Opinion and Propaganda* (Hamden, Conn.: Archon, 1948), p. 240.
2. James A. Brown, *Techniques of Persuasion* (New York: Penguin Books, 1963).
3. Shere Hite, *The Hite Report* (New York: Macmillan Publishing Co., 1976).

Section IV.   Research on the Effects of Pornography

Pornography and Repression:
A Reconsideration of "Who" and "What"

1. Amitai Etzioni, "Porn Is Here to Stay," *The New York Times*, May 17, 1977, p. 35.
2. Ibid.
3. H. Montgomery Hyde, *A History of Pornography* (New York: Farrar, Straus & Giroux, 1965), p. 1.
4. As cited by Robert Yoakum in "An Obscene, Lewd, Lascivious, In-

decent, Filthy, and Vile Tabloid Entitled *Screw*," *Columbia Journalism Review*, March/April 1977, p. 46.

5. Paul Goodman, *Utopian Essays and Practical Proposals* (New York: Random House, 1962), p. 57.

6. David Foxon, "Libertine Literature in England, 1660–1745, 'The Book Collector,'" Nos. 1, 2, 3 (Spring, Summer, Winter, 1963), p. 306.

7. Steven Marcus, *The Other Victorians* (New York: Basic Books, 1964), p. 286.

8. Kate Millett, *Sexual Politics* (New York: Doubleday, Equinox Edition, Avon Books, 1969), pp. 42–45.

9. Robin Morgan, "Goodbye to All That," in *The American Sisterhood*, Wendy Martin, ed. (New York: Harper & Row, 1972), p. 361.

10. Andrea Dworkin, *Woman Hating* (New York: E. P. Dutton, 1974), p. 78.

11. Sheila Rowbotham, *Woman, Resistance, and Revolution* (New York: Pantheon/Vintage Books, 1973), p. 30.

12. Susan Brownmiller, *Against Our Will* (New York: Simon & Schuster, 1975), p. 394.

13. Ellen Willis, "Sexual Counterrevolution I," *Rolling Stone*, March 24, 1977, p. 29.

14. Charles H. Keating, Jr., in *The Report of the Commission on Obscenity and Pornography* (Washington, D.C.: U.S. Government Printing Office, September 1970), p. 516.

15. Ibid., p. 194.

16. Ibid., p. 3

17. R. F. Cook and R. H. Fosen, "Pornography and the Sex Offender: Patterns of Exposure and Immediate Arousal Effects of Pornographic Stimuli," *Technical Reports of the Commission on Obscenity and Pornography*, Vol. 7 (Washington, D.C.: U.S. Government Printing Office, 1970), p. 168.

18. A. S. Berger, J. H. Gagnon, and W. Simon, "Pornography: High School and College Years," *Technical Reports of the Commission on Obscenity and Pornography*, Vol. 9 (Washington, D.C.: U.S. Government Printing Office, 1970), p. 168.

19. *The Report of the Commission on Obscenity and Pornography* (Washington, D.C.: U.S. Government Printing Office, September 1970), p. 139.

20. Ibid., p. 242.

21. C. E. Walker, "Erotic Stimuli and the Aggressive Sexual Offender," *Technical Reports of the Commission on Obscenity and Pornography*, Vol. 7 (Washington, D.C.: U.S. Government Printing Office, 1970), p. 111.

22. Ibid., p. 130.

23. Michael J. Goldstein and Harold Sanford Kant with John J. Hartman, *Pornography and Sexual Deviance* (Berkeley: University of California Press, 1973), p. 73.

24. Walker, op. cit., p. 128ff.

25. Goldstein and Kant, op. cit., p. 75.

26. *The Report of the Commission on Obscenity and Pornography*, op. cit., p. 221.
27. M. M. Propper, "Exposure to Sexually Oriented Materials Among Young Male Prison Offenders," *Technical Reports of the Commisson on Obscenity and Pornography*, Vol. 9 (Washington, D.C.: U.S. Government Printing Office, 1970), p. 363.
28. Garry Wills, "Measuring the Impact of Erotica," *Psychology Today*, August 1977, p. 33.
29. Cited in J. Mann, J. Sidman, and S. Starr, "Effects of Erotic Films on Sexual Behaviors of Married Couples," *Technical Reports of the Commission on Obscenity and Pornography*, Vol. 8 (Washington, D.C.: U.S. Government Printing Office, 1970), p. 217.
30. *The Report of the Commission on Obscenity and Pornography*, op. cit., p. 201.
31. P. H. Tannenbaum, "Emotional Arousal as a Mediator of Communication Effects," *Technical Reports of the Commission on Obscenity and Pornography,* Vol. 8, op. cit., p. 326.
32. *The Report of the Commission on Obscenity and Pornography*, op. cit., p. 208.
33. J. L. Howard, C. B. Reifler, and M. B. Liptzin, "Effects of Exposure to Pornography," *Technical Reports of the Commission on Obscenity and Pornography*, Vol. 8 (Washington, D.C.: U.S. Government Printing Office, 1970).
34. *The Report of the Commission on Obscenity and Pornography*, op. cit., p. 229.
35. Ibid., p. 231.
36. R. Ben-Veniste, "Pornography and Sex Crime—The Danish Experience," *Technical Reports of the Commission on Obscenity and Pornography,* Vol. 7, p. 245 (Washington, D.C.: U.S. Government Printing Office, 1970).
37. Berl Kutchinsky, "Sex Crimes and Pornography in Copenhagen: A Survey of Attitudes," ibid.
38. Victor Bachy, "Danish 'Permissiveness' Revisited," *The Journal of Communication*, Vol. 26, No. 1 (1976); and J. H. Court, "Pornography and Sex Crimes: A Re-evaluation in the Light of Recent Trends Around the World," *International Criminology and Penology*, Vol. 5, 1977, pp. 129–157.
39. F. E. Kenyon, "Pornography, Law, and Mental Health," *British Journal of Psychiatry*, Vol. 126, March 1975, p. 226.
40. Pamela Hansford Johnson, *On Iniquity*. (New York: Charles Scribner's Sons, 1967), p. 26.
41. Robert Stoller, *Perversion: The Erotic Form of Hatred* (New York: Pantheon, 1975), p. 88.

Dirty Books, Dirty Films, and Dirty Data

1. Thelma McCormack, "Machismo in Media Research: A Critical Review of Research on Violence and Pornography," *Social Problems*, Vol. XXV, No. 5 (June 1978), pp. 552–554.
2. Ibid., p. 545.

3. Ibid.
4. Ibid., p. 551.
5. Seymour Feshbach and Neal Malamuth, "Sex and Aggression: Proving the Link," *Psychology Today*, Vol. XII, No. 6 (November 1978), pp. 111–117, 122.
6. W. Cody Wilson and Herbert I. Abelson, "Experience With and Attitudes Toward Explicit Sexual Materials," *The Journal of Social Issues*, Vol. XXIX, No. 3 (1973), pp. 19–39.
7. Douglas H. Wallace, "Obscenity and Contemporary Community Standards: A Survey," *The Journal of Social Issues*, Vol. XXIX, No. 3 (1973), pp. 53–68.
8. Berl Kutchinsky, "The Effect of Easy Availability of Pornography on the Incidence of Sex Crimes: The Danish Experience," *The Journal of Social Issues*, Vol. XXIX, No. 3 (1973), pp. 163–181.
9. Donald Mosher, "Sex Differences, Sex Experiences, Sex Guilt, and Explicitly Sexual Films," *The Journal of Social Issues*, Vol. XXIX, No. 3 (1973), pp. 95–112.
10. Ibid., p. 111.
11. James L. Howard, Myron B. Liptzin, and Clifford B. Reifler, "Is Pornography a Problem?" *The Journal of Social Issues*, Vol. XXIX, No. 3 (1973), pp. 133–145.
12. Keith E. Davis and G. Nicholas Braucht, "Exposure to Pornography, Character, and Sexual Deviance: A Retrospective Survey," *The Journal of Social Issues*, Vol. XXIX, No. 3 (1973), pp. 183–196.
13. Ibid., p. 195.
14. Michael J. Goldstein, "Exposure to Erotic Stimuli and Sexual Deviance," *The Journal of Social Issues*, Vol. XXIX, No. 3 (1973), pp. 197–219.
15. Ibid., p. 216.
16. *Forcible Rape*, National Institute of Law Enforcement and Criminal Justice, U.S. Government Printing Office, March 1978, p. 49.
17. Paula Johnson and Jacqueline D. Goodchilds, "Pornography, Sexuality, and Social Psychology," *The Journal of Social Issues*, Vol. XXIX, No. 3 (1973), pp. 231–238.
18. Jay Mann, Jack Sidman, and Sheldon Starr, "Evaluating Social Consequences of Erotic Films: An Experimental Approach," *The Journal of Social Issues*, Vol. XXIX, No. 3 (1973), pp. 113–131.
19. McCormack, op. cit., p. 549.
20. Johnson and Goodchilds, op. cit., p. 238.
21. Robin Morgan, *Going Too Far* (New York: Vintage Books, 1978).
22. Don Smith, "Sexual Aggression in American Pornography: The Stereotype of Rape," paper presented at the annual meetings of the American Sociological Association, New York City, 1976.
23. Ibid.
24. Neal M. Malamuth and Barry Spinner, "A Longitudinal Content Analysis of Sexual Violence in the Best-Selling Erotic Magazines," *Journal of Sex Research*, August 1980, in press.
25. Feshbach and Malamuth, op. cit., p. 116.
26. Ibid.

27. Personal communication of October 9, 1979.
28. Neal M. Malamuth and James V. P. Check, "Penile Tumescence and Perceptual Responses to Rape as a Function of Victims' Perceived Reactions," *Journal of Applied Social Psychology,* in press.
29. Neal M. Malamuth, Ilana Reisin, and Barry Spinner, "Exposure to Pornography and Reactions to Rape," paper presented at the annual meetings of the American Psychological Association, New York City, September 1979.
30. Feshbach and Malamuth, op. cit., p. 117.
31. Ibid., p. 122.
32. Neal M. Malamuth, Scott Haber, and Seymour Feshbach, "Testing Hypotheses Regarding Rape: Exposure to Sexual Violence, Sex Differences, and the 'Normality' of Rapists," *Journal of Research in Personality,* Vol. 14 (1980), pp. 121–137.
33. Neal M. Malamuth, Maggie Heim, and Seymour Feshbach, "Sexual Responsiveness of College Students to Rape Depictions: Inhibitory and Disinhibitory Effects," *Journal of Personality and Social Psychology,* Vol. 38, No. 3 (1980), pp. 399–408.
34. Edward Donnerstein, "Pornography and Violence Against Women: Experimental Studies," *Annals of the New York Academy of Science,* 1980.
35. Edward Donnerstein and John Hallam, "The Facilitating Effects of Erotica on Aggression Against Women," *Journal of Personality and Social Psychology,* Vol. 36, 1978, pp. 1270–77.
36. McCormack, op. cit.

Pornography and Violence: What Does the New Research Say?

1. Donald Mosher, "Sex Callousness toward Women," *Technical Reports of the Commission on Obscenity and Pornography,* Vol. 8, 1971, p. 314.
2. Ibid., pp. 318, 321.
3. Donald Mosher, "Psychological Reactions to Pornographic Films," in *Technical Reports of the Commission on Obscenity and Pornography,* Vol. 8, 1971, p. 255.
4. Ibid., p. 258.
5. Ibid.
6. G. Schmidt, V. Sigusch, and S. Schafer, "Responses to Reading Erotic Stories: Male-Female Differences," *Archives of Sexual Behavior,* Vol. 2, 1973, pp. 181–199.
7. H. J. Eysenck and D. K. B. Nias, *Sex, Violence and the Media* (New York: Harper & Row, 1978), p. 258.
8. "Rape: Agony or Ecstasy?" *Response: The Photo Magazine of Sexual Awareness,* Academy Press, San Diego, Calif., pp. 8–11, 53–55.
9. Diana E. H. Russell, *The Politics of Rape* (New York: Stein & Day, 1975), p. 261.
10. Lorenne Clark and Debra Lewis, *Rape: The Price of Coercive Sexuality* (Toronto, Canada: The Women's Press, 1977).
11. Ibid., p. 142.

12. Ibid., p. 140.
13. Ibid., p. 145.
14. Eugene J. Kanin, "Male Aggression in Dating-Courtship Relations," *American Journal of Sociology*, Vol. 63, 1957, p. 197.
15. Eugene J. Kanin and C. Kirkpatrick, "Male Sex Aggression on a University Campus," *American Sociological Review*, Vol. 22, 1957, p. 53.
16. Neal Malamuth, Scott Haber, and Seymour Feshbach, "Testing Hypotheses Regarding Rape: Exposure to Sexual Violence, Sex Differences, and the 'Normality' of Rapists," *Journal of Research in Personality*, Vol. 14 (1980), pp. 121–137.
17. Seymour Feshbach and Neal Malamuth, "Sex and Aggression: Proving the Link," *Psychology Today*, November 1978, pp. 116–117.
18. Ibid., p. 117.
19. Malamuth, Haber, and Feshbach, op. cit., pp. 5–6.
20. Susan Brownmiller, *Against Our Will: Men, Women and Rape* (New York: Simon & Schuster, 1975), p. 179n.
21. Feshbach and Malamuth, op. cit., p. 112.
22. D. Zillmann. "Excitation Transfer in Communication-Mediated Aggressive Behavior," *Journal of Experimental Social Psychology*, Vol. 7, 1971; Y. Jaffe, N. Malamuth, J. Feingold, and S. Feshbach, "Sexual Arousal and Behavioral Aggression," *Journal of Personality and Social Psychology*, Vol. 30, 1974; E. Donnerstein, M. Donnerstein, and R. Evans, "Erotic Stimuli and Aggression: Facilitation or Inhibition," *Journal of Personality and Social Psychology*, Vol. 32, 1975; R. A. Baron and P. A. Bell, "Sexual Arousal and Aggression by Males: Effects of Type of Erotic Stimuli and Prior Provocation," *Journal of Personality and Social Psychology*, Vol. 35, 1977; and E. Donnerstein and G. Barrett, "The Effects of Erotic Stimuli on Male Aggression towards Females," *Journal of Personality and Social Psychology*, Vol. 36, 1978.
23. R. A. Baron. "The Aggression-Inhibiting Influence of Heightened Sexual Arousal," *Journal of Personality and Social Psychology*, Vol. 30, 1974; A. Frodi, "Sexual Arousal, Situational Restrictiveness, and Aggressive Behavior," *Journal of Research in Personality*, Vol. 11, 1977; and N. Malamuth, S. Feshbach, and Y. Jaffe, "Sexual Arousal and Aggression: Recent Experiments and Theoretical Issues," *The Journal of Social Issues*, Vol. 33, 1977.
24. Edward Donnerstein, "Aggressive Erotica and Violence Against Women," unpublished paper presented to the New York Academy of Science, October 1979, p. 4.
25. Ibid., pp. 4–5.
26. Ibid., p. 7.
27. Ibid., p. 9.
28. Ibid., p. 22
29. Ibid.
30. Edward Donnerstein, "Pornography and Violence Against Women: Experimental Studies," unpublished and undated paper, p. 13.
31. Ibid.

32. Ibid., p. 14.
33. Feshbach and Malamuth, op. cit., p. 116.
34. Ibid.
35. Malamuth, Haber, and Feshbach, op. cit., p. 7.
36. Neal Malamuth, Maggie Heim, and Seymour Feshbach, "Sexual Responsiveness of College Students to Rape Depictions: Inhibitory and Disinhibitory Effects," *Journal of Personality and Social Psychology,* Vol. 38, No. 3 (1980), pp. 399–408.
37. Ibid., p. 41.
38. Malamuth, Haber, and Feshbach, op. cit., p. 17.
39. Malamuth, Heim, and Feshbach, op. cit., p. 1.
40. Nancy Friday, *My Secret Garden* (New York: Trident Press, 1973).
41. Russell, op. cit., p. 267.
42. Neal Malamuth, "Rape Fantasies as a Function of Repeated Exposure to Sexual Violence," unpublished paper presented at the Second National Conference on the Evaluation and Treatment of Aggression, New York City, May 1979, p. 15.
43. Ibid., p. 1.
44. Ibid.
45. Ibid.
46. Ibid., p. 15.
47. G. G. Abel, et al., "The Components of Rapists' Sexual Arousal," *Archives of General Psychiatry,* Vol. 34, 1977, p. 897.
48. Ibid., p. 898.
49. D. Briddell, et al., "Effects of Alcohol and Cognitive Set on Sexual Arousal to Deviant Stimuli," *Journal of Abnormal Psychology,* Vol. 87, 1978, p. 422.
50. Ibid., p. 418.
51. Ibid., p. 427.
52. "Sexual Aggression in American Pornography: The Stereotype of Rape," unpublished paper presented at the American Sociological Association, New York City, August 1976, p. 5.
53. Ibid., p. 12.
54. Ibid., p. 10.
55. Ibid.
56. Ibid., p. 11.
57. Neal Malamuth and Barry Spinner, "A Longitudinal Content Analysis of Sexual Violence in the Best-Selling Erotic Magazines," *Journal of Sex Research,* August 1980, in press.
58. Ibid., p. 9.
59. Neal Malamuth, Seymour Feshbach, and Yoram Jaffe, "Sexual Arousal and Aggression: Recent Experiments and Theoretical Issues." *The Journal of Social Issues,* Vol. 33, No. 2, 1977, p. 129.
60. Ibid., p. 127.
61. Malamuth, Heim, and Feshbach, op. cit., p. 7.
62. Victor Cline, *Where Do You Draw the Line?* (Provo, Utah: Brigham Young University Press), p. 207.
63. Ibid., p. 208.

64. Ibid.
65. Ibid., p. 210.
66. Ibid.
67. Eysenck and Nias, op. cit., p. 190.
68. Ibid., p. 257.
69. Ibid., p. 259.
70. Martin Wolfgang, "Women's War on Porn," *Time*, August 27, 1979, p. 64.
71. Quoted in *The New York Times*, October 21, 1979, p. 41.

Section V.   Pornography and the First Amendment

Pornography and the First Amendment:
Prior Restraints and Private Action

1. 18 U.S.C. §§1461, 1462, 1465; 39 U.S.C. §§3001–3011; 19 U.S.C. §1305.
2. "An Empirical Inquiry into the Effects of *Miller* v. *California* on the Control of Obscenity," *N.Y.U. Law Review*, Vol. 52, No. 4, October 1977.
3. *Schenck* v. *United States,* 249 U.S. 47 (1919); *Dennis* v. *United States,* 341 U.S. 494 (1951); *N.Y. Times Co.* v. *United States*, 403 U.S. 713 (1971).

Section VI.   Taking Action

"We Sisters Join Together . . ."

1. Robin Morgan, "No More Miss America!" *Sisterhood Is Powerful* (New York: Vintage Books, 1970), pp. 522–524.
2. Ibid., p. 523.
3. WITCH leaflet, 1970.
4. "Protest the Madonna Whore," leaflet, August–September 1970.
5. Robin Morgan, *Going Too Far* (New York: Vintage Books, 1978), p. 62.
6. Women's Liberation leaflet, September 1969.
7. Helen Head, *Michigan Newsletter of Women's Liberation Coalition,* December 14, 1970.
8. Susan Braudy, "The Article I Wrote on Women That *Playboy* Wouldn't Publish," *Glamour*, May 1971, p. 202.
9. "Female Liberation," *Glamour*, May 10, 1979.
10. Braudy, op. cit., p. 244.
11. Claudia Dreifus, *San Francisco Chronicle*, April 27, 1970.
12. Quoted in Claudia Dreifus, *"Playboy* After the Dark Ages," *Liberation News Service*, April 29, 1970, p. 3.

Snuff—The Ultimate in Woman-Hating

1. "Letters to the Editor," *New Woman's Times*, Rochester, New York, 1977. (Thanks to Martha Gever for digging out this information.)
2. Ibid.

3. "Film of Violence Snuffed Out by Angered Pickets' Protests," *The San Diego Union*, September 29, 1977.
4. "Snuff," *Sister Courage*, April 1976.
5. "Woman's Group Picket Showing of Snuff," *The Times Herald Record*, Thursday, March 11, 1976.
6. "Obscenity Trial Ordered in Snuff Film Showing," *The Times Herald Record*, Wednesday, December 17, 1977.

Pornography and Grief

1. Georges Bataille, *Death and Sensuality* (New York: Ballantine Books, 1969), p. 10.
2. Ibid., p. 11.
3. The Marquis de Sade, *Juliette*, trans. Austryn Wainhouse (New York: Grove Press, 1976), p. 404.

Afterword

1. Elizabeth C. Stanton, Susan B. Anthony and Ida Husted Harper, eds., *The History of Woman Suffrage*, Vol. IV (Rochester, N.Y.: 1902; New York: Sourcebook Press, Collectors Editions Ltd: 1970), p. x.
2. Kathleen Barry, *Female Sexual Slavery* (Englewood Cliffs, N.J.: Prentice-Hall, 1979), p. 5.
3. Barbara Smith, tape-recorded workshop on racism and sexism, Earlham College, Ohio, April 6, 1979.
4. Michelle Cliff, ed., *The Winner Names the Age: A Collection of Writings by Lillian Smith* (New York: W. W. Norton Co., 1978), p. 204.
5. Lura Beam, *He Called Them By the Lightning: A Teacher's Odyssey in the Negro South, 1908–1919* (Indianapolis: Bobbs-Merrill, 1967), p. 172.
6. Lillian Smith, *Killers of the Dream* (New York: W. W. Norton Co., 1949), p. 145.
7. Susan Sontag, *Styles of Radical Will* (New York: Farrar, Straus & Giroux, 1969), p. 72.
8. Fran Hosken, "The Violence of Power: Genital Mutilation of Females," in *Heresies: A Feminist Publication on Art and Politics*, No. 6 (1978), pp. 28–34; Mary Daly, *Gyn/Ecology: The Metaethics of Radical Feminism* (Boston: Beacon Press, 1978), pp. 152–177.
9. Sontag, op. cit., p. 60.
10. Angela Davis, "The Black Woman's Role in the Community of Slaves," in *The Black Scholar*, December 1971, p. 7.

Bibliography

Addams, Jane. *A New Conscience and an Ancient Evil*. New York: Macmillan Co., 1914.

Armstrong, Louise. *Kiss Daddy Goodnight: A Speak-Out on Incest*. New York: Hawthorn Books, 1978.

Ashman, Charles. *The Finest Judges Money Can Buy*. Plainview, N.Y.: Nash Publishing Corp., 1973.

Bandura, Albert. *Psychological Modeling*. Chicago: Aldine Publishing Co., 1971.

Barker-Benfield, G. J. *The Horrors of the Half-Known Life: Male Attitudes Toward Women and Sexuality in the Nineteenth Century*. New York: Harper & Row, 1976.

Barreno, Maria Isabel, Maria Teresa Horta, and Maria Velho Da Costa. *The Three Marias: New Portuguese Letters*, trans. Helen R. Lane. New York: Bantam Books, 1975.

Barron, Jerome. *Freedom of the Press for Whom?* Bloomington: Indiana University Press, 1973.

Barry, Kathleen. *Female Sexual Slavery*. Englewood Cliffs, N.J., Prentice-Hall, 1979.

Beauvoir, Simone de. "Must We Burn Sade?" *The Marquis de Sade*. London: New English Library, 1972.

———. *The Second Sex*, trans. and ed. H. M. Parshley. New York: Alfred A. Knopf, 1952.

Bode, Janet. *Fighting Back*. New York: Macmillan Publishing Co., 1978.

Brady, Katherine. *Father's Days: A True Story of Incest*. New York: Seaview Books, 1979.

Brøgger, Suzanne. *Deliver Us From Love*, trans. Thomas Teal. New York: Delacorte Press/Seymour Lawrence, 1976.

Bronfenbrenner, Urie. "The Split-Level American Family," *Readings in Values Classification*, eds. Sidney B. Simon and Howard Kirschenbaum. Minneapolis: Winston Press, 1973.

Brownmiller, Susan. *Against Our Will*. New York: Simon & Schuster, 1975.

Bullough, Bonnie, and Vern Bullough. *Sin, Sickness, and Sanity*. New York: New American Library, 1977.

Calverton, V. F., and S. D. Schmalhausen, eds. *Sex in Civilization*. Garden City, N.Y.: Garden City Publishing Co., 1929.

Carter, Angela. *The Sadian Woman and The Ideology of Pornography*. New York: Pantheon Books, 1979.

Chesler, Phyllis. *About Men*. New York: Simon & Schuster, 1978.

————. *Women and Madness*. Garden City, N.Y.: Doubleday, 1972.

————, and Emily Jane Goodman. *Women, Money and Power*. New York: William Morrow & Co., 1976.

Cirino, Robert. *Power to Persuade*. New York: Bantam Books, 1974.

Clark, Lorenne M. G., and Debra J. Lewis. *Rape: The Price of Coercive Sexuality*. Toronto, Canada: Canadian Women's Educational Press, 1977.

————, and Lynda Lange. *The Sexism of Social and Political Theory: Women and Reproduction from Plato to Nietzsche*. Toronto, Canada: University of Toronto Press, 1979.

Cline, Victor B., ed. *Where Do You Draw the Line? An Exploration into Media Violence, Pornography, and Censorship*. Provo, Utah: Brigham Young University Press, 1974.

Cordelier, Jeanne. *The Life*. New York: Viking Press, 1976.

Daly, Mary. *Gyn/Ecology: The Metaethics of Radical Feminism*. Boston: Beacon Press, 1979.

Delaney, Janice, Mary Jane Lupton, and Emily Toth. *The Curse: A Cultural History of Menstruation*. New York: E. P. Dutton, 1976; paperback, New American Library.

Duncan, Carol. "The Esthetics of Power in Modern Erotic Art," *Heresies*, No. 1, January 1977.

Dworkin, Andrea. *Our Blood: Prophecies and Discourses on Sexual Politics*. New York: Harper & Row, 1976.

————. *Woman Hating*. New York: E. P. Dutton, 1974.

Eberhard, Phyllis. *Pornography and the Law*. New York: Ballantine Books, 1959.

Ellul, Jacques. *Propaganda*, trans. Konrad Kellan and Jean Lerner. New York: Alfred A. Knopf, 1969.

Ephron, Nora. *Scribble, Scribble: Notes on the Media*. New York: Alfred A. Knopf, 1978.

Ernst, Morris L., and Alan U. Schwartz, *Censorship: The Search for the Obscene*. New York: The Macmillan Co., 1964.

Eysenck, H. J., and D. K. B. Nias. *Sex, Violence and the Media*. New York: Harper & Row, 1978.

Farley, Lin. *Sexual Shakedown: The Sexual Harassment of Women on the Job*. New York: McGraw-Hill, 1978.

Figes, Eva. *Patriarchal Attitudes*. New York: Fawcett World Library, 1971.

Firestone, Shulamith. *The Dialectic of Sex*. New York: Bantam Books, 1972.

Foster, Jeannette. *Sex Variant Women in Literature*. Baltimore: Diana Press, 1975.

Frankfort, Ellen. *Vaginal Politics*. New York: Bantam Books, 1973.

————. *The Voice: Life at the Village Voice*. New York: William Morrow & Co., 1976.

————, with Frances Kissling. *Rosie: The Investigation of a Wrongful Death.* New York: The Dial Press, 1979.

Friedan, Betty. *The Feminine Mystique.* New York: Dell, 1963.

Frobenius, Lee. *African Nights: Black Erotic Folk Tales.* New York: Herder & Herder, 1971.

Gallagher, Neil. *How to Stop the Porno Plague.* Minneapolis: Bethany Fellowship, 1977.

Gardner, John. *On Moral Fiction.* New York: Basic Books, 1978.

Gilman, Charlotte Perkins. *Women and Economics.* New York: Harper & Row, 1966.

Goffman, Erving. "Gender Advertisements," *Studies in the Anthropology of Visual Communication.* Cambridge: Harvard University Press, 1979.

Goldman, Emma. *The Traffic in Women and Other Essays on Feminism.* New York: Times Change Press, 1970.

Goldstein, Michael J., Harold S. Kant, and John J. Hartman. *Pornography and Sexual Deviance.* Berkeley: University of California Press, 1973.

Gould, Lois. *Not Responsible for Personal Articles.* New York: Random House, 1978.

Greene, Gerald and Caroline. *S-M: The Last Taboo.* New York: Grove Press, 1974.

Greer, Germaine. *The Female Eunuch.* New York: McGraw-Hill, 1971.

Griffin, Susan. *Rape: The Power of Consciousness.* New York: Harper & Row, 1979.

Grimké, Sarah M. *Letters on the Equality of the Sexes and the Condition of Woman.* New York: Source Books Press, 1970. (Unabridged republication of 1838 Boston edition.)

Harris, Marvin. *Cannibals and Kings: The Origins of Culture.* New York: Vintage Books, 1977.

————. *Cows, Pigs, Wars, and Witches: The Riddles of Culture.* New York: Vintage Books, 1978.

Haskell, Molly. *From Reverence To Rape.* New York: Penguin Books, 1974.

Hite, Shere. *Sexual Honesty by Women for Women.* New York: Warner Paperback Library Ed., 1974.

————. *The Hite Report.* New York: Macmillan Publishing Co., 1976.

Holbrook, David. *The Case Against Pornography.* La Salle, Ill.: Library Press, 1974.

Horos, Carol V. *Rape.* New Canaan, Conn.: Tobey Publishing Co., 1974.

Hyde, H. M. *A History of Pornography.* New York: W. S. Heinemann, 1964.

Janeway, Elizabeth. *Between Myth and Morning: Women Awakening.* New York: William Morrow & Co., 1974.

Janus, Sam, et al. *A Sexual Profile of Men in Power.* Englewood Cliffs, N.J.: Prentice-Hall, 1977.

Jay, Karla, and Allen Young. *The Gay Report.* New York: Summit Books, 1979.

Johnson, Pamela Hansford. *On Iniquity.* New York: Charles Scribner's Sons, 1967.

Johnston, Jill. *Lesbian Nation: The Feminist Solution.* New York: Simon & Schuster, 1973.

Keating, Charles H., Jr. *Commission on Obscenity and Pornography—Dissenting Report,* September 1970.

Key, Wilson Bryan. *Media Sexploitation.* Englewood Cliffs, N.J.: Prentice-Hall, 1977.

―――. *Subliminal Seduction.* New York: New American Library/Signet, 1972.

Kirkpatrick, Clifford. *Nazi Germany: Its Women and Family Life.* Indianapolis: Bobbs-Merrill, 1938.

Lerner, Gerda, ed. *Black Women in White America: A Documentary History.* New York: Pantheon Books, 1972.

Liston, Robert A. *The Right to Know, Censorship in America.* New York: Franklin Watts, 1973.

Lloyd, Robin. *For Money or Love.* New York: Ballantine Books, 1976.

MacKinnon, Catharine A. *Sexual Harassment of Working Women: A Case of Sex Discrimination.* New Haven: Yale University Press, 1979.

Mander, Jerry. *Four Arguments for the Elimination of Television.* New York: William Morrow & Co., 1978.

Marcus, Steven. *The Other Victorians.* New York: Basic Books, 1964.

Martin, D., and Phyllis Lyon. *Lesbian/Woman.* San Francisco: Glide Publications, 1972.

Martin, Del. *Battered Wives.* San Francisco: Glide Publications, 1976.

Mead, Margaret. *Sex and Temperament in Three Primitive Societies.* New York: William Morrow & Co., 1935.

Medea, Andrea, and Kathleen Thompson. *Against Rape.* New York: Farrar, Straus & Giroux, 1974.

Michelson, Peter. *The Aesthetics of Pornography.* New York: Herder & Herder, 1971.

Miller, Casey, and Kate Swift. *Words and Women.* Garden City, N.Y.: Doubleday/Anchor Press, 1977.

Millett, Kate. *The Prostitution Papers.* New York: Basic Books, 1971.

―――. *Sexual Politics.* Garden City, N.Y.: Doubleday, 1970.

Mitchell, Juliet. *Woman's Estate.* New York: Vintage Books, 1973.

Mitscherlich, Alexander. *Doctors of Infamy: The Story of the Nazi Medical Crimes.* New York: Henry Schuman, 1949.

Moers, Ellen. *Literary Women: The Great Writers.* Garden City, N.Y.: Doubleday, 1976.

Morgan, Elaine. *The Descent of Woman.* New York: Stein & Day, 1972.

Morgan, Robin. *Sisterhood Is Powerful.* New York: Vintage Books, 1970.

―――. *Going Too Far.* New York: Vintage Books, 1978.

Nobile, Philip, ed. *The New Eroticism*. New York: Random House, 1970.

North, Maurice. *The Outer Fringe of Sex*. London: The Odyssey Press, 1970.

Oakley, Ann. *Sex, Gender and Society*. New York: Harper Colophon Books, 1972.

———. *The Sociology of Housework*. New York: Pantheon Books, 1974.

———. *Woman's Work: The Housewife, Past and Present*. New York: Vintage Books, 1976.

Packard, Vance. *The Hidden Persuaders*. New York: Pocket Books, 1976.

———. *The People Shapers*. Boston: Little, Brown, 1978.

———. *The Sexual Wilderness*. New York: David McKay, 1968.

Pankhurst, Emmeline. *My Own Story*. London: Eveleigh Nash, 1914.

Pankhurst, Sylvia. *The Suffragette Movement*. London: Virago, 1978.

Peary, Gerald. "Woman In Porn," *Take One*, September 1978, pp. 28–32. (Contains a profile of Roberta Finlay, the woman who with her husband made *Snuff*.)

Peckham, Morse. *Art and Pornography: An Experiment in Explanation*. New York: Basic Books, 1969.

Pinzer, Maimie. *The Maimie Papers*, eds. Ruth Rosen and Sue Davidson. Old Westbury, N.Y.: The Feminist Press, 1977.

Poett, James. "Deep Peep," *The Village Voice*, Vol. XXIII, No. 18, May 1, 1978, pp. 1, 19–20, 22–25.

Pomeroy, Wardell B. *Dr. Kinsey and the Institute for Sex Research*. New York: Harper & Row, 1972.

Price, Richard. *Ladies' Man*. New York: Bantam Books, 1979.

Putnam, Emily James. *The Lady*. Chicago: University of Chicago Press, 1970.

Raymond, Janice G. *The Transsexual Empire: The Making of the She-Male*. Boston: Beacon Press, 1979.

Reimann, Viktor. *Goebbels: The Man Who Created Hitler*, trans. Stephen Wendt. Garden City, N.Y.: Doubleday, 1976.

Rich, Adrienne. *Of Woman Born: Motherhood as Experience and Institution*. New York: W. W. Norton, 1976.

———. *Lies, Secrets, and Silence*. New York: W. W. Norton, 1979.

Riess, Curt. *Joseph Goebbels*. Garden City, N.Y.: Doubleday, 1948.

Rist, Ray C. *The Pornography Controversy*. New Brunswick, N.J.: Transaction Press, 1975.

Roe, Clifford G. *Panders and Their White Slaves*. New York: Fleming H. Revell Co., 1910.

Rose, Al. *Storyville, New Orleans*. University, Ala.: University of Alabama Press, 1974.

Rosner, Fred. *Sex Ethics in the Writings of Moses Maimonides*. New York: Bloch Publishing Co., 1974.

Roszak, Betty and Theodore. *Masculine/Feminine*. New York: Harper & Row, 1969.

Rowbotham, Sheila. *Hidden From History*. London: Pluto Press, 1974.

―――. *Woman's Consciousness, Man's World*. Baltimore: Penguin Books, 1973.

―――. *Women, Resistance, and Revolution*. New York: Vintage Books, 1974.

Roy, Maria, ed. *A Psychosociological Study of Domestic Violence*. New York: Van Nostrand Reinhold, 1977.

Rugoff, Milton. *Prudery and Passion: Sexuality in Victorian America*. New York: G. P. Putnam's Sons, 1971.

Russell, Diana E. H., and Nicole Van de Ven, eds. *Crimes Against Women: Proceedings of the International Tribunal*. Millbrae, Calif.: Les Femmes, 1976.

―――. *The Politics of Rape*. New York: Stein & Day, 1975.

Sanger, William W. *The History of Prostitution*. New York: The Medical Publishing Co., 1906.

Sherfey, Mary Jane. *The Nature and Evolution of Female Sexuality*. New York: Vintage Books, 1973.

Smith, Marjorie M. " 'Violent Pornography' and the Women's Movement," *The Civil Liberties Review*, January/February 1978, pp. 50–53.

Sontag, Susan. *Styles of Radical Will*. New York: Delta, 1970.

Stanton, Elizabeth, and the Revising Committee. *The Woman's Bible*. Seattle: Coalition Task Force on Women and Religion, 1975.

Stanton, Elizabeth Cady. *Eighty Years and More: Reminiscences 1815–1897*. New York: Schocken Books, 1971 (reprinted).

―――, Susan B. Anthony, and Matilda Gage Joslyn. *The History of Woman Suffrage*. New York: Source Book Press, 1970 (reprinted in 6 vols.).

Stein, Martha L. *Lovers, Friends, Slaves* . . . New York: Berkeley Medallion Books, 1975.

Stern, Susan. *With the Weathermen: The Personal Journal of a Revolutionary Woman*. Garden City, N.Y.: Doubleday, 1975.

Stoker, Bram. *Dracula*. New York: Dell, 1978.

Stoller, Robert J. *Sex and Gender*. New York: Science House, 1968.

―――. *Sexual Excitement: Dynamics of Erotic Life*. New York: Pantheon Books, 1979.

Stoltenberg, John. "Eroticism and Violence in the Father-Son Relationship," "Refusing to Be a Man," "Toward Gender Justice," in *For Men Against Sexism*, ed. John Snodgrass. Albion, Calif.: Times Change Press, 1977.

Swinburne, Algernon Charles. *Lesbia Brandon*, ed. Randolph Hughes. London: The Falcon Press, 1952.

Tawney, R. H. *Equality*. London: Unwin Books, 1964.

Tillich, Hannah. *From Time to Time*. Briarcliff Manor, N.Y.: Stein & Day, 1974.

Trilling, Diana. *We Must March My Darlings*. New York: Harcourt Brace Jovanovich, 1978.

Tripp, C. A. *The Homosexual Matrix*. New York: New American Library, 1976.

Wallace, Michelle. *Black Macho and the Myth of the Superwoman*. New York: Dial Press, 1979.

Wells, Ida B. *On Lynchings: A Red Record, Mob Rule in New Orleans: Southern Horrors*. New York: Arno, 1969. First published 1892.

Weyr, Thomas. *Reaching for Paradise: The Playboy Vision of America*. New York: Times Books, 1978.

Wollstonecraft, Mary. *A Vindication of the Rights of Women*. New York: W. W. Norton, 1967.

Woolfolf, J. P. *Male and Female*. New York: Woodford Press, 1949.

Womongold, Marsha. *Pornography: A License to Kill*. Cambridge, Mass., private publication, 1978. Send $2.00 to M. Womongold, 16 B Cedar St., Somerville, MA, 02143.

U.S. Government Report of the Commission on Obscenity and Pornography. New York: Bantam Books, 1970.

Zimbardo, Ebbessen. *Influencing Attitudes and Changing Behavior*. Reading, Mass.: Addison-Wesley Publishing Co., 1977.

Contributors

KATHLEEN BARRY is a feminist, sociologist and the author of *Female Sexual Slavery*, published by Prentice-Hall in 1979. She has worked on abortion rights, served as a women's advocate for several universities, and coauthored the *Fourth World Manifesto* and the *Stop Rape Handbook*.

PAULINE BART is a sociologist at Abraham Lincoln School of Medicine, University of Illinois, Urbana. She taught the first course on women at University of California at Berkeley in the spring of 1969, and has researched women's and health issues, especially gynecology, menopause, and rape. She is currently studying women who have been attacked and have avoided being raped, and will publish her findings in a book tentatively titled *Rape: Avoiders and Survivors* to be published by The Free Press in 1981.

JUDITH BAT-ADA received her doctorate in mass media and speech communications from Case Western Reserve University in Cleveland, Ohio. She is interested in the issue of female identity and is now writing a book entitled *Back to the Dark*. She lives in Israel.

MEGAN BOLER, ROBIN LAKE, and BRIDGET WYNNE are members of the San Francisco-based group, Women Against Violence in Pornography and Media, and have worked during the last year to fight abusive images of women in the media.

SUSAN BROWNMILLER is the author of *Against Our Will: Men, Women and Rape*.

CHARLOTTE BUNCH is a feminist activist, writer, and teacher who was a founder of DC Women's Liberation, *The Furies*, a lesbian-feminist newspaper, and *Quest*, a feminist quarterly. She has edited five feminist anthologies.

PHYLLIS CHESLER is the author of *Women and Madness*, *About Men*, and *With Child: A Diary of Motherhood*.

IRENE DIAMOND teaches political science at Purdue University in West Lafayette, Indiana. She has presented a variety of lectures and papers on pornography, including "Making Pornography a Feminist Issue" in June 1977. She is the author of *Sex Roles in the State House*, published in 1977 by Yale University Press, one of the first books on women and politics. She is currently doing research on pornography in Denmark under a Fulbright scholarship.

ANDREA DWORKIN is the author of *Woman Hating* and *Our Blood: Prophecies and Discourses on Sexual Politics*. She is a well-known feminist lecturer and activist. She currently is writing a book about pornography, scheduled for publication by Anchor/Doubleday in 1981.

341

TRACEY A. GARDNER has worked for Bay Area Women Against Rape in Berkeley, California, where she developed a perspective on the particular effects of sexual assault on communities of color. She is now on the staff of A Safe Place, a shelter for battered women in Oakland.

MARTHA GEVER and MARG HALL are members of Rochester Women Against Violence Against Women, an education and action-oriented group fighting pornography in Rochester, New York.

SUSAN GRIFFIN is a feminist poet and Emmy Award-winning playwright. Her books include *Like the Iris of an Eye* and *Voices*. She is also the author of *Woman and Nature: the Roaring Inside Her*, and is now at work on *Pornography and Silence*, to be published by Harper & Row in 1981.

ANN JONES, who holds a Ph.D. in American Literature and Intellectual History from the University of Wisconsin, wrote *Women Who Kill*, published by Holt, Rinehart & Winston in 1980.

MARGARET JOZSA has a master's degree in sociology. She has been involved in the issue of violence against women for five years. Recently she was chairperson of the Committee on Women and Violence of Southwest Women Working Together (in Chicago, Illinois).

WENDY KAMINER is a practicing attorney in New York City.

BEVERLY LABELLE is a regular contributor to *New Women's Times*, a feminist newspaper in Rochester, New York. She is the author of a long, unpublished paper, "Pornography, The Propaganda of Misogyny," from which the excerpts in this book are taken. She is now at work on a book about the image of women in female "pulp" magazines.

HELEN LONGINO teaches philosophy at Mills College in Oakland, California. She has been active in the Women's Movement since 1971, and struggles to make philosophy an instrument for social consciousness.

AUDRE LORDE is a native New Yorker who makes her home on Staten Island. Her seventh book of poetry, *The Black Unicorn*, was just released by Harper & Row. She is now working on an autobiography entitled *I've Been Standing on This Streetcorner a Hell of a Long Time*. She is Associate Professor of English at John Jay College of Criminal Justice in Brooklyn.

SUSAN LURIE is a feminist, poet, writer, and teacher who lives in Berkeley. She is coordinator of the Berkeley Women's Center Writers' Workshop, a community-based writing program for women, and publishes *Woman See'd*, a literary magazine. She is now completing her doctorate in English literature at the University of California at Berkeley.

ROBIN MORGAN is a poet and a writer of fiction and essays. A founder of this wave of feminism, she is an activist as well as a radical feminist theorist. Her books include *Monster, Lady of the Beasts, Sisterhood Is Powerful,* the now classic anthology which she compiled and edited, and, most recently, *Going Too Far: The Personal Chronicle of a Feminist*. A novel, *The Mer-Child*, and a third book of poems are forthcoming.

FLORENCE RUSH is a New York feminist, social worker, licensed therapist, and writer. She is well known for her germinal work in feminist analysis of incest. Her first book, *The Best Kept Secret: The Sexual Abuse of Children*, was recently published by Prentice-Hall.

DIANA E. H. RUSSELL is Associate Professor of Sociology at Mills College in Oakland, California. She is the author of *The Politics of Rape* and coeditor, with Nicole Van de Ven, of *The Proceedings of the International Tribunal on Crimes Against Women*.

GLORIA STEINEM is an editor of *Ms.* magazine.

LUISAH TEISH is a thirty-two-year-old Aries-Taurus who considers herself a Rational Third World Feminist. She is currently at work on a novel entitled *Dirty Laundry*—a fictionalized account of sexism within the Black Power Movement.

ALICE WALKER is a writer whose articles and short stories have appeared in *Ms.* magazine as well as other periodicals. Her latest book of poetry, *Goodnight Willie Lee, I'll See You in the Morning*, has just been published.

ROBIN YEAMANS graduated from Stanford University Law School, California, in 1969. She is a practicing attorney in San Jose, where she handles cases of personal injury and divorce. She is divorced and the mother of a seven-year-old child.

Index

345

About The Editor

Laura Lederer graduated magna cum laude from The University of Michigan in 1975. In 1976 she helped found Women Against Violence in Pornography and Media (WAVPM) in San Francisco, the first feminist organization dedicated to eliminating pornography. For three years she worked full-time as WAVPM coordinator and organizer, in which capacity, among other things, she designed, edited, and published the WAVPM *Newspage*, the first national newsletter for women on how to fight pornography. She conceived the 1978 Feminist Perspectives on Pornography conference (during which the first national Take Back the Night March was held). The conference sparked the current women's movement against pornography and served as a model for the subsequent conferences, marches, and symposia across the nation. She has spoken extensively on pornography in classrooms, at meetings and conferences, and on radio and TV shows.